STUDENT DEVELOPMENT IN COLLEGE

STUDENT DEVELOPMENT IN COLLEGE

Theory, Research, and Practice

Nancy J. Evans

Deanna S. Forney

Florence Guido-DiBrito

JOSSEY-BASS
A Wiley Company
www.josseybass.com

Published by

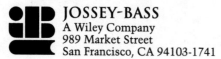

JOSSEY-BASS
A Wiley Company
989 Market Street
San Francisco, CA 94103-1741

www.josseybass.com

Jossey-Bass books and products are available through most bookstores. To contact Jossey-Bass directly, call (888) 378-2537, fax to (800) 605-2665, or visit our website at www.josseybass.com.

Substantial discounts on bulk quantities of Jossey-Bass books are available to corporations, professional associations, and other organizations. For details and discount information, contact the special sales department at Jossey-Bass.

We at Jossey-Bass strive to use the most environmentally sensitive paper stocks available to us. Our publications are printed on acid-free recycled stock whenever possible, and our paper always meets or exceeds minimum GPO and EPA requirements.

Library of Congress Cataloging-in-Publication Data

Evans, Nancy J., date.
    Student development in college : theory, research, and practice /
Nancy J. Evans, Deanna S. Forney, Florence Guido-DiBrito. — 1st ed.
      p.   cm. — (The Jossey-Bass higher and adult education series)
    Includes bibliographical references (p.   ) and index.
    ISBN 0-7879-0925-4
    1. College student development programs—United States.
2. College students—United States—Psychology.   I. Forney, Deanna
S.   II. Guido-DiBrito, Florence.   III. Title.
IV. Series.
LB2343.4.E88   1998
378.1'98—dc21   97–32507

FIRST EDITION
PB Printing 10 9 8 7 6 5

THE JOSSEY-BASS

HIGHER AND ADULT EDUCATION SERIES

Consulting Editor
Student Services

Ursula Delworth
University of Iowa

We dedicate this book

To our students, who are caring, neophyte scholars
in search of a better self:

To our past students, who let us experience them in
the classroom so that we could learn how to guide
them better along their developmental paths.

To our present students, who show us the power of
ideas and challenge us to learn and grow with them.

To our future students, who we hope develop far
beyond what we can imagine: may they take up
where we leave off and pass their learnings on and on
to the generations who follow them.

CONTENTS

PREFACE

Our student populations and the developmental issues they confront are more diverse and complex than ever in the history of higher education. The growing body of literature on student development reflects these changes, but it is scattered across disciplines. To date, the student affairs profession has lacked a single, comprehensive overview of student development theory to serve as a guide for understanding what happens to students in college and for creating intentional interventions designed to enhance student learning and development. This book is intended to fill that void.

Student Development in College will help student affairs practitioners understand the developmental challenges facing today's college students in the cognitive, affective, and behavioral domains. It will also provide them with knowledge of factors contributing to development in each of these domains. Most important, it will assist student affairs professionals in designing individual, group, and institutional approaches to work more effectively with students at various developmental levels and to facilitate student growth. As a result of reading this book, practitioners should have a better understanding of the overall needs of college students and proactive strategies for meeting these needs.

In addition, *Student Development in College* will provide academics with a comprehensive and inclusive overview of the most important student development theories and related research. As such, the book should serve as an important review and critique of the literature in the field. It will be a helpful resource to scholars in the design of future research.

Student Development in College has been written for individuals involved in student affairs work in higher education and students in college student affairs graduate programs. It will be valuable to individuals with no background in student development theory who wish to obtain a comprehensive understanding of this area as well as individuals who wish to update their knowledge. It will be particularly helpful for practitioners who work directly with students, such as student activities advisers, residence life coordinators, academic advisers, career counselors, multicultural counselors, and counseling center staff as well as individuals who supervise front-line staff and are responsible for program design and administration. University faculty interested in learning more about student development and applications of student development theory in classroom and advising settings will also find the book useful. Since examples are drawn from a variety of institutional settings, the book should have broad appeal.

Student Development in College is designed to provide a comprehensive, in-depth review of the major student development theories as they relate to student affairs practice. Because of space limitations, not all existing theories could be included. Theories were selected for inclusion using the following criteria: (1) they represent a range of philosophical and methodological perspectives, (2) they are frequently cited in the educational literature, and (3) they lend themselves to use in educational settings.

Some theories that were popular in the early history of the student development movement, such as the work of Roy Heath, Douglas Heath, and Jane Loevinger, are valuable because of the ideas they introduced but are rarely referred to in the current literature as the basis of research and practice. Other theories have been referenced over the years in the student affairs literature but have generated only limited research and application. These include James Fowler's theory of spiritual development and Robert Kegan's model of the evolving self. A final group of theories, including models of biculturalism and multiple identities as well as many of the newer racial and ethnic identity models, show great promise but have not yet been tested to any great extent. Space limitations preclude extensive discussion of these theories.

As the authors of this book, we freely admit that our personal biases have entered into the selections we made. We believe, however, that the theories we have chosen to include are ones that will provide a comprehensive grounding for the practice of intentional student development in higher education.

We include in our discussion of each theory information about its development, the basic concepts associated with the theory, assessment techniques, related research, and applications of the theory to student affairs practice. Particular attention has been paid to the applicability of various approaches to diverse student populations and diverse settings. Case studies and practical examples have been included to assist the reader in understanding the theoretical concepts being discussed and seeing their utility in the daily practice of student affairs work.

In Part One we examine the concept of student development and explore meanings attached to it in student affairs literature and practice. We also outline the historical context of student development (Chapter One) and discuss the role of theory and the uses of student development theory in student affairs practice (Chapter Two).

Successive parts examine each of the major clusters of theory—psychosocial, cognitive-structural, and typological. The introduction to each part presents the basic concepts associated with the theoretical approach being presented. Next the earliest or foundational theorist in each cluster is discussed, followed by later important theorists and researchers in the perspective. Each chapter includes discussion of applications of the theories so the reader can see how they are useful in student affairs practice.

We begin with psychosocial theories because they are content-based and seem easier for many readers to understand. These theories focus on the issues individuals face at different times in their lives. In Chapter Three we present an overview of Arthur Chickering's theory of psychosocial development, examining both his original work and his more recent revisions. In Chapter Four we introduce Ruthellen Josselson's research on identity development in women. Her study extends Erik Erikson's and James Marcia's ideas, which were based primarily on white male samples. We cover racial identity development models in Chapter Five and gay, lesbian, and bisexual identity development models in Chapter Six. Identity development models examine important and previously neglected aspects of development in college students. In Chapter Seven we review Nancy Schlossberg's transition model, which considers development across the life span. Schlossberg's life events perspective is an alternative to the age/stage theories of Chickering and other theorists in this cluster.

In Part Three we examine cognitive-structural perspectives on development. These theories examine how people perceive and interpret the events in their lives. In Chapter Eight we introduce William Perry's foundational theory concerning the intellectual and ethical development of college students. In Chapter Nine we present a number of other important cognitive-structural theories that have been built on Perry's work. First we look at Mary Field Belenky and her colleagues' study of women's intellectual development. Next we review the work of Marcia Baxter Magolda, who compared the epistemological development of men and women. Finally, we present the reflective judgment model of Patricia King and Karen Kitchener. Chapters Ten and Eleven focus on moral development, a specific component of cognitive development that deals with how people make decisions that affect their lives and the lives of others. First we review the pioneering work of Lawrence Kohlberg and researchers who have adopted his theoretical position, especially James Rest. Then we introduce Carol Gilligan's alternative explanation of moral development and examine hypothesized gender differences related to this aspect of development.

Part Four discusses typological theories. These theories call our attention to the individual differences in how students approach their worlds. In Chapter Twelve we examine David Kolb's theory of experiential learning, which helps us understand learning style differences among students. Next, in Chapter Thirteen, John Holland's theory of vocational personalities and work environments is introduced. In Chapter Fourteen we discuss the Myers-Briggs personality typology, which is based on Carl Jung's theory of personality type.

In Part Five we provide a chapter on integrating theoretical approaches to create intentional developmental environments. Examples using several theories in a comprehensive manner should help the reader pull together previously presented material in an inclusive and concrete way. Our concluding chapter examines the "state of the art" of student development theory and provides recommendations for future research and more intentional application of student development theory.

At the back of the book we have included recommendations for further reading. The works we have listed are ones we believe provide good starting points for individuals interested in obtaining a more thorough understanding of particular theories and concepts we have introduced in this book.

In conceptualizing this book, our goal was to provide a "user-friendly" introduction to student development theory that would also challenge readers to explore the topic in more depth. In addition, we intend the book to serve as an "update" for individuals who wish to learn more about recently introduced theories of student development. As student affairs professionals and other educators work together to enhance the learning environment on college campuses, an understanding of student development theory is essential. We hope that this book will make a meaningful contribution to this knowledge base.

Acknowledgments

Many people have contributed to this work in very significant ways. First, we would like to thank Gale Erlandson, our editor at Jossey-Bass, for her enthusiasm about this book and her faith in our ability to write it. We would also like to thank David Brightman, Gale's assistant at Jossey-Bass, for his good humor, support, and timely responses to all of our technical questions. Ursula Delworth, our consulting editor, has provided much support and insightful guidance throughout the project. She has been an important mentor for us all. We are also indebted to the three reviewers of our book, Marylu McEwen, Harry Canon, and a person who wished to remain anonymous. Their painstaking reviews and helpful comments have significantly improved the quality of the final version of this work.

In addition, each of us has particular individuals to thank who have supported our efforts. Nancy Evans would like to thank her husband and best friend, Jim Trenberth, for his ongoing love, support, and computer expertise and especially for his patience through long days and nights of hearing "I have to work on the book" when he would have preferred her company in other pursuits. Nancy would also like to thank her former graduate assistants Ellen Broido, Leah Temkin, and Andy Erkis, all of whom put in tedious hours hunting down library materials and reading drafts of chapters. Her student development class, who read early drafts of several chapters, also provided valuable input. Dan Salter's consultation and critique on the Myers-Briggs chapter were much appreciated. The support staff at Penn State, including Suzy Lutz, Pam Anderson, and Darla Homan, provided much support and cheerfully met all of Nancy's needs for quick turnaround on major photocopying and mailing tasks. Finally, Nancy would like to thank her former students and colleagues at Indiana University, Western Illinois University, and Penn State University for their contributions to her thinking about student development. In particular, Tony D'Augelli has been a valued colleague and has significantly influenced Nancy's thinking about the social construction of identity and the future directions of student development theory.

Dea Forney would like to thank Nancy Schlossberg and David Kolb for providing materials related to their theories. She would also like to acknowledge Becky Day for her work in typing drafts of some of the chapters and Ken Kohberger for his resourcefulness in locating library materials. Deserving special thanks is Monty Groves for his extensive assistance with library research. Finally, Dea would like to thank the students and alumni of Western Illinois University's master's program in college student personnel. Their "aha" experiences with theory, coupled with their insights and questions, have served as a source of inspiration in producing Dea's contributions to this book.

It is with great humility and gratitude that Flo Guido-DiBrito thanks two master's students who were instrumental in helping this book become reality. Adele Rodriguez spent countless hours in the library over the course of two years digging up relevant resources, creating first drafts, giving feedback, and completing some revisions. Pat Noteboom found time to assist with revisions while working on her master's thesis. Alicia Chavez, Pat Krysinski, Renee Romano, Lue Gates, Stan Carpenter, Yvonna Lincoln, Jan Freed, Scharron Clayton, Kathy Allen, Lynann Moses, James Wallace, Pat Baumgartner, Carmen Montecinos, Bob Muffoletto,

John Smith, Victoria DeFrancesco, Pie Pisano, and Sami Lynn Story offered unending moral support. The University of Northern Iowa granted Flo a 1996 summer fellowship for needed financial support and a reduced course load to help her move this project along. She is most grateful. Flo also wants to thank her parents, Toni and Cosmo Guido, and her grandmother, Florence Sirianni Guido, who let her know that a good education is the best gift they could give her, second only to their love. And last, but far from least, Flo could not have written this book without Bill, a Renaissance man who walks the untrodden path of uncompromising principles and unending patience and who wears with style the many hats of loyal partner, friend, outdoor buddy, stargazer, colleague, carpenter, poet, photographer, gourmet cook, and international education consultant (BMB).

March 1998

Nancy J. Evans
Ames, Iowa

Deanna S. Forney
Macomb, Illinois

Florence Guido-DiBrito
Greeley, Colorado

THE AUTHORS

Nancy J. Evans is an associate professor in the Department of Educational Leadership and Policy Studies at Iowa State University, associated with the program in Higher Education. She holds a B.A. degree (1970) in social science from the State University of New York at Potsdam, an M.S.Ed. degree (1972) in higher education (college student personnel) from Southern Illinois University, a Ph.D. degree (1978) in counseling psychology from the University of Missouri–Columbia, and an M.F.A. degree (1991) in theatre from Western Illinois University. She has held faculty positions in college student personnel programs at Penn State University, Western Illinois University, and Indiana University. She has also served as a practitioner in the functional areas of counseling, residence life, and student activities at Bowling Green State University, the University of Iowa, Stephens College, and Tarkio College.

Evans is a recipient of the American College Personnel Association's Annuit Coeptis Senior Professional Award. She is a past chair of the association's Commission XII–Professional Preparation and formerly served as the commission's representative to the Core Council on Professional Development. In addition, she has held several positions at the state and regional level in the American College Personnel Association and the National Association of Student Personnel Administrators.

Evans's books include *Beyond Tolerance: Gays, Lesbians and Bisexuals on Campus* (1991), with Vernon Wall; *Facilitating the Development of Women* (1987); and *The State of the Art of Professional Preparation and Practice in Student Affairs: Another Look* (1998), edited with Christine Phelps Tobin. In addition, she has published a number of journal articles and book chapters focusing on the impact of the college environment on student development, particularly with regard to members of nondominant populations.

Deanna S. Forney is a professor in the Department of Counselor Education and College Student Personnel at Western Illinois University. She earned a B.A. degree (1969) in English from Gettysburg College, an M.A. degree (1971) in English from Pennsylvania State University, and an M.A. degree (1982) and a Ph.D. degree (1989) in counseling and personnel services from the University of Maryland, College Park. Prior to becoming a faculty member at WIU, she was a student affairs practitioner at Gettysburg College, Allegheny College, the University of Delaware, and the State University of New York at Oswego.

Forney is a past chair of the American College Personnel Association's Commission XII–Professional Preparation. She has also served as ACPA's representative to the board of directors of the Council for the Accreditation of Counseling and Related Educational Programs; as a member of the ACPA-NASPA Study Group on Quality Assurance in Student Affairs, the Research Advisory Committee of the College Placement Council's Foundation, and the directorate of ACPA's Commission VI–Career Development; and as a state officer in the Association of College and University Housing Officers–International.

Forney has published several journal articles and book chapters and is a member of the editorial board of the *Journal of College Student Development*. She has also given numerous conference presentations for professional organizations and served as a consultant to colleges and universities, primarily in the areas of student development and career development. Forney is a recipient of ACPA's Annuit Coeptis Emerging Professional Award (1994) and WIU's Faculty Excellence Award (1992, 1994, and 1996).

Florence (Flo) Guido-DiBrito was recently appointed to the position of associate professor of educational leadership and policy studies in college student personnel administration at the University of Northern Colorado. She was previously assistant professor of educational leadership, counseling, and postsecondary education in student affairs at the University of Northern Iowa. Her practical experience in student affairs administration includes holding appointments as dean of students at Incarnate Word College, residence director at University of Wisconsin–Stevens Point, director of career planning and placement at Manchester College, and director of placement at St. Francis College. She received a B.A. degree (1974) in art history from Briarcliff College, an M.A. degree (1977) from Ball State University in college student personnel administration, and a Ph.D. degree (1990) from Texas A&M University in educational administration with an emphasis in higher education.

Guido-DiBrito's research endeavors have been constructivist projects examining loyalty between student affairs leaders, gender-related moral and intellectual development of student affairs leaders, and the meaning of women's education. Her scholarship has been published in a variety of student affairs and higher education journals. She also has two book chapters to her credit.

Guido-DiBrito has been a presenter at more than twenty national and regional student affairs conferences and the keynote speaker at seven regional conferences. Recently, she was appointed to the editorial board of the *Journal of College Student Development*. In 1987, she received the Annuit Coeptis Emerging Professional Award from the American College Personnel Association.

PART ONE

UNDERSTANDING AND USING STUDENT DEVELOPMENT THEORY

Regina is about to begin her master's program in student affairs administration. In addition to maintaining a 3.5 grade point average and running track, Regina was active as an undergraduate student in student government and the Association for Multicultural Understanding (AMU). When she decided early in her senior year that a career in business was not for her, the adviser to AMU suggested that she think about student affairs administration. Regina had never heard of this profession, but she enjoyed the college environment and thought that the work her adviser did was important. She wanted to have the same kind of impact on others as he had on her. So she investigated various preparation programs and ended up with an offer from one of the best programs in the country along with an assistantship in the Multicultural Affairs Office. Needless to say, she is excited but also a little scared.

Regina is hoping that the course in student development theory for which she is registered will give her some clues as to how to approach the students with whom she will be working. After her orientation to the office, all she knows is how to use the phone system, what her e-mail address is, and who the other people in her division are. No one has provided much guidance as to the issues students are facing or how to go about addressing them. At this point all she has to go on is her own experience as an undergraduate, and she is bright enough to know that students at this large research university might have different concerns than she and her peers who attended a small historically black college.

In preparation for her first class, Regina pages through her student development theory text. There are so many theories! How will she ever learn them all? Will she be able to use all these concepts meaningfully in her work? Regina is feeling somewhat overwhelmed.

As Regina has intuitively discovered, understanding student development is crucial if one is to be an effective student affairs educator. The growth and development of students is a central goal of higher education, and student affairs professionals play an integral role in its achievement. To accomplish this goal, educators must be familiar with an extensive literature base focusing on student development and be able to use relevant concepts and ideas effectively in their daily interactions with students. In addition, program planning and policy development are both enhanced when student development concepts are used as a guide. Becoming knowledgeable about student development requires serious study, including critical analysis and evaluation of theory and research.

In Part One we will set the stage for examining student development. A number of concepts will be introduced to provide a context for the study of specific student development theories presented later in the book. Though some of this material may seem abstract and confusing at first reading, readers are encouraged to refer to the text of Part One when exploring later chapters. In Part Five we will revisit many of these ideas when we examine the use of theory in practice and consider the current state of our knowledge base with regard to student development.

In Chapter One we present various definitions of student development and clarify the various ways in which the concept has been applied. To provide historical background and a sense of how and why student development became the foundation of the student affairs profession, we trace the evolution of the student development approach. A framework is then introduced for organizing the theories we examine later in the book. We also introduce the concept of paradigms and discuss their influence on student development theory and research.

In the second chapter we discuss the role of theory in practice and provide suggestions for evaluating the potential utility of specific theories. We next examine the role of research and evaluation in the development of theory. We also make a case for linking theory to practice and review the major theory-to-practice models. The interactionist paradigm, which stresses the importance of considering the interaction of person and environment, is introduced. Factors in the college environment that facilitate development are then explored. As a prelude to examining theories in the following parts of the book, we end Chapter Two with a series of cautions to keep in mind when using theory.

Though the study of student development can be overwhelming at first, the wealth of knowledge that now exists about what happens to students in college is also gratifying and exciting. We hope that Regina—and our other readers—will embark as eager explorers on their journey of discovery.

CHAPTER ONE

STUDENT DEVELOPMENT AS A FIELD OF STUDY

From the paternalistic faculty authority figure who supervised Harvard students in 1636 to the contemporary student affairs professional who uses developmental theory to examine students' human potential, student development has existed in some configuration, from cryptic to sophisticated, since the beginning of American higher education. In fact, readers are reminded by a scholar of medieval higher education (Haskins, 1957) that human development "remain[s] much the same from age to age and must so remain as long as human nature and physical environment continue what they have been. In his relations to life and learning the medieval student resembled his modern successor far more than is often supposed" (p. 93). Given the slow pace of change in higher education, it is not surprising that it took over three centuries for practitioners, theorists, and scholars to begin examination of the developmental needs of diverse students.

The purpose of this chapter is to provide an overview of the ways in which student development has been defined in the literature and to examine the origins of major student development theories created in the second half of the twentieth century. The chapter ends with a discussion of the influence of paradigms on student development theory and research.

Definitions of Student Development

The term *student development* is used extensively in student affairs practice. Professionals talk about "facilitating student development"; offices are titled "Student Development"; graduate students study "student development theories." Student development is almost universally viewed as a good thing. Parker (1974), however, criticized student affairs professionals for attaching vague and nonspecific meanings to this term and suggested that for many it has become a catchphrase with no direct application to their work. What exactly do we mean, then, when we use the expression "student development"?

In 1967, Sanford defined *development* as "the organization of increasing complexity" (p. 47). He saw development as a positive growth process in which the individual becomes increasingly able to integrate and act on many different experiences and influences. He distinguished development from *change*, which refers only to an altered condition that may be positive or negative, progressive or regressive, and from *growth*, which refers to expansion but may be either favorable or unfavorable to overall functioning. Rodgers (1990b) defined *student development* as "the ways that a student grows, progresses, or increases his or her developmental capabilities as a result of enrollment in an institution of higher education" (p. 27).

Student development, Rodgers (1990b) noted, is also a philosophy that has guided student affairs practice and served as the rationale for specific programs and services since the profession's inception. He summed up this philosophy as "concern for the development of the whole person" (p. 27).

A related application of the term *student development* is programmatic. Rodgers (1990b) said that it is what student affairs professionals do to encourage learning and student growth. In a frequently quoted definition that reflects this perspective, Miller and Prince (1976) suggested that student development is "the application of human development concepts in postsecondary settings so that everyone involved can master increasingly complex developmental tasks, achieve self-direction, and become interdependent" (p. 3).

Rodgers (1990b) also noted that the term *student development* has been used to categorize the theory and research on late-adolescent and adult development. This body of literature includes psychosocial, cognitive-structural, and typology perspectives discussed in this book. These theories expand Sanford's definition of development by identifying specific aspects of development and examining factors that influence its occurrence. Specifically, developmental theory should respond to four questions (Knefelkamp, Widick, & Parker, 1978):

1. What interpersonal and intrapersonal changes occur while the student is in college?
2. What factors lead to this development?
3. What aspects of the college environment encourage or retard growth?
4. What developmental outcomes should we strive to achieve in college?

Student development theory provides the basis for the practice of student development. Knowledge of student development theory enables student affairs professionals to proactively identify and address student needs, design programs, develop policies, and create healthy college environments that encourage positive growth in students. Because student development theories focus on intellectual growth as well as affective and behavioral changes during the college years, they also encourage the collaborative efforts of student services professionals and faculty in enhancing student learning and maximizing positive student outcomes in higher education settings.

A Brief History of the Student Development Movement

Early in the twentieth century, the newly organized disciplines of psychology and sociology were applied to the collegiate environment. Psychological theorists such as Sigmund Freud, Carl Jung, and later B. F. Skinner examined human behavior through a lens different from that of the theologians who espoused the fostering of Christian moral character (Upcraft & Moore, 1990). As the scientific study of human development evolved, the academy responded by hiring student personnel workers who were viewed as human development specialists (Upcraft & Barr, 1990). At first they focused on vocational guidance; however, the tumultuous events of the mid-twentieth century prompted significant changes in the student personnel profession and how the profession viewed student development. Influences that contributed to this renewed focus on students were an embryonic student affairs field (American Council on Education, 1937/1994a, 1949/1994b), the psychology of individual differences (Parker, 1978), and the need for institutions, particularly during the Great Depression of the 1930s, to place students in the world of work (Miller & Winston, 1991).

The 1920s Guidance Movement

In the 1920s, the vocational guidance movement began in earnest as colleges and universities graduated students who increasingly sought occupational security as plebes to the captains of business and industry. Credited with initiating the vocational guidance movement (Moore & Upcraft, 1990), Frank Parsons (1909) was the first to articulate a "match" between personal characteristics and particular occupations to determine the "best fit" for individuals in the work environment. For the next forty years vocational guidance in higher education (and elsewhere) rested on this premise.

Taking more interest in vocational preparation than developing themselves in a holistic way (Arbuckle, 1953), students in the early 1920s sought practical knowledge to propel them into the work world. At the same time, higher education and industry joined to create new knowledge and train new workers.

In reaction to student demand for work preparation and industry demand for applied research, an alarm was sounded by critics who believed that the economic ties between industry and higher education must be severed in order to preserve academic freedom and integrity (Veblen, 1918/1946). At the same time, pragmatic philosophers, who asserted that optimal learning occurs when students' rational and emotional selves are integrated (Carpenter, 1996; Knock, 1988), alerted faculty and administrators to the need to make education more than just vocational preparation for entry into the employment pipeline. Combined, these latter two forces created a moral imperative for higher education to address students' multidimensional needs rather than focusing exclusively on vocational preparation.

The Student Personnel Point of View

In 1925, representatives from fourteen institutions of higher education met to discuss vocational guidance problems in colleges and universities. World War I was over, and increased enrollments left educators scrambling for ways to evaluate students and their needs.

From 1925 to 1936, data concerning students were collected at numerous institutions. Taking advantage of empirical methods, several specialized assessment tools, such as personality rating scales, were developed to examine students' ability and performance (American Council on Education, 1937/1994a). The culmination of these efforts was the American Council on Education's 1937 statement, the "Student Personnel Point of View" (SPPV). This landmark report recognized the proud lineage of higher education's commitment to "the preservation, transmission, and enrichment of the important elements of culture" that is produced in the forms of "scholarship, research, creative imagination, and human experience" (p. 67). The report went on to assert that educators must guide the "whole student" to reach his or her full potential and contribute to society's betterment. In short, the SPPV was a reminder to the higher education community that in addition to the contributions of research and scholarship, the personal and professional development of students was (and remains) a worthy and noble goal.

In 1949, the council revised the 1937 SPPV statement to include an expanded delineation of the objectives and goals of student affairs administration. Returning to the late-nineteenth-century focus on the psychology of individual differences, the document called for faculty, administrators, and student personnel workers to effect the development of students and recognize their "individual differences in backgrounds, abilities, interests, and goals" (American Council on Education, 1949/1994b, p. 110). Furthermore, the influence of World War II was reflected in the document's call for more attention to democratic processes and socially responsible graduates.

Foundational Theory and Research of the 1960s

The 1960s saw the beginning of significant changes in student affairs and higher education as the country faced nearly a decade of social turmoil brought on by the Vietnam War and the civil rights and women's movements. While students tried to change the world, social scientists—primarily from psychology and sociology—had already begun to theorize about how students change and grow in college.

Nevitt Sanford. Psychologist Nevitt Sanford was one of the first scholars to address the relationship between college environments and students' transition from late adolescence to young adulthood (Strange, 1994). He brought forth two insights about the process of development—(1) cycles of differentiation and integration and (2) balancing support and challenge—that continue to be influential concepts when considering student development (King, 1994; Moore & Upcraft, 1990). Differentiation and integration are evident when students learn about their own personality characteristics and understand how these characteristics shape their individual identities (Sanford, 1962). Support and challenge are evident when students try to lessen the tension produced by the collegiate environment and succeed to the extent that environmental support is available (Sanford, 1967). Sanford invariably argued that "a college should be a developmental community in which the student encounters both challenges and supports" (Knefelkamp, Widick, & Parker, 1978, p. ix). Sanford's concepts help educators understand the developmental process and are discussed in greater detail in Chapter Two.

Douglas Heath. Douglas Heath's theory (1968), based on his study of male undergraduates at Haverford College, focused on the concept of maturity and described factors that contribute to the maturation process. He identified characteristics of a mature person and described the path by which a person moves from "immature" to "mature" ways of functioning (Widick, Parker, & Knefelkamp, 1978a). Heath (1977) described his model as "a classification map, a working set of categories which order the principal hypotheses which theories claim distinguish mature from immature persons" (p. 6). Heath suggested that maturation occurs along five growth dimensions in four different areas: intellect, values, self-concept, and interpersonal relationships. The growth dimensions he identified are becoming more able to represent experience symbolically, becoming allocentric (other-centered), becoming integrated, becoming stable, and becoming autonomous (Widick, Parker, & Knefelkamp, 1978a). Heath (1977) posited that the environment is influential in either facilitating or inhibiting development along these dimensions. In evaluating Heath's contributions, Widick, Parker, and Knefelkamp (1978a) stated, "Heath's work does not give specific guidance for day-to-day practice. The model is a grand design and can best be used to help us consider the outcomes of an ideal educational experience" (p. 90).

Roy Heath. Based on a longitudinal study of the experiences of undergraduate men at Princeton during the 1950s, Roy Heath (1964) introduced a typology theory that focused on how individual differences affect students' progress toward maturity. Heath suggested that two dimensions must be considered when examining development: ego functioning and individual style. He defined *ego functioning* as "the manner in which the self interacts with the world, achieves its satisfaction, and defends itself from threats to its survival" (Heath, 1973, p. 59). Individuals are hypothesized to move through three levels of maturity as they progress to an idealized state that Heath called "a Reasonable Adventurer." *Individual style* or type refers to "the manner in which the individual regulates the 'dynamic tension' between the inner, instinctual, feeling self and the outer, more rational self" (Knelfelkamp, Parker, & Widick, 1978, p. 94). Individual style is posited to influence how the person proceeds through the levels of maturity to become a Reasonable Adventurer. Although Heath's model is important in stressing individual difference as a factor to consider in development, it does not provide a clear picture of factors that contribute to movement through the levels of maturity (Knefelkamp, Parker, & Widick, 1978). Knefelkamp, Parker, and Widick (1978) also stated that little research has been conducted, other than Heath's original 1964 study, to test the model.

Kenneth Feldman and Theodore Newcomb. Sociologists during the 1960s also examined the impact of college on students (Feldman & Newcomb, 1969). Recognizing how the environment shapes a student's development, some researchers focused on the interpersonal world of college students, specifically the effects of peer groups (Newcomb & Wilson, 1966). In an exhaustive summary of research on college students, Feldman and Newcomb (1969) delineated the impact of peer group influence on individual students. They noted that peer groups help students achieve family independence, facilitate the institution's intellectual goals, offer emotional support and meet needs not met by faculty, provide contact with and practice for interacting with others who are unlike the student, reinforce student change (or not), offer another source of gratification if unsuccessful academically, affect a student's leaving or staying in college, and provide social training and personal ties that may prove useful as a student progresses down a career path. Throughout the 1960s, sociologists and psychologists offered a fresh look at students and their interaction with the campus environment while student affairs professionals moved to promoting intentional student development in institutions of higher education (Creamer, 1990).

Formal Statements About Student Development. In the late 1960s and the 1970s, professional associations, such as the Council of Student Personnel Associations (COSPA) and the American College Personnel Association (ACPA), and private groups such as the Hazen Foundation, began to reconceptualize the role and mission of student affairs. The Hazen Foundation created the Committee on the Student in Higher Education (1968), which encouraged colleges and universities to "assume responsibility for the human development of [their] students" (p. 5), something never asked of higher education before. The committee went on to proclaim that "our educational procedures rarely take cognizance of what we do know about human development" (p. 5).

At the same time, Tomorrow's Higher Education Project (T.H.E.), initiated by ACPA, explored the viability of student development as a philosophy of the profession (Brown, 1972) and specifically examined the student affairs profession's "commitment to student development—the theories of human development applied to the postsecondary education setting—as a guiding theory, and the continued attempt to ensure that the development of the whole student was an institutional priority" (Garland & Grace, 1993, p. 6).

In his influential monograph *Student Development in Tomorrow's Higher Education—A Return to the Academy,* Brown (1972) challenged college administrators and student affairs professionals to "hold up the mirror" to each other to confront the incongruities between the stated goals of higher education and what is happening to students. He questioned whether student affairs professionals should be the only ones on campus concerned about student development and, more important, whether student development can be nurtured without the support and influence of those in the academic domain. A forerunner of "The Student Learning Imperative" (1996), the T.H.E. project recommended that student affairs educators take action on such issues as moving from a focus on the extracurriculum to an emphasis on the academic, improving teaching and learning experiences, reorganizing student affairs offices and functions, being accountable by conducting outcomes assessments, and developing new sets of competencies.

Soon thereafter, the Council of Student Personnel Associations (COSPA) (1975/1994) sought to define the roles of the student development specialist and close the gap between theory and practice in the field. Miller and Prince (1976) carried the concept one step closer to implementation by highlighting the developmental tasks of college students and suggesting program options to help students reach their developmental goals. Later, instruments that focused on measuring student development outcomes (Winston, Miller, & Prince, 1979) and assessing the effect of the institutional environment on students (Pace, 1984) were developed to seek empirical evidence of the student development concept. These statements of philosophy, along with the early research, provided impetus for the student affairs field to redefine itself in ways that helped professionals meet the challenges of intentional student growth.

Student Development Theory Today

Between 1960 and the present, an explosion of developmental theory related to students found its way into the literature in numerous fields of study, including student affairs. After careful review of human development theories and models, Knefelkamp, Widick, and Parker (1978) realized the futility of designing one "comprehensive model of student development" (p. xi). Existing developmental theories do, however, tend to group into several categories, including psychosocial theories, cognitive-structural theories, and typology theories. In addition, person-environment models have been introduced that provide guidance concerning the factors that influence development. A brief description of the categories and their leading architects follows.

Psychosocial Theory. Psychosocial theory examines individuals' personal and interpersonal lives (Evans, 1996). Early psychosocial developmental research was conducted by the influential Erik Erikson (1950, 1968). He described psychosocial development as a sequence of developmental tasks or stages confronted by adults when their biology and psychology converge and "qualitatively change their thinking, feeling, behaving, valuing, and relating to others and oneself" (Chickering & Reisser, 1993, p. 2). Psychosocial theorists posit that "human development continues throughout the life span and that a basic underlying psychosocial structure guides this development" (Rodgers, 1990c, p. 122).

One of the most widely cited student development theorists is Arthur Chickering (1969). Building on the work of Erikson, Chickering described seven vectors of development that cumulatively contribute to a sense of identity. In a revision of Chickering's original theory, Chickering and Reisser (1993) pointed out that age-specific cultural norms and roles define the environmental demands placed on a developing individual, while culture and gender-related influences can vary the sequence in which adults perform developmental tasks.

Other identity models, many of which are built on the work of Erikson, are applicable to college students. Recent trends in research include an examination of the experiences of women and other diverse populations. More recent work includes Marcia's model of ego identity status (1966), Josselson's pathways to women's identity (1987a), Cross's model of African American identity (1991), Helms's model of white identity (1993d), Phinney's model of ethnic identity (1990), and models of homosexual identity by D'Augelli (1994a) and Cass (1979). All are discussed in following chapters. While these identity models all focus on the psychosocial process of self-definition, many of the models are also cognitive-structural in that individuals move through stages of increasing cognitive complexity with regard to their self-identification (Helms, 1993a).

Cognitive-Structural Theory. Cognitive-structural theories illuminate changes in the *way* people think but not *what* they think (Evans, 1996). Derived from Piagetian psychology (Piaget, 1952), these theories stress the importance of heredity and environment in intellectual development and reveal the various ways an individual develops cognitively. Cognitive-structural stages, which are "sets of assumptions people use to adapt to and organize their environments" (Evans, 1996, p. 173), always occur in sequential order regardless of cultural influence. Theorists who have helped shape student affairs perspectives of cognitive development are Perry (1968), Kohlberg (1969), and King and Kitchener (1994).

Recently, cognitive-structural theorists examining both intellectual and moral development have focused on gender differences in cognitive growth. Theorists who inform our view about gender differences in the cognitive domain include Belenky, Clinchy, Goldberger, and Tarule (1986), Gilligan (1982/1993), and Baxter Magolda (1992). The work of these cognitive-structural theorists will be reviewed in Part Three.

Typology Theory. Typology theorists "examine individual differences in how people view and relate to the world" (Evans, 1996, p. 179). Although typologies are not developmental in the psychosocial or cognitive-structural sense, innate individual differences occur in mental processing (Jung, 1923/1971)—for instance, in how individuals learn and what interests them. These differences in turn influence development in other arenas. As nonevaluative appraisals, typology theories stress that individual differences are good and healthy for the community. The assumption at their core is that each individual, representing any type, brings unique, positive contributions to each situation. Major theoretical contributions to typology theory are the Myers-Briggs theory of personality type (Myers, 1980), Holland's theory of vocational interest (1985/1992), and Kolb's theory of learning styles (1984). All are discussed in Part Four.

Person-Environment Theory. Person-environment interaction models examine not only the student and the college environment but, even more important, the interaction of the student with the environment (Rodgers, 1990b). When used in a deliberate manner to convert theory to practice, these models help the practitioner examine the different types of student development possible, "the criteria for deliberately designing environments that facilitate development, and instruments or other means for measuring development" (p. 32). The interaction of student and environment as an overriding concept is discussed in Chapter Two.

The Influence of Paradigms

McEwen (1996a) noted that theory development can occur as a result of shifting paradigms. Guba (1990) defined a paradigm as an interpretive framework, a "basic set of beliefs that guides action" (p. 17). When a particular paradigm dominates thinking, its assumptions are unquestioned and implicitly undergird the understanding of phenomena. A paradigm consists of three components: epistemology, ontology, and methodology (Denzin & Lincoln, 1994, p. 99). Epistemology examines how the inquirer comes to understand the world. Ontology explores questions about the nature of reality. Methodology focuses on how information is obtained. Guba and Lincoln (1994) pointed out that since paradigms represent basic beliefs, they cannot be proved. However, they are human constructions, subject to human error. Guba and Lincoln caution that "no construction is or can be incontrovertibly right; advocates of any particular construction must rely on *persuasiveness* and *utility* rather than *proof* in arguing their position" (p. 108).

Paradigms guide both theory and research. However, when the results of research cannot be explained within the context of the dominant paradigm, competing paradigms emerge that can better account for the findings (Kuhn, 1970). Theory and research in psychology, as well as most other fields, have been guided by the positivist paradigm for the past four centuries (Guba & Lincoln, 1994). This interpretation of the world assumes that there is an objective reality that is time- and context-free and can be stated in the form of cause-and-effect laws. A researcher is assumed to be independent of the object that is being investigated. According to this view, the investigator is able to study a phenomenon without influencing the outcome or being influenced by the object of study. The methodology used to study phenomena is experimental and manipulative. Hypotheses are formulated and subjected to empirical testing for verification. Conditions that could interfere with the results are carefully controlled.

Most of the theory and research reviewed in this book has a positivist perspective. For instance, King and Kitchener (1994) presented stages of cognitive development that they believe are apparent in the thinking of individuals regardless of the situation in which the individuals find themselves. These researchers have studied cognitive development using a standardized interview protocol that they train interviewers to present in a similar manner to all research participants. King and Kitchener have outlined a program of research based on explicitly stated hypotheses that they then test in a predetermined manner. This research is used to verify the concepts associated with their theory.

The work of King and Kitchener is excellent within the context of the positivistic tradition. However, many researchers are beginning to find such a perspective constraining. In an attempt to better explain the complexity that exists in the world today, a number of competing paradigms are emerging. Guba and Lincoln (1994) have outlined the assumptions of two of the major alternative paradigms: critical theory and constructivism. Critical theory assumes that reality is influenced by social, political, economic, ethnic, and gender-related factors. Ideas become solidified over time and are taken as "truth." Adherents of this perspective believe that research findings are inevitably influenced by the values of the inquirer. Inquiry is seen as transactional, requiring a dialogue between the researcher and the subjects of the inquiry. The purpose of inquiry is to raise consciousness and correct injustices resulting from ignorance and mistaken ideas. The work of many feminist and ethnic scholars can be situated in the critical theory paradigm. An excellent example of a study conducted within the context of critical theory is Rhoads's work, *Coming Out in College: The Struggle for a Queer Identity* (1994). Rhoads argued that our view of gay identity has been shaped by the political and cultural biases that exist in society today. He undertook an ethnographic study in which he immersed himself in gay student culture for two years. He presented his findings in a persuasive way designed to correct the misperceptions that exist about gay men. His agenda, like that of other critical theorists, is clearly political.

Constructivists view reality as relative (Guba & Lincoln, 1994). Reality is based on the specific experiences and perceptions of individuals and groups and can change over time. Investigators and subjects of investigation are viewed as linked; findings are created in the context of the investigation. Because of the variable and personal nature of social constructions, they can only be identified through interaction between the researcher and participants involved in the research. Baxter Magolda's work (1992) is constructivist. She set out to discover how students at Miami University thought about their worlds. While guided by earlier work on cognitive development, she entered her investigation without preconceived ideas about what she would find. Her findings were based on a series of in-depth interviews she conducted with 101 students over a period of several years.

In the presentation of her findings, Baxter Magolda allows her participants to present their interpretations of the world around them in their own words.

New paradigm thinking is having a profound influence on all fields, including student affairs (Kuh, Whitt, & Shedd, 1987). Student development is being reconceptualized within these new frameworks. Being familiar with the paradigmatic assumptions underlying a theory is crucial to understanding and using the theory appropriately. To give a sense of the epistemological, ontological, and methodological base of the work, throughout this book we present background about the theories and discuss the context in which they were developed. We also outline the populations and methods used in the construction of each theory reviewed.

Concluding Thoughts

Student affairs professionals appear to be the strongest and most consistent voice in the academy articulating concern for the human growth and development of students. Development of the whole student is more complex than one theory or even a cluster of theories can explain. We can only know in hindsight how our history will shape the future of student development, but for the sake of our students, we must help the academy recognize the value of the whole person concept. Student development is far too important to be recognized only as a role for student affairs professionals.

CHAPTER TWO

USING STUDENT DEVELOPMENT THEORY

Jana has recently accepted a position as coordinator of returning adult services at a large research university. Both academic and student affairs at this university focus on serving the large numbers of traditionally aged students who enroll there. In fact, Jana is the only full-time staff person in her unit. Adult students make up approximately 10 percent of the student population, but they are not highly visible on campus. Many attend classes part time while holding full-time jobs or caring for their families. They range in age from twenty-four (the age the university uses to define a returning adult student) to over sixty. Most live off campus, although a few live in married and graduate student housing. Jana quickly discovers that very few of these students use the services of her office; indeed, many do not even know of its existence. She has been charged by her vice president to develop a comprehensive and visible program to serve the needs of the adult student population. She hardly knows where to begin.

A knowledge of student development theory can be of great benefit to Jana as she addresses the challenges of her new job, but only if she uses these approaches wisely. Successfully using student development theory requires more than merely memorizing various stages, vectors, and theoretical concepts. In this chapter we provide a context for understanding and using theory that sets the stage for later chapters that examine specific theoretical approaches. We discuss several theory-to-practice models, as well as concepts considered important if development is to occur. Finally, we consider a number of factors to keep in mind when using theory in practice.

The Role of Theory

Theory is the result of the need people have to make sense out of life. It enables the organization and interpretation of the enormous amount of information that exists in the world. Each of us has a set of organizing principles, an "informal theory" that we use to make sense of our experiences. Parker (1977) defined *informal theory* as "the body of common knowledge that allows us to make implicit connections among events and persons in our environment and upon which we act in everyday life" (p. 420). As McEwen (1996a) explained, informal theories are influenced by a person's own background, experiences, and value system. These factors serve as filters through which people examine and interpret the experiences of others. Certainly, Jana brings to her position a set of ideas about the needs and concerns of adult students. These assumptions may be based on her previous interactions with adult students, her own experiences in college, the values she grew up with concerning education and what it means to be an adult, and her formal training and education.

Unfortunately, informal theory is not self-correcting (Parker, 1977). People have no basis on which to determine if their interpretations are accurate or not. Formal theories validated by research are needed to ascertain whether individuals' perceptions hold for the persons with whom they work and the situations in which they find themselves. Rodgers (1980) defined formal theory as "a set of propositions regarding the interrelationship of two or more conceptual variables relevant to some realm of phenomena. It provides a framework for explaining the relationship among variables and for empirical investigations" (p. 81). A theory is an abstract representation based on a "potentially infinite number of specific and concrete variations of a phenomenon" (Strange & King, 1990, p. 17). For instance, many theorists have examined adult development (including Erikson, 1959/1980; Neugarten, 1979; and Schlossberg, Waters, & Goodman, 1995). Jana will find these theories particularly helpful as she begins to identify the needs of her students in a systematic manner.

Theory has four increasingly powerful uses: description, explanation, prediction, and control (DiCaprio, 1974). At the first level, description, theory provides a conceptualization of what is happening. For instance, Chickering and Reisser (1993) identified a series of developmental issues, such as developing competence and managing emotions, that describe the experiences of college students. At the second level, theory can be used to explain the causes of behavior. For example, Perry's theory of cognitive development (1968) suggests that some students exhibit dualistic, either-or thinking. This information might explain why a student is having trouble in a course that involves a great deal of analysis and evaluation of arguments. At the third level, which very few theories achieve, prediction is the goal. A powerful theory might enable us to predict the developmental outcome of placing a student with certain characteristics in a particular residence hall setting. For instance, Holland's theory (1985/1992) suggests that students will perform better in an environment made up of students who have personality types that are similar to their own. The final level, which developmental theory has yet to accomplish, is control. Hypothetically, if a more comprehensive knowledge base existed, theory would enable us to produce specific developmental outcomes, such as higher levels of moral reasoning. (Some would argue, of course, that such a goal is manipulative and therefore inappropriate anyway.)

Evaluating Theory

The number of student development theories has increased significantly since 1965 (Terenzini, 1994). Not all theories are of equal value to educators. To be useful, theories must exhibit certain qualities: comprehensiveness, clarity and explicitness, consistency, parsimony, and heurism (Walsh, 1973). First, a theory should make predictions that account for a wide range of behavior. Concepts and relationships should be defined precisely. The theory should allow for inclusion of findings within a logical framework. Explanations should be simple and easy to follow. Finally, the theory should generate testable hypotheses leading to useful research. An additional and very important criterion is the degree to which the theory is useful to practitioners (McEwen, 1996a).

Knefelkamp (1978) suggested a number of questions for evaluating the utility of theory:

1. *On what population is the theory based?* It is important to determine the population on which the theory was based and whether the theory has been tested with individuals who have different characteristics. Some aspects of the theory may be specific to the original population, while other concepts may apply to people more generally.
2. *How was the theory developed?* The assessment instruments or techniques that were used in the original study should be clearly described. Assessment tools should be available for further theoretical study and evaluation of developmental outcomes.
3. *Is the theory descriptive?* Does the theory provide a comprehensive view of individuals' development and specific aspects of the developmental process?
4. *Is the theory explanatory?* Does the theory outline how development occurs?
5. *Is the theory prescriptive?* Does the theory discuss ways in which specific outcomes can be produced and lead to the prediction of events or relationships that can be verified through observation or experimentation?

6. *Is the theory heuristic?* Theory should generate research ideas.
7. *Is the theory useful in practice?* Theory should help in understanding one's clientele, in developing programs to serve them, and in evaluating the effectiveness of services provided.

Most theories fall short on one or more of these criteria. For instance, student development theories are largely descriptive, rarely explanatory or prescriptive (Parker, Widick, & Knefelkamp, 1978). McEwen (1996a) also noted that it is important to remember that no theory is really objective. Each reflects the perspective of its author. However, existing theories are sources of awareness that serve as a means of organizing one's thinking and guiding the choices that are made in working with students.

The Role of Research and Evaluation

Research plays an important role in both the development and the refinement of theory (Terenzini, 1994). Though some theories have evolved from informal observation and logic, most student development theories have been based on research specifically designed to determine what factors are important in development, how development occurs, and what environmental conditions facilitate development. Once an initial theory is outlined, research is needed to test assumptions and hypotheses that grow out of the theory. The results are then used to modify and refine the theory. Researchers also examine the applicability of the theory for different populations and explore its utility in various settings.

For example, Kohlberg (1958) conducted an initial study of boys between the ages of ten and sixteen to explore factors related to their moral reasoning. He used his findings as the basis for preliminary hypotheses about how moral development occurs (Kohlberg, 1969). He then formulated an extensive program of research to systematically test out hypotheses. The results of his studies led him to modify and refine his theory (Kohlberg, Levine, & Hewer, 1984a). Kohlberg and other researchers have also extended his theory to both men and women across the life span and from various cultural backgrounds. (See Chapter Ten for a more complete discussion of Kohlberg's work and the work of others based on his theory.)

When deciding whether a theory is valid (that is, whether it presents an accurate picture of development), practitioners should examine the research on which it was based as well as later studies that have tested the theory's assumptions, propositions, and generalizability. An important criterion of good theory is the extent to which it can be verified by research as well as its ability to generate new knowledge (McEwen, 1996a). Evaluation differs from research in that it is used to determine the effectiveness of specific programs or interventions. When used to assess the outcomes of theory-based interventions, evaluation data can contribute to our knowledge base by answering theoretical as well as practical questions. For example, a theoretically grounded evaluation might tell us not only if a program works but also for whom it works and possibly why it works for some students but not others. In this way, evaluation contributes to the refinement of theory. Kohlberg (1971) used his theory of moral development to develop moral education programs in schools. His evaluation of these programs, like his earlier validation research, led to modification of his theory. Evaluation is an important component in the design of any educational intervention.

Both research and evaluation, then, are important for the evolution of theory. Only by systematically examining theoretical concepts and propositions in practical situations involving actual human beings can we determine if the theory is a useful tool for understanding human development. Research and evaluation provide links to real life that allow for modification of existing theory and development of new theory.

Linking Theory and Practice

Student affairs practice without a theoretical base is not effective or efficient. A "fly by the seat of your pants" approach may sometimes result in beneficial outcomes, but it is just as likely to result in disaster. Jana could try to guess what the adult students on her campus need on the basis of her own experiences or the suggestions of her associates, but there are no guarantees that her guesses or theirs would be correct.

Nor can theory meaningfully exist in a vacuum. To be of any utility, theory must be related to practical situations found in real-life settings. Jana could study every adult development theory in existence, but unless she relates the theoretical principles she has learned to the specific students and university context in which she is working, she may also miss the mark.

A link is needed to connect the everyday reality of students' experiences and the conceptual frameworks provided by developmental theory. Models are designed to provide this "developmental bridge" between theory and practice (Evans, Bradley, & Bradley, 1985). Models do not define phenomena or explain relationships; they provide guidance in using the theories that do these things. Two types of models exist: *process models* consist of a recommended series of action steps for connecting theory to practice; *procedural models* present a particular way of accomplishing some aspect of student affairs practice.

Several writers have proposed models that help educators use theory effectively in practice (see Evans et al., 1985, for a complete list). Process models developed by Knefelkamp, Golec, and Wells (1985) and Rodgers & Widick (1980) and the procedural models introduced by Morrill, Oetting, and Hurst (1974) and Evans (1987) are particularly helpful to student affairs professionals and other educators.

The Practice-to-Theory-to-Practice (PTP) Model

Knefelkamp, Golec, and Wells (1985) proposed an eleven-step model for relating theory to the practical problems of student affairs practice. The authors of the model recommended identification of the issue to be addressed, tying that issue to relevant theories, analyzing the issue through a theoretical lens, designing an intervention that will facilitate development, and implementing the intervention in practice. The specific steps are as follows:

Practice

1. Identifying concerns that need to be addressed
2. Determining desired goals and outcomes

Description

3. Investigating theories that may be helpful in understanding the issue and achieving the desired goals
4. Analyzing relevant student characteristics from the perspective of the theories identified
5. Analyzing characteristics of the environment associated with the issue from the perspective of identified theories

Translation

6. Identifying potential sources of challenge and support, taking into account both student and environmental characteristics, and recognizing factors that produce a balance

Prescription

7. Reexamining goals and outcomes in light of the theoretical analysis
8. Designing the intervention using methods that will encourage achievement of goals

Practice

9. Implementing the intervention
10. Evaluating the outcomes of the intervention
11. Redesigning the intervention if necessary

The PTP model works equally well in designing classroom strategies, developing programming, and determining services to be provided by various student services units. Jana could certainly use this model as a guide as she identifies services needed by the adult students on her campus. Adult development theories would be especially useful in determining the developmental issues faced by the students with whom she is working. This assessment could then be used, for example, to develop an orientation program or ongoing workshop series. A specific intervention developed using the PTP model is presented in Chapter Fifteen.

The Grounded Formal Theory Model

Rodgers and Widick (1980) proposed a similar model for using student development theory to enhance student affairs practice. Their Grounded Formal Theory model differs from the PTP model in that it involves using theoretically based measurement methods to assess students' developmental levels and developing interventions based on the obtained data. This model is particularly helpful when a specific population needing a service can be identified and assessed. The steps in the Grounded Formal Theory model are as follows:

1. *Focusing on a problem, context, and population.* This step involves examining all factors related to the situation of concern or interest. For example, one of the problems Jana faces is the low number of adult students using her service. The context would be the conditions that exist on her campus, and the population would be the adult students on campus.

2. *Selecting useful and usable formal theories.* The chosen theories should include those related to both the content of the problem and student development. In the scenario at the start of this chapter, for example, Astin's involvement theory (1984) would relate to the content of the problem of low usage. The transition theory of Schlossberg, Waters, and Goodman (1995) would be helpful in examining the developmental issues of adults.

3. *Grounding theories in the context.* Methods of measurement associated with the chosen theories are used to assess the needs and developmental levels of the students who will be participating in the intervention. The data obtained are used to conceptualize the problem. In the example, Jana might look for an instrument designed to assess the involvement level of students. A second instrument could be used to determine developmental issues facing the students. Let's say her assessment reveals very low involvement and a lack of self-confidence in academic ability among the adult students at her university. Jana might hypothesize that students aren't getting involved because they are worried about their ability to perform academically and are afraid to do anything outside of the classroom.

4. *Formulating goals.* In this step, both developmental and content-related goals are identified. In the scenario, a developmental goal might be to enhance

the academic self-confidence of adult students while a content-related goal would be to increase the involvement of adult students in the activities of the Office for Returning Adult Students.

5. *Designing interventions or programs.* Theoretical concepts guide development of both the content of the program and the process (that is, the way in which the program is presented). For instance, knowing that adult students often "recycle" through developmental issues also faced by younger students (Chickering & Reisser, 1993), Jana might refer to Chickering's theory to learn more about the developmental task of achieving competence. This information could be used in the context of a program designed to address this need among adult students. In addition, knowing that it is important that students feel as if they matter to someone (Schlossberg, 1989a) might guide Jana to design the program to involve peer mentors to work with students in their academic areas.

6. *Examining theory-in-use of staff and conducting process evaluation.* The assumptions, beliefs, knowledge base, and skills of the individuals implementing the program are checked to make sure that they are effectively carrying out the program as it was designed. To carry out this step, Jana might conduct interviews with selected adult students and their peer mentors to determine what has been happening during their meetings.

7. *Evaluating the intervention and selected theoretical questions.* The outcomes of the program are assessed to determine its impact and to answer theoretical questions of interest. Jana will want to develop a systematic plan for evaluating the peer mentor program. Her plan might include a review of retention rates and grade point averages for participants compared to those of nonparticipants. An instrument designed to measure academic self-confidence could also provide information. Jana might also want to assess whether adult students involved in the peer mentoring program were attending other programs sponsored by her office and whether the overall numbers of students using her office's services had increased.

The Cube

Morrill, Oetting, and Hurst (1974) introduced a model to assist student affairs professionals in developing interventions designed to enhance student learning. Referred to as "the Cube" because its three dimensions are often arranged along the sides of a cube when the model is diagrammed, the model is designed to encourage greater variety in the creation of student affairs interventions. The three dimensions of the Cube model are the target of the intervention, the purpose of the intervention, and the method of the intervention.

The target of the intervention may be (1) *individual students,* (2) *primary groups* (such as roommates, couples in committed partnerships, or families), (3) *associa-*

tional groups that come together for a purpose (such as classes or student organizations), or (4) *institutions or communities* that have an identity but do not bring their members together in a systematic way (such as a particular college, university, or neighborhood).

The purpose of an intervention may be (1) *remediation* of an existing problem (such as tutoring to assist a student who is failing a class), (2) *prevention* of a potential problem (such as the development of a study skills program for high-risk students), or (3) *development* of skills (such as an academic enrichment program for students interested in pursuing a topic in greater depth than is possible in a regular classroom).

The method of intervention may be (1) *direct service,* where a professional provides the service (such as an academic adviser assisting a student with the preparation of his or her schedule); (2) *consultation and training,* where the professional consults with or trains other individuals to provide the service (such as a career counselor training peer counselors to assist students in preparing résumés); or (3) *media,* where materials are prepared to provide information (such as a videotape series on stress management).

The Cube model provides a vehicle for tying "programs and activities together with some unifying direction or purpose" (Morrill, Hurst, & Oetting, 1980, p. 85). It "not only provides a framework within which alternative modes of intervention can be both classified and understood" but "also implicitly carries with it the stimulation to consider various targets, purposes, and methods so that the best all-around intervention procedures will be developed" (Morrill, Oetting, & Hurst, 1974, p. 359). The Cube model can be a way to organize existing programs and services designed to enhance development, a tool for evaluating "holes" in existing program offerings, and a stimulus for creative program development.

The Developmental Intervention Model

Evans (1987) presented a framework for facilitating development that encourages student affairs professionals to use a variety of strategies. She noted that developmental interventions can be targeted at either the individual or the institution, that they can be either planned or responsive, and that the approach used can be either explicit or implicit. These three components are defined as follows:

Target of intervention. Individual interventions focus on the attitudes, knowledge, or behavior of specific students. For instance, Jana could develop a study skills workshop for returning adult students that would improve their skills in reading comprehension and note taking, and increase their confidence in their ability to successfully handle college-level coursework.

Institutional interventions are designed to create a developmental environment on campus. Giving attention to the developmental implications of university policy is a particularly powerful way to affect the climate (Coomes, 1994). For example, knowing that returning adults are at a disadvantage when taking standardized tests, Jana might chair a task force designed to reevaluate a university policy requiring all students to submit SAT scores for admission.

Type of intervention. Planned interventions are intentional, proactive, and structured. They anticipate problems or developmental needs that students are expected to face in college. Since research indicates that many adult students return to school when they are experiencing life transitions such as divorce, loss of a job, or having children leave home (Schlossberg, Lynch, & Chickering, 1989), Jana might plan a series of workshops on these topics to take place throughout the semester.

Responsive interventions are reactive; they make use of, or respond to, opportunities or issues as they arise. Noticing that a group of adult students have remained after an orientation program to talk and share concerns, for example, Jana might suggest to the students that they form a support group to meet on a weekly basis.

Intervention approach. Explicit interventions address developmental issues directly. The workshop series as a planned intervention uses an explicit approach; developmental issues suggested by adult development theory and research are specifically addressed.

Implicit interventions approach developmental issues indirectly. For instance, the lack of confidence experienced by many adult learners could be addressed by asking adult students who had been enrolled for several semesters to serve as peer counselors for new adult students. Through this intervention, more experienced students would discover that they have much to offer to new students, and new students would be provided with successful role models.

Considering various combinations of target, type, and approach leads to a comprehensive program of interventions that can have a powerful developmental impact on students. The Developmental Intervention model encourages student affairs professionals to think in purposeful and creative ways as they consider applications of theoretical concepts and approaches.

The Interactionist Perspective

The famous equation $B = f(P \times E)$ is the cornerstone on which our understanding of student development is based. Introduced by Kurt Lewin (1936), the formula states that behavior (B) is a function (f) of the interaction ($\times$) of person (P) and environment (E). To understand why people behave as they do and to facilitate their development, such factors as their characteristics, background, and developmental level must be examined. Factors related to the environment in which the person is living, studying, or working must also be explored. Most important, the interaction of these variables must be considered; not every person will experience an environment in the same way.

Let's consider the adult students with whom Jana works. For example, a twenty-five-year-old single mother working in a factory and registering for one evening class a semester may have almost no impression of the campus as a whole. Her class is only one of the many demands on her time and energy. In contrast, a twenty-four-year-old army veteran attending classes full time and living in a residence hall is likely to be greatly influenced by his living arrangements, his classes, and the students with whom he interacts on a regular basis. In all likelihood, it will be much easier for Jana to reach the veteran than the single mother since the veteran is much more involved in campus life and sees himself primarily as a student. Jana will need to make more of an effort to establish contact with the single mother and to let this student know that support services are available to assist her.

Student development theories help describe the "person" aspect of Lewin's equation. They provide information about issues people are facing and ways in which individuals think about and process those issues. However, we must not neglect the "environment" side of the equation, for it is environments, in the form of physical surroundings, organizational structures, and human aggregates, that present the experiences that either retard or facilitate development (Strange, 1996). And by intentionally attending to the "design" of the environment (Banning, 1989) through implementation of policy, creation of programs, and training and supervision of staff, educators can help ensure that the person-environment interaction is healthy and developmentally enhancing.

Environmental Factors Influencing Development

Several conditions that are found (or not found) in the college environment can have a major impact on students' growth and development. These include the concepts of challenge and support, involvement, marginality and mattering, and validation. These concepts are helpful to consider in relation to their impact on aspects of development to be discussed in later chapters in this book.

Challenge and Support

Nevitt Sanford (1966) was one of the first developmental theorists to pay attention to the idea of student development as a function of person-environment interaction. He proposed three developmental conditions: readiness, challenge, and support. With regard to readiness, he hypothesized that individuals cannot exhibit certain behaviors until they are ready to do so. Readiness results because of either the internal processes associated with maturation or beneficial conditions in the environment.

In discussing the influence of the environment, Sanford (1966) suggested that the goal should be to find the range of optimal dissonance for the person. If the environment presents too much challenge, individuals tend to regress to earlier, less adaptive modes of behavior; polarize and solidify current modes of behavior; escape the challenge if possible; or ignore the challenge if escape is impossible. If there is too little challenge in the environment, individuals may feel safe and satisfied, but they do not develop.

The amount of challenge a person can tolerate is a function of the amount of support available (Sanford, 1966). The range of optimal dissonance for any particular person varies, depending on the quality of the challenge and support that the environment provides as well as the characteristics of the individual. For example, adult students such as the single mother mentioned earlier are already facing many challenges when they choose to enter college. They are in need of support to succeed in their educational endeavors. If the university environment fails to provide such support or if the students do not obtain the available support, the additional challenge of taking classes on top of the stresses of work and family life may be too great, leading students to drop out of college. Being aware of this possibility, Jana might think about sponsoring a support group for adult students and more vigorously publicizing the services her office provides.

Involvement

Astin (1984) stressed the role of student involvement in development. He defined involvement as "the amount of physical and psychological energy that the student devotes to the academic experience" (p. 297). He further clarified that involvement refers to behavior, what the student actually does, rather than the student's feelings or thoughts. Astin's theory has five postulates (p. 298):

1. "Involvement refers to the investment of physical and psychological energy in various objects." An object can be anything from the student experience as a whole to a specific activity, such as an intramural volleyball game.
2. "Regardless of the object, involvement occurs along a continuum." Some students will invest more energy than other students, and any particular student will be more involved in certain activities than others.
3. "Involvement has both quantitative and qualitative features." A quantitative aspect of involvement would be the amount of time devoted to an activity,

whereas a qualitative component would be the seriousness with which the object was approached and the attention given to it.

4. "The amount of student learning and personal development associated with any educational program is directly proportional to the quality and quantity of student involvement in that program." Basically, the more students put into an activity, the more they will get out of it.

5. "The effectiveness of any educational policy or practice is directly related to the capacity of that policy or practice to increase student involvement."

Rather than examining development itself, Astin's approach focuses on factors that facilitate development. He argued that for student learning and growth to take place, students need to actively engage in their environment. Student affairs professionals and other educators need to create opportunities for involvement to occur, both in and out of the classroom.

Astin's ideas provide further support for Jana's efforts to create programs that would further engage the adult students at her institution by providing opportunities for active involvement.

Marginality and Mattering

Nancy Schlossberg (1989a) pointed to the importance of considering the concepts of marginality and mattering when examining the impact of the college experience on student development. Feelings of marginality often occur when individuals take on new roles, especially when they are uncertain about what a new role entails. Marginality can be defined as a sense of not fitting in and can lead to self-consciousness, irritability, and depression. For members of minority groups, marginality is often a permanent condition; others, such as new college students from dominant populations, may temporarily experience these feelings.

Schlossberg (1989a) suggested that when individuals feel marginal, they worry about whether they matter to anyone. Schlossberg defined mattering as "our belief, whether right or wrong, that we matter to someone else" (p. 9). Drawing on the work of Rosenberg and McCullough (1981), Schlossberg investigated four aspects of mattering: *attention,* the feeling that one is noticed; *importance,* the belief that one is cared about; *ego extension,* the feeling that someone else will be proud of what one does or will sympathize with one's failures; and *dependence,* the feeling of being needed. Based on her own research, Schlossberg added a fifth dimension: *appreciation,* the feeling that one's efforts are appreciated by others.

Schlossberg (1989a) stressed that institutions of higher education need to help people feel like they matter. She saw this goal as a precursor to students' becoming involved in activities and academic programs that would facilitate development and learning. Schlossberg would caution Jana, for instance, that the adult students with whom she is working would need to feel like they mattered before they would become involved in activities. Personal attention in the form of phone calls to individual students might be one strategy that Jana could use to create a sense of mattering.

Validation

In a study examining the experiences of students in college, Rendón (1994) discovered that whereas traditional students expressed few concerns about being academically successful, nontraditional students (those from diverse racial, ethnic, and cultural backgrounds) were often doubtful of their academic ability. She found that active intervention in the form of validation was needed to encourage nontraditional students to become involved in campus life and to enhance their self-esteem. Rendón defined validation as "an enabling, confirming and supportive process initiated by in- and out-of-class agents that foster academic and interpersonal development" (p. 46). Students who were validated developed confidence in their ability to learn, experienced enhanced feelings of self-worth, and believed that they had something to offer the academic community. Validation can occur in a variety of settings, including the classroom, student organizations, or the community. Validating agents can be instructors, classmates, student affairs staff, relatives, friends, or other people who are significant to the student in some way.

Rendón (1994) viewed validation as a developmental process rather than a goal. She suggested that "the more students get validated, the richer the academic and interpersonal experience" (p. 44). Validation is most powerful when offered during the early stages of the student's academic experience, preferably during the first few weeks of classes.

The need for validation is likely to apply to adult students, who are often first-generation college students experiencing many doubts about their ability to succeed. Jana needs to keep this factor in mind as she talks with students and develops programs to meet their needs. Often a few words of encouragement can make a significant impact on a person who has no other source of support.

Cautions in Using Theory

Using student development theory appropriately takes time and practice. Several cautions may assist individuals as they undertake this complex process.

This book introduces a number of important student development theories. As mentioned in the Preface, there are others that could also be used to guide educational practice. In the future, new theories will be added to the list. The probability of learning and understanding each of these theories well enough to use them all in practice is low. Initially identifying a few theories that make sense and seem to explain development in a way that is logical and useful is generally a good strategy for determining which theories to study in depth and use in practice. However, it is important to be aware of the limitations of these theories and to consider populations and settings for which they are not appropriate.

Theory can rarely be "applied" in "whole chunks" (Weith, 1985). Specific concepts and ideas associated with a particular theory will be useful in certain cases while other concepts from that theory will not.

Kuh, Whitt, and Shedd (1987) cautioned against the use of labels. Too often terms such as *dualist* or *introvert* are used to describe a person without much thought being given to what the concept really implies. *Introvert* becomes incorrectly equated with *antisocial, dualist* with *stubborn,* and so on. It is important to explain the meaning of terms carefully and to present evidence to support their use. Better yet, educators could forgo the use of labels altogether and talk about individuals' behavior. As Kuh et al. correctly noted, once applied, labels are difficult to change.

In 1978, Parker et al. outlined three cautions in using theory that are still important to keep in mind. First of all, theories are descriptive. They do not indicate what behaviors or changes are best for students. It cannot be assumed that specific kinds of change predicted by theory ought to be encouraged, particularly in light of the Eurocentric value system on which these theories are based.

Second, whereas theories attempt to describe universal phenomena, students are unique individuals. As Strange and King (1990) noted, "Theory cannot be an accurate description of any specific reality, but only an approximate representation of many" (p. 18). Theoretical concepts must be evaluated in light of individual differences. The person should always take precedence over the theory. This caution is particularly important to keep in mind when working with groups of students who may exhibit different levels of development and individually vary from theoretical predictions.

Third, educators must avoid the tendency to view students as inert substances that can be manipulated in desired directions. The role of educators is to provide growth-enhancing conditions that empower students, not to make their decisions for them. Hunt (1978) presented a particularly persuasive argument for recognizing the role students play in their own development. He first described a way in which theory is too frequently used: "The theorist describes and then prescribes to the practitioner who, in turn, delivers the services to the client who is the passive recipient" (p. 252). The client "is usually not informed about the nature of the theory or program so such issues as his wishes to 'be developed' are rarely considered" (p. 255). Hunt argued that "taking account of a client as person puts the client's developmental stage (knowledge and competence) into the context of his intentions. Perhaps the most important implication is to understand the client's motives for change and his perception of how it might occur. Also, taking account of the client's intentions is more likely to emphasize the importance of self-matching procedures in which the client is an active participant in the decision-making process" (p. 260).

In a statement that concluded his final exam in a course on student development theory, Weith (1985) wrote, "Probably because the student development literature has offered us so much, we tend to pick it apart when it fails as an end-all. Was it ever meant as such?" Reality is complex. Student development theory does not explain all behavior. Both its benefits and its limitations must be acknowledged.

PART TWO

PSYCHOSOCIAL AND IDENTITY DEVELOPMENT THEORIES

Two students nervously enter the career development center to attend a workshop on career planning that is being offered this evening. The first person, Adrianne, is a thirty-five-year-old returning adult student. She had originally dropped out of school after her first year to get married, quickly had two children, and stayed at home to raise her family. After an unexpected and difficult divorce, she returned to school last fall. Her children are now fifteen and twelve, and she is finding it difficult to balance all the demands on her time, what with their school activities, her studies, and her part-time job as a receptionist. She is doing OK in school, although she really feels out of place with all the younger students and isn't too secure about her study skills. She hasn't decided on a major or a future career but knows she needs something stable and well paying so that she can provide for her children and be able to send them to college. She doesn't want to waste her time or money, both of which are pretty limited, so the need to decide on a career direction and a major feels rather urgent.

The second student, James, is also a sophomore. He is nineteen, the youngest of six children and the first person in his family to go to college. He is African American and attended an all-black inner-city high school. James struggled his first year because of his poor academic background but persisted because he didn't want to let down his family or the people in his church who encouraged him to go to college so that he could make a contribution to his community. James had never really thought about race much in his all-black neighborhood, but he has really been struggling to find his place and overcome his feelings of being different at the predominantly white university he attends. He doesn't know any African American men who have a college degree, so he has few ideas of what he can do with his major in sociology, a field he picked in the hope that he could use what he learned to help his community. People keep asking James what he intends to do when he finishes college, and he is feeling pressured to come up with an answer soon.

In Part Two we discuss psychosocial theories of development. Psychosocial theorists examine the *content* of development, the important issues people face as their lives progress, such as how to define themselves, their relationships with others, and what to do with their lives. Not all issues are equally important throughout a person's life. Rather, development takes place across the life span in a series of age-linked sequential stages. In each stage, particular issues, called developmental tasks, arise and present compelling questions that must be resolved (Erikson, 1959/1980).

Examined from Erikson's psychosocial perspective, Adrianne and James are in different stages of development. James, at age nineteen, is in an earlier stage, identity versus role confusion, dealing with such developmental tasks as determining a vocational direction and identifying a personal set of beliefs and values. Adrianne, at age thirty-five, is facing the developmental issues associated with the stage of generativity versus stagnation, including finding ways to actively nurture her offspring and contribute in a productive way to society.

Each new stage occurs when internal biological and psychological changes interact with environmental demands, such as social norms and roles expected of individuals at certain ages in particular cultures. A developmental crisis, or turning point, in the person's life is associated with each stage (Erikson, 1968). The dissonance, disequilibrium, and anxiety associated with the crisis create a need within the individual to do something to resolve the issue. For James, making a decision about a career is the developmental crisis at this point in his life. This issue has become more urgent because of conditions that are present in his environment. James is feeling a lot of pressure from his significant others to determine his vocational direction. So he decides to attend the career planning workshop to help resolve this issue.

What issues arise, the order in which they are experienced, and their relative importance in a person's life are strongly influenced by society, culture, and gender (Erikson, 1959/1980). Adrianne, for example, decided to get married and raise a family when she was nineteen. In all likelihood, this decision was influenced by societal norms concerning appropriate roles for women. As a result, making a career decision is a developmental task she is undertaking much later in life.

The attitudes individuals have toward developmental issues, and how and when they choose to respond to them, also vary with the person's cultural background, current environment, and gender (Widick, Knefelkamp, & Parker, 1980).

James, for instance, is strongly influenced by his background and environment. Family, community, and church are highly valued in his particular African American subculture, and the desire to "give something back" is clearly influencing his career decision making.

Resolution of developmental tasks is influenced by how successful the individual is in developing appropriate coping skills. An optimal balance of challenge and support in the environment facilitates such development (Sanford, 1966). Both Adrianne and James are currently facing significant challenges: Adrianne is having trouble balancing many responsibilities and is the sole supporter of her children; James is struggling to survive and find a place in a predominantly white university. Perhaps the career planning workshop will provide important support that will enable these students to focus on their future plans and begin to develop the skills they need to successfully plan their careers.

Each crisis offers a heightened opportunity as well as increased vulnerability for the individual (Erikson, 1968). How people resolve each crisis influences how they view themselves and their place in their environment and also affects in a cumulative way how they resolve tasks at later stages. Successful resolution of the dissonance and anxiety associated with each developmental crisis leads to the development of new skills and attitudes. Inadequate resolution, however, can lead to stress and inappropriate behavior, contribute to a negative self-image, and decrease the likelihood that future developmental crises will be successfully addressed. For instance, if James fails to find an acceptable career in which he can make a contribution to his community, he might decide that his struggle to succeed in college is not worth the effort and that dropping out to find immediate employment would be a better way to help his family. Such a decision might in turn compromise his sense of self-worth and integrity.

Regression to earlier stages, readdressing of developmental tasks, and relearning of coping skills frequently occur when individuals are placed in new and stressful situations (Erikson, 1968). In returning to college, Adrianne revisited the competence issues she faced seventeen years earlier as a first-year student. She had to brush up on both her study skills and her interpersonal skills to handle the situations she faces as a returning adult student. She is now addressing the issue of making a career decision, something she postponed at age nineteen when she got married.

Psychosocial theories are helpful in understanding the issues individuals face at various points in their lives. For example, student affairs staff working with an African American student like James who has never experienced a predominantly white educational setting might anticipate that his transition could be difficult. Knowing that family and church are important components of the African American worldview would help student affairs professionals understand the central role these institutions play in James's support system as he confronts a strange and often hostile environment.

Psychosocial theories can also provide guidance concerning topics for programs and workshops for particular groups of students. Understanding that returning adult students, like Adrianne, often need to readdress competence issues may suggest that programming on study skills for this population would be appropriate.

Because life events play such an important part in psychosocial development, it is particularly important that these theories be examined in light of the person's culture and background. Recent work, such as Josselson's research examining identity resolution in the lives of women (1987a), has examined the applicability of psychosocial theories for women. New theoretical work in this domain has focused particularly on racial, cultural, and lesbian, gay, and bisexual identity development as well as the interaction of minority identity development with other aspects of psychosocial development. The examination of psychosocial development across the life span, rather than just during the traditional college years, is another trend in this literature. Most of the work that extends student development theory to diverse populations has focused on psychosocial development.

Part Two begins with an examination of Chickering's theory of psychosocial development, the first major theory to specifically examine the development of college students. Both Chickering's landmark 1969 work and his recent revisions (Chickering & Reisser, 1993) are discussed in Chapter Three. In Chapter Four we review Josselson's identity development model (1987a), which extends to women work done by Erikson (1959/1980) and Marcia (1966) based on white male samples. Racial identity development models, which explore the interaction of personal and racial group identity formation, are discussed in Chapter Five. In Chapter Six we examine gay, lesbian, and bisexual identity development. The theories of Cass (1979) and D'Augelli (1994a) are outlined in detail. In the final chapter in this section, development across the life span is examined, as described in the transition model of Nancy Schlossberg (Schlossberg, Waters, & Goodman, 1995).

CHAPTER THREE

CHICKERING'S THEORY OF IDENTITY DEVELOPMENT

Melissa has just been elected educational chairperson for her sorority. This is her first leadership role, and she is anxious to do a really good job of providing programs that will be of benefit to the women in her house. Melissa asks for ideas at the first chapter meeting after her election. Some of the seniors immediately speak up. They want information about putting together résumés and conducting job searches as well as the pros and cons of going to graduate school. Some of the sophomores and juniors are more interested in how to go about deciding on a career direction that is right for them. Sandy, a second-semester student, is obviously frustrated with these suggestions. She blurts out that she is still struggling with study skills and adjusting to college classes; she is nowhere near ready to think about careers and job searches. The group moves on to discuss another area: establishing meaningful relationships. Many of the women complain that all the guys they have been meeting are superficial and immature. They want help in learning how to develop a relationship that has some depth. A few of the younger members indicate that they haven't even been able to talk comfortably with guys at mixers or in class, let alone establish a relationship. A number of the women also mention that they have been having trouble with their parents, who just don't seem ready to let them grow up. They want to remain close to their folks, but they also feel like they are ready to make their own decisions. Shari hesitates but then mentions that she thinks the sorority needs to work on understanding differences. She refers to last year's rush period when the sorority struggled over whether to accept an African American woman as a pledge. Carla mentions that she is really struggling to define "who she is." Other people see her as a "party girl" because she is a member of a sorority. She used to be OK with that image, but she is coming to realize that life needs to be more than parties. Lisa chimes in that she, too, is trying to decide what she really values in life. She used to go along with what the rest of her sorority sisters thought, but lately she has discovered that some of her ideas are different. She wants to discuss how values affect life decisions. Though Melissa appreciates the honesty of all her sisters, she is a bit overwhelmed. "Wow," she thinks, "this is a big job. Everyone seems to have such different needs. How in the world can I address all these issues?"

The issues Melissa's sorority sisters raised during their chapter meeting are similar to those experienced by many college students, particularly individuals between the ages of eighteen and twenty-four. In his theory of psychosocial development, Arthur Chickering (1969) provided an overview of the developmental issues faced by college students and went on to examine environmental conditions that influence development. Building on Erikson's discussion of identity and intimacy (1959/1980), Chickering saw the establishment of identity as the core developmental issue with which students grapple during the college years. Resolution of a number of issues contributes to the person's growing sense of identity. Establishment of identity in turn allows the person to address issues that may arise later in the developmental process. Chickering also identified key aspects of the college environment that influence development and suggested ways to enhance student growth.

Chickering's theory has been widely used in student affairs since its introduction in 1969. It has served as the foundation for extensive research as well as practical application. The original theory and its revisions (Chickering & Reisser, 1993) are the focus of this chapter, along with related assessment techniques, research, and applications.

Historical Overview

Chickering's theory was first outlined in his landmark book, *Education and Identity* (1969). The theory is based on research Chickering conducted between 1959 and 1965 while he was employed at Goddard College (Thomas & Chickering, 1984). At Goddard, Chickering was responsible for evaluating the impact of innovative curricular practices on student development. He administered sixteen hours' worth of achievement tests, personality inventories, and other instruments to students at the end of their sophomore and senior years. He also asked selected students to keep diaries of their experiences and thoughts and conducted detailed interviews with other students. He began writing *Education and Identity* in 1963 in an attempt to provide a conceptual framework for his findings as well as other research that had been conducted on college students.

From 1964 to 1969 Chickering served as director of the Project on Student Development in Small Colleges (Thomas & Chickering, 1984). The data he obtained from studies of thirteen dissimilar small colleges across the country were incorporated into the latter half of *Education and Identity,* which focused on the influences of the college environment on development.

Chickering targeted faculty in the preparation of *Education and Identity.* His goal was to provide them with ideas concerning the organization of educational programs to more systematically enhance student development (Thomas & Chickering, 1984). In fact, Chickering noted, "student affairs professionals as an audience were not in my mind at all. . . . It was entirely by chance that *Education and Identity* made a significant contribution to those professionals" (p. 393). In a later interview (Krivoski & Nicholson, 1989), Chickering admitted that his first awareness of student affairs as a profession came as a result of being asked to address a National Association of Women Deans and Counselors conference in 1967. As a result of invitations during the late 1960s and early 1970s to speak to professionals in student affairs, Chickering learned about the field that would come to have the most impact on his later thinking and would do the most to implement his ideas in practice (Thomas & Chickering).

In several interviews during the 1980s (Garfield & David, 1986; Krivoski & Nicholson, 1989; Thomas & Chickering, 1984), Chickering discussed areas that he would expand or adjust if he were to revise his theory. He mentioned the need (1) to incorporate findings from recent research on gender, race, and national origin; (2) to acknowledge the greater range of options students now have; (3) to adjust the theory to fit adult learners as well as traditional-aged students; and (4) to alter the definitions of several of the vectors to reflect changes in societal conditions and to acknowledge the work of other theorists.

Working with Linda Reisser (1995), Chickering revised his theory to incorporate new research findings, to summarize the work of other theorists as it relates to his theory, and to be more inclusive of various student populations. The revised edition (Chickering & Reisser, 1993) adheres to the basic premises of the original work but includes 90 percent new material (Schuh, 1994).

Chickering's Theory

Chickering proposed seven vectors of development that contribute to the formation of identity. Chickering (1969) used the term *vectors of development* "because each seems to have direction and magnitude—even though the direction may be expressed more appropriately by a spiral or by steps than by a straight line" (p. 8). He called these vectors "major highways for journeying toward individuation" (Chickering & Reisser, 1993, p. 35). Chickering noted that students move through these vectors at different rates, that vectors can interact with each other, and that students often find themselves reexamining issues associated with vectors they had previously worked through. Although not rigidly sequential, vectors do build on each other, leading to greater complexity, stability, and integration as the issues related to each vector are addressed. Chickering's work takes into account emotional, interpersonal, ethical, and intellectual aspects of development.

The Seven Vectors

Chickering's seven vectors, as presented in his revised theory (Chickering & Reisser, 1993), paint a comprehensive picture of psychosocial development during the college years.

Developing Competence. Chickering and Reisser (1993) likened competence to a three-tined pitchfork, the tines being intellectual competence, physical and manual skills, and interpersonal competence. The handle of the pitchfork, necessary if the tines are to do their work, is "a sense of competence" that "stems from the confidence that one can cope with what comes and achieve goals successfully" (p. 53). Intellectual competence involves acquisition of knowledge and skills related to particular subject matter, development of "intellectual, cultural, and aesthetic sophistication" (Reisser, 1995, p. 506), and increased skill in areas such as critical thinking and reasoning ability. Physical competence comes through athletic and recreational activities, attention to wellness, and involvement in artistic and manual activities. Interpersonal competence includes skills in communication, leadership, and working effectively with others.

Melissa's sorority sisters who indicated that they did not yet feel comfortable with their study skills seem to be dealing with intellectual competence issues, while those who couldn't talk to men are experiencing interpersonal competence concerns.

Managing Emotions. In this vector, students develop the ability to recognize and accept emotions, as well as to appropriately express and control them. In addition, students learn to act on feelings in a responsible manner. Chickering's original theory (1969) focused on aggression and sexual desire. His recent work addresses a more inclusive range of feelings including anxiety, depression, anger, shame, and guilt, as well as more positive emotions such as caring, optimism, and inspiration.

Sandy, the young woman in the scenario who became annoyed at her sisters who wanted information on job searches and career exploration, seems to be having trouble appropriately expressing and controlling her emotions. She is not handling anxiety about her intellectual competence in an effective manner.

Moving Through Autonomy Toward Interdependence. This aspect of development results in increased emotional independence, which is defined as "freedom from continual and pressing needs for reassurance, affection, or approval from others" (Chickering & Reisser, 1993, p. 117). Students also develop instrumental independence, which includes self-direction, problem-solving ability, and mobility. Finally, they come to recognize and accept the importance of interdependence, an awareness of their interconnectedness with others. Chickering's revised theory places a greater emphasis on the importance of interdependence. To underscore this change, he has renamed this vector, which was previously called Developing Autonomy.

The sorority women who indicated that they were having trouble redefining relationships with their parents seem to be wrestling with questions of independence and interdependence. They want to be viewed as adults capable of making their own decisions while still maintaining positive relationships with their families.

Developing Mature Interpersonal Relationships. This vector, which in the original version of the theory was called Freeing Interpersonal Relationships and followed the Establishing Identity vector, has been placed earlier in sequence to acknowledge that experiences with relationships contribute significantly to the development of a sense of self. The tasks associated with this vector include development of intercultural and interpersonal tolerance and appreciation of differences, as well as the capacity for healthy and lasting intimate relationships with partners and close friends. Reisser (1995) noted that both tasks "involve the ability to accept individuals for who they are, to respect differences, and to appreciate commonalities" (p. 509).

Shari's concern about learning to appreciate differences, arising from controversy in the sorority over accepting an African American pledge, is an example of a task related to developing mature interpersonal relationships. The concerns of other sorority women over the lack of depth in their relationships with men is another example.

Establishing Identity. Establishing identity builds on each of the vectors that comes before it. In Chickering's revised theory, this vector has taken on added complexity to acknowledge differences in identity development based on gender, ethnic background, and sexual orientation. Identity includes comfort with body and appearance, comfort with gender and sexual orientation, a sense of one's social and cultural heritage, a clear self-concept and comfort with one's roles and lifestyle, a secure sense of self in light of feedback from significant others, self-acceptance and self-esteem, and personal stability and integration.

Carla is beginning to address identity issues. She is rejecting an identity given to her by others and looking for roles and a lifestyle that is meaningful to her.

Developing Purpose. This vector consists of developing clear vocational goals, making meaningful commitments to specific personal interests and activities, and establishing strong interpersonal commitments. It includes intentionally making and staying with decisions, even in the face of opposition. The term *vocation* is used broadly to refer to paid or unpaid work within the context of a specific career or more generally as a person's life calling. Lifestyle and family influences affect the decision-making and goal-setting processes involved in developing purpose.

The sorority women who were interested in career exploration are dealing with issues of purpose. They are attempting to find a life direction that makes sense for them.

Developing Integrity. This vector includes "three sequential but overlapping stages" (Chickering & Reisser, 1993, p. 51): humanizing values, personalizing values, and developing congruence. First, students progress from rigid, moralistic thinking to the development of a more humanized value system in which the interests of others are balanced with one's own interests. Next a personalized value system is established in which core values are consciously affirmed and the beliefs of others are acknowledged and respected. In developing congruence, values and actions become congruent and authentic as self-interest is balanced by a sense of social responsibility.

Lisa is examining integrity issues. She is moving away from a value system dictated by her sorority sisters and beginning to establish a personal value system. She is becoming aware that her values have implications for her actions.

Environmental Influences

Chickering argued that educational environments exert powerful influences on student development. He proposed seven key factors.

Institutional objectives. Clear and specific objectives to which personnel pay attention and use to guide the development of programs and services have a powerful impact. They lead to greater consistency in policies, programs, and practices while making evident the values of the institution. Students and other constituencies are then able to agree with or challenge these values.

Institutional size. Significant participation in campus life and satisfaction with the college experience are important if development is to occur. Chickering and Reisser (1993) argued that "as the number of persons outstrips the opportunities for significant participation and satisfaction, the developmental potential of available settings is attenuated for all" (p. 269).

Student-faculty relationships. Extensive and varied interaction among faculty and students facilitates development. Students need to see faculty in a variety of situations involving different roles and responsibilities. Such interaction leads students to perceive faculty as real people who are accessible and interested in them beyond the classroom.

Curriculum. A relevant curriculum is needed, one that is sensitive to individual difference, offers diverse perspectives, and helps students make sense of what they are learning. The assumptions about student learning that underlie the curriculum and the process by which learning takes place have as much impact on outcomes as the specific curricular content.

Teaching. For development to occur, teaching should involve active learning, student-faculty interaction, timely feedback, high expectations, and respect for individual learning differences. Such teaching strategies affect cognitive development in the form of active thinking and integration of ideas. They also encourage interdependence, cooperation, and interpersonal sensitivity.

Friendships and student communities. Meaningful friendships and diverse student communities in which shared interests exist and significant interactions occur encourage development along all seven vectors. Communities may be informal friendship groups or more formal groups such as residence hall floors, student organizations, or classes. To have maximum positive benefit, the community should "[encourage] regular interactions between students," "[offer] opportunities for collaboration," be "small enough so that no one feels superfluous," "[include] people from diverse backgrounds," and "[serve] as a reference group" (Chickering & Reisser, 1993, p. 277).

Student development programs and services. Collaborative efforts by faculty and student affairs professionals are necessary to provide developmental programs and services. Chickering and Reisser (1993) "recommend that administrators of student programs and services redefine themselves as educators and refer to themselves as 'student development professionals'" (p. 278).

Chickering and Reisser (1993) introduced three principles that underscore the factors just listed:

Integration of work and learning. Since most students today work as well as take classes, collaborative relationships are needed between business, the community, and institutions of higher education that will maximize the developmental potential of work and volunteer experiences.

Recognition and respect for individual differences. Chickering and Reisser (1993) stated, "It is clear that diversity will only increase in the years ahead. It is also clear that if we are unable to deal with it, we are likely to face increasing conflict, a two-tier society, and economic stagnation" (p. 473). Educators must be cognizant of the different backgrounds and needs of their students and adjust their interactions and interventions to address these differences.

Acknowledgment of the cyclical nature of learning and development. Learning involves periods of differentiation and integration, equilibrium and disequilibrium. New experiences and challenges provide opportunities for new perspectives and more complex understanding to occur. Chickering and Reisser (1993) cautioned that "signs of discomfort and upset are not necessarily negative. On the contrary, they often signal that developmentally fruitful encounters are occurring, that stimuli for learning are at work" (p. 479).

Assessment Techniques

Because psychosocial development is multidimensional and complex, its assessment is not easy (Miller & Winston, 1990). Development is continually occurring in many different arenas, and assessment can provide only a limited evaluation of a particular aspect of that development at a specific point in time. Cognitive development also interacts with psychosocial development in that individuals at different levels of cognitive development will interpret their experiences differently (Mines, 1985). In addition, psychosocial development is influenced by the environmental context in which it occurs (Miller & Winston). Cultural values, setting, and historical time affect development and must be considered in the construction of assessment techniques.

Efforts to assess psychosocial development as outlined in Chickering's theory (1969) have been made by teams located at the University of Georgia and the University of Iowa (Miller & Winston, 1990). In addition, Reisser (personal communication, March 1997) has indicated that she is currently working on new measures to reflect the recent modifications in Chickering's theory (Chickering & Reisser, 1993). Instruments currently available include the Student Developmental Task and Lifestyle Inventory (SDTLI) (Winston, Miller, & Prince, 1987) and the Iowa Student Development Inventories (Hood, 1986).

Student Developmental Task and Lifestyle Inventory

The SDTLI is the latest iteration of a counseling tool developed at the University of Georgia to assist students in their psychosocial development. Earlier versions, which are no longer in print, include the Student Developmental Task

Inventory (SDTI) (Prince, Miller, & Winston, 1974) and the SDTI–2 (Winston, Miller, & Prince, 1979). Although designed to be used in counseling students, the SDTLI and its earlier versions have also been used extensively in research.

The SDTLI assesses three developmental tasks: Establishing and Clarifying Purpose, Developing Mature Interpersonal Relationships, and Academic Autonomy. A task on the SDTLI is defined as "an interrelated set of behaviors and attitudes which the American culture specifies should be exhibited at approximately the same time by a given age cohort in a designated context" (Winston & Miller, 1987, p. 8). The Establishing and Clarifying Purpose task has five subtasks: Educational Involvement, Career Planning, Lifestyle Planning, Cultural Participation, and Life Management. The Developing Mature Interpersonal Relationships task includes three subtasks: Peer Relationships, Tolerance, and Emotional Autonomy. Academic Autonomy is defined as the ability to manage one's life in order to achieve goals and fulfill responsibilities. The SDTLI has three scales in addition to the three tasks: Salubrious Lifestyle, Intimacy, and Response Bias. The Salubrious Lifestyle scale focuses on health and wellness practices. The Intimacy scale examines capacity to love and be loved and to make commitments, regardless of sexual orientation. It is considered an experimental scale. The Response Bias scale is used to determine if a person is attempting to portray himself or herself in a unrealistically positive light when taking the instrument.

Available reliability data include estimates of internal consistency and temporal stability. Winston (1990) reported internal consistency (Cronbach's alpha coefficients) based on a sample of twelve hundred students enrolled in twenty colleges and universities in the United States and Canada as being above .70 for the three tasks and the two scales (excluding the Response Bias scale). Alpha coefficients for the subtasks were somewhat lower, ranging from .80 to .45. Test-retest data were obtained from five samples of twenty-seven to ninety-six students each who were tested at periods ranging from two weeks to twenty weeks. Coefficients for the three tasks and two scales ranged from .87 to .80 over a two-week period and from .80 to .62 over a twelve-week period.

Validity of the SDTLI has been tested by examining factor structure and intercorrelations as well as correlational studies. The Establishing Purpose and Mature Interpersonal Relationships tasks have been found to be relatively independent of each other, while the Academic Autonomy task has been found to be moderately correlated with the other two tasks, suggesting that it is not totally independent (Winston, 1990). The SDTLI tasks and the Salubrious Lifestyle scale have been found to correlate significantly with instruments that measure related concepts. Only limited support has been found for the validity of the Intimacy scale, however.

Winston (1990) pointed out that although the SDTLI is based on Chickering's constructs in a general way, it "does not completely conform to the vector structure proposed in 1969" (pp. 108–109). The series of revisions made in the instrument on the basis of data collected from college students has resulted in new and redefined developmental tasks. Researchers interested in assessing Chickering's theoretical constructs should therefore use caution when using the SDTLI. Winston also delimits the SDTLI to student populations between the ages of seventeen and twenty-four. The context for the instrument is "the fundamentally middle-class environment of colleges and universities" (p. 109).

Iowa Student Development Inventories

Faculty, staff, and students at the University of Iowa have developed six instruments, each measuring a specific vector of development. No instrument exists to measure the last vector, Developing Integrity (Hood, 1986). The instruments are based on Chickering's original definitions of the vectors.

Iowa Developing Competency Inventory (Hood & Jackson, 1983a). This scale consists of seventy items divided into three subscales: Self-Confidence (SC), which examines ease of communication with others and interactions with authorities and peers; Competency in Writing (CW), which focuses on self-confidence about and enjoyment of writing; and Competency in Math (CM), which deals with self-confidence in and enjoyment of math. Reported coefficient alphas are .94 for the total scale, .92 for SC, .92 for CW, and .96 for CM. No validity studies have been reported to date.

Iowa Managing Emotions Inventory (Hood & Jackson, 1983c). A sixty–item scale, this inventory examines the emotions of depression, anger, frustration, happiness, and attraction. The following concepts are addressed for each emotion: recognition of emotions, exploration of emotions, and insights into emotions. Because these three subscales were found to be highly correlated, only a total score is reported. Coefficient alpha for the total inventory is .95. Coefficient alphas reported for the five emotion scales were .85 for Depression, .79 for Anger, .81 for Frustration, .80 for Happiness, and .76 for Attraction (Miller & Winston, 1990). No validity studies have been reported.

Iowa Developing Autonomy Inventory (Hood & Jackson, 1983b). This ninety–item inventory includes six subscales: Mobility, Time Management, Money Management, Interdependence, Emotional Independence—Peers, and Emotional Independence—Parents. Reported coefficient alphas for each of these scales were .87, .85, .81, .80, .77, and .88, respectively. The reliability for the entire scale was .94. No validity information has been reported.

Erwin Identity Scale (Erwin, 1979). This scale is composed of fifty-eight items arranged into three subscales: Confidence, Sexual Identity, and Conceptions About Body and Appearance. Confidence focuses on self-awareness and a feeling that one can handle aspects of one's life. Sexual Identity has to do with acceptance and control of sexual feelings. Conceptions About Body and Appearance involves accurate self-assessment and acceptance of one's appearance. Total scale reliability is .91 (Hood, 1986), reliability coefficients for the three subscales ranging from .75 to .81 (Erwin, 1979). Convergent validity studies (Erwin & Schmidt, 1982) have found moderate correlations between Confidence and Sexual Identity and other measures of related concepts. Longitudinal studies (Erwin, 1982; Erwin & Kelly, 1985) have demonstrated that scores increase on the Confidence scale throughout the first year of college and from the first year to the senior year.

Mines-Jensen Interpersonal Relationship Inventory (Mines, 1977). Two subscales, Tolerance and Quality of Relationships, make up this forty-two-item inventory. Tolerance is defined as greater openness and acceptance of difference, and Quality of Relationships involves a move from extreme dependence or independence toward interdependence. Four content areas are included: peers, adults, friends, and significant others. Reliabilities ranging from .65 to .87 have been reported for different samples. Longitudinal studies have demonstrated increased scores on both scales during the first year of college and from the first year to the senior year.

Developing Purposes Inventory (Barrett, 1978). This inventory has forty-five items arranged into three subscales: Avocational-Recreational, which deals with development of nonvocational activities and openness to new areas of interest; Vocational, which explores commitment to a career choice; and Style of Life, which looks at the relationship between the student and others in his or her community. Goal setting is also examined. Coefficient alphas ranged from .68 to .80, three-month test-retest reliabilities ranged from .55 to .82, and six-month test-retest reliabilities ranged from .55 to .75. Validity studies examining correlations with demographic, behavioral, and attitudinal data have been conducted (Miller & Winston, 1990).

Research

Schuh (1994) speculated that over the past twenty-five years, Chickering's theory (1969) has generated as much research as any work in the field of student development. Researchers have investigated the validity of Chickering's theory, including its applicability to various student populations, factors related to psychosocial development, and the relationship of psychosocial development to cognitive development.

Validity of the Theory

White and Hood (1989) examined the validity of Chickering's vectors of development by administering the six Iowa instruments plus an objective measure of cognitive development to 225 students. A factor-analytic procedure provided only limited support for Chickering's theory. Factors generally paralleled the Developing Purpose, Developing Integrity, and Establishing Identity vectors. Overlapping of various dimensions assessed by the Iowa instruments was evident.

Women's Development

Researchers examining the applicability of Chickering's theory to women have found that women's development differs from men's, particularly regarding the importance of interpersonal relationships in fostering other aspects of development. On the basis of data from their study of African American and Caucasian women, Taub and McEwen (1991) concluded that development of mature interpersonal relationships may begin earlier for women than for men and that development of autonomy may occur later than Chickering suggests. In a longitudinal study, Blackhurst (1995) found support for this argument. In her study, scores of women students on the Mature Relationships task of the SDTLI increased significantly over the course of their first semester in college while the scores of men on this task did not change significantly. For many women, developing mature interpersonal relationships seems to precede developing autonomy (Greeley & Tinsley, 1988; Straub, 1987; Taub, 1995), and many women achieve autonomy through the development of healthy relationships (Straub & Rodgers, 1986; Taub, 1995).

Women college students also score higher on intimacy than men college students do (Greeley & Tinsley, 1988; Utterback, Spooner, Barbieri, & Fox, 1995). And at historically black colleges, African American women scored higher than African American men on interpersonal relationships, autonomy, and life purpose (Jordan-Cox, 1987). But in a longitudinal study over four years of college, men experienced greater increases in identity development on the Erwin Identity Scale than women did (Hood, Riahinejad, & White, 1986).

Development of Students from Various Racial and Ethnic Groups

Several writers have questioned the applicability of Chickering's theory for students who are not from white, middle-class backgrounds, and some researchers have examined aspects of the psychosocial development of African American students. Development of racial and ethnic identity is of particular importance to African American students, often delaying other aspects of psychosocial development (Taub & McEwen, 1992). McEwen, Roper, Bryant, and Langa (1990) and Gibbs (1974) also suggested that the role of assimilation, acculturation, and cultural awareness in development must be considered. McEwen et al. stressed that identity, for African Americans, includes both personal and collective elements that result from social interaction and group identifications. For African

Americans, developing independence and autonomy seems to occur in the context of interpersonal relationships, affiliation plays an important role in development, and family and extended family exert a pervasive influence (Branch-Simpson, 1984; Hughes, 1987). Religion, spiritual development, and social responsibility also take on significance for African Americans (Branch-Simpson; Hughes).

A few researchers have investigated the influence of the college environment on African American development. Generally, researchers have found that African American students are better adjusted at historically black institutions than at predominantly white schools (Fleming, 1984; Hughes, 1987). Fleming found that isolation and loneliness affected the establishment of interpersonal relationships for African American students on white campuses, with African American men being particularly at risk. On predominantly white campuses, black women were found to score lower than white women on intimacy; however, the authors of this study question the appropriateness of the measuring instrument for African American students (Taub & McEwen, 1991).

Sedlacek (1987) found that noncognitive variables related to psychosocial development, such as confidence, realistic self-appraisal, and a solid ethnic identity, were crucial to the success of African American students on predominantly white campuses. In contrast to other research, Cheatham, Slaney, and Coleman (1990) found that African American students at a predominantly white institution scored higher on emotional and academic autonomy, as well as cultural participation, than African American students at a historically black college.

Unfortunately, research concerning the applicability of Chickering's theory to other racial and ethnic groups is very limited. Utterback et al. (1995) found that whites score higher on intimacy than Native Americans, African Americans, and Hispanic Americans. Sheehan and Pearson (1995) found that Asian international first-year students scored significantly lower than American students, for whom race or ethnicity was not specified, on the Establishing and Clarifying Purpose and Developing Mature Interpersonal Relationships tasks and the Intimacy scale of the SDTLI. No differences were found on the Academic Autonomy task.

Development of Gay, Lesbian, and Bisexual Students

Although Chickering and Reisser (1993) have expanded the description of establishing identity to include becoming comfortable with one's sexual orientation, almost no research has been done to examine the suitability of Chickering's theory for nonheterosexual populations. In a small exploratory study, Levine and Bahr (1989) found evidence that development of sexual identity may retard other components of psychosocial development for gay, lesbian, and bisexual students. Certainly, vectors such as Managing Emotions, Developing Mature Interpersonal

Relationships, Establishing Identity, and Developing Purpose would be affected by how one felt about one's sexual orientation (Evans & D'Augelli, 1996).

D'Augelli (1994a) has stressed that gay, lesbian, and bisexual youth face the added pressure of giving up a majority identity and developing a new minority identity. Coming out—acknowledging and disclosing one's sexual orientation—is another developmental task not experienced by heterosexual students (Wall & Evans, 1991).

Factors Related to Development

Academic experiences have been shown to be related to psychosocial development. Confidence (on the Erwin Identity Scale) is significantly correlated with academic satisfaction and classroom performance (Erwin & Delworth, 1982; Erwin & Kelly, 1985). Students enrolled in remedial programs scored lower than regularly admitted students on the Appropriate Educational Plans subtask of the Developing Purpose task of the SDTI–2, indicating that they are less able to realistically evaluate their educational setting and goals (Pollard, Benton, & Hinz, 1983).

Involvement on campus is also related to psychosocial development. Fox, Spooner, Utterback, and Barbieri (1996) found that first-year students who remain on campus on weekends report higher levels of autonomy than students who leave campus. Several researchers (Hood et al., 1986; Hunt & Rentz, 1994; Williams & Winston, 1985) have demonstrated that students who are more involved in extracurricular activities score higher on scales measuring confidence, developing purpose, developing mature interpersonal relationships, and intimacy. In addition, active engagement in work and study is related to Establishing and Clarifying Purpose on the SDTLI (Niles, Sowa, & Laden, 1994).

Involvement is not always positively related to development, however. Sowa and Gressard (1983) found that students who participated in intercollegiate athletics scored lower than nonathletes on the Educational Plans, Career Plans, and Mature Relationships scales of the SDTI. And in a longitudinal study, Kilgannon and Erwin (1992) found that sophomore men in Greek organizations scored lower on the Confidence subscale of the Erwin Identity Scale than non-Greek men did. In may be that development in this area occurs after the sophomore year, as the Hood et al. (1986) study suggested.

Previous life experiences also relate to psychosocial development. Women who reported unwanted childhood sexual experiences scored lower on the Career Planning and Intimacy scales of the SDTLI, and Sexual Identity scores were lower for women who experienced incest (White & Strange, 1993). Another study (Heyer & Nelson, 1993) demonstrated that students with divorced parents scored higher on the Confidence and Sexual Identity scales of the Erwin Identity Scale.

Higher levels of psychosocial development seem to be related to career commitment. Erwin and Kelly (1985) found such a relationship with Confidence on the Erwin Identity Scale. Long, Sowa, and Niles (1995) also demonstrated a connection between having made a career decision and academic autonomy, sense of purpose, vocational identity, and occupational information.

Psychosocial Development and Cognitive Development

Buczynski (1991) examined the relationship between cognitive development and the development of identity in first-year students. She found an inverse relationship: the more complex a student's level of cognitive development, the less well developed his or her identity. However, the objective measure of cognitive development used in this study is somewhat suspect.

Polkosnik and Winston (1989) carried out an exploratory longitudinal study to examine the connection between intellectual and psychosocial development. They failed to find a direct link between these aspects of development. Development in various arenas seems to occur at varying rates and to be influenced by a variety of life experiences.

Applications

Chickering's theory has generated a number of student affairs applications, particularly in the area of programming. Interventions to facilitate particular aspects of development have been introduced, as have general programming strategies. Chickering has also provided examples of ways that several of the key environmental factors can be implemented.

Programming

Chickering's model is particularly effective in developing overall program priorities and strategies. For instance, Evans (1982) used Chickering's vectors as a basis for the development of a needs assessment instrument to be used in residence hall program planning. Hurst (1978) suggested that programming on campus be targeted to address each of the seven vectors using a variety of different approaches outlined in the Cube model (Morrill, Oetting, & Hurst, 1974).

Chickering's theory can also be used to evaluate and explain the impact of programmatic efforts. Chickering (1977) discussed ways in which college union programs affect various aspects of development, particularly competence, autonomy, interpersonal relationships, and humanitarian concern. Klepper and Kovacs

(1978) built on his ideas to suggest ways that programs offered by student unions across the country connect to each of the seven vectors. Similarly, Todaro (1993) outlined how a recreational sports program can encourage development along each vector.

Programs have also been designed to help students address specific developmental issues. Lott (1986) discussed the Freshman Home Reentry program at Valparaiso University designed to help students with the transition of returning home for the summer after their first year in college. Developmental issues related to establishing identity and freeing interpersonal relationships were discussed. Lemons and Richmond (1987) went a step further to help students deal with "sophomore slump," which the authors related to problems with achieving competence, developing autonomy, establishing identity, and developing purpose. Mentoring and individual counseling interventions were introduced. Cognitive-behavioral counseling techniques, such as assertiveness training and self-mastery techniques, have been suggested for women who are dealing with autonomy issues (McBride, 1990). The unique developmental programming needs of students with disabilities are discussed by Huss (1983) and Perreira and Dezago (1989).

Student affairs professionals should be aware, however, that students don't always take advantage of developmental programs. Hess and Winston (1995) found that students tended to take part in programs focusing on developmental tasks that, for them, were already well developed and that they were unmotivated to attend programs designed to enhance their less developed skills. Similarly, Rice and Brown (1990) found that students who were most likely to become involved in a mentoring program were those least likely to need it. Students with low self-esteem and less well-developed interpersonal relationships were less likely to enroll in the program.

Environmental Interventions

Chickering introduced the idea of a "residential learning contract" at George Mason University (Krivoski & Nicholson, 1989). As part of the application process, students were asked to outline the learning outcomes they wished to achieve by living in university housing. At the end of the year, both students and staff evaluated the extent to which the developmental goals were achieved, with continued occupancy being contingent on good-faith efforts to accomplish the goals established.

Recently, Chickering has been involved in designing the University Learning Center at George Mason (Chickering & O'Connor, 1996). One of the main goals of the center is to foster collaboration among individuals who normally do not interact.

In a book geared to students about to enter college, Chickering and Schlossberg (1995) explained the areas of development that should occur during college and ways that students can structure their environment to achieve these development goals. Key environmental factors, such as relationships with faculty, active learning, and collaboration with other students, are stressed. In addition, Schlossberg, Lynch, and Chickering (1989) suggested programs and services designed to meet the needs of adult students in college.

Critique and Future Directions

Chickering's theory provides a comprehensive picture of the developmental tasks college students face. His work not only helps explain the issues and concerns with which students are dealing but also suggests steps that student development educators can take to foster student growth.

Chickering and Reisser's revisions do much to update the theory. In his review of the second edition of *Education and Identity*, Schuh (1994) applauded Chickering and Reisser for their willingness to revise the definitions and order of the seven vectors to reflect research findings. He was particularly pleased to see the incorporation of material related to women's development and the development of African American and Hispanic students. Schuh noted, however, that Asian American and Native American students are still being overlooked. Schuh is also critical of Chickering and Reisser for not clearly indicating the sources of the quotes they provide as examples.

Chickering's theory is empirically grounded and comprehensive; however, it lacks specificity and precision. Even in the newer version, definitions of vectors are often quite general. Developing Integrity is particularly hard to grasp and therefore to measure. Chickering also fails to address the different motivational levels of students to address issues or the process by which they accomplish developmental tasks.

More research to test the validity of Chickering's theory is warranted, particularly in light of its recent revision. Most current research is correlational and designed to focus on one or two vectors rather than the overall pattern of development. More longitudinal research, examining development over time, is needed. Factors that influence development also need further study.

Reisser (1995) acknowledged that more research is needed on the interrelationships among age, gender, sexual orientation, race, culture, and aspects of psychosocial development. She called for broad inclusive theories rather than narrow group-specific ones. However, much of psychosocial development is culture-specific. It may not be possible to develop a theory that is totally valid for everyone.

Research is only as good as the instruments and techniques on which it is based. Although the Iowa instruments show promise as objective measures of six of the seven vectors, further work is needed to validate them. It is also important to note that they are based on the earlier definitions of the vectors. The Student Developmental Task and Lifestyle Inventory measures only three vectors and defines those vectors differently than Chickering does; therefore it measures Chickering's theory in only a limited way. Further efforts are needed to develop reliable and valid assessment tools to study aspects of Chickering's theory.

Qualitative approaches should also be considered to examine psychosocial development, particularly as it occurs for members of different multicultural populations. Rather than trying to fit Chickering's theory onto groups different from the one on which it is based, we need to start from scratch to determine what is important in the lives of people from different backgrounds. This goal is best accomplished using phenomenological techniques.

Chickering's theory has had a significant impact on the development of proactive and intentional interventions in higher education. Because of the practical approach Chickering has taken, his theory is easy to understand and use. As a result, he has become perhaps the most highly regarded student development theorist to date.

CHAPTER FOUR

JOSSELSON'S THEORY OF IDENTITY DEVELOPMENT IN WOMEN

Maryann, Nan, Sinead, and Ramey are female students facing difficult decisions or crises in their lives. They decide to attend a counseling center women's group that meets weekly in the Peace Center on campus. Each of the women is unsure about who she is, what she believes, and how to make meaning of her life. Each woman comes to the group seeking assistance for different reasons.

Maryann, a junior elementary education major, is outwardly committed to little outside her family and her future career. Raised in an extended Italian Catholic enclave, she feels a tight connection to her family and never questions their religious beliefs. She routinely attends Sunday Mass while at college. Following in her mother's footsteps, she wants to become a teacher so she can empower young children in learning. From the time Maryann was a young girl, she assumed that she would teach until she married and became pregnant. She is proud of being a virgin and believes that sex is a sacred act saved for marriage. However, Maryann is concerned about never dating a man more than once and wants to know what she can do to find a partner.

Nan, a sophomore, is active in the Experiential Learning and Volunteer Services Center on campus. As a first-year student, she helped build a home for a family in dire need of housing and medical care in a rural area near her college. After her first year, she dropped her business major against the protest of her parents and enrolled as a pre-med major in order to help those who desperately need medical attention. Last summer, again against her parents' wishes, she accompanied a group of holistic physicians to deliver volunteer medical treatment to Indian peasants in Central American clinics. While in Guatemala, Nan met Kent and now hopes that her relationship with him will lead to marriage. Nan believes that sex is permissible when experienced in the context of a loving relationship, although she knows her parents would disapprove if they knew. The overwhelming guilt she feels about having an intimate sexual relationship with Kent is affecting her grades. She comes to the women's group seeking emotional relief.

Sinead, a first-year psychology major, was politically active during her first semester at college. She hoped someday to win a Nobel Peace Prize for her international contributions to social change through activism. However, José, her boyfriend, thought her political activism was irresponsible and took too much time away from her studies. After hours of discussion with José, Sinead relented and became inactive. Although her relationships with men are important, she does not plan to marry and trusts her instincts to know with whom and when to have sex. She experiences her mother as overprotective but adores her father. Sinead chose psychology as a major to help her understand the continuing rocky relationship with her mother. Her emotional reactions to her roller-coaster relationships left her searching for answers. After several months, she realized that she could not "fix" herself by studying psychology, and that left her wondering about her academic and vocational future. Since Sinead's parents are paying for her education, she feels tremendous guilt because she has no idea who she wants to be or what she wants to do when she graduates. She joins the women's group to seek advice.

Ramey, a second-semester sophomore, is thinking about dropping out of college. After a semester as a political science major, another as a pre-med major, and a third as a biology major, Ramey feels like she is floating through college and finds it difficult to commit to a field of study. In fact, she finds it difficult to commit to anything. Raised in an Orthodox Jewish family, Ramey quit going to synagogue when she entered college. Although she knows her parents would condemn her behavior, she marches in campus protests for liberal political causes and experiments with sex. She criticizes her parents for being too strict. Ramey thinks anyone who is a virgin at twenty-two must be abnormal. On occasion, Ramey drinks to excess and smokes marijuana with her friends. Although she sees little need to join the women's group, Ramey agrees, after weeks of persuasion by her friend Sinead, to attend for consultation.

They are not likely to know it, but Maryann, Nan, Sinead, and Ramey all seek assistance in developing their identity. Each woman represents one of Ruthellen Josselson's four identity statuses (1987a): Identity Diffusion, Foreclosure, Moratorium, and Identity Achievement, in ascending order of development. Thus Diffusers are the least mature, and Achievers are the most mature. Although student affairs professionals do not always witness the private moments of students' internal selves, understanding the content and process of how women create themselves through their ideological separations and connections will help us serve them better.

Historical Overview

Erik Erikson (1959/1980, 1963, 1968) was the first clinical psychologist to address the identity development journey from adolescence through adulthood. Basing his research on Freud's psychoanalytic perspective of individual development, Erikson deviates from Freud in at least one significant way (Widick, Parker, & Knefelkamp, 1978b). He predicates individual development on *both* internal dynamics and external environment. Erikson puts the developing person in a social context, addresses the influences of significant others and social institutions across the life span, and grounds these conditions in a historical foundation.

Erikson (1959/1980) described eight stages through which identity develops over the life span. Each stage is distinguished by a psychosocial crisis that must be resolved by balancing internal self and external environment. Although his theory is not the focus of this chapter, a rudimentary review, with a special emphasis on the young adult, may be helpful to understand Josselson's contribution to our knowledge of the life stages that make up the psychosocial developmental journey.

Erikson sees the first four stages coalescing in childhood to form the basis of identity. Stage 1 (basic trust versus mistrust) occurs during the first year of life when infants and caregivers deal with the issue of trust. In Stage 2 (autonomy versus shame and doubt) and Stage 3 (initiative versus guilt), children learn that they are the masters of their bodies and pursue curiosity without fear. In Stage 4 (industry versus inferiority), children learn in school to evaluate themselves as workers. When these early issues are resolved successfully, a child is a "collector of basic building blocks, a self that is essentially trusting, basically autonomous, able to act and strive toward goals without excessive fear, and able to achieve capacities and attitudes which seem necessary prerequisites to establishing identity" (Widick et al., 1978b, p. 4).

Stage 5 (identity versus identity diffusion) is a transition between childhood and adulthood that signals a call to define the self. Erikson (1959/1980) described how identity development is influenced by the interrelatedness of the first four stages and their successful completion. He stated that "the emerging ego identity bridges the early childhood stages, when the body and the parent images were given their specific meanings, and the later stages, when a variety of social roles becomes available and increasingly coercive" (p. 96). Josselson's theory of women's identity development (1987a) flows from this fifth stage.

The remaining stages of Erikson's theory describe how individuals interpret the meaning of love, care, and wisdom in their lives after identity is resolved. Stage 6 (intimacy versus isolation) occurs when the young adult must decide whether or not to fuse identity with another to create a union. Stage 7 (generativity versus stagnation) happens in midlife when the adult actively engages in giving back to society and must decide what legacy to leave behind. Stage 8 (integrity versus despair) is based on a need in old age to affirm one's existence and the meaning of one's life.

In defining identity, Erikson (1959/1980) recognized the internal relationship we have with ourselves as well as the external relationships we have with others. He believed identity "connotes both a persistent sameness within oneself (selfsameness) and a persistent sharing of some kind of essential character with others" (p. 109). Identity, Erikson stated, is ever-changing from birth to death, but as each crisis is successfully resolved, commitment to an established identity becomes even stronger. At a minimum, identity formation embodies "commitment to a sexual orientation, an ideological stance, and a vocational direction" (Marcia, 1980, p. 160). Although highly descriptive, Erikson's stages are difficult to study empirically.

Grounding his research in Erikson's stage theory, psychologist James Marcia (1966) was the first to create a "prototype of needed empirical study" (Widick et al., 1978b, p. 11) on the identity development of young adults, contributing significantly to our knowledge of the identity resolution process. *Exploration* (questioning values and goals defined by the parents) and *commitment* (attaching ownership to pronounced values and goals) are critical variables in describing individual identity formation (Bilsker, Schiedel, & Marcia, 1988). Exploration is often referred to as a "crisis, defined in terms of the presence or absence of a decision-making period" (Marcia, 1980, p. 161). After a crisis period, commitment is the personal investment in the decision. Marcia (1980) suggested that crisis and commitment in political, religious, and occupational decision making are the primary content of identity. Based on their study of women, Schenkel and Marcia (1972) added sexual decisions to political, religious, and occupational commitments as a fourth basis for forming individual identity.

The two interacting variables of crisis and commitment create the basis for Marcia's four identity states (1966, 1980), which inspired those of Josselson (1987a): Diffusion, Foreclosure, Moratorium, and Achievement. Unlike Erikson's stage theory, Marcia's identity states are not necessarily progressive, but neither must they be permanent. A person's identity status may or may not change over the life span. A dichotomy of healthy and unhealthy choices exists in each state. Individuals in the state of Foreclosure do not question but rather accept parental values; their commitment comes without crisis. They are viewed as "steadfast or rigid, committed or dogmatic, cooperative or conforming" (Marcia, 1980, p. 161). People in the state of Diffusion refuse or are unable to commit; they have not made a commitment, although they may experience crisis. People experiencing Diffusion may be thought of as "carefree or careless, charming or psychopathic, independent or schizoid" (p. 161). Individuals in the Moratorium state actively question parental values in order to form their identity; this crisis comes without commitment. They are seen as either "sensitive or anxiety-ridden, highly ethical or self-righteous, flexible or vacillating" (Marcia, 1980, p. 161). The state of Achievement comes after a period of crisis in which crucial choices are made and strong commitments are achieved. A secure ego identity is evident in this state. Viewed as the healthiest psychological status one can obtain, "Identity Achievements for the most part, are seen as strong, self-directed, and highly adaptive" (Marcia, 1980, p. 161).

Josselson's Theory

In 1971, Ruthellen Josselson set out "to understand the internal and developmental roots of identity formation in women" (1987a, p. 33). Her journey led her to the exploration of the internal differences among the four identity groups described by Marcia (1966) to explain why some resolve their identity crisis while others avoid creating identity or fail to move beyond the crisis. Over a three-year period, data were gathered by clinical psychologists who interviewed sixty randomly selected female college seniors between twenty and twenty-two years of age from four different colleges and universities. Josselson became curious about the accuracy of her predictions for these women after ten years of presenting and examining her findings. Thus she conducted a follow-up study of thirty-four women from the original study who agreed to participate. The following are patterns and themes identified in her two studies and their application to the female students in our women's Peace Center group.

Foreclosures: Purveyors of the Heritage

Foreclosures are women who graduate from college with identity commitment but without experiencing identity crisis. From an early age they know what they want and pursue it "with single-minded determination" (Josselson, 1987a, p. 43). Childhood assumptions and identifications serve as the bases for the confidence in the direction of their lives. They make choices without doubt or hesitation and without questioning the basic messages from their childhood. Typically, women in Foreclosure automatically adopt their parents' standards about sexual morality and choose an occupation and religion that reflect parental beliefs and preferences. They are not likely to risk disappointing their parents, who may hold a similar view of Foreclosures' perception of themselves (Josselson, 1987a).

Women interviewed twelve years later in this group were all classified again as Foreclosures. They experienced little identity change, as they were unable to imagine a life different from the one they lived as a child. Foreclosure women are described as "hardworking, responsible, and capable" (Josselson, 1987a, p. 60). Their careers expressed a "preoccupation with the care of others," but the main focus of their lives was "in their private worlds" (p. 59).

Foreclosures seek security in relationships not in work, even when successful in a career. Most Foreclosure women choose a partner who shares their perception of family harmony. As devoted mothers and wives, Foreclosures are psychologically tied to the centrality of family in their lives and their role in this tightly knit group. Few have relationships outside the family. Those relationships tend not to last, and Foreclosures eventually return to the comfort of familial bonds.

One student in our women's group, Maryann, is a Foreclosure. Despite her solid and strong character structure, she is building her identity on an unchallenged ego organization and gives few indications of psychological growth (Josselson, 1982). Maryann's security lies in her relationships, not in her chosen teaching career. Her life is consumed with a strong sense of family, tradition, and moral values. Grounded in identification with family rather than individuation, she does not distinguish her values from those of her family. She believes that other people make her who she is. Maryann discovers herself through her beloved parents rather than through self-discovery and differentiation. It is hard for her to form lasting relationships with peers of both sexes because her moral standards are demanding and her expectations are circumscribed. Although she is in the enviable position of having little inner conflict or ambivalence, she speaks of life in an idealized way and naively insists that everything in her life be "right."

Identity Achievements: Pavers of the Way

Identity Achievement women break the psychological ties to their childhood and form separate, distinct identities. Separation is painful, for it means giving up what is known and trusted about themselves while simultaneously opening up to the unpredictable and unknown possibilities that lie ahead. As the psychological bonds to parental identification are broken, Identity Achievement women reorganize their sense of self and identity. During adolescence, Identity Achievement women go through the process of reshaping, modifying, adding to, and mixing together the individuated and unindividuated aspects of the self. After critical examination of the childhood identity assigned to them by their parents, these women create identity in their own way after considering who they were in the past and who they want to become in the future.

Identity Achievement women follow a developmental course that leads them "to renounce the self-esteem derived from pleasing parents and to struggle for maturity" (Josselson, 1987a, p. 97). Rather than experience an intense identity crisis, many test their options silently and internally. Interestingly, Identity Achievement women have no higher intelligence or talent than any other group (Josselson, 1987a). However, they are found in more difficult college majors than Diffusers (Marcia & Friedman, 1970). In contrast to the other identity groups, Achievers value their own competence "and the role they give it in their personality structure" (Josselson, 1987a, p. 97). What matters to these women is feeling pride in themselves, not seeking others' pride to affirm their self-worth.

As adolescents, Identity Achievement women are likely to make decisions contrary to parental expectations. Although they feel guilty, Identity Achievement women are committed to a life of their own and therefore develop the capability of tolerating intense guilt. Interaction with others outside the family, such as teachers and peers, results in new ways of experiencing the self without abandoning the old self. As traditional college students, they are likely to be somewhat depressed and sad over the psychological separation from their parents. As adults, the depression disappears as they move through guilt and sorrow to maturity.

Relationship is primary for Identity Achievement women. They tend to marry men whom they consider partners and are likely to structure relationships on the basis of partnership needs rather than societal images of the "ideal" marriage. Childhood memories of Identity Achievement women suggest a combination of dependence and connection that reflects the integration of "the self-in-the-world and the self-in-relation" (Josselson, 1987a, p. 102). As an adult, what they do is secondary to securing a close relationship from which to draw strength. Yet the hallmark of Identity Achievement women is the balance they strike among work, relationships, and interests.

By the end of college, Identity Achievement women commit to aspects of psychosocial identity, including occupational identity. Many women find that the career they choose is unsatisfactory and initiate a change. Most Identity Achievement women in this study realized that they could not reach their goals within the bureaucratic structure of their work environment and, after another crisis period, retrained and obtained realistic work opportunities better suited to a more harmonious identity. Although this may seem inconsistent with Identity Achievers, other research (for example, Schenkel & Marcia, 1972) consistently demonstrates "that for women occupational identity is less predictive of overall identity status than is ideological and interpersonal identity" (Josselson, 1987a, p. 101). In short, once women Achievers commit to who they are in relation to others and decide how they want to contribute to others' lives, occupational identity becomes a way to express the self.

The success of Identity Achievement women comes from their capacity to construct their own identity. In doing so, women move toward maturity through "a tolerance for ambiguity, a resignation to what is outside one's control, and increasing confidence in the capacity to affect what can be controlled" (Josselson, 1987a, p. 104). Identity Achievement women are flexible in their identity as they develop and move toward the future. They are likely to continue to differentiate and explore other paths to identity. In effect, Identity Achievement women are forever becoming.

Our women's group participant, Nan, is an Identity Achiever. She struggles to set free the part of her personality that wrestles with exploration and making her own choices. She is flexible in recombining personality elements to form an exceedingly personal identity. In her quest for independence, Nan abandons childhood ego gratifications in order to form new ties. Her developmental work is based on internal liberation not readily identifiable in her behavior (Josselson, 1987a). Feeling trust and love toward her parents, she can appraise them realistically. Nan demonstrates a high tolerance for guilt when she makes decisions contrary to her parents' wishes, like the change of her major from business to pre-med and her summer trip to Latin America. She wants to stay connected and "be her own person" simultaneously. As she distances herself from her parents, Nan looks to Kent for ego support and to replace her self-esteem lost in the break from parental identification (Josselson). With Kent, she integrates her needs both for relatedness and for self-assertion (Orlofsky & Frank, 1986). She feels connected to Kent because he encourages her to be herself and to take pride in her accomplishments.

Moratoriums: Daughters of the Crisis

The Moratorium state is an unstable time of experimenting and searching for new identities. Moratorium status occurs when the individual internalizes the paradox that there are many ways "to be right." After internalizing the values of the family, Moratoriums are convinced of the rightness of these values. When a Moratorium woman learns that there are other legitimate ways of being, she goes into a tailspin. Many who remain in Moratorium at the end of college are caught in identity conflict, paralyzed to move beyond it. Some need additional time beyond college to resolve identity conflict. Of these women, some will remain searching, some will regress to a previously prescribed self-identity, and some will move on to Identity Achievement (Josselson, 1996).

In college, Moratorium women describe their childhoods as ones surrounded by overprotective mothers who indulge and overvalue them. Most do not consciously want to be like their mothers (who, ironically, dedicated their lives primarily to their daughters). In their efforts to assert independence, Moratorium women work to ensure not becoming like their mothers. Oddly, they are closer to their mothers as adults than the members of any other identity status group. Nevertheless, while rejecting identification with Mother, these women are likely to idealize their father. For them, Father represents a romantic notion of strength and success. More than any other group, Moratoriums talk about daydreams of stupendous magnitude. They speak of discovering a cure for cancer and being an ambassador to Russia. Glorified aspirations of childhood are a "necessity for some sort of idealized perfection" (Josselson, 1987a, p. 135). While in college, many Moratorium women behave in ways that do not win approval of either parent. Their cost is omnipresent guilt.

Our women's group member, Sinead, identifies with a Moratorium identity status. She experiences herself in relation to others. Although emotionally tied to her parents, she tries to individuate and looks to José for new identifications. She does not look to José for security but for approval, a kind of structure to build her life around. Although Sinead has illusions of grandeur about becoming a Nobel Peace Prize recipient, she invests little of herself in personal achievement. She desperately seeks others to define and differentiate her. Experiencing developmental growth as an external battle between herself and her mother, Sinead does not see the internal fight for her emerging identity. Through emotional support and validation, José helps her deal with her guilt and uncertainty.

Identity Diffusions: Lost and Sometimes Found

Marked by lack of crisis and commitment, Identity Diffusion college women are a varied and complex group. Evidence suggests that they score lowest among the four identity status groups "on all measures of healthy psychological functioning" (Josselson, 1987a, p. 140). They rank lowest in ego development (Hopkins, 1982), have the most difficulty establishing relationships (Kacerguis & Adams, 1980), and rank highest in anxiety (Schenkel & Marcia, 1972), field dependency (making decisions based on external stimuli) (Schenkel, 1975), and undifferentiated in sex-role orientation (Orlofsky, 1977). Little is known about why Identity Diffusion women have so much difficulty, but a critical review of nearly thirty studies examining the identity diffusion pattern tells us that one commonality among them is a tendency to withdraw from situations (Bourne, 1978a, 1978b).

When interviewed as college seniors, Identity Diffusion women in this sample were a diverse group who followed one of four different patterns: severe psychopathology, previous developmental deficits, Moratorium Diffusion, and Foreclosed Diffusion. Women in the first two groups fell outside the normal range of a healthy personality and were considered to have "borderline personality disorders" (Josselson, 1987a, p. 141). Early emotional scars, such as emotional neglect or loss of a caretaker, caused feelings of powerlessness that excluded women in these two subgroups from forming healthy identities. Since these women were "impulsive, avoiding guilt at all costs, they were unable to make identity commitments because of the instability and unreliability of their capacity to organize and integrate their experiences" (p. 142). For the most part, Identity Diffusion women with unhealthy psychological functioning are unable to develop positive identification with their parents over time.

Women in the third subgroup, Moratorium Diffusion, experience a crisis in identity but not in areas typical of psychosocial functioning. These women are in severe conflict about the choices in their lives, and philosophical questions about the meaning of life perplex them most. More experimental than Moratoriums, they try different ways to experience the world, "liberally employing drugs, sex, and fringe religious groups to this end" (Josselson, 1987a, p. 142). Although these women do not resign themselves to their impulses, they appear to vacillate between Moratorium (seriously searching) and Diffusion (drifting) statuses.

Ramey, our final women's group member, is an example of a Moratorium Diffusion. She fails to internalize her varied experiences, a stasis of her internal self. For example, although she renounces Judaism, she does not search for new religious beliefs to replace her old beliefs. Her broad experience does not produce learning or change. As she has little attachment to her inner self, she rejects nothing and follows her impulses to experiment with sex and drugs, which lead to little consistency in understanding her later experiences.

The fourth and last subgroup, Foreclosed Diffusions, drift through life neither in crisis nor able to commit. Foreclosed Diffusions appear to lack the will to construct a harmonious path for their lives. Lack of parental direction from a very early age leaves them disoriented rather than independent. Sensing their parents' lack of conviction and poor decision-making ability, Foreclosed Diffusions ironically cling to their parents for safety. These women feel so little control in their lives that they wait passively on deck for someone else to take the helm.

Assessment Techniques

An extensive review of the literature revealed no assessment techniques specifically devised to measure the four statuses of Josselson's theory of identity development in women. However, to understand the assessment roots of determining identity status, a review of Marcia's development and validation of measures of ego identity (1966) is helpful. Marcia created measures and criteria consistent with Erikson's notion of identity resolution as a psychosocial task. Measures included a semistructured interview to determine an individual's identity status and a sentence-completion form to serve as a measure of identity achievement. Using the concepts of crisis and commitment to establish identity status, Marcia applied these variables to occupational, political, and religious choices of eighty-six males enrolled in psychology, religion, and history courses at a small coeducational liberal arts college.

First, a fifteen- to thirty-minute semistructured interview, taped and heard by at least three raters, was administered in order to categorize participants' identity statuses. Each participant was rated by the presence or absence of crisis and the degree of commitment to occupational, religious, and political ideology. Twenty randomly selected participants produced a 75 percent agreement rate among three judges in the analysis of interjudge reliability.

Second, using the Ego Identity Incomplete Sentences Blank (EI-ISB) to measure overall ego identity, participants completed sentences and were encouraged to express their true feelings when given a leading phrase. Interrater reliability for twenty protocols among three judges produced an "average item-by-item correlation of $r = .76$, an average total score of $r = .73$, and an average percentage of agreement of 74" (Marcia, 1966, p. 554).

Another instrument used in this experiment was Concept Attainment Task (CAT) performance as measured by the D score, also called attainment discrepancy (Bruner, Goodnow, & Austin, 1956; Weick, 1964). The D score "reflects the algebraic average" (Marcia, 1966, p. 554) of the difference between a participant's aspirations and performance. A significant difference among identity statuses in D score was found using analysis of variance ($F = 5.10$, df $= 3/80$, $p < .01$).

Next, participants were placed in a combination of two stress conditions. Stressed participants scored significantly more poorly than nonstressed participants ($t = 2.61$, df $= 54$, $p < .02$). Finally, the Self Esteem Questionnaire (SEQ-F), a twenty-item test developed by de Charms and Rosenbaum (1960), reports the degree of endorsement a participant is willing to give statements about self-confidence and worthiness. A significant relationship was identified between EI-ISB score and the SEQ ($r = .26$, df $= 84$, $p < .01$). As measured by the EI-ISB and identity status, an analysis of variance among the four statuses ($F = 5.42$, df $= 3/82$, $p < .01$) was used to measure the relationship with overall ego identity.

Research

The bulk of research related to psychosocial maturity and identity development stems from Erikson's theoretical framework (1959/1980, 1963, 1968). Most of the research on identity development in young adults conducted between 1950 and 1970 examined late-adolescent men at prestigious colleges from an Eriksonian perspective and generalized the findings to women. Since that time, little research has been conducted on women's identity, and even less has been done using Josselson's theory as a theoretical base. Because much of the research discussed in this section was conducted so long ago, caution is warranted in applying the results to today's students.

Josselson's Research on Women's Identity

Much of the research on Josselson's theory was conducted by the researcher herself (for example, Josselson, 1973, 1982, 1987a, 1987b; Josselson, Greenberger, & McConochie, 1977). Josselson identified what is fundamental to women's experience to produce a uniquely feminine identity and how this may vary within identity statuses. She found that women, in creating their identity, are more likely to focus on "the kind of person to be" (Josselson, 1973, p. 47) rather than their occupational decisions, sexual identifications, political ideologies, religious convictions, or ideological beliefs. Thus a woman's relationship with herself is sewn together by who she is and not by the decisions she makes.

Josselson (1973) also tapped the tacit intricacies of how women relate to others. She found that women are in relationship with others for the sake of the relationship, not as a means to something else. These interpersonal relationships elicit autonomous satisfaction, giving a woman a better sense of her individual identity. By simultaneously merging autonomy and connectedness, women demonstrate a symbiotic process in their psychological lives.

One study conducted by Josselson, Greenberger, and McConochie (1977) revealed a difference in low- and high-maturity eleventh-grade girls. The researchers found that low-maturity girls' present and future lives are consumed by two primary goals: material things and fun. Desiring to be protected from themselves, these young girls seek their parents' counsel for support and protection. Showing similarities to Foreclosure women, low-maturity girls seek external guideposts for decision making rather than looking to themselves.

In contrast, high-maturity girls underemphasize material possessions and pleasure and spend energy reflecting on where they come from and where they are going. They find reflection on their own growth meaningful, whereas low-maturity girls find it threatening. Showing similarities to Identity Achievement women in their determination to obtain abstract goals, high-maturity girls "are more able to delay gratification" and "are more concerned with discovering a manner of being that is uniquely satisfying to themselves" (Josselson et al., 1977, p. 163).

In a study of personality structure and identity status as examined through college women's early memories, Josselson (1982) found that in contrast to Foreclosures, Moratorium women show more ego development. Dependence and safety are conflict areas for Foreclosures, who hold on to the past when forming their identity and current perceptions of self. Moratorium women concentrate on their own abilities and have tremendous capacity to bear anxiety compared to

Foreclosures. Confirming these findings, other research suggests that Identity Achievement and Moratorium women possess a more advanced ego development than women in Foreclosure and Diffusion (Ginsburg & Orlofsky, 1981).

At the most developed status, the inner self of women Identity Achievers integrates the need for relatedness with the need to assert the self. In finding this balance, Achievement women are best characterized by "rapprochement, a pattern wherein closeness is maintained to the persons from whom the individual is separating and individuating" (Josselson, 1982, p. 298). Rapprochement is considered by some to be the final step to a healthy identity consolidation. To their credit, Achievement women moving toward rapprochement blend Moratorium and Foreclosure patterns.

Identity Differences Between Women and Men

The literature on identity development tells of distinct differences between the identity development of women and men college students. Constantinople's classic study of psychosocial development in three hundred undergraduate women and men at one university (1969) claimed that men develop a greater degree of psychosocial maturity than women as they matriculate through college. Contradicting Constantinople's findings, several follow-up studies demonstrated that college seniors show greater psychosocial maturity than first-year students and that college women generally score higher in psychosocial development than men (Whitbourne, Jelsma, & Waterman, 1982; Zuschlag & Whitbourne, 1994). Other research suggests that women and men in Foreclosure and Diffusion score lower in achievement motivation and self-esteem than women and men Identity Achievers and Moratoriums (Orlofsky, 1978).

Waterman and Waterman (1971) found that college men progress from developmentally less mature identity statuses to more mature statuses during their first year in college. Maturation in the first year was confirmed by the decrease in men identified as Diffusions and the increase in men identified as Moratoriums in their occupational decision making. A second study of the same men in their senior year found significantly more students in Identity Achievement and significantly fewer students in Moratorium and Foreclosure statuses than in the first year (Waterman, Geary, & Waterman, 1974). An increasing number of male Identity Achievers during the college years suggests that achievement status is the most mature and likely "the final step in the process of development at this stage of life" (Prager, 1986, p. 32).

Women and men college students appear to resolve the processes of intimacy and identity development differently (Hodgson & Fischer, 1979). Late-adolescent males tend to discover their identity through issues of competence and knowledge.

Men's competence evolves from choosing a career and securing a stable future, and their knowledge comes about through the confidence gained by development of an ideology. Women, by contrast, find their identity by relating to others and have the capacity to experience higher levels of intimacy than men.

In a different study of identity status and occupational decision making in college students, men more frequently identified as Achievers, and women more frequently identified as Foreclosed or Diffuse (Hodgson & Fischer, 1979). In regard to religious beliefs of college students, men (Hodgson & Fischer, 1979) and women (Orlofsky, 1978) are both likely to be Identity Achievers. Examination of college students' political ideology suggests that men more often become Achievers (Hodgson & Fischer, 1979) and women are overrepresented as Foreclosures (Adams & Fitch, 1982). College students' attitudes toward premarital sex seems to vary developmentally as well (Schenkel & Marcia, 1972); women more frequently report Identity Achievement status than men, whereas men are more frequently Foreclosed or Diffuse (Orlofsky, 1978; Waterman & Nevid, 1977).

Applications

An inclusive review of the literature uncovered a dearth of information related to applying Josselson's theory in practice. Weston and Stein (1977) examined women's Identity Achievement status and its relationship to structural factors within the college environment. Contrary to their expectations, these researchers found that structural factors such as type of housing, type of institution, and academic classification were not related to women's Identity Achievement status. Yet this research did reveal that women's participation in college activities is related to achievement identity. Three facets of participation were examined: number of organizational memberships, degree of activity, and leadership functions performed. Of these three dimensions, "degree of activity was the most useful in predicting identity achievement of college women" (Weston & Stein, p. 23). Women students heavily involved in campus organizations appear to have already accomplished identity and participate as an expression of the self, rather than using organizational involvement to search for Identity Achievement status.

Marcia (1989) offers some insight into establishing psychological interventions to promote identity development that are easily adapted to student affairs practice. He encourages primary efforts in the sociocultural domain of "seeking to eliminate harmful circumstances that might *eventually* produce psychological difficulty" (p. 405). From his perspective, identity statuses may not be as significant as their underlying components of exploration and commitment. Students face difficult decisions about ideology, occupation, sexuality, and interpersonal beliefs that lead to a naturally occurring disequilibrium in their lives. Student affairs professionals can capitalize on this predictability and offer safety, structure, facilitation, and guidance while students experiment with their choices of becoming. In order to make a commitment, young adults need a safety net to catch them when they fail and retreat and a caring environment to nurture them back to psychological health.

Marcia (1989) makes the important point that classrooms must be staffed with teachers who are nourished in a supportive environment where they can face identity, intimacy, and generativity issues. Easily translated to a student affairs context, professionals in the field must be concerned with setting the stage for and taking action on their own identity development as well as that of the students they serve. To do less undermines the learning process and deprives us all of being the best we can be.

Critique and Future Directions

The paucity of research and assessment conducted on the identity development of women leaves this area ripe for exploration. Although considerable research has been conducted involving both women and men, no research using Josselson's theory exists that addresses race.

The application of identity research, for women and men, is important for student affairs professionals who want to create meaningful developmental experiences to help students form a healthy identity. It is especially important to understand how autonomy, connectedness, and decision making are psychologically manifest in an individual's quest (or lack thereof) for identity in late adolescence and early adulthood.

Josselson's recent contribution to the literature (1992) enriches our understanding of relatedness as a positive aspect of the self. Through use of intensive interviews with women and men and their self-reported diagrams of "relational space," she examines how positive, healthy relationships are formed for women and men. She identifies eight dimensions of relationships (holding, attachment, passions, eye-to-eye validation, idealization and identification, mutuality and resonance, embeddedness, and tending) and their pathological poles to show their evolution over time. She asserts that relatedness is central in the lives of women and men but connections with others are manifest in qualitatively different ways for each sex. For example, women see relationships as fluid and dynamic, and they feel and describe their connections to others "as multifaceted, complex, and often contradictory and paradoxical" (Josselson, 1992, p. 223), whereas men view relationships as permanent structures that are likely to continue in roughly the same way once they are formed.

Others claim that identity formation is different for women and men and more measures are needed that take sex differences into consideration (Cella, DeWolfe, & Fitzgibbon, 1987; Orlofsky & Frank, 1986). Still others point out the need for research that not only examines women's identity but also explores the identity formation of the numerous and diverse student subpopulations (Jones, 1995; Kroger, 1985). Without a doubt, more research in the areas of psychological relatedness, connection, intimacy, interdependence, autonomy, and independence is needed in order to better understand our students and ourselves in this fast-paced, technologically connected world. It will help us set the stage for women's growth and development in our colleges and universities and help women like Maryann, Nan, Sinead, and Ramey make the difficult decisions in their lives.

CHAPTER FIVE

RACIAL AND ETHNIC IDENTITY DEVELOPMENT

Violent hate crimes aimed at racial minority group students find administrators, faculty, and students pondering the level of civility at Kando University. With fists and beer bottles flying, several African American and Latino students receive multiple wounds and lacerations in the most recent eruption. Student affairs administrators responsible for campus discipline ask the Student Government Association (SGA) to take an active role in helping to resolve this campus crisis. Student government leaders, who are primarily white, decide to sponsor a public forum and appoint representative leaders of the African American, Latino, and American Indian student unions to begin a focused dialogue on this campus crisis.

There is no standing room left when the gathering commences. Emotions are intense. Opinions vary. Before the moderator starts an open dialogue among community members, the four student representatives draw straws to determine the order of their five-minute presentations.

Roshana goes first. She is an African American student with long braided hair and traditional Nigerian dress. To Roshana, white male professors are the enemy and represent the arrogant supremacy of Western culture. She refuses to enroll in any classes taught by these white oppressors. Her anger also focuses on white male administrators who converted the African American Cultural Center to the Multicultural Education Center because she believes they are prejudiced against blacks.

Roshana begins. In a passionate way, she describes the recent condition of her roommate, whom she found at 3:00 A.M. beaten, raped, and left in an alley behind a white fraternity house. She is angry that women students, particularly minority women, face the scary prospect that this will happen to them. Through her tears, she condemns the actions of white men and pleads with the community to take a moral position that respects the right of individual differences.

Tomás, a Latino Student Union member, speaks next. He tells of an encounter with hostile white peers who accused him of filling an unwritten university admissions minority quota. When Tomás ignores their name calling, he is kicked during intramural soccer competition when the referees look away. In a quavering voice, Tomás courageously tells the roomful of people that he fears for his safety but thinks nothing will be done if he does not come forward now. With anger in his voice, he states that he has not experienced this kind of blatant racism before and pleads for acceptance of people for who they are and not rejection based on skin tone or accent.

Joleen, a proud Lakota woman and representative of the American Indian Union, is third to address the crowd. Last year she convinced the board of trustees to change the university team name from the Chiefs to the Lions. She is still mocked by classmates who revere dominant-culture traditions and cannot comprehend that some words are sacred to indigenous peoples and consequently can offend when used out of context.

Joleen's voice is heard clearly over the whispers as she ceremoniously begins an ancient tribal chant. The two hundred people in the room are spellbound by the tone and cadence of her strong, calm voice. When Joleen stops, she explains that the chant was sung by warring tribes before reconciliation. She hopes a similar result will come from this meeting. Her stories reveal the plight of American Indian students and exemplify the public and private indignities they experience on campus.

Katy, the SGA representative, speaks last. She knows few people of color on this predominantly white campus. She explains that she comes from a small, white farming community in the Corn Belt and has no firsthand experience of racial discrimination at Kando University. She condemns the hurtful treatment of minority students but believes that students of color may bring the "uproar" on themselves. Katy thanks the union representatives for educating her about their difficult confrontations with racism on campus. Last year, Katy's flashy roommate was robbed and abducted in a fraternity alley. She wonders aloud if the rape Roshana described was behavior brought on by the student's unawareness of her sexuality rather than a racial incident. Katy closes her remarks by asking the anxious crowd to take responsibility for bringing peace to the community before more harm occurs. She desperately wants the campus to leave the conflict behind. She turns the discussion over to the moderator to discuss ways to heal the community and reinstate respect and civility.

In the beginning of this century, W.E.B. du Bois (1903/1995), the first African American to earn a Ph.D. degree at Harvard, accurately predicted that "the problem of the Twentieth Century is the problem of the color line" (p. 41). Thus not surprisingly, studying the psychological constructs of individuals in the context of an ethnically diverse society has been mostly ignored. In a broad sense, individual "identity is a cognitive map that functions in a multitude of ways to guide and direct exchanges with one's social and material realities" (Cross, 1995, p. 117). All of the students in the opening scenario are influenced by their racial and ethnic identity development. Although often used interchangeably, "the terms *race* and *ethnicity* represent different constructs with different meanings" (McEwen, 1996b, p. 193). The definitions and manifestations of racial and ethnic identity do not originate in biology but are in fact social constructions based on an individual's heritage and reflected in white domination of racial and ethnic minorities.

Due to the confusion caused by the many definitions of racial and ethnic identity, it is important to highlight them prior to introducing specific models explaining the process of development. We will also describe biracial and bicultural identity. Finally, a brief summary of work being done on racial and ethnic identity development will be followed by a more complete examination of three well-known models, those of Cross (1971, 1991, 1995), Helms (1992, 1993a, 1995), and Phinney (1990).

Historical Overview

Racial identity, traditionally referred to as a biological condition (Casas, 1984; Krogman, 1945), is more accurately defined as "a sense of group or collective identity based on one's perception that he or she shares a common racial heritage with a particular racial group" (Helms, 1993b, p. 3). Racial identity theory comes from "the tradition of treating race as a sociopolitical and, to a lesser extent, a cultural construction" (Helms, 1995, p. 181). Thus an underlying assumption about race in the United States presupposes that racial groups experience either domination or oppression.

Katy, the white student who clearly does not understand her racial status, has never had reason to think about being white and its implications. She is not alone. White people rarely give much thought to membership in their racial group (Frankenberg, 1993). A rare exception, Lois Stalvey (1970/1989) detailed the account of confronting her role as an oppressor in the white culture during the 1960s.

Exploring whiteness through white women's life histories, Frankenberg (1993) argued that being white "refers to a set of locations that are historically, socially, politically, and culturally produced and, moreover, are intrinsically linked to unfolding relations of dominance" (p. 6). Indeed, white people's historical, social, political, cultural, and economic dominance has brought about racism and oppression in the United States. Yet there are several ways white people can work to eliminate the many overt and covert acts of individual and institutional racism (McIntosh, 1989). Whites can abandon the "myth of meritocracy" (p. 11), reexamine their unacknowledged privileged status, and expose the "invisible systems conferring dominance" (p. 10) on them. For example, Katy could benefit from more self-reflection on how her white racial status oppresses other racial groups at Kando University and what risks she can take to uproot the evolution of white privilege and power in the university system.

In contrast to racial identity, ethnic identity is defined as identification with "a segment of a larger society whose members are thought, by themselves or others, to have a common origin and to share segments of a common culture and who, in addition, participate in shared activities in which the common origin and culture are significant ingredients" (Yinger, 1976, p. 200). Although ethnic identity does not place primary emphasis on oppression, it "may include the prejudices and cultural pressures that ethnic individuals experience when their ways of life come into conflict with those of the White dominant group" (Sodowsky, Kwan, & Pannu, 1995, p. 133). Tomás, verbally and physically abused by his Anglo peers on the soccer field because he is Latino, feels the pain of prejudice and cultural pressure.

In the psychological literature, ethnic identity is many-faceted (Phinney, 1990), although empirical research on the topic is inconclusive and fragmented. Most of the psychological research examines "attitudes toward racial or ethnic groups other than one's own and particularly . . . stereotyping, prejudice, and discrimination" (p. 499). The psychological relationship of racial and ethnic group members within their own group is a less studied aspect of diversity. This concept, broadly known as ethnic identity, is attested to by numerous writers who struggle to understand their ethnicity (for example, du Bois, 1903/1995; Malcolm X, 1970; Rodriguez, 1982; TwoTrees, 1997).

The number of racially mixed people in the United States has risen dramatically since 1967 when the U.S. Supreme Court repealed the laws against miscegenation (race mixing) (Root, 1992). Children born to parents of different races are considered biracial, which "most appropriately signifies the presence of two racial backgrounds in a nonjudgmental manner" (Kerwin & Ponterotto, 1995, p. 201). First-generation offspring tend to carry this blended identity, although multigenerational individuals may, too (Daniel, 1996). Space restrictions limit detailed consideration here, but other developmental models that address the needs and experience of persons from more than one racial group include those by Poston (1990) and Kerwin and Ponterotto (1995). Like similar models, Kerwin and Ponterotto's suggests that during the college years, biracial students are likely to embrace one culture and reject the other. As personal identity becomes more secure, biracial college students are likely to reject the expectations of others and develop a healthy biracial identity.

Biculturalism, a concept grounded in the work of Ramirez (1983) and Szapocznik and Kurtines (1980), is defined by Torres (1997) as "a synthesis of two cultures and languages out of which arises a third reality that was not present before" (p. 1). The concept of biculturalism is more relevant to describe minority students who retain significant aspects of the culture from which they come while moving toward acculturation into the academy. Roshana and Joleen, students participating in the forum at Kando University to help create a healthy community on campus, show signs of synthesizing their "birth" culture (Nigerian dress and ancient tribal chants, respectively) with the college culture (representing their culture at the forum). Biculturalism is discussed more fully in our description of Phinney's Ethnic Identity Development Model later in this chapter.

In the past twenty years, the racial identity development of persons of color and white persons has attracted increasing attention in the literature (McEwen, 1996b). Building on the work of Erik Erikson (1950, 1968) and James Marcia (1966, 1980), researchers began to examine models of racial development (for example, Arce, 1981; Cross, 1978, 1991; Helms, 1993a; Kim, 1981; Thomas, 1971) and ethnic development (for example, Atkinson, Morten, & Sue, 1993; Phinney, 1989, 1990) to better understand those who successfully resolve identity issues. Although it is beyond the scope of this chapter to include the burgeoning number of racial and ethnic identity models, an expanding number of models exist that are related to specific groups such as Hispanics (Bernal & Knight, 1993; Casas & Pytluk, 1995; Padilla, 1995; Ruiz, 1990), Asians (Kim, 1981; Sodowsky, Kwan, & Pannu, 1995; Sue & Sue, 1990) and American Indians (Choney, Berryhill-Paapke, & Robbins, 1995).

Racial and Ethnic Identity Development Models

It is impossible to include in this chapter all of the theories and models related to racial and ethnic identity. The models presented here were selected because of their applicability to many minority group and non–minority group students and because they are frequently referred to in the literature. Specifically, Cross's Model of Psychological Nigrescence (1971, 1991, 1995), Helms's Model of White Identity (1992, 1993d, 1995), and Phinney's Model of Ethnic Identity (1990) are discussed. These three models give insight into the complex undertaking of racial and ethnic identity formation. The four students described in the racial forum at Kando University are discussed as appropriate with each model.

The Cross Model of Psychological Nigrescence

During the social movements of the late 1960s and early 1970s, scholars began to examine the concept of psychological Nigrescence. Nigrescence is a "resocializing experience" (Cross, 1995, p. 97) in which the healthy individual's identity is transformed from one of non-Afrocentrism to Afrocentrism to multiculturalism. More akin to a cyclical journey than a linear one, changes occur over the lifetime in the African American individual's psyche (Parham, 1989).

One of the most prevalent models of psychological Nigrescence was developed and later revised by Cross (1971, 1991, 1995). He described this positive conversion as a five-stage sequential process. The five stages, which address the psychology of Nigrescence, are Preencounter, Encounter, Immersion-Emersion, Internalization, and Internalization-Commitment.

Stage 1: Preencounter. In the first stage, individuals view race as unimportant and prefer to be accepted as "human beings." Viewing the world from a Eurocentric perspective, this "deracinated" frame of reference influences the individuals' social, political, cultural, and psychological behavior. In other words, the individuals' thoughts and actions are pro-white and anti-black. Attitudes and values reflect the white normative standard, thereby devaluing or denying "Blackness—that is, [African Americans'] social group identification within the social context of racism" (Hardiman & Jackson, 1992, p. 22).

In Cross's revised model (1995), Preencounter African Americans tend to range from low-salience (race-neutral, where being black does not play a significant role in life) to anti-black. One permutation of low-salience individuals is African Americans who also see "race as a problem or stigma" (p. 98). They are likely to work hard to eliminate the social stigma connected to their blackness. At the other extreme, anti-black African Americans look at blacks in a way similar to that of a white racist (Cross, 1995). Anti-blacks see blackness through a telescope of adverse racial stereotypes, whereas they see whiteness as the preferred racial status.

Stage 2: Encounter. The second stage involves an encounter that shatters an individual's current identity and worldview (Cross, 1995). Often it is not a singular event that destroys a person's identity equilibrium but rather multiple small encounters that eventually have the cumulative effect of throwing a baseball through a plate glass window. This experience creates a sense of disequilibrium that causes vulnerability to a new interpretation of identity. For example, if an African American student identifies as "nonblack" or "just a human being" and is called derogatory racial names on a basketball court, anger will likely cause an examination of the appropriateness of the old identity and worldview. As exploration for a new worldview begins, black identity emerges.

This stage occurs in two steps: (1) undergoing an encounter and (2) being affected by it in a powerful way. In the first step, the individual is the "object of an encounter event or activity" (Cross, 1995, p. 105); in the second step, the individual personalizes the encounter to the point of interpreting the world though a new lens. The encounter may be positive (for instance, discovering African American historical or cultural information previously unknown) or negative (for example, racist acts against the individual). After a period of anger at whites and anxiety over the "kind" of black person to become, the African American is energized and takes action to seek information about, and affirmation of, a new black identity.

Stage 3: Immersion-Emersion. The third stage is a watershed period in which the individual discards remnants of the old identity and commits to personal change (Cross, 1995). In effect, individuals simplify, fantasize, and romanticize new black self-images. Neophyte converts are captivated by the new identity and its symbols such as clothing, hairstyle, language, attendance at black events, involvement in black organizations, and glorification of African heritage. Paradoxically, it is these new converts who are the most blatant about the outward symbols of their changing black identity (Cross, 1995). Individuals in Immersion-Emersion tend to disparage white people and white culture as they withdraw from contact with other ethnic groups. Though the degree of immersion into blackness is very high, internalization of the new identity is minimal.

Stage 3 has two phases: the first involves total immersion into blackness while withdrawing from other groups, particularly whites. In this stage, individuals experience feelings of rage (at white people and their culture), guilt (for believing what white society told them about themselves), and pride (in black people and culture). Roshana, the African American Student Union representative at the forum, can easily be identified in Stage 3. Her Nigerian dress and braided hair are manifestations of her immersion into black culture. She mocks whiteness by enrolling in courses taught only by minority professors, preferably African American scholars. Her reaction at the forum was emotion-filled, aiming rage at whites.

The second phase of Stage 3 highlights a progression out of a dualistic, reactionary mode into a more critical analysis of the new black identity. In truth, the individual cannot continue locked in this highly charged emotional state and is predisposed to seek out other worldviews to stabilize the intensity. Greater control over emotions and attitudes takes hold as this difficult transitional period passes. Effectively, a shift occurs from the outward signs of the new identity to an internalization of the new identity when the convert "begins to comprehend immersion as a period of transition rather than an end state" and "seems to understand that continued growth, perhaps of a less emotional nature, lies ahead" (Cross, 1995, p. 111).

Stage 4: Internalization. The fourth stage marks the beginning of a resolution between the old identity and the new black worldview. As anti-white feelings give way to a nonracist perspective, the individual achieves a sense of inner security and self-confidence about being black. Feelings of hostility and emotional turmoil begin to subside. It is not that converts' basic personality structure changes but that race and culture take on greater salience in their lives.

Individuals in this stage are characterized by their ideological flexibility, psychological openness, and a more tranquil and secure demeanor. Though the primary reference group is still black, the individual moves to a more pluralistic perspective. For individuals in Internalization, "Blackness becomes one of several (biculturalism) or many (multiculturalism) saliencies" (Cross, 1995, p. 113). Relationships with white associates and people from other ethnic groups are renegotiated as internalization of the new black identity takes hold.

Stage 5: Internalization-Commitment. The final stage in Cross's conversion experience (1991) translates the new identity into meaningful activities that address concerns and problems shared by African Americans and other oppressed peoples. A continuing involvement in these activities and issues promotes a lasting potential significance of the new black identity. The individual replaces an "I" or egocentric perspective with a "we" or group perspective. Although the process of psychological Nigrescence does not necessarily end with Stage 5, development may level off at Stage 4 as the individual internalizes a new identity but does not continue to be involved in relevant issues. Empirical studies that address a sustained commitment to psychological Nigrescence are nonexistent (Cross, 1995).

Helms's White Identity Development Model

Janet Helms (1993d) proposed a model of white racial identity development based on the process of moving toward a nonracist white identity and hence the abandonment of racism. That racism is the central theme of white identity development is not in doubt (McEwen, 1996b). Jones (1972, 1981) identified three types of racism: (1) *individual racism,* in which personal attitudes, beliefs, and behaviors are designed to assure the individual of the superiority of whites and the inferiority of nonwhites; (2) *institutional racism,* in which social policies, laws, and regulations maintain the economic and social privileges of whites over nonwhites; and (3) *cultural racism,* in which social beliefs and customs promote the idea that the white culture is superior to nonwhite cultures.

Helms's White Identity Model (1993d) features two primary phases: abandonment of racism and defining a nonracist white identity. The search for white identity is a process that involves complex interactions of attitudes, emotions, and behaviors. As individuals change from racist to nonracist, they acknowledge racism and become conscious of whiteness. As progress is made through each status, the individual completes the developmental tasks necessary for a healthy white identity. These tasks include an expulsion of internal individual racism, recognition of and oppo-sition to institutional and cultural racism, awareness and acceptance of whiteness as a part of one's identity, and internalization of a positive white identity.

The Helms model (1995) is a six-status process of development. In her orig-inal model, Helms (1993d) described an individual's movement through "stages" rather than what she now calls "statuses." She found *stage* a limited concept be-cause individuals struggling with their racial identity appear to be in more than one stage at a time (Parham & Helms, 1981); the term implies a static condition rather than the dynamic interplay of cognition and emotion (Helms, 1995); and racial identity theory does not support the idea of mutually exclusive stages (Helms, 1993a).

Phase I: Abandonment of Racism. The first phase of the Helms model has three statuses.

Status 1: Contact. The first status of Phase I is Contact, which occurs when the individual encounters the idea or actuality of black people. Depending on family background, a white person may enter this status with naive curiosity or timidity about blacks and a superficial and inconsistent notion of whiteness. During the Contact status, the white person may not be aware that he or she automatically benefits from institutional and cultural racism. Consequently, individuals may enjoy being racist more than persons in other statuses because they have not con-fronted moral dilemmas resulting from a racist identity. Behaviors typical of a white person in Contact include limited interracial social or occupational inter-actions with blacks (unless with persons who "seem white") and generally positive feelings about the "idea" of blacks and fair treatment of them, combined with anxiety over spending time with them.

Our SGA representative, Katy, is in the Contact status of Helms's model. She does not see herself as white or as a member of any race. Her limited experience has not exposed her to interracial social or occupational contexts. She expresses general feelings of acceptance for and fair treatment of minority students but feels uncomfortable in their presence. Katy believes that if students like Roshana would amend their behavior (to conform to white society), their problems with white people would end.

The length of time whites spend in this status depends on the types of inter-actions they encounter with blacks and with racial issues generally. If whites con-tinue to interact with blacks, sooner or later they will experience conflict with significant others who make it known that interaction with blacks is unacceptable behavior. Eventually, individuals in the Contact status must acknowledge that blacks are treated differently from whites in the United States. When whites reach this point, they can move to the next status.

Status 2: Disintegration. Disintegration, the second status of Helms's white identity development model, involves the conscious, though conflicted, acknowledgment of one's whiteness while recognizing the moral dilemmas associated with being white. At this point, the individual experiences emotional discomfort caused by the incongruence between what society teaches (for example, freedom, democracy, all people are created equal) and what the individual observes and experiences (such as racism, sexism, homophobia). Eventually, it becomes apparent to the white person that the social skills taught in this culture may not result in successful interactions with blacks. The conflicts experienced between beliefs, feelings, attitudes, and values lead to a state of dissonance marked by feelings of guilt, depression, anxiety, and helplessness. To reduce the uncomfortable state of dissonance in Disintegration, the white person may avoid further contact with blacks, attempt to explain to significant others that blacks are not so bad, or seek information to suggest that racism does not exist or that it is not the fault of white people. As white persons attempt to develop new beliefs, they enter the Reintegration status.

Status 3: Reintegration. During Reintegration, the white person consciously acknowledges a white identity. While selectively attending to information to confirm societal stereotypes of African Americans, the individual accepts the belief of white racial superiority and black inferiority. Any remnants of guilt feelings about blacks are transformed into feelings of fear and anger. These feelings and beliefs may be expressed passively, by removing oneself from an environment where there are blacks, or actively, by treating blacks as inferior. White behavior may include acts of violence or exclusion in order to protect white privilege. A person can stay in Reintegration until a jarring event causes abandonment of a racist identity. As white people begin to question the definition of whiteness and the justifiability of different forms of racism, they enter into Phase II of white racial identity development.

Phase II: Defining a Nonracist White Identity. The second phase of the Helms model also has three statuses.

Status 4: Pseudo-Independence. Pseudo-Independence, or White Liberalism, is the first status defining a positive white identity. Actively questioning the assumption that blacks are inherently inferior to whites, the individual begins to acknowledge white persons' responsibility for racism while trying to understand the ways in which white people perpetuate racism. During this time of intellectualization, the individual sublimates previous feelings of dissonance. Feelings regarding racism take the form of empathy with blacks and agitation regarding racial issues while in white peer groups. White people in this status may seek greater interaction with blacks. However, often this interaction involves trying to get blacks to act more like whites regarding criteria for success and acceptability.

Pseudo-Independent individuals view racial differences through a white standard while expecting blacks to explain and seek solutions to racism. Thus in this status, individuals may unwittingly perpetuate different forms of racism and possess neither a negative nor a positive white identity or consciousness. As such, the white person may be viewed suspiciously by both whites and blacks and feel marginalized. As whites seek a more productive definition of whiteness, they enter the next status.

Status 5: Immersion-Emersion. During Immersion-Emersion, whites replace white and black stereotypes with more accurate information about what it means to be white in the United States. The individual begins to ask, "Who am I racially?" and seeks out the stories of other whites who have experienced similar identity journeys. During Status 5, the focus shifts from trying to change blacks to trying to change whites. As emotional and cognitive restructuring occurs, an individual begins to seek a new identity through engagement with other whites and by reading and studying biographies and autobiographies or joining consciousness-raising groups. Status 5 individuals reexperience distorted or underground emotions. As negative feelings are expressed, a feeling of euphoria sets in. These positive feelings allow the individual to confront and fight against various forms of racism and oppression.

Status 6: Autonomy. The final status of white identity development is Autonomy. This status requires white people to internalize, nurture, and apply the new definition of white identity. Race no longer poses a threat; therefore the individual no longer feels compelled to oppress, idealize, or denigrate nonwhites. Personal, cultural, and institutional racism is abandoned as one's worldview broadens and becomes more flexible. Actively seeking learning opportunities involving other cultural groups, understanding how other forms of oppression are related to racism, and working to eliminate all "isms" are behaviors included in Autonomy. Although Status 6 is the highest level of white racial development, it is an ongoing process in which white individuals continue to be open to new ways of thinking about culture and race.

Phinney's Model of Ethnic Identity Development

Jean Phinney (1990) maintains that the issue of ethnic identity is important to the development of a positive self-concept for minority adolescents. Based on Erikson's theory (1968), Phinney's model is consistent with Marcia's identity development model (1980) and other ethnic identity models (Atkinson, Morten, & Sue, 1993; Cross, 1991; Helms, 1993a).

The ethnic identity construct focuses on what people learn about their culture from family and community (Torres, 1996). Ethnic identity develops from the shared culture, religion, geography, and language of individuals who are often connected by strong loyalty and kinship. Theories of ethnic identity formation examine how "individuals come to understand the implications of their ethnicity and make decisions about its role in their lives, regardless of the extent of their ethnic involvement" (Phinney, 1990, p. 64).

As part of the process of committing to an ethnic identity, minority youth must resolve two basic conflicts that occur as a result of their membership in a nondominant group. The first conflict involves stereotyping and prejudice on the part of the majority white population toward the minority group. Negative attitudes and prejudicial treatment pose a threat to the self-concept of minority youth. The second conflict involves a clash of value systems between majority and minority groups and the manner in which the minority adolescent negotiates a bicultural value system. This issue, too, will influence minority adolescents' self-concept and sense of ethnic identity.

Phinney's model of ethnic identity development (1990) is made up of three distinct stages: Diffusion-Foreclosure, Moratorium, and Achievement. Minority adolescents who are able to actively explore their identity and resolve the inherent conflicts can develop an Achieved identity. Those who fail to move through this process develop a Diffused or Foreclosed identity.

Stage 1: Diffusion-Foreclosure. Individuals in the first stage of ethnic identity development have not explored feelings and attitudes regarding their own ethnicity. There may be a lack of interest in examining ethnic feelings, or it may be seen as a nonissue that leads to diffusion. The individual may have acquired attitudes about ethnicity in childhood from significant others that lead to foreclosure. Adolescents who accept the negative attitudes displayed by the majority group toward the minority group are at risk of internalizing these values. However, for the most part, this stage is marked by a disinterest in ethnicity.

Stage 2: Moratorium. During the second stage of ethnic identity development (Phinney, 1990), the individual becomes increasingly aware of ethnic identity issues. Stimulated by an experience that causes an exploration, a new awareness causes an individual to examine the significance of her or his ethnic background. The experience may be harsh, such as an encounter with overt racism, or it may be more indirect, such as the gradual recognition (as a result of less dramatic incidents) that the individual is perceived as "less" by the dominant culture. As a result of this awakening, the adolescent begins an ethnic identity search or moratorium. During this time, individuals seek more information about their ethnic or racial group while attempting to understand the personal significance of ethnic identity. This stage is characterized by emotional intensity, including anger toward the dominant group and guilt or embarrassment about their own past lack of knowledge of racial and ethnic issues.

Tomás, the representative from the Latino Student Union, is in Stage 2 of Phinney's Ethnic Identity Model. Since his arrival at Kando University, he has become increasingly aware of his Mexican heritage. The intentional racism he described at the forum caused him to explore his ethnic background. Seeking familial roots, Tomás wants to unlock the door of his ethnicity. Healing the wounds of his anger toward whites is a major step to the last stage of ethnic identity development. Speaking out about his personal experiences with racism at the forum, especially in light of potentially more physical abuse, helps Tomás move to the next level of growth.

Stage 3: Identity Achievement. In the final stage of ethnic identity development, the adolescent achieves a healthy bicultural identity. Individuals resolve their identity conflicts and come to terms with ethnic and racial issues. As individuals accept membership in the minority culture, they gain a secure sense of ethnic or racial identification while being open to other cultures. The intense emotions of the previous stage give way to a calmer and more confident demeanor.

Joleen, the American Indian student who voiced her views at the forum, is assigned Identity Achievement status based on Phinney's model. Before her fight with the board of trustees to change the team name from the Chiefs to the Lions, she was estranged from her culture and religion. Her security is marked now by singing a tribal chant at the forum. The culmination of Joleen's identity resolution process left her comfortable with a bicultural identity.

Assessment

Although many constructs of racial and ethnic identity are abstract and difficult to operationalize, a growing number of instruments designed to assess these variables are found in the literature (for example, Baldwin & Bell, 1985; Claney & Parker, 1989; Constantinou & Harvey, 1985; Garcia, 1982; Milliones, 1973; Teske & Nelson, 1973; Ting-Tomey, 1981; Zak, 1973). Since these instruments are far too numerous to discuss in depth, only instruments derived from Cross's black identity, Helms's white identity, and Phinney's ethnic identity models are reviewed here.

The instrument used most often to measure black racial identity formation, the Black Racial Identity Attitude Scale (RIAS-B), is based on Cross's early work on black identity (1978). Developed by Parham and Helms (1981), the RIAS-B is basically an attitude scale that attempts to measure the range of positive, negative, and mixed feelings of blacks toward other blacks and toward whites and how those attitudes change as an individual moves through the stages. The instrument has thirty items and uses a five–point Likert scale (1 = strongly disagree, 5 = strongly agree). Respondents are asked to indicate the extent to which each item is descriptive of them. Cronbach's alpha reliability coefficients for the four scales—Preencounter, Encounter, Immersion-Emersion, and Internalization—were .67, .72, .66, and .71, respectively, in Parham and Helms's study (1981). In a later study by Helms and Parham (1996), the following Cronbach's alphas were reported: Preencounter = .69, Encounter = .50, Immersion-Emersion = .67, and Internalization = .79. Helms (1993c) presented the following evidence of the validity of the RIAS-B: (1) correlations between RIAS-B scales support racial identity as a process occurring in stages (that is, stages next to each other are more highly correlated than those that are farther apart), and (2) a multidimensional scaling process demonstrated that items tend to align in a way that indicates a stagewise developmental process. Helms also noted that scores on the RIAS-B generally predict behaviors and values that Cross's theory suggests should be related to racial identity. Although evidence to support the existence of all stages except, in some cases, the Encounter stage, was reported by Helms (1993c) and other researchers (Ponterotto & Wise, 1987), some observers challenge the idea that ethnic and racial identity, as a personality trait, can be measured by an attitudinal instrument like the RIAS-B (Akbar, 1989). Helms (1993c) also cautioned that research to date has focused on college students and therefore the scale's generalizability to other populations is unknown.

The White Racial Identity Attitude Scale (WRIAS), one of only two instruments available to measure white racial identity (Rowe, Behrens, & Leach, 1995), assesses "attitudes related to the original five stages of white racial identity development proposed by Helms" in the early 1980s (Helms & Carter, 1993, pp. 67–68). Examining development that moves from a lack of sensitivity toward race to race consciousness and from least to most healthy, the WRIAS is characterized by white persons' attitudes about themselves and their relationship to black persons. Respondents are asked to describe themselves on ten items using five-point Likert scales (1 = strongly disagree, 5 = strongly agree) for each of five subscales (Contact, Disintegration, Reintegration, Pseudo-Independence, and Autonomy) for a total of fifty attitudinal statements. Comparison of women's and men's scores for each subscale suggested that men score higher on Autonomy ($F = 3.59$, df $= 1/504$, $p = .06$) and Pseudo-Independence ($F = 2.94$, df $= 1/504$, $p = .09$) (Helms & Carter, 1993). Among participants in a counselor preference study, reliabilities ranging from .65 (Pseudo-Independence and Autonomy) to .76 (Disintegration) were found (Helms & Carter, 1991).

Paradoxically, as the WRIAS became the measure of choice for white racial identity researchers, mounting evidence of its psychometric deficiencies were uncovered. For example, several researchers found low reliabilities on the Contact scale, ranging from .18 to .33 (Alexander, 1993; Davidson, 1992; Ottavi, Pope-Davis, & Dings, 1994). In addition, the interscale correlations of the remaining scales have been so high that there may be scant justification for considering them separate scales (Gilchrest, 1994; Grandner, 1992; Tokar & Swanson, 1991). Certainly, evidence suggests that new assessment tools for examination of white racial identity are needed.

The first version of the Multigroup Ethnic Identity Measure (MEIM) was derived from the Objective Measure of Ego Identity Status (Adams, Bennion, & Huh, 1987) and "developed to assess ethnic identity search and commitment" (Phinney, 1992, p. 161). The goal of several revisions and administrations of the instrument (see Phinney, 1989; Phinney & Alipuria, 1990; Phinney & Tarver, 1988) was to produce a scale to be used with diverse samples of high school and college students of African American, Asian American, and white descent and to permit "assessment and comparison of ethnic identity and its correlates both within and across groups" (Phinney, 1992, p. 163).

The MEIM, using a four–point scale from strongly agree to strongly disagree, contains fourteen items that assess different aspects of ethnic identity: positive ethnic attitudes and sense of belonging (five items), ethnic identity achievement (seven items), and ethnic behaviors and practices (two items) (Phinney, 1992, p. 163). Cronbach's alphas were calculated to determine the overall reliability for the fourteen-item scale, and correlations of .81 for the high school sample and .90 for the college sample were found. Reliabilities were .75 for the high school students and .86 for the college students on the Affirmation/Belonging scale. For the seven–item Ethnic Identity Achievement scale, reliabilities were .69 for the high school students and .80 for the college students. Although the Ethnic Behavior scale consisted of only two items and was not calculated, "separate analysis showed that the ethnic behavior items increased the overall reliability of the measure" (p. 165). Phinney concluded that the MEIM is a reliable measure of late adolescents' and young adults' degree of identification with their own ethnic group.

Research Based on Racial and Ethnic Identity Models

Little empirical research conducted on racial and ethnic identity of college students is reported in the mainstream psychological or developmental literature. African American and white racial identities have received the most attention. For instance, Cross's work, derived from the 1960s civil rights era, has become a popular theoretical model to understand the black experience. Yet the amount of empirical evidence related to racial and ethnic identity remains small, although it is increasing.

Much of the research on college students' racial identity examines the phenomenon in counseling situations. For instance, Helms's excellent summation of black and white identity (1993a) includes discussions of how racial identity is framed within the counseling context including attitudes and behaviors within a black-white interaction model, how racial identity attitudes influence the counseling process in different-race dyads (Carter, 1993), and black client racial identity attitudes and white therapist cultural sensitivity in cross-racial therapy dyads (Bradby & Helms, 1993).

Another study of black college students in a counseling context led to the conclusion that in general, "possession of racial identity attitudes influences Black people's acceptance of Black and White counselors" (Parham & Helms, 1981, p. 255). Using self-assigned racial identity attitudes from Cross's racial identity model, this research suggests that as African Americans become more comfortable with their identity, their preference for a counselor of a certain race becomes less pronounced.

A study of black college students grounded in Cross's model lends partial support to the hypothesis that racial identity stage and self-esteem are related (Parham & Helms, 1985). The study found that black college students in the Preencounter and Immersion stages tend to have low self-esteem, whereas those in the Encounter stage tend to have positive self-esteem.

Little attention has focused on how racial identity affects students' daily lives and decision making. However, one study examined the relationship between black students' racial identity and their participation in cultural (black-oriented) and noncultural campus organizations (Mitchell & Dell, 1992). As the researchers hypothesized, students whose scores on the RIAS-B indicated they were in the Encounter, Immersion, or Internalization stage were likely to be involved in cultural organizations, whereas students in the Preencounter stage were unlikely to be involved in these organizations. A significant positive correlation was also found between scores on the Internalization scale and participation in noncultural campus activities, indicating that students who are at this higher level of identity development are more likely to seek both cultural and noncultural involvement.

Other researchers have examined components of African American student development unrelated to Cross's model. One study found a difference between African American and white alumni perceptions of growth during the college years (Placier, Moss, & Blockus, 1992). Results indicated that African American alumni perceive proportionally more growth than their white counterparts. Looney (1988) asserted that African Americans with strong egos define themselves, whereas those with weak egos are defined by others. Being aware of this challenge, student affairs administrators can intentionally design developmental interventions to assist in the growth and development of African American students and help increase black student retention.

McEwen, Roper, Bryant, and Langa (1990) outlined nine dimensions of African American student development to enrich the discussion of psychosocial theories related to college students' development. They suggested nine dimensions related to developmental tasks black students face: development of racial and ethnic identity, interaction with the dominant culture, cultural aesthetics and awareness, development of identity, social responsibility, interdependence, spirituality, fulfillment of affiliation needs, and survival in an intellectually competitive environment. McEwen et al. warned student affairs administrators of the pitfalls of using traditional theories based on European Americans' experiences and assumptions or based on a theory that assumes that blacks are inherently inferior. Being mindful of black Americans' African roots, they recommended that practitioners develop African American theories of student development that work in practice.

Drawn from a spectrum of literature, including social identity, acculturation, culture conflict, and identity formation, Phinney (1990) conducted an extensive review of the empirical literature related to ethnic identity in adolescents and adults. Though the majority of the studies she reviewed deal with members of white ethnic groups, she found a dearth of research conducted on the ethnic identity of dominant-group members. Black subjects were the second largest group represented, and Asian Americans, Hispanics, and American Indians were underrepresented. In fact, the research she described represents "a picture of fragmented efforts by many authors working individually with particular ethnic groups and developing measures of limited generality" (p. 500). Of more importance, however, this body of studies gives researchers, teaching faculty, and administrators a starting point for understanding the many ways to examine ethnic identity.

Application

Unfortunately for the practitioner, few research studies or resources are available that demonstrate the applicability of racial and ethnic identity models to student affairs or higher education. However, as institutions of higher education become increasingly more diverse, the failure of student affairs practitioners and faculty to understand students' racial and ethnic identity development "can lead to inappropriate and ineffective responses to volatile racial situations on campus" (Hardiman & Jackson, 1992, p. 21). The hate crime scenario at the beginning of this chapter is one example.

Several scholars have applied racial identity to the college classroom and encourage faculty to learn more about their own and their students' racial and ethnic development to improve classroom climate (Tatum, 1992). Hardiman and Jackson (1992) were clear about the appropriate responses to the conflicts created by students' (and sometimes faculties') clashing stages and statuses of racial identity development. They offered some helpful suggestions that are easily adaptable to student affairs.

For example, a primary goal of all educators (this includes student affairs administrators) is to "facilitate development in students, not stifle it or hide from it" (Hardiman & Jackson, 1992, p. 34). Enhancing the development of students in Stage 3 (Immersion-Emersion) of Cross's model can be particularly difficult. Students in Stage 3, who are often rightfully angry about racism on campus, are sometimes objects of offensive white supremacy acts. White administrators, whom students view as the power elite and toward whom they often direct their anger, must not dismiss these hostile acts by white students as "college pranks." Student affairs administrators must make it possible for racial and ethnic minority students to express their emerging worldview peacefully without fear of retribution from other students, faculty, or administrators. Hardiman and Jackson contended that to enhance the development of students, faculty and administrators must examine these stages in light of their own experiences, consider the role of stages and statuses as they watch students proceed down their individual developmental paths, and understand the large differences between social groups and students' different relationships to these groups.

Some of the recent discussion on college campuses centers around white identity development and how institutions of higher education can break the gridlock of white domination and racism. Clayton and Jones (1993) recommended workshops that focus on unlearning racism for student affairs administrators and students in graduate preparation programs. Participation in these experiences will allow white students to become ethnic learners as their worldview shifts from viewing other racial groups as if they do not exist or in some stereotypical way to respecting, appreciating, and celebrating ethnically and racially different others. Ultimately, the goal of racism unlearning workshops is the demise of white domination and oppression of racial and ethnic minorities in the academy. Educators can improve the quality of life inside and outside the classroom by "being more cognizant of and responsive to the developmental nature and implications of the ethnic identity process, [by being] more astute in diagnosing students' attitudes and behavior within this developmental paradigm, and by matching curriculum content and instructional style with ethnic identity stage" (Gay, 1985, p. 55).

Helms offered help for whites who want to take appropriate responsibility for ending racism in a powerful little book titled *A Race Is a Nice Thing to Have: A Guide to Being a White Person or Understanding the White Persons in Your Life* (1992). She clearly articulated how whites are hurt by dominating and oppressing others and "how ending [racism] serves White people's best interests" (p. i). Through a wide variety of poignant educational activities, Helms leads white people through a growth process to help them identify the various forms of racism and to replace it with other options. In addition, she presents excellent examples of how each white identity status is translated into practice and states in clear language what it means to have a positive white identity.

Critique of Models and Future Directions

In recent years, the explosion of racial and ethnic identity models has highlighted individual differences in our pluralistic student populations. As research reveals more about these differences, understanding of how students develop identity around race and ethnicity becomes clearer. Yet the theories and models available (such as the Cross, Helms, and Phinney models) represent only a tiny portion of what student affairs administrators need to know to ease the racial tensions prevalent on many campuses like Kando University and to create healthy campus environments in which students can explore this important dimension of their identity.

Most administrators and faculty are not trained in an environment that emphasizes cultural pluralism, and as well intentioned as they may be, they are likely to be ethnocentric (Ponterotto & Casas, 1991). Although many whites recognize that minorities are placed at a disadvantage in the systems created by whites, few acknowledge, much less attempt to change, systems that confer dominance on whites (Sue, 1995). Since institutions of higher education traditionally maintain the status quo, theories and models that explain how whites move from a racist to a nonracist perspective are important in creating equality and changing the power imbalance embedded in colleges and universities.

Closer scrutiny of nonwhite racial and ethnic identity theories is also necessary to improve understanding of the rapidly growing minority student populations that will become the majority in U.S. institutions of higher education in the twenty-first century. More must be known about the identity and acculturation processes of diverse students from a "dynamic perspective—the affective and cognitive manifestations and their implications for an individual's psychological well-being and personality and/or characterological development from both a short- and a long-term perspective" (Casas & Pytluk, 1995, p. 176). Moreover, the tendency to generalize, particularly African American identity models, to other minority groups, such as Chinese Americans, Japanese Americans, Hispanics/ Latinos/Chicanos, and American Indians, has created identity transformations for these groups with "cultural oppression as the common unifying force" (Sue & Sue, 1990, p. 95).

Furthermore, research that focuses on minorities who are biracial, biethnic, women, gay, lesbian, or bisexual is lacking the necessary depth to provide an understanding of the complex interaction patterns of multiple identity development. To approach identity development from a broader scope, future research should explore majority-minority ethnic identity models as Smith (1991) has. Helping majority students, like Katy, find avenues for exploring their identity can help curb and eventually eliminate violent hate crimes and other discriminatory practices against racial and ethnic minorities on college and university campuses as all students move toward multiculturalism.

CHAPTER SIX

GAY, LESBIAN, AND BISEXUAL IDENTITY DEVELOPMENT

A meeting of the Gay, Lesbian, and Bisexual Student Alliance was about to begin. Since it was the first meeting of the fall semester, the agenda consisted of setting goals and planning activities for the year. Returning members greeted each other, expressing relief at being back at school where they could "be themselves." Many told "war stories" of summers spent with families with whom they had to be "closeted," being grilled about who they were dating, and having to be constantly vigilant about what they said and how they acted. A few new members were present; they tended to sit in the back by themselves, and they looked uncomfortable. Some of the older members "checked them out" for their potential as dating partners. Outside the room where the meeting was taking place, Angela stood by the door and tried to hear the conversation and get a look at the people who were there. She desperately wanted to go in, but she was afraid; after about ten minutes she decided she couldn't do it and left.

James, the group's chairperson, began a brainstorming session about goals for the year. Marty, the political director, started with an impassioned plea that it was time for the organization to make its presence known on campus. He was in favor of taking a strong activist stance to see that "queer rights" were achieved. He favored demonstrations and rallies that would get the attention of the campus. Gretchen, chairperson of the women's caucus, advocated making sure that issues facing lesbians on campus were addressed. She was "sick of being a second-class citizen" in the GLBSA. Rudolfo, a Latino member, mentioned the importance of addressing racism in the gay, lesbian, and bisexual (GLB) community. Patrick, a younger and less vocal member of the group, was getting a bit uncomfortable with the direction of the discussion. He wasn't quite ready to be speaking at protest rallies. He was seeking friendship and social interaction with other GLB students. Jessica, a first-year student at her first meeting, was totally overwhelmed. She was looking for a place where she could talk privately with others about her newly discovered bisexuality. She hoped that the meeting would end soon so that she could get away from these radicals. James, appreciating the frustration of the returning members and their desire for action, also recognized that the newer attendees seemed uncomfortable with the direction the discussion was taking. He remembered what it felt like when he was beginning to explore his own homosexual feelings. He hoped that he could create an atmosphere where all members felt valued and accepted.

The scenario just presented illustrates part of the complexity of being gay, lesbian, or bisexual in college. Many GLB students begin or accelerate exploration of their identities during college (Evans & D'Augelli, 1996). Although individuals may have been aware of their orientation earlier in their lives, college is often seen as a "safer" environment in which to explore and "come out" than the home and family environment. Research indicates that as many as 10 percent of all college students identify as gay, lesbian, or bisexual and that others may be questioning their sexuality (Ellis, 1996); consequently, student affairs professionals must understand the developmental challenges these students face and provide appropriate supports to assist them in navigating what is often a hostile and uneducated environment (Obear, 1991).

Following a brief review of early research examining homosexuality and some of the first models of homosexual development, this chapter will present an in-depth look at gay, lesbian, and bisexual identity development from two perspectives: the social psychological model, exemplified by Vivienne Cass (1979), and the life span approach, outlined by Anthony R. D'Augelli (1994a).

Historical Overview

The first important studies of homosexuality, which was at the time considered pathological, focused on identifying its "cause" in order to find a "cure" (L. S. Brown, 1995). Another major and important debate in the literature has centered around the question of whether sexual orientation is innate (the essentialist argument) or fluid and changeable over time in response to context and interpersonal experiences (the constructionist position) (L. S. Brown, 1995; Kitzinger, 1995). Essentialists argue that the homosexual is a type of person who has been with us throughout history, while constructionists believe that the concept of "the homosexual" is socially constructed and changes as social definitions change (Kitzinger,

1995). This debate has important political implications in that the fight for gay civil rights has been based on the essentialist argument that people do not "choose" their sexual orientation and that it cannot be changed.

In the early 1970s, interest shifted away from the etiology of sexual orientation to the development of homosexual identity (Cass, 1983–1984). Homosexual *identity* was distinguished from homosexual *acts* because many people engage in homosexual behavior without identifying themselves as homosexual (Cass, 1983–1984). Researchers began to examine what it means to be homosexual and how people adjust their lives as they take on this identity.

Klein (1990) stressed that sexual orientation encompasses much more than sexual activity. He noted that emotional preference, social preference, lifestyle, and self-identification as well as sexual attraction, fantasy, and behavior at different times in a person's life must all be considered to provide an accurate picture of sexual orientation.

The expression "homosexual identity" is found in earlier literature and generally refers only to the type of behavior in which persons engage. Later theorists examined gay, lesbian, and bisexual identities that encompass emotional, lifestyle, and political aspects of life as well as sexual contact. This broader perspective is usually preferred in the GLB community because it has a more positive and less clinical connotation (Levine & Evans, 1991). To avoid confusion, terms used by the original theorists are repeated in this chapter.

Models of identity development can be loosely grouped into two categories: sociological and psychological (Levine & Evans, 1991). Sociological theories tend to focus on the impact of community, development of social roles, and managing stigma. Sociological theorists include Warren (1974) and DuBay (1987). Other sociological theorists, including Dank (1971), Lee (1977), Hencken and O'Dowd (1977), and Coleman (1981–1982), focused specifically on the coming-out process.

Psychological theories concentrate on internal changes experienced by individuals as they come to identify as homosexual. They examine growing self-awareness, formation of a homosexual self-image, and personal decisions about identity management. Psychological approaches include those of Plummer (1975), Minton and McDonald (1984), and Troiden (1989).

Many models present specific stages of development (for example, Lee, 1977; Coleman, 1981–1982; Minton & McDonald, 1983–1984; Plummer, 1975; Troiden, 1989). After reviewing these models, Levine and Evans (1991) identified four general developmental levels: first awareness, self-labeling, community involvement and disclosure, and identity integration.

Several problems exist with these early models of identity development (Levine & Evans, 1991). First, many reflect the social and political forces of the 1970s when they were developed and may not reflect the social realities of the current era.

Second, little research exists actually testing the models. Third, most of the early work on homosexual identity development centered on gay men. And finally, these models were based almost exclusively on white Eurocentric populations.

Gay, Lesbian, and Bisexual Identity Development Theories

The most frequently cited theory of homosexual identity development is that of Vivienne Cass (1979, 1983–1984). Cass's model is more complex than other models, integrating psychological and social aspects. Cass (1983–1984) also tested her theory empirically. D'Augelli (1994a) has recently introduced a life span model of gay, lesbian, and bisexual identity development that overcomes some of the weaknesses of earlier stage models.

Cass's Model of Homosexual Identity Formation

Cass (1979) presented a model of homosexual identity formation based on her clinical work with gays and lesbians in Australia. She does discuss the applicability of her model to bisexual men and women.

Defining identity formation as "the process by which a person comes first to consider and later to acquire the identity of 'homosexual' as a relevant aspect of self" (p. 219), Cass's model is based on the assumption that acquisition of a homosexual identity is a developmental process resulting from the interaction between the individual and his or her environment. She identified six stages of perception and behavior, moving from minimal awareness and acceptance of a homosexual identity to a final stage in which homosexual identity is integrated with other aspects of the self (Cass, 1979). Prior to the first stage, individuals perceive themselves as heterosexual. As their perceptions change, increased conflict occurs between self-concept, behavior, and the perceptions of others. This conflict results either in movement to a new stage or identity foreclosure that consists of either staying at the current stage or retreating to an earlier one.

Cass (1983–1984) noted that homosexual identity varies "from person to person, from situation to situation, and from period to period" (p. 111). She cautioned that not all individuals progress through all the stages, stressing that individuals make choices and play an active role in the development of their identities. Cass (1979) noted that development is influenced by social factors. She suggested that movement from one stage to the next is based in part on the individual's attempt to resolve inconsistencies between perceptions of self and others. She also indicated that sex-role socialization might result in differences in how males and females negotiate the developmental process and suggested that societal attitudes at different historical periods would influence how the individual approached identity formation.

Cass's stages (1979) have both a cognitive component reflecting how individuals view themselves and an affective component indicating how they feel about their own and others' perceptions. The stages are labeled and defined as follows:

Stage 1: Identity Confusion. This stage begins with individuals' first awareness of homosexual thoughts, feelings, and attractions. It is accompanied by confusion and anxiety. Individuals may react positively to their newly identified feelings by seeking more information, in which case movement to the next stages occurs. Negative reactions, such as rejecting evidence of homosexuality, lead to foreclosure.

In the opening scenario, Angela is a Stage 1 individual who is seeking information by approaching the GLBSA meeting, but her fear keeps her from entering the room. A Stage 1 person who rejects his or her homosexual feelings may sometimes engage in "gay bashing" activities or aggressively pursue heterosexual sexual activity.

Stage 2: Identity Comparison. Movement from Stage 1 to Stage 2 occurs once individuals have accepted the possibility that they might be gay or lesbian. They are now confronted with the issue of how to manage the social alienation that accompanies a homosexual identity and may try to address this problem in several ways: they may seek out other gay and lesbian individuals to learn what it means to be gay or lesbian, they may continue to maintain a public identity that is heterosexual while attempting to "explain" their homosexual behavior, they may attempt to change their homosexual behavior, or they may totally inhibit their own homosexual behavior and denigrate homosexual behavior in general.

Jessica, in the opening example, is in Stage 2. She is seeking out other supportive people with whom to explore her bisexual feelings.

Stage 3: Identity Tolerance. Individuals entering Stage 3 have acknowledged that they are probably gay or lesbian and seek out other gay and lesbian people to reduce their feelings of isolation. The nature of this contact can determine how individuals come to feel about themselves and their newfound identity. Negative interactions may lead persons to identity foreclosure; positive experiences will propel them into the next stage.

Patrick, in the opening example, is in Stage 3. He is seeking out social interactions with other gay and lesbian individuals. If these interactions are positive, perhaps he will become more public about his identity. If they are not positive, he may withdraw from the group and remain "in the closet."

Stage 4: Identity Acceptance. A positive connotation is placed on homosexual identity in this stage. Contacts with other gay and lesbian people are frequent, and friendships develop. The norms and behavior of individuals' social groups influence how they choose to present themselves, particularly in mainstream heterosexual society. Some individuals may choose to continue to "pass" as heterosexual, some may be selectively out to others, and some may be more public about their identity.

The returning members of the GLBSA appear to be at least in Stage 4. They accept their gay and lesbian identities, although they often choose to remain closeted in their home environments. On campus, however, the norms of the group encourage being out. Individuals who are just entering identity acceptance would likely be influenced to adopt a public gay or lesbian identity if they wished to fit in with the rest of the group.

Stage 5: Identity Pride. In this stage, individuals focus on gay issues and activities and minimize contact with heterosexuals. Feelings of both pride in things gay and anger at things "not gay" propel individuals into activism and confrontation with an oppressive society. Unconcerned with the impressions of others, individuals are publicly and vocally out. Individuals at this stage whose disclosures are received negatively generally foreclose.

Marty, the political director in the opening scenario, is in Stage 5. He is angry at the treatment of gays, lesbians, and bisexuals on campus and in society, and he wants to attack heterosexism and homophobia using forceful confrontational strategies. Highly politicized gay, lesbian, and bisexual student organizations often have many Stage 5 members.

Stage 6: Identity Synthesis. In the final stage of development, homosexual and heterosexual worlds are less dichotomized and individuals are judged on the basis of their personal qualities rather than solely on the basis of their sexual identity. Individuals' public and private identities become more congruent as they become comfortable and secure in who they are. Homosexual identity is now seen as just one aspect of self rather than as one's entire identity.

James, the GLBSA chairperson, is in Stage 6. Though he understands the feelings of the Stage 5 members, he also recognizes that there are nonpolitical issues the group must address. He is concerned with his role as leader and role model in assisting newer members.

D'Augelli's Model of Lesbian, Gay, and Bisexual Development

D'Augelli (1994a) argued against the essentialist notion of identity development that holds that identity is formed in sequential stages, achieved by early adulthood, and then endures throughout life. Instead, he views identity as a "social construction," shaped to varying degrees by social circumstances and environment and changeable throughout life.

D'Augelli (1994a) pointed out that the social invisibility of sexual orientation and the social and legal penalties associated with homosexual expression represent two unique and powerful barriers to self-definition as gay, lesbian, or bisexual. To develop a positive gay, lesbian, or bisexual identity, persons must first give up the prescribed heterosexual identity they have assumed since birth. Exiting a heterosexual identity entails giving up the privileges and social approval associated with this identity while taking on an identity that is denigrated by mainstream society. Societal oppression based on *homophobia*, a fear and loathing of non-heterosexual individuals (Pharr, 1988), and *heterosexism*, a belief in the superiority of heterosexuality (Lorde, 1983), contribute in powerful ways to feelings of panic, anxiety, and denial that individuals experience when they first become aware of homosexual thoughts and desires. As a result of these cultural norms, the process of giving up a heterosexual identity and accepting a gay, lesbian, or bisexual identity is slow.

D'Augelli (1994a) presented a life span model of lesbian, gay, and bisexual identity development that takes into account "the complex factors that influence the development of people in context over historical time" (p. 317). In this model, individuals shape their environments as well as react to them.

Three sets of interrelated variables are involved in the formation of identity: personal subjectivities and actions, interactive intimacies, and sociohistorical connections.

Personal subjectivities and actions include individuals' perceptions and feelings about their sexual identities as well as actual sexual behaviors and the meanings attached to them. In the opening example, Patrick perceives his gayness in social terms, while for Marty it is a political experience.

Interactive intimacies include the influences of family, peer group, and intimate partnerships and the meanings attached to experiences with significant others. In the opening example, the students in the GLBSA talk extensively about the influence of their families on their behavior and feelings. They are also influenced by one another in the group setting.

Sociohistorical connections are defined as the social norms, policies, and laws found in various geographical locations and cultures as well as the values existing during particular historical periods. Students today have more opportunities to come together and live in a society that is more open about sexual orientation than students in earlier decades of this century, when an organization such as GLBSA could never have existed.

Assumptions of D'Augelli's Model. Accepting the assumptions of more general life span models (for example, Baltes, 1987), D'Augelli (1994a, 1994b) sees development of sexual orientation as a lifelong developmental process. Multiple changes can occur over time in attitudes, feelings, and behavior.

"Developmental plasticity" is important in D'Augelli's model (1994a). This concept suggests that "human functioning is highly responsive to environmental circumstances and to changes induced by physical and other biological factors" (p. 320). At certain times, sexual identity may be very fluid, whereas at other times, it will be more solidified. Hormonal changes, social circumstances, and peer relationships at different life stages are three factors that may influence developmental plasticity.

A third concept that D'Augelli (1994a, 1994b) borrows from the life span perspective is the idea of individual difference—the idea that no two people travel the same developmental path. D'Augelli suggests that there may be more similarities in sexual self-definition in certain periods of life, such as late adulthood; in certain kinds of families, such as those that do not value difference; in certain communities, such as those that are highly homogeneous; and in certain historical periods, such as the 1950s. The degree of difference tends to increase in late adolescence and adulthood as persons are exposed to more models of behavior and have more choices about how to live their lives.

Finally, D'Augelli (1994a, 1994b) stresses the impact that individuals have on their own development. People not only react to social circumstances but also make choices and take action. Lesbians, gay men, and bisexual people, particularly, shape their own identity because our heterosexist culture provides no socialization for being gay, lesbian, or bisexual. In the GLBSA, the students are defining for themselves what it means to be gay, lesbian, and bisexual personally and on their campus.

The Identity Development Process. D'Augelli (1994a) identified six interactive processes (not stages) involved in lesbian, gay, and bisexual identity development.

1. *Exiting heterosexual identity* requires recognition that one's feelings and attractions are not heterosexual as well as telling others that one is lesbian, gay, or bisexual. Angela is at the beginning of this process, starting to acknowledge her feelings but not yet ready to share them with others.

2. *Developing a personal lesbian/gay/bisexual identity status* involves a "sense of personal socio-affectional stability that effectively summarizes thoughts, feelings, and desires" (D'Augelli, 1994a, p. 325). One must also challenge internalized myths about what it means to be gay, lesbian, or bisexual. Developing a personal identity status must be done in relationship with others who can confirm ideas

about what it means to be nonheterosexual. Jessica is looking for such validation but is afraid she won't find it in the highly politicized environment of the GLBSA.

3. *Developing a lesbian/gay/bisexual social identity* consists of creating a support network of people who know and accept one's sexual orientation. Determining people's true reactions can take time. Reactions may also change over time and with changing circumstances, such as whether an individual is involved in an intimate relationship.

To some extent, all of the students attending the GLBSA come seeking a support network. This need is more salient for students like Patrick who are less ready to be publicly out than others. Gretchen and Rudolfo, too, are struggling with the issue of social support. Though they fit into the group because they identify as lesbian and gay, respectively, they are also marginalized as members of other oppressed groups (Angela is a woman and Rudolfo is Latino). Sexism and racism within the GLBSA have led them to feel less valued than their white male counterparts.

4. *Becoming a lesbian/gay/bisexual offspring* involves disclosing one's identity to parents and redefining one's relationship after such disclosure. D'Augelli (1994a) noted that establishing a positive relationship with one's parents can take time but is possible with education and patience.

This developmental process is particularly troublesome for many college students who depend on their parents for financial as well as emotional support. Our GLBSA members were struggling with the issue of how to be themselves in their home environments without losing their parents' love and acceptance.

5. *Developing a lesbian/gay/bisexual intimacy status* is a more complex process than achieving an intimate heterosexual relationship because of the invisibility of lesbian and gay couples in our society. D'Augelli (1994a) noted, "The lack of cultural scripts directly applicable to lesbian/gay/bisexual people leads to ambiguity and uncertainty, but it also forces the emergence of personal, couple-specific, and community norms, which should be more personally adaptive" (p. 327).

The college years are often a time when individuals establish their first meaningful relationships (Evans & D'Augelli, 1996). In addition to its other reasons for existence, the GLBSA also serves the purpose of being a place to meet potential romantic partners.

6. *Entering a lesbian/gay/bisexual community* involves making varying degrees of commitment to social and political action. Some individuals never take this step; others do so only at great personal risk, such as losing their jobs or housing. Marty, the political director, has made this commitment, while others are not as far along in this aspect of development.

In summarizing his theory, D'Augelli (1994a) stated, "A revision of our operational definition of sexual orientation must occur, allowing for study of the continuities and discontinuities, the flexibilities and cohesiveness, of sexual and affectional feelings across the life span, in diverse contexts, and in relationship to culture and history" (p. 331).

Assessment Techniques

Most of the early theories of homosexual and gay, lesbian, or bisexual identity development were based on interviews that asked individuals to recall experiences that led to the formation of their identities (for example, Coleman, 1981–1982; Warren, 1974). No standardized measures of the theorized developmental sequences were developed to allow for validation of the models.

Cass (1984) did attempt to assess the validity of her model by developing two measures, the Stage Allocation Measure and the Homosexual Identity Questionnaire. The Stage Allocation Measure consists of one-paragraph descriptions of each of the six stages in Cass's model (1979) plus a pre–Stage 1 identity. Individuals are asked to select the paragraph that best describes how they see themselves.

The Homosexual Identity Questionnaire (HIQ) contains 210 multiple-choice and checklist items that describe feelings, thoughts, and actions, responses to which Cass categorized as indicative of specific stages in her model. Cass (1984) examined the degree to which scores on the six scales of the HIQ reflected self-definitions obtained on the Stage Allocation Measure. Though her findings suggest a general correspondence between the two instruments, some stages on the HIQ were more clearly identified than others. Six stages were identifiable in her data. Cass (1984) indicated that she was refining the questionnaire, but no further work has been reported.

In 1983, Brady independently developed a measure of Cass's model (1979) for gay men called the Gay Identity Questionnaire (GIQ). After a series of pilot tests and refinement of the instrument, the GIQ now consists of forty-five true-or-false items (Brady & Busse, 1994), forty-two of which (six items per stage) are used to assign individuals to one of the six stages in Cass's model and three of which are used to verify that individuals have homosexual thoughts, feelings, or behavior.

In a validity study involving 225 gay men (Brady & Busse, 1994), too few Stage 1 and Stage 2 individuals were identified to allow assessment of these stages. Interitem consistency for the other four stages ranged from $r = .44$ to $r = .78$. The authors also found significant relationships between stage and assessments of psychological well-being and adjustment to a homosexual identity, as predicted by Cass's model. Levine (1997) demonstrated the utility of Brady's instrument for measuring the last three stages of lesbian identity development. Preliminary construct validity seems promising for this instrument, but much more research is needed.

No measure exists for D'Augelli's model of gay, lesbian, and bisexual identity development (1994a). He stressed the importance of using multiple measures to assess each of the factors that influence development across the life span (D'Augelli, 1994b). D'Augelli cautioned that studying the individual is not enough to provide an accurate measure of development. He also advocated the use of longitudinal studies to investigate development over time.

Research

Little research has examined identity development as it specifically relates to college students. However, researchers have examined the coming-out process and associated developmental milestones in the lives of gay and lesbian persons. Factors influencing and associated with gay and lesbian identity development have also been investigated. Researchers are beginning to explore cultural and gender differences in the development of sexual identity as well as the process of identifying as bisexual.

Developmental Milestones, Timing, and Patterns

In support of a life span perspective, researchers have documented many different patterns of GLB identity development and provided evidence that such development occurs over a wide age range (D'Augelli, 1994b; Savin-Williams, 1995).

Comprehensive reviews of research examining the coming-out process (Cohen & Savin-Williams, 1996; Savin-Williams, 1995; Troiden, 1989) indicate that most lesbian and gay adults felt "different" from their peers in childhood because they did not adhere to typical gender-related behavioral norms. Increasing awareness of attraction to individuals of the same gender tends to occur around puberty, but youth are reluctant to label themselves as gay, lesbian, or bisexual because they fear social rejection (Cohen & Savin-Williams; Troiden). Many more youth experience same-gender erotic attractions, "experiment" with same-sex behavior, and report being unsure about their sexual orientation than label themselves as gay, lesbian, or bisexual (Savin-Williams).

Recent research reviewed by Savin-Williams (1995) suggests that many youth are coming out at younger ages (midteens) than previously reported, with gay males reporting earlier homosexual activity (early teens) than lesbians (midteens). Most often, youth first come out to a best friend, usually a girl. Most youth do not come out widely until they leave the parental home, and they report that telling their families is the greatest challenge they face with regard to being gay (D'Augelli, 1991). McDonald (1982) reported that an average of eleven years passed for gay men between first awareness of same-gender feelings and developing a positive gay identity. Research indicates that coming out to oneself relatively early but waiting to selectively reveal one's identity to others when the environment is likely to be somewhat supportive (usually after high school) is psychologically and sociologically best (Cohen & Savin-Williams, 1996).

Factors Influencing GLB Identity Development

Individuals who do not adhere to gender norms related to appearance, interests, and behavior are likely to question their sexual orientation earlier than gender-typical youth (Troiden, 1989). And because urban youth have more opportunity to meet GLB individuals and to be exposed to gay culture, they also tend to come out earlier than youth living in rural communities (Savin-Williams, 1995; Sears, 1991; D'Augelli, 1991).

Troiden (1989), Kahn (1991), and Rhoads (1994) reported that supportive family and friends facilitate formation of a positive GLB identity and self-disclosure. In addition, youth raised in more liberal societies (Sweden, Finland) developed more positive self-concepts than youth from more conservative and homophobic societies (Australia, Ireland) (Ross, 1989). Troiden's research review also suggests that positive homosexual experiences facilitate gay, lesbian, or bisexual self-definition and negative experiences inhibit such identification.

Identity Development and Psychological Well-Being

The early stages of identity development are often associated with feelings of isolation, anxiety, and confusion (Buhrke & Stabb, 1995; Troiden, 1989). Rhoads (1994) reported that keeping their identity hidden greatly retarded development of deep relationships for gay and bisexual male students. Alcohol and drug abuse as well as suicide attempts and suicidal ideation have been reported to be higher for GLB youth, although these studies have been challenged on methodological grounds (Buhrke & Stabb).

Self-identification as gay or lesbian has been found to be positively associated with self-esteem and adjustment (Cohen & Savin-Williams, 1996; Rhoads, 1994; Troiden, 1989). Brady and Busse (1994) found a positive relationship between stage of identity development in Cass's model and psychological well-being in gay males. However, as Rhoads discovered, for gay and bisexual men, being open about one's identity also puts one at risk of being harassed and discriminated against.

Levine and Bahr (1989) found that students in the middle stages of Cass's model of homosexual identity formation scored lower on the three scales of the SDTI–2 (Developing Purpose, Developing Autonomy, and Developing Mature Interpersonal Relationships) than students in either the earlier or later stages of homosexual identity development, indicating that sexual identity issues take precedence over other issues during the emotionally laden middle period of development. Being gay, lesbian, or bisexually identified influences many other aspects of development, including career decision making, interpersonal relationships, dating behaviors, family relationships, and religious involvement (Wall & Evans, 1991).

Identity Development and Behavior

Positively gay-identified men participated more in gay culture and were more likely to disclose their orientation to others (McDonald, 1982). Gay and bisexual men who were open about their identity also tended to be more political and confrontational in the struggle for gay rights (Rhoads, 1994).

Cain (1991) identified a number of situational and relational concerns that influenced whether and how a man disclosed his sexual orientation to family, friends, and distant others. These factors were largely independent of stage of gay identity development. Cain cautioned against assuming that self-acceptance necessarily leads to self-disclosure or that lack of disclosure indicates lack of self-acceptance.

Cultural Differences in GLB Identity Development

The extent of cultural influence on gay, lesbian, and bisexual identity development is much greater than has been acknowledged in existing models (Chan, 1995). For instance, definitions of what constitutes homosexual and bisexual behavior differ in Hispanic cultures from definitions in white culture. Latinas and Latinos more often identify as bisexual than as gay or lesbian; the latter concepts are seen in the Latino culture as applying to whites only (Morales, 1989). Strong family and religious influences also inhibit the coming-out process for Hispanics (Wall & Washington, 1991).

In black communities, conformity to traditional gender roles is a significant pressure for men that often precludes their self-identification as gay (Icard, 1985–1986). Family and religious influences also make coming out especially difficult for African Americans (Wall & Washington, 1991). However, Manalansan (1996) reported that the African American community is often tolerant of gay black men as long as they keep their identities quiet.

In Asian cultures, the idea of sexual identity beyond the familial expectation for procreation is nonexistent, and homosexuality can be expressed only if it doesn't interfere with the person's prescribed role within the family (Chan, 1995). In line with this cultural norm, Wooden, Kawasaki, and Mayeda (1983) identified their thirteen gay male Japanese American interviewees as being in Cass's third and fourth stages, Identity Tolerance and Identity Acceptance, but they were not active politically and were reluctant to reveal their gay identity to their parents.

However, Manalansan (1996) cautioned against assuming that all Asian Americans hold similar views of homosexuality and presented evidence that being gay was not a problem for many Filipino American men he interviewed. In general, Asian Americans who openly identify as gay, lesbian, or bisexual are likely to be more acculturated to American values and are more likely to come out to non-Asians than to Asians (Chan, 1989).

In contrast to the cultures just discussed, Native American cultures, which refer to homosexual individuals as "two-spirit persons," accept and value the contributions of these people (Williams, 1996). In Native American cultures, sexuality is valued as a form of recreation, relaxation, and expression of intimacy as well as reproduction. Two-spiritedness is viewed as inborn, and families play an important part in helping youth learn the unique role they will play in their society. Two-spirit people are particularly valued for their economic and caretaking contributions to the family.

Integrating two central identities has been found to be an important issue for gay, lesbian, and bisexual people who are also members of racial or ethnic minority groups (Loiacano, 1989). Wall and Washington (1991) noted that it is difficult for gay, lesbian, or bisexual persons of color to find a balance that allows them to feel good about both of their identities.

Conflict between ethnic identity and lesbian and gay identity has been reported by Cuban women (Espin, 1987), African Americans (Loiacano, 1989), and Japanese Americans (Wooden et al., 1983) who experience racial discrimination in the gay and lesbian community and homophobia and heterosexism in their respective racial or ethnic communities.

Lesbian Identity Development

Studies of lesbian identity development are few. Those that have been conducted demonstrate greater variability in timing and ordering of developmental experiences and self-labeling than for men (Kahn, 1991; Sophie, 1985–1986). These research studies argue for recognition of flexibility in sexual orientation and the importance of viewing sexual orientation in context, ideas proposed by D'Augelli (1994a) and other social constructionists. Golden (1996) found that some lesbians believed that their sexual orientation was beyond their control and others felt that they had consciously chosen to be lesbians. Some of the "elective" lesbians now saw their attraction to women as a central, enduring aspect of their identity, while others saw their sexuality as fluid and changeable. Golden and Weise (1992) both reported that women who previously identified as lesbian sometimes shift to a bisexual identity after becoming attracted to men later in life. Laura S. Brown (1995) stated that "evidence exists that lesbian identity development is a process with not only several different initial stages, but variations in later stages as well" (p. 8).

Because of the strong socialization of young women into heterosexual roles, involvement in a significant lesbian relationship and same-gender physical or sexual contact is generally necessary before lesbians acknowledge their sexual orientation (Buhrke & Stabb, 1995). Unlike gay men, women usually identify as lesbian before they actively enter the gay and lesbian community (Gramick, 1984; Ponse, 1980). Because lesbians often become aware of their identity later in life, they have often resolved other developmental issues and have an easier time handling the coming-out process than men do (Paul, 1984).

Bisexual Identity Development

Initially, developmental theorists viewed bisexuality as a form of foreclosed identity or a transitional stage between heterosexual and gay or lesbian identification (Fox, 1995). More recently, bisexuality has been acknowledged as a distinct sexual orientation. However, lack of acceptance by gays and lesbians as well as heterosexual individuals make bisexual identity development particularly challenging (Paul, 1996).

Using three studies conducted in the 1980s, Weinberg, Williams, and Pryor (1994) identified three stages associated with bisexual identity development: initial confusion, finding and applying the label, and settling into the identity. They also indicated that a fourth stage, continued uncertainty, is characteristic of many bisexual people because of the lack of validation of this sexual orientation.

Most researchers, however, have concluded that bisexual identity development is a complex process that does not lend itself to a linear stage interpretation. Social context, relationships in which individuals are involved, and how open individuals are about being bisexual all influence how they interpret their identity at various times (Fox, 1995). Adult sexual orientation among bisexuals is much less closely tied to preadult sexual feelings than it is for gays and lesbians (Bell, Weinberg, & Hammersmith, 1981). Whereas most bisexual women first identify as heterosexual and later in life discover their homosexual feelings, many men experience the opposite pattern (Bell et al.; Rust, 1993).

Bisexual people self-identify two to three years later than gay or lesbian individuals (Fox, 1995). Most bisexual people in the Bell et al. (1981) study reported experiencing conflict in balancing the many variables related to their sexual attractions and behavior but became more secure in their identities with time. Bisexuality seemed less problematic for women than for men.

Applications

Little attention has been paid to enhancing the experiences of gay, lesbian, and bisexual students on college campuses, and almost none of the existing literature is theory-based. Most of the literature that does exist discusses therapeutic interventions with GLB clients in counseling settings. Only one book (Evans & Wall, 1991) focuses on interventions in other student affairs settings. D'Augelli (1996) presented a comprehensive plan for addressing the needs of GLB youth that includes individual, small group, organizational, and institutional strategies. Buhrke and Stabb (1995) discuss methods for conducting needs assessments with GLB students.

Literature on counseling gay, lesbian, and bisexual students stresses the importance of being familiar with the issues students face at various stages of development, particularly the challenges involved in relating to parents and family, development of a peer group, establishing intimate relationships, exploring career plans, and coming out to self and others (Browning, 1987; Hetherington, 1991; Sophie, 1982). The importance of therapists' recognizing and working through their own feelings about homosexuality and providing a supportive environment for client self-exploration is stressed (Eldridge & Barnett, 1991; Groves & Ventura, 1983). Openly gay, lesbian, and bisexual staff are also crucial in college counseling centers since many GLB students feel safer discussing issues with staff who share a common identity (Evans & D'Augelli, 1996).

D'Augelli (1996) noted that students who are in the earliest stages of development are often the hardest to reach. Angela's fear of entering the GLBSA meeting comes to mind. D'Augelli suggested providing public lectures on human sexuality and sexual orientation and telephone help lines to assist such students. Curricular integration of material about gay, lesbian, and bisexual issues can also normalize homosexuality for these students as well as for heterosexual students.

Gay, lesbian, and bisexual student organizations provide an important vehicle in which students can explore their sexual identity. However, as illustrated in the opening scenario, because students are at different developmental stages, disagreement about activities and agendas is often prevalent in such organizations (Gose, 1996). On larger campuses, a variety of gay, lesbian, and bisexual groups with different purposes would make sense. Options could include discussion or support groups for students who are just beginning to explore their sexuality as well as more politically oriented groups for those who are more secure in their identity (D'Augelli, 1996; Scott, 1991).

"Safe space" in which students can explore their identities and associate with other GLB people as well as allies is an important need. Professionally staffed gay, lesbian, and bisexual student centers have been started on a number of campuses (D'Augelli, 1996; Evans & D'Augelli, 1996). Other institutions have established networks of individuals who identify themselves as available to provide support and information to GLB students.

Bourassa and Shipton (1991) and Evans and D'Augelli (1996) stress the importance of hiring staff who are sensitive to the needs of GLB students and of providing ongoing training and staff development related to issues these students face. Policy and programming should also be reviewed to ensure that it is inclusive and equitable. Bourassa and Shipton (1991) and Schreier (1995) provide examples of affirming residence hall programming.

Critique and Future Directions

In recent years, research and theory about gay, lesbian, and bisexual identity development has increased, both in quantity and in quality. Models are much more sophisticated and inclusive than initial attempts to describe the homosexual experience. The two theories reviewed in depth in this chapter, those of Cass and D'Augelli, explore the interaction of psychological and sociological variables in the formation of identity and take into account individual and cultural differences in the process. D'Augelli, in particular, takes issue with the rigidity of earlier stage models and presents an alternative that allows for fluidity and variation in identity development.

Problems remain, however. First, far too few attempts have been made to validate the theoretical propositions that have been advanced. Measurement of identity and of factors related to identity development is preliminary at best. Cass's model has found acceptance in part because instruments exist to identify her stages of development. More effort needs to be focused on development of assessment instruments and completion of validation research.

Current research suggests that the developmental process is different for gay men, lesbians, and bisexuals. Much more work needs to be done to understand factors involved for each group and how psychological variables and socialization differentially influence men and women. The issues of transgender individuals are only beginning to be discussed (Carter, 1997) and deserve serious consideration. Cultural influences on development also warrant further exploration. Of particular interest is the effect of acculturation on development of gay, lesbian, and bisexual identity for second- and third-generation Americans.

A careful review of this chapter will underscore that most of the research related to gay, lesbian, and bisexual lives has been done by developmental psychologists. Very few studies have examined the experiences of college students or ways in which gay, lesbian, and bisexual development can be enhanced in the college setting. Higher education scholars are encouraged to build on the research that is available and to develop and evaluate appropriate interventions designed to facilitate the development of gay, lesbian, and bisexual students.

CHAPTER SEVEN

SCHLOSSBERG'S TRANSITION THEORY

Marie is a forty-year-old student who has returned to school after a twenty-year absence. She left college at the age of twenty to marry. Recently, Marie and her husband divorced. Her return to college was precipitated by the need to secure full-time employment and her desire to achieve her original career goal of becoming a teacher. Marie is concerned about simultaneously maintaining her roles as a mother and a student. She was awarded primary custody of her children, a daughter, twelve, and a son, sixteen. Financial and time concerns are also in her mind as she anticipates the challenges inherent in continuing her part-time secretarial job and raising her children while adding the responsibilities of being a full-time student. She is finding that the emotional toll of the divorce is still an issue as well.

It's been a rough semester for Eric, a twenty-one-year-old senior. Within the past two months, his father was killed in an automobile accident, and he failed to gain admission to any of the medical schools to which he applied. To become a doctor was a lifelong dream for Eric, a dream that was shared by his family. Eric thought things were starting to look a little brighter when he began going out with Jason, but Jason has since indicated that he doesn't wish to pursue their relationship further.

College students, whether traditionally or nontraditionally aged, face many changes that can have short- and long-term effects on their lives. Nancy Schlossberg's transition theory provides insights into factors related to the transition, the individual, and the environment that are likely to determine the degree of impact a given transition will have at a particular point in time. The nature of the supports available to facilitate coping, as well as strategies that can be used to assist individuals experiencing change, are also addressed.

Schlossberg's is typically categorized as a theory of adult development. Given the integrative nature of the work in relation to preexisting theories of adulthood, this classification is appropriate. However, the theory is also relevant to traditionally aged college students. Educators should avoid creating a false dichotomy between "adult development" and "college student development" when identifying theories that can be helpful in understanding and working with students.

Historical Overview

Schlossberg (1984) identified "operationalizing the notion of variability" as a primary goal of her development theory. She felt the need for a framework that would facilitate an understanding of adults in transition and lead them to the help they needed to cope with the "ordinary and extraordinary process of living" (p. vii).

Fassinger and Schlossberg (1992) described four categories of adult development theory, based on the extent to which each portrays continuity versus variability in the life course, that are useful in understanding Schlossberg's work in the context of adult development theory. The *contextual perspective* highlights the influence of the social environment on individual lives. The *developmental perspective* portrays the sequential nature of change during the adult years and consists of three subtypes: *age-related* (for example, Levinson, 1986); *stage* (for example, Erikson, 1950); and *domain-specific* (for example, Perry, 1968; Helms, 1993a). The *life span perspective* emphasizes the individuality of continuity and change. Finally, the *transitional perspective* focuses on both cultural components (for example, social norms as described by Neugarten & Neugarten, 1987) and individual life events involving change (for example, Schlossberg, 1984).

Schlossberg, Waters, and Goodman (1995) also discussed these different clusters of adult development theory as a preliminary to presenting the revised version of Schlossberg's work. They noted that current theories related to adulthood offer "interesting but essentially untested predictions about the course of adult life" (p. 4).

In their discussion of the contextual perspective, Schlossberg et al. (1995) cited Bertaux's study of French bakers (1982) in which the lives of the bakers and their wives were directly shaped by the structure and nature of the men's work world. They also pointed out that work by Kanter (1977) and Rosenbaum (1979) reinforces a contextual perspective by finding evidence that the environment, specifically the impact of organizations on people, rather than intrapsychic influence, was responsible for the so-called midlife crisis. A broader perspective related to the impact of context can be found in Mayer and Schoepflin's writing on the role of the state in individual lives (1989). Schlossberg et al., citing Mayer and Schoepflin, noted that through legislation, economic regulation, and social programs, the state provides a general framework for the individual life course. For example, the state defines parameters for entering into and exiting from the educational system and marriage.

A final example of the contextual perspective comes from Hagestad and Neugarten (1985). According to Schlossberg et al. (1995), Hagestad and Neugarten maintained that cultures have different age systems that form norms that regulate status and roles across the life span. Schlossberg et al. asserted that an understanding of cultural age norms and age constraints, as well as an understanding of individual, family, and historical time (Hareven, 1992), is important in understanding transitions. They concluded that in focusing on individuals in relation to transitions, it is important also to understand the sociological and ecological factors that affect them.

Schlossberg et al. (1995), in discussing the developmental perspective, referred to subcategories of age and domain-specific theories, but they deviated from Fassinger and Schlossberg's descriptions (1992) by referring to the third subcategory as being based on resolution of specific, crucial issues. They viewed the developmental perspective as consisting of stage theories that can be divided into the three categories identified earlier. They mentioned that overlap exists among these categories.

In considering age-related theories, Schlossberg et al. (1995) pointed out that while Levinson's theory (1986) allows for some variation, the emphasis is on the similarity of experience and the sequential order of the six life stages presented for all adults. These stages are Early Adult Transition, or Leaving the Family (ages sixteen to twenty); Entering the Adult World (ages twenty-one to twenty-nine); Settling Down (ages thirty to thirty-four); Becoming One's Own Person (ages thirty-five to thirty-nine); Midlife Transition (ages forty to forty-two); and Restabilization (ages forty-three to fifty).

Schlossberg et al. (1995) also cited works that question the applicability of Levinson's theory to women (Roberts & Newton, 1987), based on evidence of greater variations for this population, and to people of color (Gooden, 1989; Ross, 1984). Gooden studied professional and working-class African American men and cited limitations in Levinson's theory in regard to race and socioeconomic status. Ross, while finding that the general sequence of stages seemed to apply to Mexican immigrants, also found that important differences existed in areas such as education attained, occupational goals, and the role of family.

Schlossberg et al. (1995) included Erikson's theory (1950) as an example of ones in which development is based on the resolution of specific, crucial issues. Though not linked precisely with chronological age, an invariable sequence of stages characterizes development. As examples of domain-specific development, which is characterized by movement through sequences of stages representing qualitative differences in the way people view the world, Schlossberg et al. included theories such as Fowler's on faith development (1981), Loevinger's on ego development (1993), and Helms's on racial identity development (1993a).

The life span perspective, with its attention to the individuality of continuity and change, includes theorists such as Neugarten (1982), who emphasizes variability; Pearlin (1982), who also endorses individuality and variation; and Whitbourne (1995), who sees adaptation as the result of continuous evaluation of life experiences rather than the product of reactions to specific events. Schlossberg et al. (1995) also stated that the life span perspective offers promise in addressing death and dying. Citing the work of Kastenbaum (1985), they noted that to maintain a sense of continuity and selfhood over the life span, aging individuals must learn to manage transitions related to death and loss.

Finally, Schlossberg's work (1984) serves as a primary example of the transition perspective. Schlossberg et al. (1995) also cited the work of Fiske and Chiriboga (1990) and Lazarus and Folkman (1984) as providing support for this perspective. Fiske and Chiriboga found evidence that transitions, or life events, are more important than age in understanding individual behavior, and Lazarus and Folkman emphasized the importance of cognitive appraisal in both assessing the impact of a transition and coping.

In relation to the traditional body of college student development theory, Schlossberg's work can be viewed as psychosocial and as a counterpoint to age/stage perspectives. Transitions provide opportunities for growth and development, but a positive outcome for the individual cannot be assumed.

Schlossberg's earliest extended treatment of her conceptualizations appeared in *The Counseling Psychologist* in 1981. Describing her model as a vehicle for "analyzing human adaptation to transition" (p. 2), Schlossberg asserted that adaptation was affected by the interaction of three sets of variables: the individual's perception of the transition, characteristics of the pretransition and posttransition environments, and characteristics of the individual experiencing the transition. The perceptions, environmental characteristics, and personal characteristics could each include some components that might be considered assets, liabilities, a mix of the two, or neutral in regard to influence on the ability to cope with a particular transition.

Schlossberg incorporated the feedback received in the critiques that appeared in the same issue and reconceptualized her model as dealing with "response to transition" since adaptation may not always be achieved. In 1984, a book-length treatment, *Counseling Adults in Transition,* appeared. Along with chapters that placed her approach in the broader context of adult development theory in general and provided programmatic examples of applications, this more extensive discussion of the theory was accompanied by a chapter linking transition theory to the contemporary version of Egan's helping model (1982). This connection provided substantial support for theory-to-practice efforts of a counseling or programming nature.

Overwhelmed (1989b) represented a popular press rendition of Schlossberg's work and was particularly significant for introducing several of the modifications that have since been integrated into the latest version of the theory (Schlossberg et al., 1995). In *Overwhelmed,* Schlossberg presented the transition process as having three components: approaching change, taking stock, and taking charge. The "taking stock" section introduced the "4 *S*'s": situation, self, support, and strategies. The 4 *S*'s represent a reframing of Schlossberg's previous discussions (1984) of coping resources as variables characterizing the transition, the individual, and the environment. The "taking charge" section introduced the terminology of "moving in," "moving through," and "moving out" to describe the phases of transitions.

Schlossberg, Waters, and Goodman produced the second edition of *Counseling Adults in Transition* in 1995. Geared to a counselor audience, this edition is divided into three sections: "What Do We Need to Know?" "What Are We Likely to Hear?" and "What Can We Do with What We Know and Hear?" The first part presents the revised version of transition theory in the context of adult development theory in general; the second part considers individual, relationship, and work transitions; and the third part includes an integration of the transition framework with Cormier and Hackney's counseling model (1993)—in lieu of Egan's model (1982)—and related applications.

Transition Theory

Schlossberg et al. (1995) defined a transition as "any event, or non-event, that results in changed relationships, routines, assumptions, and roles" (p. 27). In the scenario at the start of this chapter, Marie's divorce is an example of an event, something that happened that has changed her life. She has, for example, taken on the new role of student and lost the role of wife. She is concerned about her relationship with her children as her routine has been dramatically changed by the absence of the marriage relationship and the addition of academic responsibilities. Eric's not receiving a medical school acceptance represents a nonevent, something desired and anticipated that did not happen. The reality of not going to medical school requires Eric to rethink the life he had envisioned for himself, including the assumption that he would become a physician.

Schlossberg et al. (1995) stress the role of perception in transitions, noting that a transition exists only if it is so defined by the individual experiencing it.

Changes may occur without the individual's attaching much significance to them. Such changes would therefore not be considered transitions.

Type, Context, and Impact

Schlossberg et al. (1995) noted that to understand the meaning that a transition has for a particular individual, one needs to consider the type, context, and impact of the transition. Three nondiscrete types of transitions are described: (1) *anticipated transitions*, ones that occur predictably, such as Eric's expected graduation from college; (2) *unanticipated transitions*, which are not predictable or scheduled, such as Marie's divorce and the sudden death of Eric's father; and (3) *nonevents*, transitions that are expected but do not occur, such as Eric's failure to be admitted to medical school. Nonevents can be classified as *personal*—related to individual aspirations; *ripple*—felt due to a nonevent of someone close; *resultant*—caused by an event; and *delayed*—anticipating an event that might still happen. Schlossberg and Robinson (1996) pointed out that nonevents are associated more with probability than with possibility. Only when an event is likely to occur but fails to occur does it qualify as a nonevent.

The meaning attached to transitions by different individuals is relative, as is the way in which the transition is categorized by type. Again, the role of perception is important.

Context refers to one's relationship to the transition (one's own or someone else's) and to the setting in which the transition takes place (work, personal relationships, and so forth). *Impact* is determined by the degree to which a transition alters one's daily life. Both positive and negative transitions, as perceived by the individual, produce stress. The presence of multiple transitions, as in the case of Eric's father's death, rejection by medical schools, and loss of a prospective partner, can compound the stress. The impact of such stress is dependent on the ratio of the individual's assets and liabilities at the time.

The Transition Process

Whereas a transition may be precipitated by a single event or nonevent, dealing with a transition is a process that extends over time. Essentially, the individual moves from a preoccupation with the transition to an integration of the transition. The time needed to achieve successful integration will vary with the person and the transition. Transitions may lead to growth, but decline is also a possible outcome, and many transitions may be viewed with ambivalence by the individuals experiencing them. Integrating the work of other authors, Schlossberg et al. (1995) endorsed the concept of transitions consisting of a series of phases and term theirs "moving in," "moving though," and "moving out."

The 4 *S*'s

Schlossberg et al. (1995) identified four major sets of factors that influence a person's ability to cope with a transition: situation, self, support, and strategies, known as the "4 *S*'s." The individual's effectiveness in coping with transition depends on his or her resources in these four areas—in other words, his or her assets and liabilities— at that time. The ratio of assets to liabilities helps explain "why different individuals react differently to the same type of transition and why the same person reacts differently at different times" (Schlossberg et al., p. 49).

The authors note that the individual's appraisal of the transition is an important determiner of the coping process. Two types of appraisals are made. Primary appraisal has to do with one's view of the transition itself; is it regarded as positive, negative, or irrelevant? Secondary appraisal is a self-assessment of one's resources for coping with the transition. Both types of appraisal are subject to change as the individual proceeds through the transition process. The 4 *S*'s provide a framework for an individual's appraisal process.

Situation. In examining an individual's situation, the following factors are considered important:

Trigger: What precipitated the transition?

Timing: Is the transition considered "on time" or "off time" in terms of one's social clock? Is it viewed as happening at a "good" or a "bad" time?

Control: What aspect of the transition does the individual perceive as being within his or her control (for example, the transition itself or reaction to it)?

Role change: Is a role change involved, and if so, is it viewed as a gain or a loss?

Duration: Is it seen as permanent, temporary, or uncertain?

Previous experience with a similar transition: How effectively did the person cope then, and what are implications for the current transition?

Concurrent stress: Are other sources of stress present?

Assessment: Who or what is seen as responsible for the transition, and how is the individual's behavior affected by this perception?

Self. Factors considered important in relation to the self are classified into two categories: personal and demographic characteristics and psychological resources. *Personal and demographic characteristics* are described as affecting how an individual views life. This category includes socioeconomic status, gender, age (emphasizing psychological, social, and functional age over chronological) and stage of life, state of health, and ethnicity. *Psychological resources,* aids to coping, include ego development; outlook, in particular optimism and self-efficacy; and commitment and values.

Support. Support is composed of three facets: types, functions, and measurement. "Support" in this model really refers to social support, and four types are cited: intimate relationships, family units, networks of friends, and institutions and communities. Affect, affirmation, aid, and honest feedback serve as the functions of support. Incorporating the work of Kahn and Antonucci (1980), Schlossberg et al. (1995) suggested that social support can be measured by identifying the individual's stable supports, supports that are to some degree role dependent, and supports that are most likely to change.

Strategies. In discussing the fourth S, strategies, Schlossberg et al. (1995) endorsed Pearlin and Schooler's descriptions (1978) of coping responses as essentially falling into three categories: those that modify the situation, those that control the meaning of the problem, and those that aid in managing the stress in the aftermath. In relation to the differing goals reflected by these categories, individuals may also employ four coping modes: information seeking, direct action, inhibition of action, and intrapsychic behavior. Schlossberg et al. emphasized that effective copers demonstrate flexibility and use multiple methods. (Exhibit 7.1 provides a summary of the transition model.)

Aspects of transition theory can be used to assist the two students in our opening scenario. To help Marie and Eric take stock of their assets and liabilities, a helper could guide them through a consideration of each of the 4 S's. Regarding her situation, Marie may consider the timing of the divorce good if she felt control in initiating the process. Eric, by contrast, is unlikely to find the timing good, considering that the loss of his father, the rejection by medical school, and the terminated relationship with Jason were all beyond his control. Relatedly, Eric is likely to view his role changes as losses, while Marie has the potential to find something positive in her new role as student. Duration of the transitions may pose challenges for both Marie and Eric. Marie is juggling the multiple roles of student, single parent, and employee, a demanding combination even on a temporary basis, and Eric is confronted by the permanent loss of a parent along with rejections on the professional and personal levels. He may be able to achieve acceptance to medical school in the future and to find a new partner, but most immediately, these are uncertain prospects. Concurrent stress represents a challenge for both students, given Marie's multiple roles and Eric's multiple losses.

In regard to self, physical health can be assumed to be a desirable asset for both Marie and Eric. In addition, a higher socioeconomic status tends to be an asset. On the downside, gender, age, and ethnicity represent variables that are

EXHIBIT 7.1. SCHLOSSBERG, WATERS, AND GOODMAN'S TRANSITION MODEL.

Transitions

- Events or nonevents resulting in changed relationships, routines, assumptions, or roles
- Meaning for the individual based on
  Type: anticipated, unanticipated, nonevent
  Context: relationship to transition and the setting
  Impact: alterations in daily life

The Transition Process

- Reactions over time
- Moving in, moving through, and moving out

Coping with Transitions

- Influenced by ratio of assets and liabilities in regard to four sets of factors:
  Situation: trigger, timing, control, role change, duration, previous experience, concurrent stress, assessment
  Self: personal and demographic characteristics (socioeconomic status, gender, age, stage of life, health, ethnicity), psychological resources (ego development, outlook, commitment, values)
  Support: types (intimate, family, friends, institutional), functions (affect, affirmation, aid, honest feedback), measurement (role dependent, stable and changing supports)
  Strategies: categories (modify situation, control meaning, manage stress in aftermath), coping modes (information seeking, direct action, inhibition of action, intrapsychic behavior)

Source: Adapted from Schlossberg, Waters, and Goodman, 1995.

open to interpretation. Do Marie and Eric view these as assets, liabilities, or mixed blessings for themselves, and do these aspects have an impact on the options open to them to aid in coping? In considering psychological resources, more advanced levels of ego development imply a maturity that would be an asset in coping. Similarly, a positive outlook, seeing the glass as half full rather than half empty, and a belief in one's own ability to have an impact (self-efficacy) are considered assets. Commitments, which are subject to change, and values and beliefs can also play a role. For example, if Marie saw herself as very committed to her marriage and if she holds religious beliefs that are critical of divorce, her difficulty in dealing with her transition is heightened. Similarly, Eric presents becoming a doctor as a lifelong dream. Especially if this value was accompanied by a significant commitment to academic achievement, the denial of medical school admission represents a severe blow.

Examining social supports for Marie and Eric is the next step. The amount of support available to Marie may depend to some degree on how the loss of the marriage relationship affects other already established relationships. For example, will friends whom she and her ex-husband have in common maintain their relationships with her? At the same time, her resumption of her student status opens the door to a new form of institutional support—from the college itself. Assuming that Eric will be relocating, he will soon lose the supports provided by his college, but he has access to services while he is still enrolled. Similarly, his network of friends is likely to be disrupted by his impending graduation. If Eric returns home, family has the potential to be a source of support. However, more would need to be known about family reactions to the father's death, Eric's medical school situation, and other life circumstances for the likelihood of support to be accurately assessed. Marie's remaining in the same location is likely to afford her access to preexisting and new supports, while Eric's loss of relationships and the pervasive impact of graduation and relocation pose additional challenges in his transition.

Both Marie and Eric may benefit from using strategies that help them manage current stress and control the meaning of the situation. Both could fall into self-defeating thinking ("poor me"). Marie could become discouraged by the weight of her multiple responsibilities, and Eric could become despondent by concluding that all is lost. Marie may benefit from reinforcing the message that her situation is temporary, and Eric from believing that he will find a career alternative or try for medical school again and that future relationships are possible. Eric may benefit from seeking career information and from inhibiting the urge to give up. Marie may benefit from learning more about services available to her and taking action to enhance her time management and stress management skills.

The Cormier and Hackney Model

In integrating the transition model with the Cormier and Hackney (1993) counseling model, Schlossberg et al. (1995) provided a useful vehicle for identifying effective actions that can be taken to support individuals in transition. The 4 *S*'s of situation, self, supports, and strategies supply a structure for considering what helpers can do in each stage of the Cormier and Hackney model to assist individuals in transition. These five stages are (1) relationship building, (2) assessment, (3) goal setting, (4) interventions, and (5) termination and follow-up.

Schlossberg et al. (1995) suggested the following integration of the two models. In relationship building, helpers use basic listening skills. In assessment, the second stage, areas to assess include the individual's environment (situation), internal resources (self), external resources (support), and current coping skills (strategies). In Stage 3, goal setting, individuals may find it helpful to set goals related to each of the 4 *S*'s. Schlossberg et al. provided the examples of modifying the environment (situation), regaining a sense of balance or equilibrium (self), increasing support (support), and developing an action plan (strategies). For the fourth stage, interventions, Schlossberg et al. suggested the following possible helper behaviors: reframing, or changing the individual's interpretation of the meaning of the situation; conducting an assessment of the individual's assets (self); referral to a support group (support); and generating problem-solving strategies (strategies). Finally, in regard to termination and follow-up, the helper can aid the individual in reviewing what has happened so far and planning next steps.

Some of the language in the Cormier and Hackney (1993) model may sound more clinical than that used in the Egan (1982) model in the first edition. In relation to sharing with paraprofessionals and general student audiences for their use, though, this resource could be adapted by substituting language that is less clinical, as was done in the preceding paragraph, and using examples relevant to students.

The updated Egan model (1994) remains a helpful tool to be used in conjunction with the transition model. As Schlossberg (1984) discussed, the three stages of Egan's model essentially involve exploration, understanding, and coping. Therefore helpers can assist individuals in transition explore what is happening to them by providing an unbiased relationship as well as listening and responding; understand what is happening by offering a more objective perspective; and cope by influencing appropriate action or inaction.

To summarize, a transition is an event or a nonevent that results in change. Dealing with such change is a process that evolves over time and that includes phases such as moving in, moving through, and moving out. Perception plays a crucial role in how the transition itself is viewed and how the individual goes about coping. The individual's ratio of assets and liabilities in terms of situation, self, supports, and strategies determines his or her coping effectiveness. The process of providing assistance to individuals in transition can be guided by counseling models such as those proposed by Cormier and Hackney (1993) or Egan (1994).

Assessment Techniques

Informal and formal assessment techniques may be used in relation to this theory. Although psychometrically sophisticated instruments are not available—a fact that may pose some limitations in relation to traditional research—methods of self-assessment to support individual coping can be readily accessed.

The *Transition Coping Questionnaire* (1993) and its companion *Transition Coping Guide* (1993) are available. In the explanatory material, Schlossberg is mentioned as a cocreator of the instrument, though authors are not cited formally. In relation to the transition of concern at the moment, users of the instrument are asked to respond to Likert scale items for each of the 4 *S*'s. The "situation" section solicits information about how the user views the transition; the "self" section focuses on "who you are" and includes, along with the typical Likert items, some questions about life priorities and the impact of the transition on them; "supports" assesses help that is perceived to be available from others; and "strategies" solicits self-ratings on items related to coping skills. Scores are produced based on the Likert ratings (1–5), and the *Coping Guide* converts these scores to classifications of "high," "medium," or "low" in relation to the user's coping resources for each of the 4 *S*'s. No psychometric information is given about how these categories were derived. The remainder of the *Guide* offers suggestions related to coping.

In the "Taking Stock" section of *Overwhelmed*, Schlossberg (1989b) offered a series of yes-or-no questions to aid in assessing each of the 4 *S*'s. Informal questions geared to assessing each of the 4 *S*'s are also included in Schlossberg et al.'s discussions of these concepts (1995).

Student affairs professionals interested in providing a structure for self-assessment for individuals experiencing transitions could easily create a worksheet by taking each of the 4 *S*'s and listing under each important aspects for the individual's reflection and discussion. For example, under "situation," factors such as trigger and timing could be included; under "self," personal and demographic characteristics and psychological resources could be listed; under "support," the four types could be given; and under "strategies," the three categories and examples of each could be mentioned, along with an "other" category to encourage the identification of any additional resources. If desired, a plus-and-minus system or the "assets" and "liabilities" labels could be used to help individuals identify supports and challenges or obstacles.

Research

Research in support of early theory development included studies such as Schlossberg and Leibowitz's study (1980) of men who lost their jobs at NASA and the resulting impact of a support program and Charner and Schlossberg's study (1986) of clerical workers, which emphasized an exploration of coping strategies. Schlossberg and Leibowitz conducted interviews with NASA employees one week after they had lost their jobs due to a reduction in force. Follow-up interviews were conducted six months later. Participants were asked about their perceptions of the transition, available supports, and their coping styles. The importance of institutional supports, in this case counseling workshops and placement assistance, was endorsed. These interviews also reinforced that the transition process often has both positive and negative components for the same individual.

Charner and Schlossberg (1986) conducted interviews with clerical workers on a university campus. Women made up 75 percent of the sample, and 98 percent of the sample was white. Ages ranged from twenty-seven to over sixty-five. Participants were asked to identify and discuss a transition in their lives and how they coped. A structured transition instrument was used, and content areas, reflecting the theory, included identifying and examining the transition; exploring the impact of the transition, personal resources and options, support systems, and coping strategies; assessing the transition and the transition process; and identifying personal characteristics. Of the sample, 62 percent reported that their most recent transitions were planned, and family represented the context for the transition for half of the participants. Nearly 75 percent of the respondents, asked to describe their outlook on transitions, characterized themselves as "fighters." Most frequently used strategies for coping included reflecting on the situation (90 percent), relaxing (90 percent), embracing the change (80 percent), and yelling, crying, or laughing (72 percent). Charner and Schlossberg concluded that one implication for practitioners would be the importance of helping individuals learn new and multiple coping strategies. Another implication cited was the usefulness of the transition model in helping practitioners and their clients understand how to create a ratio of liabilities and assets that will aid in successful resolution of the transition process.

Schlossberg (1981) also conducted a pilot study of transitions related to geographical mobility. Interviews were conducted with couples who had recently relocated. The most important factors related to coping were sex and sex-role identification, perceived duration of the move, interpersonal supports, and degree of control. The results also reinforced the concept that transitions often involve both positive and negative aspects for the same person.

In her first published presentation of the model, Schlossberg (1981) also discussed the research of Lyons (1980) and Merikangas (1980). Both of these projects involved the design, implementation, and evaluation of programs to aid coping with transitions in the workplace. Lyons developed a workshop to facilitate effective entry into the first job, and Merikangas created a planning seminar for employees nearing retirement. Both projects were implemented at NASA's Goddard Space Flight Center.

More recently, Swain (1991) conducted a study of athletes withdrawing from sports and found support for aspects of the transition model, including the "process over time" concept, the similarity and variability of individuals' transitions, and the significance of the different coping resources. Swain suggested adding education, skills, activities, and interests to the list of coping resources; he also recommended the addition of chance encounters as an environmental variable. In addition, he found that much attention was needed at the beginning of the transition experience to aid in coping.

In relation to higher education, Schlossberg, Lynch, and Chickering (1989) provided support for their conceptual framework via interview information obtained from adult learners. Schlossberg, Waters, and Goodman (1995) pointed out that these interviews also served as another confirmation that transitions often include both positive and negative aspects for the same person. Given the limited amount of research to date, studies, perhaps of a qualitative nature, that examine the transition experiences of college students have the potential to be very informative.

Applications

Schlossberg et al. (1989) provided a detailed approach to how transition theory can be used to support the higher education experiences of adult learners. Using the transition model as a framework for service provision, these authors emphasized the variety of environmental responses needed to accommodate the heterogeneity of adult learners and the different points at which they may find themselves in the transition process. A common theme is transitions as triggers for college attendance. Payoffs for the institution (for example, retention, involvement, and alumni support) also receive attention.

Champagne and Petitpas (1989) provided another example of how Schlossberg's theory can be used as a design tool for developmental interventions for adult learners. Recognizing the need for adult learners to understand and deal with numerous transitions and receive support in the process, Champagne and Petitpas recommended that student affairs staff perform eight functions in relation to adult learners: provide specialized services (adapted for adult needs), education (information and skills related to adult development, transitions, and the college experience), advocacy, a clearinghouse (campus services and resources), referrals (institutional and community), program planning (including support groups), networking and mentoring, and counseling (including outreach and peer support).

Although applications of the theory in support of adult learners are certainly valuable, it is important not to pigeonhole the theory as one that is meaningful *solely* in designing interventions for adults. As in *Improving Higher Education Environments for Adults* (Schlossberg et al., 1989), Chickering and Schlossberg, in *How to Get the Most Out of College* (1995) conceptualized the process of college attendance as involving phases of moving in, moving through, and moving out, with certain transitions and accompanying supports being characteristic of each period. This publication, which is packed with self-assessment exercises, shows the applicability of transition theory to students of all ages.

Pearson and Petitpas's application (1990) of Schlossberg's theory as a support for designing developmental interventions for the anticipated and unanticipated transitions of athletes (for example, not making the team, injury) represents an approach that could be readily adapted to collegiate athletes and provides an example of use of the theory to address the needs of a specific population.

Applications of Schlossberg's transition theory can take many forms. Schlossberg et al. (1995) discussed the relevance of the model for program and workshop development, consulting, advocacy, and self-help groups. The approach taken by Schlossberg (1989b) in presenting the theory in *Overwhelmed* also renders it useful as a self-help vehicle. For example, this book served as a support to a student convalescing in a hospital after an automobile accident.

Schlossberg's theory can be easily taught to organization officers, resident assistants, and other student leaders to support their efforts in assisting their peers as well as to general student audiences to aid them in understanding and responding to their own experiences. For example, for resident assistants (RAs), the model can serve as a general guide for designing programming to support dealing with environmental changes, such as a series of programs planned on buying cooking equipment, preparing low-budget meals, and other relevant matters for residents of a hall that had recently been renovated to form suites with kitchens. The links to helping models (Cormier & Hackney, 1993; Egan, 1994) can also provide RAs with a way to think about and approach individuals who may have experienced a potentially traumatic transition, such as the loss of a loved one in an automobile accident, as in the example involving Eric.

Orientation programs for entering students can use the transition model, especially the "moving in" component, as a design tool. Similarly, transition programs for seniors approaching graduation can be designed, paying particular attention to the challenges inherent in "moving out" (for example, Forney & Gingrich, 1983).

Given the constancy of change in the lives of college students, the potential for use of this model for programmatic and counseling purposes far exceeds the examples that have appeared in the literature, which have been directed primarily toward adults.

Critique and Future Directions

Schlossberg (1981, 1984) and Schlossberg et al. (1995) have evolved an excellent model to facilitate understanding and action. The work reflects their ability to identify, extract, and integrate core ideas. The framework is comprehensive in scope, highly integrative of other theoretical contributions, and conceptually and operationally sound. The authors have taken a vast array of writings and gleaned the most important concepts from them, added their insights, and created a dynamic model that can provide a solid foundation for practice that is responsive to both commonalities and idiosyncrasies. Schlossberg's openness to criticism and her willingness to revise and extend her theory since its inception have resulted in a very practical resource for assisting college students in dealing with change.

Because the structure of the theory places so much emphasis on consideration of the individual's perspective and the specifics of his or her own situation, Schlossberg has provided a tool that readily allows for the integration of individual and cultural differences.

For the future, an expansion of the research base related to Schlossberg's theory would be helpful. Though the complexity of the model (for example, the number of variables included) may pose some challenges in regard to design, both quantitative and qualitative studies are needed. In particular, more research related to diverse student populations, such as students of color, students with disabilities, lesbian, gay, and bisexual students, and international students, has the potential to increase our understanding of and hence our ability to assist with various transitions that these students experience while moving into, through, and out of our higher education settings.

PART THREE

COGNITIVE-STRUCTURAL THEORIES

Kyle and Kathy, twenty-two-year-old student leaders who are about to graduate, are discussing their future plans and reminiscing about the past four years:

Kathy: Do you remember when we met in the orientation course our first year? I was sure scared that I would never make it in college. I registered for that course because I thought the teacher would tell me what to do to succeed in college.

Kyle: That first year I spent a lot of time talking to the seniors on my floor about what activities I should get involved in and what courses and instructors to take. I tried to follow their advice, but it was really confusing when they all gave me different suggestions. Then I began to think that no one knew anything.

Kathy: I know what you mean. I went through a period during my sophomore year where no one could tell me anything. I figured that my ideas were just as good as everyone else's. I was on hall government at the time and was always fighting with our adviser because she wanted us to justify our budget requests and I had no idea what she meant.

Kyle: I started to understand the importance of supporting my position when I was on the judicial board my junior year. We would hear so many cases where the situation and circumstances made a difference in our decision. Listening to all the different perspectives of the other members of the board really made me think about where I stood and why I felt that way.

Kathy: Now that I am interviewing for positions with different companies, I really see how important it is to consider all the different aspects of a decision and to weigh my options. Each job situation has its pros and cons, and I can certainly see that there is no perfect situation. I have to do what seems best for me at this point in my life.

Kyle: Yes, and I know that the choices I am making now are only tentative. I have decided to attend grad school in California to study microbiology, but once I finish my degree, I'll have a whole new set of choices to make. Life is sure complex, isn't it?

Cognitive-structural theories help explain the changes in Kyle and Kathy's thinking. Rooted in the work of Piaget (1952), cognitive-structural theories examine the process of intellectual development during the college years. These theories focus on *how* people think, reason, and make meaning of their experiences.

The mind is thought to have structures, called *schemata* by Piaget (1952), *positions* by Perry (1968), and *stages* by others. These structures are sets of assumptions by which persons adapt to and organize their environments. They act as filters or lenses for determining how people perceive and evaluate experiences and events. Structures change, expand, and become more complex as the person develops. Kyle and Kathy, as first-year students, assumed that there was one right way to get through college and looked to others for answers. As seniors, they realize that decision making is a complex process in which individual circumstances and context play important roles. They are also aware that they are responsible for their own decisions. These changes reflect their movement from simple to complex cognitive structures.

Cognitive-structural stages are viewed as arising one at a time and always in the same order, regardless of cultural conditions. The age at which each stage occurs and the rate of speed with which the person passes through it are variable, however. Each stage derives from the previous one and incorporates aspects of it; thus each successive stage is qualitatively different and more complex than the stages before it (Wadsworth, 1979).

Cognitive-structural theorists posit that change takes place as a result of assimilation and accommodation. Assimilation is the process of integrating new information into existing structures, rounding them out and contributing to their expansion (a quantitative change). Accommodation is the process of modifying existing structures or creating new structures to incorporate stimuli that will not fit into existing structures (a qualitative change) (Wadsworth, 1979). Equilibrium, a balance between assimilation and accommodation, is necessary if the person is to interact efficiently with the environment. Disequilibrium, or cognitive conflict, occurs when expectations are not confirmed by experience. When conflict is experienced, the individual first tries to assimilate the new information into the existing structure; if assimilation is not possible, accommodation occurs to regain equilibrium (Wadsworth). Often a transition period occurs as the person struggles to accommodate but is not quite able to create a new thinking structure. During such a transition, a person's thinking may seem inconsistent.

In his effort to succeed the first year, Kyle initially tried to follow the advice given to him by the seniors on his floor, since following the advice of more experienced individuals had always worked for him before (assimilation). When this strategy didn't work because the suggestions he received conflicted, he changed his way of interpreting the situation by deciding that nobody really had the right answer and that his ideas were as good as anyone else's (accommodation). During the transition period between assimilation and accommodation, Kyle's thinking process likely vacillated. One day he might have "known" that no one had the answer, yet the next day he would be seeking out yet another senior for advice.

Piaget (1952) stressed the importance of neurological maturation in cognitive development but also noted the significant role played by the environment in providing experiences to which the individual must react. Social interaction with peers, parents, and other adults is especially influential in cognitive development, as illustrated by the experience of Kathy and Kyle with their advisers, teachers, and peers. Wadsworth (1979) stated, "Equilibration (attaining equilibrium) is seen as an internal self-regulation system that operates to reconcile the roles of maturation, experience, and social interaction" (p. 35).

Cognitive-structural theories can help student affairs professionals understand how students view situations they are experiencing and provide guidance about how to communicate effectively with students. Knowing that students interpret their experiences differently, depending on their level of intellectual development, can help student affairs professionals understand the variations in feedback they receive from students about activities, classes, and other experiences and will assist them in advising students about available options. A student at a lower level of development, for example, will feel more comfortable and may do better in a more highly structured setting (Widick, Knefelkamp, & Parker, 1975).

Knowledge of students' reasoning processes will also help student affairs professionals understand students' decision making with regard to their own lives as well as their interactions with others. Students such as Kyle and Kathy who have progressed to higher levels of cognitive development by their senior year are more complex thinkers who will generally make informed decisions. Students at lower levels of development, however, often look to others for advice and may need more support. This difference may explain, for example, why a first-year student calls home every weekend and decides to major in business because that is what her father wants her to do.

Cognitive-structural theories can be very helpful in the design of workshops and classes (Rodgers & Widick, 1980; Widick, et al., 1975). For instance, a workshop for first-year students on how to choose a major would probably enroll students at lower levels of development who need a great deal of structure and a personalized atmosphere to feel comfortable. A senior-level seminar, by contrast, could be more loosely structured and rely on input from more cognitively advanced students.

The initial cognitive-structural theories of Piaget (1952) and Perry (1968) were developed mainly on samples of white males. Since cognitive-structural theories focus on how people think about the experiences and issues in their lives, rather than the content of those experiences and issues, theorists and researchers have hypothesized that cultural conditions have less influence on cognitive-structural development than they have on psychosocial development. Gender variation in cognitive development has been studied (Baxter Magolda, 1992; Belenky, Clinchy, Goldberger, & Tarule, 1986; Gilligan, 1982/1993; King & Kitchener, 1994), and researchers have explored moral development in other countries and cultures (Rest, 1986b); however, little work has tested the assumption that cognitive-structural theory is universally applicable to all racial and cultural groups.

Part Three begins with an examination of the work of William Perry (1968), the first cognitive-structural theorist to focus on the intellectual development of college students. In the following chapter, the work of several theorists who have built on Perry's theory is discussed. First we review the contributions of Belenky and her colleagues (1986), who investigated women's development. Then we examine the theory of Baxter Magolda (1992), which incorporates gender-related differences in intellectual development. Finally, King and Kitchener's reflective judgment model (1994) is discussed. The last two chapters in this part review moral development theories that focus on how individuals make decisions that affect themselves and others in significant ways. First we look at the pioneering work of Kohlberg (1984) and then examine Gilligan's approach (1982/1993), which focuses on the moral development of women.

CHAPTER EIGHT

PERRY'S THEORY OF INTELLECTUAL AND ETHICAL DEVELOPMENT

Lee, a junior, is the president of the university union's student programming board, having served as a member during his freshman and sophomore years. Lately, Lee has been experiencing some frustration. His board is currently composed primarily of freshmen and sophomores. Lee values the group's energy, but he has difficulty dealing with some of their attitudes and behaviors. For example, while they are eager to do whatever work needs to be done, they have difficulty making decisions about the types of programs to offer, appropriate marketing strategies, and other important matters. Some of the board members have very strong opinions about what the group should do, and often these opinions conflict.

A recent meeting became deadlocked when one faction took the stance that programming funds should not be given to the university's Black Student Association for special orientation programming designed for students of color and proposed as a supplement to the university's standard orientation activities. The programming board members who opposed this allocation indicated that they believed that since the university's orientation activities were for *all* students, it would be wrong to fund additional activities designed for only *some* students. One of these board members tried to call for a vote on the issue before alternative points of view could be presented. When Lee suggested that it seemed only fair to listen to other opinions on the subject, he was cut off by one of the more vocal members of the opposing group. The student asserted that "what's right is right and what's wrong is wrong, so why waste time talking about it?"

Some of the other board members wanted to consult with their adviser, Miriam, who was unable to attend the meeting. Lee found this attitude frustrating as well. He saw these students as always wanting Miriam to tell them what to do—what programs to offer, how to advertise them, every little detail. "Can't they ever think for themselves?" Lee wondered. Lee was also willing to admit to himself that he felt a bit offended that these students consistently turned to Miriam and not to him for advice. After all, he thought, his opinions were just as valid as hers.

As an entering student, Audrey feels intimidated by the academic experience. She loves literature and loves to read, but her experience so far with her Introduction to Literature class has been stressful. She enjoys the class when she can sit and listen to the professor lecture on the lives of famous authors and facts related to the writing of the works they are reading. But she has difficulty with the expectation that students speak regularly in class discussions and offer their own interpretations of the literature. What could she possibly have to offer? The professor is the expert. She wants to hear what he thinks. Besides, he knows which interpretation is correct, and she would feel dumb if she gave an incorrect interpretation. Consequently, she often sits in silence, staring down at her notebook, hoping the professor won't call on her to speak.

Jordan is in the same class. He's a sophomore who is taking the course to fulfill a distribution requirement. He's not a big fan of literature, but he loves the discussion component of the class, and he is very willing to offer his own views. After he heard the professor's explanation of the graded assignments—discussion contributions, papers on interpreting excerpts from the literature, and so forth—he thought this class would be an easy A. All he would have to do is present his own opinion. Having now received two papers back from the professor, Jordan is angry. Both papers received grades of C. The professor indicated that while Jordan made creative interpretations, he failed to offer evidence from the literature to support his perspective. Jordan thinks the professor is unfair. How can he give a low grade? It's all just opinions anyway.

Jerome, another student in the class, is a senior. He is also taking the course for a distribution requirement. He knows that most students completed their distribution requirements by the end of their sophomore year, but he is actually glad he waited. Initially, he thought an intro course might seem kind of Mickey Mouse to him, as a senior. Instead, Jerome has found that he really connects with the professor's approach to the course. He is enjoying the literature, but what really excites him is the opportunity to hone his analytical skills. Jerome is planning to attend law school, and he finds that presenting and backing up his interpretations both verbally, in class, and in writing, in his papers, is good practice for the analytical and persuasive skills he believes he will need to be a successful attorney. Though he thinks that some students in the class, such as Jordan, just talk to hear themselves talk and wouldn't know a well-developed and well-presented interpretation if they ran head on into one, he appreciates the feedback he receives from the professor. This feedback is helping him understand his strengths in presenting his views as well as his areas for improvement in presenting an effective argument.

Clearly, how students make meaning can have a profound impact on both themselves and others, both inside the classroom and beyond it. William Perry's theory of intellectual and ethical development (1968) can greatly aid our understanding of meaning-making processes. It can also serve as a resource for appropriate ways of responding to student differences in meaning making, including possible approaches to assisting students with further growth in the area of cognitive complexity.

Historical Overview

During the 1950s and early 1960s, while serving as the director of Harvard's Bureau of Study Counsel, William G. Perry Jr., along with his associates, engaged in research examining how students interpret and make meaning of the teaching and learning process. From this research, Perry and his colleagues formulated what he has described as "the typical course of development of students' patterns of thought" (1981, p. 77) and "unfolding views of the world" (1968, p. ix). Perry holds academic degrees in the humanities and counts a translation of the *Iliad* among his published works. The influence of Perry's background in literature can be seen in his writing on cognitive development as he described his scheme as "a 'Pilgrim's Progress' of ways of knowing" (1981, p. 77).

Perry (1968) acknowledged indebtedness to Piaget and other developmental psychologists, such as Kohlberg. Because little had been done that addressed the adolescent-to-adulthood transition, Perry made particular mention of the influence of the work of Nevitt Sanford (1962, 1966) and Roy Heath (1964) in the higher education setting.

Although students from both Harvard and Radcliffe formed the sample for Perry's longitudinal study, a series of year-end interviews conducted with students over the course of their four years at the institution, Perry (1968) noted that with few exceptions, only the interviews with Harvard men were used in validating the theory and in illustrating it.

From Perry's own comments can be derived the image of a somewhat reluctant theorist. Early on in his book, he stated, "Our initial intent was purely descriptive, and not even systematically so" (1968, p. 6).

Perry has published two major discussions of his theory. The first, *Forms of Intellectual and Ethical Development in the College Years: A Scheme* (1968), is the book-length treatment of the theory and contains detailed explanations and examples of the concepts that comprise the theory, along with procedural information about the study itself. The second, a chapter in *The Modern American College* (1981), presents a more condensed, though equally richly textured, treatment of the theory. Both of these publications require that the reader be willing to engage actively with the material and be challenged by some complex concepts and some sophisticated writing.

Perry's Theory

Perry (1968) referred to "forms" of intellectual and ethical development. "Forms" are the structures that shape how people view their experiences. He described his scheme as beginning with simplistic forms in which the individual interprets the world in "unqualified polar terms of absolute right-wrong, good-bad" (p. 3). The scheme concludes with complex forms through which the individual seeks to affirm personal commitments "in a world of contingent knowledge and relative values" (p. 3).

The continuum of development that provides the foundation for Perry's theory consists of nine "positions." Perry (1968) chose the term *position* over *stage* for several reasons. First, no assumption about duration is made. Second, because individuals may demonstrate some range in structures manifested at a given point in time, *position* can represent "the locus of a central tendency or dominance among these structures" (p. 48). Finally, Perry considers *position* to be consistent with the image of a point of view from which one looks at the world.

Perry (1981) has labeled his positions as follows:

1.   Basic Duality
2.   Multiplicity Prelegitimate
3.   Multiplicity Legitimate but Subordinate
4a.   Multiplicity Coordinate
4b.   Relativism Subordinate
5.   Relativism
6.   Commitment Foreseen
7–9. Evolving Commitments

It is important to note that Perry regards the positions themselves as static, with development occurring not in the positions but during the transitions between them. He conjectured, "Perhaps development is all transition and 'stages' only resting points along the way" (1981, p. 78).

In relation to application of Perry's theory to student affairs practice and the classroom, the degree of precision and some of the more subtle differences that characterize the nine positions can be viewed as representing more detail than may be needed to render Perry's scheme a usable tool for understanding and interacting with students. A simplified version of the theory portraying the basic differences in the primary modes of meaning making, along with an explanation of the deflections that can impede cognitive growth, seems sufficient to facilitate active use of Perry's ideas.

From Perry's labeling of his positions, certain key words, representing fundamental differences in the process of meaning making, can be noted: *duality, multiplicity,* and *relativism. Commitment* is another key word, which also signifies an important concept within the scheme.

The following descriptions of basic concepts in the Perry scheme are based on discussions by Perry himself (1968, 1981) as well as those by King (1978) and Knefelkamp and Cornfeld (1979).

Dualism represents a mode of meaning making that tends to view the world dichotomously: good–bad, right–wrong, black–white. Learning is essentially information exchange because knowledge is seen as quantitative (facts) and authorities (including people and books) are seen as having and dispensing the right answers. In the scenarios at the start of this chapter, Audrey has this view of her instructor as the expert. One interpretation of literature is correct, and the professor knows that correct answer and should share it with her.

The essence of dualism can be seen in the tongue-in-cheek response of a student affairs graduate student who, when asked by an instructor to explain dualism, retorted, "You're the teacher. You tell us." Dualistic meaning makers believe that right answers exist for everything. The transition to multiplicity begins when cognitive dissonance occurs. For example, when experts disagree or when good teachers or authority figures don't have all the answers or express uncertainty, disequilibrium is introduced into the meaning-making process for dualistic thinkers.

Multiplicity is sometimes misunderstood and described as an "anything goes" mode of making meaning. In reality, Perry characterizes multiplicity as honoring diverse views when the right answers are not yet known. All opinions are equally valid, from a multiplistic perspective, in such instances. As individuals move through multiplicity, they tend to shift their conception of the role of the student from that of one who learns how to learn and works hard to one who learns to think more independently. During this progression, peers become more legitimate sources of knowledge and individuals are likely to improve their ability to think analytically.

In the opening scenarios, Lee demonstrates some examples of multiplistic thinking when he pronounces his opinion as being as valid as that of Miriam, the adviser. He is frustrated by the board members who look to Miriam for answers, and his description of these students portrays them as dualistic thinkers, by contrast. If these students are dualistic in their thought processes, Lee, as a peer, is unlikely to be seen as an expert. To them, his opinions will not be considered as valid as Miriam's. He would need to establish himself as an authority figure in their eyes if he is to receive the same regard from them, which apparently has not yet happened.

For multiplistic thinkers, the transition to *relativism* is initiated by a recognition of the need to support opinions. All opinions no longer appear to be equally valid. Relativistic thinkers acknowledge that some opinions can be of little value, yet reasonable people can also legitimately disagree on some matters. Knowledge is now viewed more qualitatively; it is contextually defined, based on evidence and supporting arguments.

In the opening scenario, Jerome manifests relativistic thinking. He values developing well-founded arguments, and he also welcomes critical feedback that points out flaws in his analysis. By contrast, Jordan has difficulty distinguishing between any opinion and a well-developed argument. His thinking appears to be multiplistic.

The oppositional students on the programming board could appear to be dualistic thinkers. They don't want to hear differing opinions, and they express some dichotomous views—for example, what's right is right and what's wrong is wrong. It seems important, however, to come to such a conclusion only tentatively. Because their views could be seen as less inclusive or politically incorrect, their mode of meaning making might be assumed to be less complex. As Knefelkamp, Widick, and Stroad (1976) pointed out, however, the content of one's views should not be confused with the degree of complexity of the thought process used to come to one's conclusions. In reality, individuals who think dualistically and individuals who think relativistically can resemble each other on the surface. Both may demonstrate "strong" views. At issue as a distinguishing factor is the degree of examination and reflection that has gone into formulating those views. If ideas have essentially been "swallowed whole" from authorities such as parents, teachers, advisers, or textbooks, and if little or no questioning has been part of the process of adopting these beliefs, the process demonstrates a dualistic mode—"the ideas are right because I have been told that they are right." By contrast, a relativistic thinker may have been presented with ideas by an authority figure and may have come to adopt them as his or her own. However, along the way, the ideas have been critically examined and perhaps even rejected for a period. The rationale for current adherence to the beliefs will reflect a more complex process of coming to conclusions, a process that includes some questioning and a contextual basis for the stance taken.

King (1978) has noted that beyond Position 5 in Perry's scheme, a shift away from cognitive development occurs because movement beyond Position 5 does not involve changes in cognitive structures. In other words, the individual who moves beyond Position 5 does not become different in terms of cognitive complexity. Therefore, the movement from relativism to the process of *commitment in relativism,* which involves making choices in a contextual world, can be viewed as initiating the "ethical development" identified in the title of Perry's scheme.

The commitment process involves choices, decisions, and affirmations that are made from the vantage point of relativism. Perry (1981) stated, "It is in one's way of affirming Commitments that one finds at last the elusive sense of 'identity' one has searched for elsewhere" (p. 97). Two aspects characterize students' thinking about commitments: area and style (Perry, 1968). Area refers to social content—decisions about major, career, religion, relationships, politics, and so forth. Style has to do with balancing in regard to both the external (for example, relative time use, nature of relationships) and the subjective (for example, action versus contemplation, control versus openness).

Consistent with his view that development does not occur in a linear fashion, Perry also described three deflections from cognitive growth. Temporizing represents a "timeout" period. Movement is postponed. Perry (1968) acknowledged that some temporizing may be needed to allow for lateral growth or development within a particular stage *(horizontal décalage)* or to provide a rest period for one's system. With temporizing, cognitive development is essentially "put on hold"; a plateau is maintained. Escape, another deflection, involves an abandonment of responsibility characterized by alienation. Retreat, the third deflection, involves a temporary retreat to dualism.

Assessment Techniques

An array of methods is available to assess development from the vantage point of Perry's theory. These include both production and recognition formats. In the original study, Perry (1968) and his colleagues conducted open-ended interviews, beginning with a question such as "Would you like to say what has stood out for you during the year?" (p. 7) and following up with probes seeking specific examples.

After the scheme was conceptualized from a qualitative analysis of early protocols, a manual was developed and subsequent ratings were done by independent judges (Perry, 1968). The time and expense involved in conducting interviews and doing ratings of protocols for assessment purposes limited widespread use of the technique. As alternatives to the interview approach, several paper-and-pencil measures of the Perry scheme have been developed.

Knefelkamp (1974) and Widick (1975) developed and refined a production-oriented instrument that came to be known as the Measure of Intellectual Development (MID), which measures the first five Perry positions. The MID consists of three essays that ask students to describe the best class they have taken, the last time they had to make an important decision, and important considerations in making career decisions. These essays are evaluated by two independent raters. Each essay is assigned a three-digit rating that reflects a stable Perry position as well as transitional steps. Mines (1982) has stated that the MID is more reliably scored than most instruments that assess complex data. He provided information on three categories of reliability studies conducted on the MID: correlations with interview ratings, correlations with external experts, and interrater reliability data of various kinds. Considering absolute agreement on the three-digit rating the most stringent criterion, he reported correlations ranging from .43 to .64. However, Mines also indicated that the authors of the MID consider agreement on the dominant position the most reasonable measure, and their reported correlations ranged from .73 to 1.00. Mines has also reported convergent/divergent validity data for the MID by summarizing results from several studies. Correlations for the MID and other constructs are as follows: conceptual level, .51; moral development, .13, .45; ego development, .30; empathy, .14, .32; and locus of control, −.19, −.54. Mines concluded that the developmental dimensions represent reasonably distinct domains and that the relationships with empathy and locus of control provide additional evidence to support validity.

Baxter Magolda and Porterfield's Measure of Epistemological Reflection (MER) (1985), another production instrument, also measures the first five positions of the Perry scheme. Via a series of short-answer essay questions, six domains of the learning process are examined: decision making, the role of the learner, the role of the instructor, the role of peers, evaluation, and the nature of truth. Follow-up questions probing for rationales and elaborations are included for each domain. Scoring is done by using a standardized rating manual to reduce the amount of inference in rating the instrument (Baxter Magolda, 1987). Baxter Magolda and Porterfield (1985) have reported evidence to support reliability and validity of the MER. They reported a correlation coefficient of .80 for interrater reliability. An analysis of variance revealed differences in MER results by level of education that were significant at the .01 level, thereby supporting validity.

Erwin's Scale of Intellectual Development (SID) (1983) represents an early effort to create a Perry measure comprised of recognition tasks. The SID consists of 119 items with four–point Likert scale responses. These responses are categorized into dualism, relativism, commitment, and empathy. Internal consistency coefficients (Cronbach's alpha) were as follows for the scales: Dualism, .81; Relativism, .70; Commitment, .76; and Empathy, .73 (Erwin, 1983). Both Baxter Magolda (1987) and King (1990) have expressed concern about the validity of the instrument as a measure of the Perry scheme. Specifically, multiplicity is not included, resulting in what King has described as a reductionistic approach.

Another Perry measure that uses the recognition format is Moore's Learning Environment Preferences Measure (LEP) (1989). Five sentence stems are each followed by a series of statements that respondents are asked to rate on a four–point Likert scale in regard to their significance in the respondent's ideal learning environment. Respondents are then asked to identify and to rank the three most important statements for each stem. These stems represent the domains of view of knowledge and course content, role of the instructor, role of the student and peers in the classroom, classroom atmosphere, and role of evaluation. A scoring index is used to produce a score on a scale of 200 to 500, corresponding to Positions 2 through 5 of the Perry scheme. Moore reported Cronbach's alpha reliability coefficients ranging from .72 to .84 for these four positions. In relation to concurrent validity, the correlation of this measure with the MID was .36 (Moore). An analysis of variance produced significant results across class groups at the .01 level, providing further data to support validity (Moore).

The time, expense, and expertise required to implement production-oriented assessments typically render them impractical for applied uses in the classroom or student affairs settings. By contrast, recognition-oriented assessments are likely to be viewed as more viable when formal assessment is desired in a context other than academic research. However, the option of informal assessment also seems important to note.

Interactions with students in the classroom, residence halls, student organizations, counseling relationships, judicial conferences, and so forth are likely to provide clues as to how students make meaning. Such impressionistic information can be valuable in trying to understand students' perspectives and work with the differences manifested in an effective manner. It is not necessary to conduct a formal assessment to form some tentative impressions of where students may be in terms of their cognitive development and to use Perry's theory as a support in responding. As King (1990) has cautioned, one does run the risk of error in conducting informal assessments. It is therefore important to use such information tentatively and empathically and to be willing to recognize the possibility of mistaken impressions. Informal assessments that are done responsibly would seem to be preferable to giving no consideration to where students may be in their cognitive development simply to avoid the risk of error.

Research

Much research has been done involving Perry's theory. This section focuses on early groundbreaking research and examples of the types of research conducted more recently.

Perry and his colleagues replicated their original work with the Harvard-Radcliffe entering class of 1971 and again with the class of 1979 (Perry, 1981). Though some variations were noted when comparing these samples to the original, Perry concluded that the scheme of cognitive and ethical development seemed to be a constant phenomenon in a pluralistic culture.

Perry (1981) credited James Heffernan as the first to use the scheme for research purposes by incorporating it into an outcome study of a residential college at the University of Michigan. Joanne Kurfiss is also identified (King, 1978; Perry) as a researcher who conducted early work based on the Perry scheme. She examined conceptual properties and the comparative rates of development within individuals in relation to moral values, counseling and advice, evaluation (grading) of essays, the responsibility of the professor in regard to knowledge, and the nature of knowledge. Kurfiss found disparities in the levels of development within individuals that reflected correlations among the more abstract (moral values, nature of knowledge) and the more concrete areas (the remaining three) but not across the two groups.

Pierre Meyer (1977) was another researcher who used Perry's theory early on. He studied the religious development of students with a common religious preference who attended two small colleges (one private, one public). Perry position was found to correlate positively with measures of moral judgment and conceptual complexity. The content base of the structured interview used to assess position in the Perry scheme was religious in nature. King (1978) has noted that this study shows that an understanding of religious issues can serve as an indication of intellectual development.

Bateman and Donald (1987) conducted a study of construct and empirical validity of the Perry scheme. Students at a Canadian institution were given a questionnaire intended to measure dualism, multiplicity, relativism, and commitment. The questionnaire included items taken from Perry interview transcripts and from Kurfiss's work as well as some items specifically developed by the researchers. Rather than stages of development, the authors found two positions that students took toward knowledge: a view of knowledge as facts and data that professors should supply; and a view that knowledge is a quest in which students have responsibility for their own learning and should be able to judge the validity of arguments and take their own position and defend it. Questioning the construct validity of the scheme, the authors suggested that the items might more appropriately be considered measures of attitudes rather than measures of intellectual development.

Another study (Lavallée, Gourde, & Rodier, 1990), also conducted at a Canadian institution, included an examination of the generalizability of Perry's model to other areas of reflection. The authors found that Perry's scheme was applicable to the domain of social role as well as to the domains of knowledge and education. Also, no significant developmental differences were found between house-wives and female workers entering the university for the first time and a tradi-tional student group with two years of completed university study, indicating that environments other than higher education can also elicit development.

Use of Perry's scheme as an outcome measure is also represented in the re-search. For example, the MID was used to assess the impact on cognitive devel-opment of a program designed to enhance the professional identity of medical students (Swick, 1991). The SID was used to assess the impact of a semesterlong career planning course for vocationally undecided students (Jones & Newman, 1993). Finally, the MID was used to measure the impact of a yearlong interdisci-plinary program at Daytona Beach Community College (Avens & Zelley, 1992).

An early and extensive use of the Perry scheme as an outcomes measure oc-curred at Alverno College (Mentkowski, Moeser, & Strait, 1983). Perry's scheme was used, along with other developmentally oriented instruments, as a measure of student growth at an institution with an outcome-centered curriculum. A five-year longitudinal study involving 750 women aged seventeen to fifty-five was con-ducted, and the basic finding was that students do change on the Perry scheme during their time in college. Development was found to be differential, depend-ing on the area of development (for example, career development versus class-room learning).

Finally, Piper and Rodgers (1992) conducted a study that found that student affairs practitioners who use Perry in their work are more likely to be Perry rela-tivists and Myers-Briggs feeling and perceiving types. In addition, they found that Myers-Briggs sensing types were more likely to be dualistic, while intuitive types were more likely to be multiplistic or relativistic. They offer several recommen-dations related to staff development, such as encouraging judging and thinking types to use theory and fostering cognitive growth since relativistic thinking might be a necessary condition for integrating a complex theory and using it in practice.

Applications

First we will examine the Developmental Instruction model and then move on to discuss both classroom and student affairs applications.

The Developmental Instruction Model

Knefelkamp and Widick's creation of the Developmental Instruction (DI) model (Knefelkamp, 1984) provided a valuable resource to aid in operationalizing Perry's model. As "second-generation" theorists, they can be credited with translating Perry into a usable form for the classroom and other instructional settings. Knefelkamp and Widick produced a model for instructional design that is grounded in an analysis of Perry's discussion of student learner characteristics.

The four variables of challenge and support that characterize the model are structure, diversity, experiential learning, and personalism. Each variable can be viewed as existing on a continuum that symbolizes greater or lesser amounts of the variable itself.

Structure refers to the framework and direction provided to students. The continuum represents the movement from a high degree to a low degree of structure. Examples of ways in which structure can be provided are placing the course in the context of the curriculum, affording an opportunity to rehearse evaluation tasks, giving detailed explanations of assignments, and using specific examples that reflect the students' experience. Students in the earlier positions in Perry's model will value structure as a support, and students who have advanced further may consider structure limiting and prefer a more open-ended approach that gives them latitude.

Diversity has to do with alternatives and perspectives that are presented and encouraged. Two dimensions characterize diversity: quantity and quality. Quantity refers to amount, and quality to complexity. Consequently, the two-dimensional continuum reflects these two dimensions and ranges from a few simple pieces of information to many highly complex concepts or tasks. Diversity can be introduced via variety in readings, assignments, points of view presented, and methods of instruction.

Experiential learning relates to the concreteness, directness, and involvement contained in learning activities. This continuum ranges from direct involvement to vicarious learning. Experiential learning's purpose is to help students make connections to the subject matter. Methods include case studies, role plays, and exercises that facilitate reflection on and application of the material. As Knefelkamp (1984) pointed out, though all students can benefit from experiential learning, students in the early stages of cognitive development are more in need of this form of support, which can be lacking in the traditional college classroom.

The final variable, personalism, reflects the creation of a safe environment where risk taking is encouraged. This continuum moves from high to moderate, since an impersonal learning environment is not considered facilitative for any student. Personalism is manifested in an interactive environment that demonstrates enthusiasm for the material, instructor availability, and comprehensive feedback. Although personalism has value throughout the cognitive development process, it is especially important for students in the early stages.

By drawing on these four challenge and support variables, both faculty and student affairs practitioners can create learning activities and environments that can connect with where students are in the cognitive development process and also support their potential to develop further.

Another useful resource in the design process is the analysis of learner characteristics presented by Knefelkamp and Cornfeld (1979). For dualistic, multiplistic, and relativistic ways of making meaning, they describe each perspective's view of knowledge, role of the instructor, and role of the student and peers in the learning process, as well as evaluation issues, primary intellectual tasks, and sources of challenge and support.

The DI model could aid the instructor who is working with Audrey, Jordan, and Jerome in the opening scenario focusing on the classroom. For example, for Audrey, the variable of personalism can be an important support. An instructor who is approachable, available, and encouraging of participation rather than demanding of it may help her move toward confidence in the legitimacy of her own opinion. Also, an assignment that would require Audrey to read two dissenting interpretations of a literary passage, both written by individuals perceived to be experts in literary criticism, could represent a use of the variable of diversity to challenge her appropriately. Asking Audrey to report to the class on her findings reflects the variable of experiential learning. Because she is asked to report the opinions of others, this task would not represent the potentially overwhelming challenge of reporting her own ideas. Drawing on the variable of structure by giving detailed instructions for the verbal report could be an effective way to provide support to Audrey to mediate some of the challenge inherent in having to speak before the class and her instructor.

An assignment that would require Jordan and Jerome to work together to develop and present an interpretation of symbolism in a work of literature has the potential to aid Jordan in gaining an increased understanding of the need to support opinions. Because of Jordan's current multiplistic thinking, peers would be considered legitimate sources of knowledge. Jerome, because of his relativistic thinking, has the potential to have an impact on Jordan because he is likely to manifest the "plus-one staging" concept without even being aware of it. Plus-one staging, a concept described by Knefelkamp, Widick, and Stroad (1976) and attributed to Kohlberg (Stonewater, 1988), refers to the idea that individuals can typically understand and even be attracted to reasoning that is slightly more advanced than their own. Jordan's current dissatisfaction with his instructor could also render Jerome a more viable teacher. For Jerome, this assignment can reinforce his sense of mastery of the intellectual tasks involved. If the instructor presents the assignment as an opportunity for students to share views and practice the ability to support arguments, Jerome is likely to see relevance to further skill development for his chosen career of the law.

Classroom Applications

Examples of and arguments for use of Perry's theory to enhance the teaching and learning process in the classroom are abundant. The typical application consists of using Perry's work to design learning experiences that provide a match or a developmental mismatch, given the cognitive complexity represented among the students in the course. The use of plus-one staging can serve as a means of providing a developmental mismatch and facilitating further cognitive growth. Relativistic reasoning used with a dualistic thinker will make little sense to that person. This would be a nondevelopmental mismatch. Too much challenge is present. By contrast, multiplistic thinking can have an impact on dualistic thinkers who are approaching a point of transition. It is important to remember that Perry's positions represent a continuum. Movement is fluid rather than a sudden and complete shifting of gears at a particular point in time. Therefore progress along the continuum can be supported and even encouraged by using an appropriate combination of challenge and support.

Widick and Simpson (1978) described in detail the design work done by Knefelkamp (1974) and Widick (1975) in the initial classroom application of the DI model in an interdisciplinary course focusing on themes in human identity.

Use of Perry's theory in the classroom has been advocated in relation to teaching content areas such as philosophy (Rapaport, 1984), art and art history (Crawford, 1989), writing (Burnham, 1986; Dinitz & Kiedaisch, 1990; Hays, 1988), music (Brand, 1988; Cutietta, 1990), literary analysis (Plummer, 1988), foreign languages (Jacobus, 1989), home economics (Mullis, Martin, Dosser, & Sanders, 1988), library instruction (McNeer, 1991), economics (Thoma, 1993), public speaking (Hayward, 1993), abnormal psychology (Van Hecke, 1987), and chemical engineering (Woods, 1990).

Knefelkamp (1982) has noted that inherent in Perry's theory is the assumption that learning is an ego-threatening task; she added that teaching is as well. Relatedly, an understanding of Perry's scheme and effective approaches to dealing with differences in students' levels of cognitive complexity, such as the DI model provides, has the potential to help faculty form connections with students and in turn help students form connections with the subject matter and the learning process.

In conducting workshops, we have occasionally encountered faculty members who question the need to learn and use models such as Perry's. Skeptical comments can include statements such as "It's my job to teach, and it's the student's job to learn." Such challenges have been countered with the question, "Do you see yourself teaching subject matter, or do you see yourself teaching students?" Clearly, if an instructor is genuinely concerned about effective teaching and learning, knowledge and use of Perry's ideas and the DI model can result in increased satisfaction and success for both students and faculty. A compelling argument for the integration of Perry's work into the teaching and learning process was eloquently presented by Knefelkamp (1982). She argued for student development theory as a source of a common language that can assist faculty and students in hearing each other's voices.

Student Affairs Applications

Knefelkamp and Slepitza (1976) introduced an early application of Perry's theory in a student affairs setting. They demonstrated how Perry's work could be used to understand how students make meaning in the context of career counseling. The shift from an external to an internal locus of control that characterizes forward movement in the Perry scheme is particularly noteworthy in understanding the differing expectations that students bring to the career development process. For example, dualistic thinkers are likely to believe that one "right" career exists for them and that the career counselor, as the expert, knows what that career should be. Multiplistic thinkers are more likely to look to the career counselor to provide a process by which decisions can be made. The level of cognitive complexity necessary to make commitments helps explain the reluctance to commit that is evident in some students. Perry (1978) himself discussed the affective component in choice and commitment when he noted the need to grieve for the loss experienced in giving up the roads not taken. He expressed a desire to rewrite vocational theory so that it addresses "not . . . how you choose what you are going to do, but . . . how you give up all the other selves you are not going to be" (p. 271).

Touchton, Wertheimer, Cornfeld, and Harrison (1977), using Knefelkamp and Slepitza's work (1976) and integrating the DI model, designed an undergraduate career planning course that deliberately included challenge and support components deemed appropriate for the level of cognitive complexity characterizing their students.

Stonewater (1988) presented a very valuable application of Perry's theory in the residence halls. She provided useful descriptions of the different ways in which students who are dualistic, multiplistic, and relativistic thinkers are likely to view the residence hall staff, discipline, and roommate conflicts. In her work, too, the Developmental Instruction model is integrated, and ways of providing challenge and support using diversity, direct experience, and structure are discussed.

Also in relation to residence halls, Ricci, Porterfield, and Piper (1987) applied Perry's theory to staff supervision. They described characteristics related to knowledge, authority, the learning process, peer acceptance, and evaluation for staff members who are dualistic, multiplistic, and relativistic in their thinking. Also included are implications for the staff members themselves in each group, as well as strategies for supervisors for working with staff members in each of the three groups.

Cosgrove (1987) used Perry's model to support group advisement responsibilities, such as those performed by student activities professionals. He noted that since students don't learn differently in student organizations than in the classroom, Perry's theory can be useful to advisers who are trying to hear students and to provide learning environments for them. Areas of application include offering feedback, designing and developing programs, diagnosing and managing group conflict, and adjusting advising styles.

Knefelkamp, Widick, and Stroad (1976) drew on considerations in Perry's work to support the process of counseling women. They advocated recognizing the difference between the content of one's beliefs and developmental stage as well as the use of plus-one staging.

Saidla (1990) explained how Perry's theory can be useful in understanding behavior in groups over the course of the group development process. Tuckman's group stages (1965) form the basis for discussion of group development. The different ways of making meaning represented in Perry's scheme are integrated to explain how cognitive complexity can affect individual behavior in each stage of the group development process. This information is relevant to counseling groups as well as task groups (for example, classroom projects, committees) or student organizations.

Hillman and Lewis (1980) have applied Perry's theory to the process of academic advising. Even the functional area of financial aid has been identified as one that could benefit from having Perry's theory available as a resource for understanding the student clientele (Coomes, 1992).

What most of these applications have in common is a recognition of the value that the Perry scheme has in creating an understanding of how students interpret their experiences and how practitioners can deal constructively with such differences in designing developmental responses, typically with the aid of the DI model, in group-based learning environments or in one-to-one interactions. It is important to remember when using Perry's theory to design student affairs applications that movement along Perry's scheme is slow. Consequently, a one-shot program with a goal of increasing students' cognitive complexity would be misdirected. As Mines (1982) pointed out, change is gradual and uneven across different content areas. Sustained interventions are needed to promote growth. Measurement of impact should be done in relation to a specific content area and on the micro level.

Returning to the scenario involving Lee and the union programming board members, one can formulate some approaches that Miriam, the adviser, might use to support further cognitive growth for the students involved. For Lee, Miriam could serve as a role model and teacher. She can help him comprehend the dualistic thinking that seems to characterize many of the board members. She can model helpful responses and advise him on appropriate approaches that he might take. In interacting with the group during meetings and in other situations, Miriam needs to be sensitive to supporting Lee's leadership position. The dualistic thinkers will look to her for answers. One approach she could take would be to reinforce Lee's legitimacy as a source of knowledge by asking for his thoughts when such questions are raised.

Miriam can also assist the group by encouraging group members to brainstorm alternatives, an activity likely to result in the viability of more than one approach in relation to programming decisions, marketing strategies, and so forth. Sharing information about successful approaches used at other institutions is another way that Miriam can introduce the legitimacy of multiple strategies.

Making contextually appropriate choices is likely to be beyond most of the board members, given their dualistic thinking. Lee, by contrast, could be ready to develop these skills. One approach to encouraging contextually appropriate thinking is to have the group develop a list of items that would be important to consider in relation to the institution when making the programming decision. Each person is likely to suggest the factors that she or he considers important. The group as a whole may or may not embrace the entire list, depending on how individuals perceive the "rightness" of the items. The absence of more complex thinkers in the group may pose a dilemma for Miriam. As the adviser, does she honor a trial-and-error approach if important institutional considerations are not endorsed, or does she intervene in the decision-making process to try to minimize the potential for failure? Clearly, a group composition that included more students who are further along in their cognitive development would be advantageous because more complex views could come from several of the student group members themselves. As this group is currently composed, the aspect of giving priority to the students' own growth and development could come in conflict with the task-oriented nature of the student organization itself and any related political dynamics, including the expectations of supervisors.

Critique and Future Directions

Legitimate concern can be expressed about Perry's samples' lack of inclusiveness. Clearly, attempting to generalize from a study of primarily traditionally aged white males at a prestigious institution is a risky business. Using Perry's theory tentatively in relation to women, people of color, and other nondominant groups is recommended. At the same time, Perry's ways of making meaning do intuitively make sense, and student affairs practitioners and graduate students readily recognize these modes in the students with whom they interact and even in themselves.

Another concern can be raised as a consequence of Perry's scheme's including two constructs rather than one. To combine both intellectual and ethical development can result in some confounding, particularly in terms of what is perceived as being "more developed." As King (1978) noted, the positions associated with Perry's commitment process are no longer measuring or portraying increased cognitive complexity. Structurally, positions beyond relativism do not represent cognitive change. Instead, these positions reflect the second construct of "ethical" growth or the development of commitment. Relatedly, evidence to support the existence of the most advanced positions, the "committed" positions, is limited (King). Whether this is a weakness of the measurement instruments or of the theory itself is uncertain.

The heuristic value of Perry's theory deserves mention. Perry's work has influenced Belenky, Clinchy, Goldberger, and Tarule's research on women (1986), Baxter Magolda's examination of the cognitive development of both men and women in the college setting (1992), and King and Kitchener's development of the Reflective Judgment Model (1994), all discussed in the next chapter.

Clearly, Perry's work is of great value for gaining a basic understanding of how students make meaning. The concepts of dualism, multiplicity, relativism, and commitment in relativism are easy to grasp and to recognize, at least tentatively, in students. Equally important is Knefelkamp and Widick's effort (Knefelkamp, 1984) to operationalize Perry's theory. They provided the information needed to go beyond understanding to action. The impact of how students make meaning can be felt in the classroom, in interactions with student affairs staff, and in their contacts with each other. In turn, Perry's theory can be used to support practice in any of these arenas.

Finally, concerns can be raised that Perry's theory simply "labels" students and that efforts to facilitate development are misdirected. For example, after a faculty development workshop in which Perry's work was promoted, a colleague commented, "They want us to put numbers on students." In regard to the issue of labeling, if Perry's descriptions are used empathically rather than judgmentally in relation to students, faculty and student affairs practitioners will not "pigeonhole" them but attempt to understand how they make meaning and respond appropriately. With this knowledge, one can more effectively contribute to students' learning processes. As to whether or not development should be facilitated, faculty and student affairs practitioners need to recognize that students cannot be dragged kicking and screaming through a developmental sequence. They are agents on their own behalf and cannot be forced to grow. At the same time, higher education is about growth and development. Many institutional mission statements make reference to character and to producing responsible citizens. Enhanced cognitive complexity supports such a goal. Perry (1978) himself asked, "What's so good about advancing along such a series of discoveries (or any other scheme of development . . .)?" (p. 269). In answering his own question, Perry argued that the world is a complicated place and that it is better in trying to function in it to have "a matching set of complicated ideas" (p. 269) rather than simple ideas that don't fit. Do educators not have some obligation to attempt to help students equip themselves with complicated ideas that are both self-supporting and inclusive of others?

At the same time, all cognitive structural theories that are available in relation to college students will benefit from continuing research efforts that are inclusive of the diversity inherent in today's and tomorrow's campus.

CHAPTER NINE

LATER COGNITIVE-STRUCTURAL THEORIES

This chapter will examine three more recent cognitive-structural theories: Belenky, Clinchy, Goldberger, and Tarule's *Women's Ways of Knowing;* Baxter Magolda's Epistemological Reflection Model; and King and Kitchener's Reflective Judgment Model. The scenarios that began the Perry chapter will also receive attention in this chapter for purposes of comparison and contrast with Perry's theory (1968).

Belenky, Clinchy, Goldberger, and Tarule's Women's Ways of Knowing

Belenky, Clinchy, Goldberger, and Tarule (1986) began their research in the late 1970s when they "became concerned about why women speak so frequently of problems and gaps in their learning and so often doubt their intellectual competence" (p. 4). At the same time, the authors were also aware that for many women, formal education was not central to their development. Instead, they noted that the most valuable lessons were derived from relationships, crises, and community involvements.

The authors cited the work of both Carol Gilligan and William Perry as influential in shaping their own efforts. They built on Gilligan's landmark contribution (1977) of including woman's voice in human development theory and acknowledged Perry's research (1968) for the opportunity provided to see what women might have in common with men. Belenky et al. (1986) in turn focused on *what else* might be important to note about women's intellectual development, as well as on "alternative routes" (p. 9) that are not elucidated by Perry's work.

These authors described themselves as being both psychologists and academic feminists. They stated their intent as being "to share not prove our observations" (p. 16). In this spirit, they undertook a study involving lengthy interviews with 135 women, some of whom were students in or recent graduates of academic institutions and some of whom were affiliated with human service agencies that provided support to women in parenting.

The results of this research are presented in their compelling book *Women's Ways of Knowing: The Development of Self, Voice, and Mind* (1986). The authors noted that the book is about "pain and anger and static lives" (p. 4) and about "the 'roar which lies on the other side of silence' when ordinary women find their voice and use it to gain control over their lives" (p. 4).

The Theory

In presenting their theory, Belenky et al. (1986) referred to the different ways of knowing as "perspectives" rather than stages. They maintained that more work is needed to determine if "stagelike qualities" (p. 15) characterize these perspectives. They also put forth several disclaimers about the five perspectives by acknowledging that their categories may not be fixed, exhaustive, or universal; that by nature of their abstractness, the categories do not portray the unique and complex aspects of a given individual's thought process; that similar categories may be found in men's thinking; and that others might organize the observations in a different way. But the authors stated with conviction their finding that for women, the development of voice, mind, and self are "intricately intertwined" (p. 18). And *voice* assumes a meaning beyond "academic shorthand for a person's point of view" (p. 18). Women used the metaphor of voice to describe their intellectual and ethical development.

From the study of women of "diverse ages, circumstances, and outlooks" (Belenky et al., 1986, p. 13) emerged the following five "epistemological perspectives from which women know and view the world" (p. 15): silence, received knowledge, subjective knowledge, procedural knowledge, and constructed knowledge.

The perspective of *silence* is characterized as mindless, voiceless, and obedient. Access to language is limited, and silence represents powerlessness. In this perspective, women find themselves subject to the whims of external authority. Though rare as a current way of knowing among the women interviewed, the perspective of silence was described in retrospect by some interviewees. Belenky et al. (1986) noted that these women were found through the social service agencies and not on the college campus. They were among "the youngest and most socially, economically, and educationally deprived" (pp. 23–24) of the interviewees.

Listening to the voices of others is a predominant trait of the perspective of *received knowledge.* Learning consists of listening to others, and truth resides in others, not in the self. A lack of self-confidence is evident in the belief that one is capable of receiving and reproducing knowledge imparted from external authorities but not of creating knowledge on one's own. Similarities can be seen between received knowers and Perry's dualistic thinkers (1968), as Belenky et al. (1986) pointed out. Some differences can also be observed. Both the men in Perry's study and the women in this study stood in awe of authority figures. However, the women identified less with these authorities than Perry's men did. Belenky et al. speculated that this lack of identification may reflect the fact that the women were less privileged in regard to social class than Perry's men were or the fact that few women were included in the "authorities" group. Another distinction is that women as received knowers focus on listening, while Perry's dualistic men were described by Belenky et al. as lecturing more than listening. In the scenarios at the start of Chapter Eight, Audrey, along with manifesting characteristics of Perry's dualistic thinkers, also exhibits the emphasis on listening that is characteristic of Belenky et al.'s received knowers.

With the perspective of *subjective knowledge,* the pendulum swings, and truth is now seen as residing in the self. One's own inner knowledge is considered superior to the knowledge of others. Belenky et al. (1986) stated that if and when the shift into subjectivism occurs for women, it is particularly significant. A frequently cited element in the shift into this perspective by the women who held it is a failed male authority figure, such as a father who commits incest or an abusive husband. The authors again noted a parallel to Perry's scheme by citing a similarity between subjective knowing and multiplicity. Inherent in the process of subjective knowing for women is a quest for the self, often including the element of "walking away from the past" (p. 76), an act of choosing self over other.

In looking at the classroom scenario at the beginning of Chapter Eight, Jordan, a multiplistic thinker, may have a female counterpart of sorts in another hypothetical classmate, Rose, who also places great value in her own views. She trusts her own voice over the voice of others. She is skeptical of her male professor as a source of knowledge and wisdom. Rose is finding college particularly stressful this semester because her father, only a few weeks before she returned to school, abandoned her mother and several younger siblings to pursue a relationship with another woman. She had very much looked up to her father and sought his advice regularly; she was heartbroken by his actions. Rose would seem to fit several aspects of the description of subjective knowers.

The perspective of *procedural knowledge* involves learning and applying objective procedures for receiving and conveying knowledge. Two approaches are evident in this mode. The first, separate knowing, is grounded in impersonal procedures for establishing truth. Separate knowing is characterized by critical thinking; listening to reason, though an adversarial tone is implicit; and self-extrication, in the sense that "procedures for meaning making are strictly impersonal" (Belenky et al., 1986, p. 109). Separate knowing often involves doubting. The second, connected knowing, is based on truth emerging in the context of personal experience and being grounded in empathy and care. Connected knowing is grounded in the belief that knowledge is derived from personal experience rather than from authorities. Connected knowers display trust and patience toward others in the process of knowing. Connected knowing often involves believing. The women interviewed tended to shift between these two voices. Those who favored separate knowing tended to be college graduates from elite liberal arts colleges, often women's institutions. Separate knowers are described as refusing "to play the conventional female role" (p. 104). In groups, separate knowers tend to try to separate the personality of the perceiver from the perception, whereas connected knowers view personality as enhancing the perception.

In reconsidering the scenario of Lee and the student programming board that opened Chapter Eight, one might find among the board members two juniors, Sarah and Susan. In the meeting that dealt with the issue of providing programming funds for a special orientation program for students of color, Sarah took an analytical approach. She listened carefully to the points of view presented and tried to ignore the fact that she personally dislikes one of the major spokespersons on one side of the issue so that she could try to draw a conclusion based on the merits of the argument alone. Sarah would appear to be a separate knower. Susan also wanted to be objective in reaching a decision on this issue. She remembered the feelings of exclusion that a student of color who lives on her residence hall floor had expressed to her about the traditional orientation program. This experience seemed important to her as she worked toward reaching a decision on the issue. Susan appears to be demonstrating aspects of connected knowing.

Constructed knowledge, as a perspective, involves the integration of subjective and objective knowledge, with both feeling and thought present in ways of knowing. Belenky et al. (1986) asserted that "it is in the process of sorting out the pieces of the self and of searching for a unique and authentic voice" (p. 137) that women discover the two basic insights of constructivist thought. These insights are that all knowledge is constructed and that the knower is an intimate part of what is known. The authors described the women who displayed this way of knowing as articulate, reflective, caring, self-aware, concerned with separation and connection, engaged in a struggle to balance the extremes in their lives, and fighting to find their own voices. Constructivists are also portrayed as "passionate knowers" who distinguish between didactic talk and "real talk." Significantly, the authors characterized constructivists as able to listen to others without losing the ability to also hear their own voices.

The authors found that common family experiences characterized each of the different perspectives. In other words, women who share an epistemological position have some similarities in their family histories. For example, Belenky et al. (1986) noted that themes emerged related to the "politics of talk" (p. 156), forms of discussion that a family encourages and those that it discourages. In addition, certain themes related to learning emerged. Such themes included the need for confirmation of the self as knower from early on in the educational process, a need for honoring the voice of experience as a legitimate source of knowledge, and a need for structure without an accompanying excessive degree of control by others that negates the need for freedom.

Assessment Techniques

Belenky et al. (1986) proceeded phenomenologically in their research and used an "intensive interview/case study approach" (p. 11) that resulted in interviews that varied from two to five hours in length. Modeled on Perry's method (1968), each interview started with the question, "Looking back, what stands out for you over the past few years?" (Belenky et al., p. 11). Other questions explored "self-image, relationships of importance, education and learning, real-life decision-making and moral dilemmas, accounts of personal changes and growth, perceived catalysts for change and impediments to growth, and visions of the future" (p. 11). Along with Perry's work, work by Gilligan (1982/1993) and Kohlberg (1984) was also influential in the design of the interview format. Consequently, the potential existed to view the interviewees in the context of these theories' conceptions of development as well as to determine inadequacies in these approaches.

The sections of the interview designed to assess development as outlined in the theories of Perry, Gilligan, and Kohlberg were scored using masked coding (the raters knew nothing about the individuals whose protocols they were scoring). The researchers discovered that women's thinking could not be adequately described by the Perry scheme. Unlike Perry's men with the common influence of Harvard; Belenky et al.'s women represented such widely differing circumstances that "universal pathways are far less obvious" (1986, p. 15).

After the Perry, Gilligan, and Kohlberg assessments were completed, a contextual analysis was performed. Coding categories were developed to classify how women regard themselves as developing beings and how they experience learning environments. Included in the coding categories were ten bimodal dimensions labeled "educational dialectics" (p. 16). Examples are "process-oriented versus goal-oriented" and "support versus challenge." The authors anticipated that for women one mode would tend to predominate, while educational practice would tend to favor the opposite mode.

Buczynski (1993) developed a paper-and-pencil instrument to measure the five women's ways of knowing. Named the Ways of Knowing Instrument, the objective measure was designed to be simple to administer and score. A four-point Likert scale (strongly disagree to strongly agree) is provided to respond to a total of forty-eight items. Items were designed to represent the five ways of knowing, and items judged by experts and potential participants as ambiguous or not representative were previously eliminated. Reliability coefficients for the subscales representing each mode of meaning making ranged from .69 to .80. Buczynski cited the need for further work related to validity and reliability as well as the need to use the instrument with larger and more diverse samples.

Research

At this writing, Belenky et al.'s own work constitutes virtually the entire available research base.

Applications

Belenky et al. (1986) concluded their book by advocating "connected teaching" (p. 214). Connected teachers can help women nurture their own voices by emphasizing connection rather than separation, understanding and acceptance rather than assessment, and collaboration rather than debate; respecting and supporting firsthand experience as a source of knowledge; and encouraging student-induced work patterns rather than imposing their own expectations and requirements.

Underlying the proposed approach is a recognition of the need for women to see models, female and male, of the thinker in process rather than of thoughts as fully formed outcomes. Belenky et al. (1986) maintained that women "need models of thinking as a human, imperfect, and attainable activity" (p. 217). Relatedly, they suggested the role of teacher as midwife, one who assists students "in giving birth to their own ideas" (p. 217). "Connected" classes are described as providing cultures for growth. Class discussions that encourage the expression of diverse opinions represent a means of implementing connected teaching. The authors noted that in contrast to writings that describe doubt as a factor in cognitive development, connected teachers demonstrate belief and trust in their students' thinking. While Belenky et al. noted the legitimacy of cognitive conflict as a stimulus for growth and underscored its impact on their own development, they stressed that the midwife approach to teaching was more prevalent as a stimulus among the women included in their study.

Ortman (1993) used principles of connected teaching in an undergraduate learning theory course conducted at a women's college. She included *Women's Ways of Knowing* as a text and employed a discussion format, case studies, group presentations, a cooperative evaluation system, and a final paper rather than an exam. Regarding the course as fairly successful for a pilot effort, Ortman did note several anticipated changes for the future, including increased attention to theories via lecture, elimination of the collaborative evaluation component, and the imposition of more conditions to create collaboration. Ortman suggested the desirability of using the connected teaching methods in a coeducational or all-male class for comparative purposes.

Another example of a classroom application of connected teaching is Crowley's description (1989) of a small group exercise used in a graduate-level group dynamics course. The exercise was designed to help students develop their own thinking and validate knowledge coming from firsthand experience. In addition, Tedesco (1991) explained how the theory can be useful in working with students of composition, and Crawford (1989) discussed uses of the theory in teaching art and art history.

Ursuline College (Gose, 1995), in an institutionwide application, introduced a core curriculum, the Ursuline Studies Program, based on Belenky et al.'s work, which emphasizes group discussions and collaborative learning in a freshman seminar format.

In her review of *Women's Ways of Knowing*, Forrest (1988) asserted that student affairs professionals can support women's development if they place greater emphasis on issues of connection than on issues of separation when working with women. One way to do so is to adopt the midwife role and help students produce their own ideas. Fried (1988) also contended that Belenky et al.'s theory can be applied in almost all student affairs work settings because the need to understand women's intellectual and emotional development is pervasive. Consequently, the absence of student affairs–related applications in the literature is noteworthy.

Critique and Future Directions

Given the reality that Perry (1968) drew almost exclusively on information from men in presenting his theory, an examination focused exclusively on women can be considered a logical next step. Belenky et al.'s research presents perspectives worthy of examination by higher education personnel. At the same time, aspects of the methodology used pose some limitations. For example, King (1987) has criticized the lack of detail in the discussion of procedures used and the presentation of the data. Also, Evans (1996) has noted that because the study was not conducted longitudinally, the question remains as to whether the perspectives found are in fact sequential and hierarchical.

Perhaps *Women's Ways of Knowing* can be used most constructively as *a* source rather than *the* source of information about women and meaning making. The authors themselves were modest in their own claims. For faculty, a sensitivity to the need for differing instructional methods to facilitate the development of at least some women is a reasonable implication for practice that can be derived from Belenky et al.'s work. Along with a similar understanding to support their role in formal learning environments, student affairs practitioners can benefit from using *Women's Ways of Knowing* as a framework for listening and responding to women in many other interactions.

Baxter Magolda's Model of Epistemological Reflection

Marcia B. Baxter Magolda traced her interest in students' ways of knowing to her graduate school experience. For her dissertation, she sought to create a practical means to assess students' thinking. The manual that resulted received some criticism, according to Baxter Magolda (1992), because her interpretations of over one thousand student essays deviated at times from those of Perry (1968). Informed by both her experiences with her own students and the work of Belenky et al. (1986), Baxter Magolda came to believe that her interpretations were not inaccurate but simply different from Perry's because the voices she heard in the essays were different, particularly the women's voices.

Baxter Magolda (1992) indicated that she was struck by both the gender similarities and differences that emerged from Perry's work on men (1968) and Belenky et al.'s work on women (1986). Kitchener and King's research involving both men and women (1981, 1990) also influenced Baxter Magolda because of the differing conception of the nature of knowledge that emerged. However, because gender was not at the core of Kitchener and King's research, Baxter Magolda believed she had identified an important gap in the research to date: the need to address gender in a study of cognitive development that would include both men and women. From this realization came a longitudinal study involving students from Miami University in Ohio. Naturalistic inquiry and postmodern feminist literature served as additional influences in this undertaking (Baxter Magolda).

The most extensive treatment of Baxter Magolda's work is her book, *Knowing and Reasoning in College: Gender-Related Patterns in Students' Intellectual Development* (1992). Baxter Magolda did not stop there, however, and further reporting has been done (Baxter Magolda, 1995).

Early on, Baxter Magolda (1992) stated, "Understanding college students' intellectual development is at the heart of effective educational practice" (p. 3). By presenting a detailed examination of gender similarities and differences while also devoting half her book to academic and student affairs implications, Baxter Magolda supplied information that both increases this understanding and provides supports for enhancing practice.

The Theory

In *Knowing and Reasoning in College*, Baxter Magolda (1992) presented the results of a five-year longitudinal study of 101 students at Miami University. Interviews began in 1986, during the students' first year, and continued annually through the first year after graduation. Seventy students participated for the entire five-year period. Baxter Magolda reported that the random sample of entering students consisted of fifty-one women and fifty men. Three of the 101 were nonwhite.

Baxter Magolda (1992) identified six guiding assumptions in the development of her model: (1) ways of knowing and patterns within them are socially constructed; (2) ways of knowing can best be understood through the principles of naturalistic inquiry; (3) students' use of reasoning patterns is fluid; (4) patterns are related to, but not dictated by, gender; (5) student stories are context-bound; and (6) ways of knowing are presented as "patterns." *Patterns* refers to Marilyn Frye's belief (1990) that generalization is problematic, given the variations of each individual's experience. Consequently, Baxter Magolda adopted Frye's term *patterns* as a way to "make sense of experience but stop short of characterizing it in static and generalizable ways" (p. 17).

The Epistemological Reflection Model that resulted from Baxter Magolda's research (1992) contains four stages, with gender-related patterns reflected in the first three. In the first stage, *absolute knowing*, knowledge is viewed as certain. Instructors are seen as authorities with the answers, and the purpose of evaluation is to reproduce what the student has learned so that the instructor can determine its accuracy. Two patterns, *receiving knowledge* and *mastering knowledge*, were found in this stage.

Receiving knowledge, a more private approach, was used by more women, and mastering knowledge, a more public approach, was used by more men. Receiving knowledge involves "minimal interaction with instructors, an emphasis on comfort in the learning environment, relationships with peers, and ample opportunities to demonstrate knowledge" (Baxter Magolda, 1992, p. 82). Baxter Magolda noted that one could argue that the voices of receivers are silent. However, she also pointed out that these knowers do have more independent perspectives in their view of knowledge. At the same time, these views, perhaps because of socialization, are not expressed. Audrey, in the scenario at the start of Chapter Eight, may be a receiver; however, she doesn't seem to acknowledge the value of her own perspective. Mastering knowledge is characterized by a verbal approach to learning, a willingness to be critical of instructors, and an expectation of peer and instructor interactions that facilitate the mastery of knowledge. Baxter Magolda stated, "The combination of the certainty of knowledge, the use of logic to arrive at answers, and the view of self as autonomous led to a style of interaction that appeared on the surface to be competitive" (p. 98).

In essence, as Baxter Magolda (1992) observed, receiving pattern and mastery pattern knowers differ in three ways. First, they differ in voice, with mastery pattern knowers attempting to express themselves by imitating authority figures and receiving pattern knowers listening carefully. Second, they vary in identification with authority, with less identification among receivers. Finally, the two groups exhibit different relationships with peers, with collaboration for receivers involving more support and collaboration for mastery knowers involving more mutual challenge.

The second stage, *transitional knowing,* involves an acceptance that some knowledge is uncertain. A realization that authorities are not all-knowing is a turning point from absolute knowing. Transitional knowers expect instructors to go beyond merely supplying information to facilitate an understanding and application of knowledge. A utilitarian perspective motivates students, with investment in learning determined by perceived future usefulness. Evaluation that focuses on understanding is endorsed over that which deals only with acquisition. *Interpersonal knowing* and *impersonal knowing* are the two patterns in this stage.

Interpersonal knowing, used by more women, is characterized by an involvement in learning that includes gathering ideas from others, peer interaction to hear and share ideas, a valuing of rapport with instructors to facilitate self-expression, a preference for evaluation geared to individual differences, and an approach to resolving uncertainty that employs personal judgment. Impersonal knowing, used by more men, involves a desire to be forced to think, a preference for debate as a vehicle for sharing views with instructors and peers, an endorsement of evaluation that is fair and practical, and an approach to resolving uncertainty that uses logic and research.

Baxter Magolda (1992) found that students in both patterns of transitional knowing had developed their voices more fully than in absolute knowing. However, interpersonal knowers separated more from authority, whereas impersonal knowers tended to reflect authority in the expression of their respective voices. Also, whereas relationships are central to the learning process for interpersonal knowers, impersonal knowers value challenge over relationships.

In *independent knowing,* the third stage, knowledge is viewed as mostly uncertain. The preferred role of the instructor shifts to that of providing the context for the exploration of knowledge. Promoting independent thinking and the exchange of opinions in class are valued instructor behaviors. Independent knowers believe that evaluation should reward their thinking and not penalize views that diverge from the instructor or textbook authors. The two patterns found in this stage are *interindividual* and *individual*.

Interindividual knowing, used more by women, contains a dual focus on the value of one's own ideas as well as the ideas of others. Baxter Magolda (1992) stated, "The interindividual pattern has as its defining theme a connection between the knower and others that maintains the integrity of both" (p. 155). Individual knowing, used more by men, also values the interchange with peers and instructors, but more attention is given to the individual's own thinking. Baxter Magolda noted that sometimes listening to others involves an element of struggle for individual knowers. Jerome, a student in the classroom scenario at the beginning of Chapter Eight, would seem to be manifesting some characteristics of individual knowers. He respects his professor, but he especially values the opportunity to develop and refine his own thinking. Although interindividual knowers lean toward connection and individual learners toward separation, Baxter Magolda emphasized that they are moving closer together than in previous ways of knowing.

Contextual knowing, the final stage, reflects a convergence of previous gender-related patterns. Demonstrated only rarely among undergraduate students, contextual knowing involves the belief that the legitimacy of knowledge claims is determined contextually. The individual still constructs a point of view, but the perspective now requires supporting evidence. The role of the instructor now involves the creation of a learning environment that endorses contextual applications of knowledge, discussions that include evaluation of perspectives, and opportunities for mutual critiques by students and instructor. Evaluation that accurately measures competence contextually and that permits the mutual involvement of instructor and student is endorsed. Because only 12 percent of the postgraduation interviews contained indications of contextual knowing, Baxter Magolda (1992) considered the data insufficient to explore gender patterns at the time of the writing of her book.

In a more recent discussion of the postcollege phase of her research, Baxter Magolda (1995) indicated that the relational and impersonal patterns of knowing that characterized the preceding stages become integrated in the stage of contextual knowing. She stated, "When young adults in this study faced the limitations of their pattern of knowing, they learned how to use the alternative and then integrate the two" (p. 215).

Baxter Magolda (1992) emphasized that she found more similarities than differences in men's and women's ways of knowing. In addition, she stressed that variability exists among members of a particular gender. Therefore, patterns are related to, but not dictated by, gender.

In regard to the evolution of the ways of knowing, Baxter Magolda (1992) found that absolute knowing was most prevalent in the first year of college (68 percent). Among sophomores, 53 percent were transitional knowers. Transitional knowing was also the most prevalent mode among both juniors (83 percent) and seniors (80 percent). Independent knowing was most represented in the year following graduation (57 percent).

Quite appropriately, Baxter Magolda (1992) discussed the limitations of her findings for diverse student populations. She noted that her model is based on information supplied by traditionally aged students, typically from white, middle-class families and existing in a student culture where high involvement, academic focus, and tradition are valued. She also recognized that ways of knowing are socially constructed. As a result, she cautioned that the model generated cannot be transferred automatically to other young adults.

Baxter Magolda (1992) did maintain that three underlying story lines "form the foundation of parallels" (p. 191) between her study participants and other young adults. These story lines are the development and emergence of voice, changing relationships with authority, and evolving relationships with peers. She also described two broad contexts in which she believes such parallels might occur. These contexts are dominance-subordination and socialization.

Dominance-subordination is presented as a context in which voice and relationships can be affected. The three story lines can be affected by the following dominant-subordinate relationships: educator and student, objectivist and social constructionist perspectives, and majority and minority parties. Essentially, students who are placed in the subordinate role are less likely to express their own voices. The context of socialization is related to how upbringing can affect voice and relationships. For example, gender-related socialization can encourage the expression of voice for men and the suppression of voice for women, and African American children may be given messages of inferiority. In relation to any other student population, Baxter Magolda (1992) cautioned that "true transferability can only be judged through dialogue with students" (p. 192).

Assessment Techniques

Interviews formed the foundation of Baxter Magolda's research. The protocol for the first-year interview contained nine general questions designed to assess epistemological development by exploring the six domains addressed by Baxter Magolda and Porterfield's Measure of Epistemological Reflection (MER) (1985), described in Chapter Eight. Roles of the learner, instructor, peers, and evaluation in the learning process and decision making were directly addressed; the nature of knowledge was explored only if the student brought up the subject. All the questions were used, Baxter Magolda noted, but the order deviated based on the student's responses.

Modifications to the interview format were made in each following year. Study participants were also asked to complete the MER after the interview (two weeks to three months) to afford an opportunity for them to write about their perspectives and to provide a comparative base for the interviews.

Research

Baxter Magolda's own work represents the primary research done in relation to her model.

Applications

Baxter Magolda (1992) devoted the second half of her book to higher education applications. Both academic and student affairs are addressed as she uses "educational practice" to include both curricular and cocurricular aspects. Four major findings are presented as having implications for educational practice.

First, validating students as knowers is essential to encouraging the development of their voices. Baxter Magolda found this concept to be consistent with other professional literature, including Belenky et al.'s concept of the teacher as midwife (1986). Second, Baxter Magolda (1992) found that "situating learning in the students' own experience legitimizes their knowledge as a foundation for constructing new knowledge" (p. 378). This concept is important because it provides for a linkage between the world of the student and academic knowledge, and it allows for students to be legitimate sources of knowledge. This finding also provides insight regarding why students regard their cocurricular experiences as such important avenues for learning. Baxter Magolda observed that cocurricular involvements place the student's experience in the forefront, thereby legitimizing it as a basis for constructing new knowledge.

Baxter Magolda's third finding is that "defining learning as jointly constructed meaning empowers students to see themselves as constructing knowledge" (1992, p. 380). Her final major point for educational practice is that the relational component in the three previous findings is essential if students are to become empowered to construct knowledge.

Baxter Magolda (1992), however, cautioned that there are issues within higher education that can impede implementation of her findings. Six concerns are discussed: the need for educators to have a better understanding of diverse student populations; the need for educators to understand the impact of context on learning; the importance of studying specific students in specific contexts if an understanding of student development and learning is to be achieved; the need for an encouraging environmental structure if voice is to develop; the perceived conflict between promoting the development of voice and learning content; and the need to address broader educational issues, such as the separation of academic and student affairs, if efforts to promote the development of voice are to succeed.

Baxter Magolda's suggestions (1992) for improving educational practice have at their core the realization that learning is a relational activity and that education is often not relational. She provided many specifics to improve the learning environment, addressing the dimensions of professors' attitudes, professor-student interaction, teaching strategies, classroom structure, evaluation, and knowledge discrepancies. For absolute knowers, she advised: demonstrate helpfulness, provide opportunities for students to know the professor, make the classroom active and relational, and help students understand grading. For transitional knowers, she recommended: relate to and demonstrate care for students, engage in positive interactions with students, get students involved, build in peer involvement, promote thinking rather than memorization, and introduce contradictory views. For independent knowers, she advocated: treat students as equals, establish genuine relationships with students, connect learning to real life, create opportunities for independence, critical thinking and peer collaboration, allow for freedom of expression, and value contradictory views. Finally, for contextual knowers, she suggested: engage in collegial relationships with students, create opportunities for mutual responsibility, look at the big picture, and create opportunities for interdependence.

Baxter Magolda (1992) acknowledged the need for both challenge and support in the development of voice, and she applied Kegan's concepts (1982) of confirmation, contradiction, and continuity in the environment. In this process, confirmation of students' abilities is necessary, as is contradiction of the image of authority (for example, faculty or student affairs practitioners) as omnipotent. Continuity represents the need to persevere with students as they work toward constructing knowledge.

Because many students' most meaningful experiences were cocurricular in nature, confirmation, contradiction, and continuity can play significant roles in this arena as well. Baxter Magolda (1992) synthesized implications for student affairs practitioners from her interviews in the categories of peer relationships, student organizations, living arrangements, internship or employment experiences, educational advising, general campus environment, and international experiences.

For absolute knowers, she emphasized: create opportunities for positive peer interaction and student responsibility, and balance opportunity for responsibility with support. For transitional knowers, she offered: encourage the development of support networks of friends, help students respond to peer influence and learn as much as possible about diversity, promote leadership development, offer opportunities for practical experience, recognize student organizations as a source of friendships and dealing with diversity, and organize living arrangements around themes of responsibility and community. She also recommended: use internships and employment to build human relationship skills and offer practical experience, provide direct experience and stress management assistance to help students make decisions, provide opportunities for self-discipline, and use international and cultural exchange to provide direct encounters with diversity.

For independent knowers, she recommended: support peer interaction that fosters appreciation of diversity, encourage efforts to balance personal needs and others' needs, teach students how to create support networks, validate voice through leadership opportunities, help students process insights gained, use internships and employment to reinforce self-confidence, and use international and cultural exchange to create opportunities for students to evaluate their beliefs. Finally, for contextual knowers, she advised: reinforce peers as a legitimate source of knowledge, provide freedom to exercise choice, reinforce expanding horizons via internships and employment, and create possibilities for freedom and development of voice.

Critique and Future Directions

A primary strength of Baxter Magolda's work is her inclusion of both men and women in her sample, permitting the identification of gender similarities and differences in ways of knowing. Certainly, the restriction of her focus to only students from Miami University and the minimal representation of students of color even within that sample pose limitations in terms of traditional generalizability to other groups of students. Baxter Magolda acknowledged this problem and also provided cautions and suggestions regarding efforts to determine the validity of the information for other students.

Baxter Magolda's work does seem to represent an integration and enhancement of the work of Perry (1968) and Belenky et al. (1986). Her stages bear similarities to Perry's positions, and her patterns reflect Belenky et al.'s concepts of separate and connected knowing. McEwen (1994), however, expressed concern that these earlier works are not acknowledged as fully as they could be.

Devoting so much space to excerpts from student protocols can also be regarded as a strength. Although some readers may argue that this approach provides more detail than they desire, the passages that depict students through their own voices afford ample opportunities for readers to grasp what the different ways of knowing and the patterns within them truly sound like.

Another strength is the substantial attention devoted to implications for educational practice. Concrete "nuts and bolts" suggestions for the classroom and beyond are given considerable treatment. As McEwen (1994) pointed out, however, this discussion would have been strengthened by devoting some attention to gender patterns. Suggestions are made only for the four ways of knowing in general. The implications of the differing patterns in the first three stages are not addressed in relation to improving educational practice.

King and Kitchener's Reflective Judgment Model

In their 1994 book *Developing Reflective Judgment*, King and Kitchener mentioned that they had begun their work more than fifteen years before, initiating it in a graduate seminar conducted by Clyde Parker at the University of Minnesota. The authors cited several influences in the development of their model: the individuals whom they interviewed about epistemic assumptions, their interest in understanding the process of and rationale for the evolution of different forms of reasoning from the perspective of other theorists, and their efforts to identify the differences between their own and other approaches.

Dewey's conceptualizations (1933, 1938/1960) related to reflective thinking and Piaget's assumptions (1956/1973) about stage-related development were both influential in King and Kitchener's work, as was Kohlberg's work (1969) on cognitive and moral development. Their model also builds on previous theories developed by Perry (1968); Broughton (1975); Harvey, Hunt, and Schroder (1961); and Loevinger (1976).

Central to King and Kitchener's model is the observation that "people's assumptions about what and how something can be known provide a lens that shapes how individuals frame a problem and how they justify their beliefs about it in the face of uncertainty" (1994, p. xvi). The authors indicated a desire to have their work reach a broad audience since their research, originally focused on college students, has applicability for populations spanning the period from late childhood through adulthood.

The need for King and Kitchener's work is evident in their reference in the title of the first chapter to reflective judgment as "a neglected facet of critical thinking" (1994, p. 1). Furthermore, they asserted, "one of the most important responsibilities educators have is helping students learn to make defensible judgments about vexing problems" (p. 1).

The Theory

The Reflective Judgment Model (RJM) was developed by King and Kitchener to respond to the question, "How do people decide what they believe about vexing problems?" (1994, p. 2). King and Kitchener adopted Dewey's notion (1933,

1938/1960) that reflective judgments are made to bring closure to situations that can be characterized as "uncertain," where there is uncertainty about a solution. They distinguished between reflective thinking and critical thinking on the basis of reflective thinking's emphasis on epistemological assumptions and ill-structured problems. Problem structure refers to how completely a problem can be described and to the degree of certainty with which a solution can be considered correct. Well-structured problems have single correct answers that are ultimately available. "Ill-structured problems cannot be described with a high degree of certainty" (p. 10). King and Kitchener cited overpopulation, hunger, pollution, and inflation as examples of ill-structured problems. The RJM therefore describes "the development of epistemic cognition," or "a developmental progression that occurs between childhood and adulthood in the ways that people understand the process of knowing and in the corresponding ways that they justify their beliefs about ill-structured problems" (p. 13).

Seven stages characterize the RJM. Each stage represents a distinct set of assumptions about knowledge and the process of acquiring knowledge, and each set of assumptions results in a different strategy for solving ill-structured problems. Increasingly advanced stages signify increasing complexity. The seven stages may be clustered into the categories of prereflective thinking (Stages 1, 2, and 3), quasi-reflective thinking (Stages 4 and 5), and reflective thinking (Stages 6 and 7).

Prereflective thinkers do not acknowledge or possibly even realize that knowledge is uncertain. Consequently, these individuals don't recognize the existence of real problems that lack an absolute correct answer. They also don't use evidence in reasoning toward a conclusion. *Quasi-reflective thinkers* realize that ill-structured problems exist and that knowledge claims about such problems include uncertainty. Consequently, quasi-reflective thinkers can identify some issues as genuinely problematic. At the same time, though they use evidence, they have difficulty drawing reasoned conclusions and justifying their beliefs. *Reflective thinkers* maintain that knowledge must be actively constructed and that claims of knowledge must be viewed in relation to the context in which they were generated. Reflective thinkers maintain that judgments must be based on relevant data and conclusions should be open to reevaluation.

If the students in the classroom scenario in Chapter Eight were asked to reason about ill-structured problems, it can be conjectured that Audrey might display prereflective thinking, Jordan quasi-reflective thinking, and Jerome reflective thinking. Audrey places great faith in the knowledge of experts, such as her instructor. She may not recognize the existence of uncertainty, and her ability to construct her own argument using evidence seems limited. Jordan seems to have the potential to recognize that uncertainty exists. At the same time, he appears to have difficulty using evidence effectively to justify his beliefs. Jerome demonstrates an understanding and valuing of the need to use evidence well in constructing arguments.

Stages within the RJM are presented as qualitatively different and as building on the skills of previous stages while also providing the groundwork for the increasing complexity of subsequent stages. King and Kitchener (1994) provided capsule summaries of the views of knowledge and concepts of justification that characterize each stage of their developmental model, along with a representative quote for each.

For *Stage 1*, knowledge is absolute and can be secured by observation, and beliefs require no justification because truth and what is believed are identical. "I know what I have seen" (King & Kitchener, 1994, p. 14). In *Stage 2*, knowledge is certain but may not be immediately accessible. Knowledge may be obtained through the senses or from authority figures. Beliefs are either unjustified or justified by their adherence to those of an authority figure. "If it is on the news, it has to be true" (p. 14). Knowledge is certain or temporarily uncertain in *Stage 3*. Knowledge comes from authorities, and when knowledge is temporarily uncertain, personal beliefs are legitimate. When certainty exists, beliefs are justified by their consistency with those of authorities, and personal opinions may serve as justification when uncertainty is present. "When there is evidence that people can give to convince everybody one way or another, then it will be knowledge; until then, it's just a guess" (p. 14).

In *Stage 4*, the first manifesting quasi-reflective thinking, knowledge is uncertain. Knowledge claims are considered idiosyncratic to the individual because situational variables (such as lost data) dictate that knowing always contains some ambiguity. Justification involves reasoning and evidence; however, idiosyncratic tendencies are evident in the selection of evidence to support the belief. "I'd be more inclined to believe evolution if they had proof. It's just like the pyramids: I don't think we'll ever know. Who are you going to ask? No one was there" (King & Kitchener, 1994, p. 15). For *Stage 5*, knowledge is contextual and subjective since only interpretations of evidence, events, or issues may be known. Justification involves context-specific interpretations of evidence. "People think differently and so they attack the problem differently. Other theories could be as true as my own, but based on different evidence" (p. 15).

Stage 6, the beginning of reflective thinking, contains a view of knowledge as constructed into individual conclusions about ill-structured problems. Interpretations involve evaluation across contexts and evaluation of the opinions of reputable others. Justification involves a comparison of evidence and opinion across different contexts and the construction of solutions based on weight of the evidence, utility, or need for action. "It's very difficult in this life to be sure. There are degrees of sureness. You come to a point at which you are sure enough for a personal stance on the issue" (King & Kitchener, 1994, p. 15). Finally, in *Stage 7*, knowledge results from a process of reasonable inquiry involving construction of solutions to ill-structured problems. Solutions are evaluated for adequacy based on what is reasonable, considering current evidence, and these solutions are subject to reevaluation, should new evidence become available. Justification involves a consideration of probability in light of weight of evidence, explanatory value of interpretations, risk of erroneous conclusions, and consequences of alternative judgments. "One can judge an argument by how well thought out the positions are, what kinds of reasoning and evidence are used to support it, and how consistent the way one argues on this topic is as compared with other topics" (p. 16).

King and Kitchener (1994) pointed out that their model of "a developmental progression in people's assumptions about how and what they can know" (p. 20) provides some evidence of epistemological positions beyond relativism. Examples of such reasoning were found in some interviews with graduate students and college faculty.

Assessment Techniques

The Reflective Judgment Interview (RJI), designed to gather information about individuals' assumptions about knowledge and how it is obtained, was used to conduct King and Kitchener's research on the Reflective Judgment Model. The authors indicate that to elicit ratable data, the RJI consists of four ill-structured problems and a standard set of follow-up questions. The four standard problems use these issues: "how the Egyptian pyramids were built," "the objectivity of news reporting," "how human beings were created," and "the safety of chemical additives in food" (King & Kitchener, 1994, p. 100). The authors indicated that a fifth problem concerning the disposal of nuclear waste has also been used in more recent research. King and Kitchener clarified that the intent in the original choice of problems was to focus on how people reason about intellectual issues. Consequently, ill-structured problems concerning moral, social, and identity issues were not included. Each problem included is defined by two contradictory points of view.

The interview is characterized by a semistructured format and is designed to be conducted by a trained interviewer. After a standard introductory statement, problems are read and interviewees are asked to explain and justify their own points of view on the issues and then respond, after each, to the six follow-up questions. Examples of follow-up questions are "How did you come to hold that point of view?" and "Can you ever be sure that your position on this issue is correct? How or why not?" If any responses to the six questions are incomplete or ambiguous, the interviewer is instructed to ask for clarification.

King and Kitchener (1994) emphasized that the standard RJI does not measure an individual's optimal level of performance, where the opportunity is provided to think extensively and develop careful explanations of one's views, but instead elicits how the individual would typically reason about the issue, in a situation where thinking, expressing, explaining, and defending must be done quickly.

Masked responses to each problem were independently rated by two certified raters. Responses to each of the six follow-up questions were also rated. Scores for each transcript were eventually summarized into a three-digit code, which represents stages used in the ratings. For example, if among the seven scores possible for each problem, five of the seven ratings were at Stage 3 and two were at Stage 4, the rating would be 3–3–4 (King & Kitchener, 1994).

King and Kitchener (1994) reported several kinds of reliability data for the RJI. They indicated that interrater reliability coefficients have averaged in the high .70s, test-retest reliability has been found to be acceptable (.71), and internal consistency coefficients were typically in the high .70s to mid-.80s. King and Kitchener concluded that the RJI is a reliable instrument that is suitable for decision making about groups; however, they advised caution in relation to potential use in individual decision making such as counseling and advising.

Information related to validity is implicit in the process of development of the RJM that King and Kitchener (1994) described. They explained that they have used what is called a "bootstrapping method" (p. 46) by "using theoretical accounts of the nature and development of reasoning to understand and interpret the way people solve ill-structured problems, and then using these natural accounts to revise the theory" (p. 46). To construct the stage descriptions of the RJM, King and Kitchener indicated that they began by examining the scoring rules describing Perry's positions (1968) as developed by Knefelkamp (1974) and Widick (1975), omitting those related to addressing ethical and identity concerns and revising the remainder, in keeping with their belief that there were "structural and epistemic aspects that superseded relativism" (p. 46). They used the work of other theorists such as Popper (1969), Dewey (1933, 1938/1960), and Harvey, Hunt, and Schroder (1961) in formulating Stages 6 and 7. After pilot testing, scoring rules were revised. In 1985, the scoring system was again revised after examination of extensive longitudinal data.

Research

King and Kitchener (1994) indicated that more than seventeen hundred people, representing varied student and nonstudent subgroups, had participated in Reflective Judgment Interviews at the time of their writing. Much research on the RJM has been conducted by King and Kitchener and others. These studies are described in the 1994 book.

King and Kitchener (1994) conducted a ten-year longitudinal study, which involved eighty participants, from 1977 to 1987. These participants ranged in age from sixteen to twenty-eight at first testing. Focusing on whether the ability to make reflective judgments develops over time, this study provided an opportunity to examine whether involvement in higher education contributes to higher levels of reflective judgment.

The sample contained twenty high school juniors, forty college juniors, and twenty third-year doctoral students. The high school and college groups were matched to the graduate sample by gender (half male, half female) and by academic aptitude. The authors hypothesized that different ways of reasoning, as represented by the RJM, should be evident with these individuals based on their range of educational levels. If no differences were found, by contrast, the RJM or its measurement (or both) would be called into question. Testing was conducted in 1977, 1979, 1983, and 1987, at which time 70 percent of the original sample participated. Several measures, including the RJI, were administered, with some variations from testing to testing.

King and Kitchener (1994), in examining group scores, concluded that "these patterns suggest that the development of reflective thinking as measured by the RJI evolves slowly and steadily over time among individuals engaged in educational programs" (p. 132). For individuals, they reported, "this pervasive pattern of upward change in RJI scores over the ten years of this longitudinal study shows that the vast majority of the individuals who participated in the study improved in their ability to make reflective judgments over time" (p. 137). The researchers also found that individuals do demonstrate reasoning that is characteristic of more than one stage of the RJM at a time. For example, an individual who typically approaches problems with Stage 4 assumptions, such as "opinions can't be evaluated," may also present a carefully balanced perspective, characteristic of Stage 5 reasoning. King and Kitchener noted that the fact that people commonly use multiple ways of reasoning can give educators a framework for understanding variability within their individual students. Relatedly, they suggested that educational interventions should be geared to the leading edge of development rather than to the central tendency.

Some evidence of gender differences was found in both the 1983 and 1987 testings. King and Kitchener (1994) suggested that the differences in educational achievement of the men and the women in the sample may have contributed to the differences in RJI scores (favoring the men). The researchers also identified a strong linear relationship between age and RJM stage. However, they cautioned that the role of age should not be overstated because members of the sample were actively involved in educational pursuits during the study's time period, demonstrated a high level of scholastic aptitude, and hence are not representative of the general adult population.

King and Kitchener (1994) offered several cautions related to their longitudinal study. Regarding the sample, participants were restricted to white adolescents and adults from the upper Midwest, and the students involved possessed unusually high academic aptitude scores. At the same time, King and Kitchener concluded that there was strong evidence to support the development of reflective thinking and that the observed changes in reasoning were consistent with the RJM. The ability to think reflectively was found to develop in a sequential fashion (rather than to emerge fully formed), and earlier stages both build on prior stages and provide a foundation for subsequent stages. Finally, King and Kitchener maintained that this study also raised new questions about the development of college-educated adults, including the influence of age, the role of specific collegiate experiences, and the effects of other life experiences on reflective thinking.

King and Kitchener (1994) also reported on six other longitudinal studies that encompassed twelve different samples totaling 241 people, most of whom were tested twice at intervals ranging from three or four months to four years. Findings from these studies provided additional evidence that reflective judgment develops slowly and steadily over time and that increases in scores are not an artifact of practice or selective participation.

Results of cross-sectional studies are also reported by King and Kitchener (1994). High school students, traditional-aged college students, nontraditional-aged college students, graduate students, and nonstudent adults are all represented in these studies. Key findings include that RJI scores increase slowly but steadily from high school to college to graduate school; average RJI score was higher for adults with a college degree than for those without a degree; adult learners were not dramatically different from younger students in their reflective thinking; and freshmen demonstrated reasoning reflective of Stages 3 and 4 of the RJM, while for seniors, Stage 4 thinking was prevalent.

Fourteen studies supplied information related to gender differences, with seven reporting that no differences were found. Of the seven that reported finding differences based on gender, six indicated that males scored higher; the other found a class-by-gender interaction, with female traditional-aged juniors and nontraditional-aged freshmen scoring higher than their male counterparts. King and Kitchener (1994) noted that the findings suggest that men and women may develop at different rates and that these rates may be different between cohorts of women and men. Data also suggest that differences in timing may characterize developmental changes in men and women. King and Kitchener called for more research in this area.

One cross-cultural study involving the RJI was reported by King and Kitchener (1994). Using a German sample, this study provided preliminary evidence of "the cross-national applicability" (p. 179) of the RJM.

In their summary of the research reported in their book, King and Kitchener (1994) noted the following general findings: "people who are engaged in educational activities tend to improve in their reasoning about ill-structured problems";

"development typically follows the stage-related patterns described by the Reflective Judgment Model"; and "being in an educational setting seems to facilitate development" (p. 187).

Applications

King and Kitchener (1994) asserted, "Teaching students to engage in reflective thinking and to make reflective judgments about vexing problems is a central goal of higher education" (p. 222). They offered suggestions to support the efforts of both faculty and student affairs practitioners and identified seven assumptions that underlie these suggestions: individuals actively interpret and attempt to make sense of what they experience; how individuals interpret events is affected by their epistemic assumptions; people's ways of making meaning develop over time; individuals function within a "developmental range" of stages; interactions with the environment strongly affect an individual's development; development is stimulated when an individual's experiences do not match his or her expectations; and development in reflective thinking occurs within the context of the individual's background, previous educational experiences, and current life situation.

In offering their suggestions, King and Kitchener (1994) emphasized that their intent is to share observations rather than advocate a single best method for teaching reflective thinking. Eleven primary suggestions were discussed. First, they recommended showing respect for students as people regardless of the developmental levels that they may be demonstrating. They noted the importance of emotional acceptance to students' ability to be receptive to feedback and to take risks. Second, they stressed the importance of understanding that students differ in regard to their epistemic assumptions. In turn, responding to individual differences is important for educators working both inside and outside the classroom. King and Kitchener offered several examples from student affairs settings of how educational strategies can be selected to match students' assumptions about knowledge. For example, understanding these concepts can be helpful when advising student groups. Advisers can help group members understand that differences in points of view can occur for legitimate reasons rather than only because individuals deliberately bias information, as Stage 4 thinkers are likely to believe. Advisers can encourage members to share the details of the reasons for their perspectives and also have members generate reasons for and against alternatives when controversial decisions must be made.

Their third recommendation was that educators familiarize students with ill-structured problems in their own disciplines or areas of expertise. They maintained that ill-structured problems should be viewed as essential aspects of undergraduate education. Fourth is the suggestion that multiple opportunities for students to examine different points of view on a topic be created so that students can practice paying attention to the evidence used and emphasized in various perspectives. Fifth, opportunities should be created and encouragement provided for students to make judgments and explain what they believe. Sixth, educators are advised to informally assess students' assumptions about knowledge and how beliefs should be justified.

Next educators should acknowledge that students work within a developmental range of stages and target expectations and goals accordingly. Educators are reminded that assessments are affected by the context of the assessment, and they should therefore rely on multiple measures rather than a single measure. In addition, King and Kitchener recommended that educators provide multiple examples in which higher-level reasoning skills are used so that students can receive feedback and encouragement to practice higher-level skills. In relation to targeting educational efforts, educators are advised to aim at both functional and optimal levels of students' reasoning.

The eighth and ninth suggestions are related. Educators should provide both challenge and support in interacting with students, and challenge and support can be grounded emotionally as well as cognitively. Appropriate challenges and supports differ with students' developmental levels. For example, King and Kitchener (1994) noted that students using Stage 3 reasoning, who believe that points of view are arbitrarily selected, would find it easy to defend a point of view different from their own. A challenging task would be for these students to have to create an argument based on evidence.

The tenth recommendation is that educators be aware of which skills are required for various activities and assignments. The final suggestion is that a climate that promotes thoughtful analysis of issues throughout the campus be fostered. To aid in facilitating processes supportive of promoting reflective thinking, King and Kitchener (1994) provided exhibits for Stages 2 through 6 that describe characteristic assumptions of each stage, sample instructional goals, examples of difficult tasks for individuals at this stage, sample assignments (challenges) to stimulate development, and supportive activities that would complement the challenges in the process of trying to achieve the instructional goals.

For example, for Stage 2, a characteristic assumption would be that knowledge is certain but some people do not have access to it. A sample instructional goal would be for students to accept that several opinions may exist about a controversial issue, none of which is known to be absolutely correct. A difficult task would be recognizing the existence of legitimate differences of opinion about some issues, and a sample developmental assignment would be considering two interpretations of a historical event. A support would be to legitimize students' feelings of anxiety when confronting multiple perspectives on an issue.

For Stage 5, a characteristic assumption is that beliefs may be justified only within a given context or from a given perspective, and an instructional goal would be learning to relate alternative perspectives on an issue to each other by comparing and contrasting them and evaluating their strengths and weaknesses. A difficult task would be recognizing that choosing one alternative doesn't deny the legitimacy of other alternatives. A sample developmental assignment would be comparing and contrasting two competing and unequal points of view, citing and evaluating evidence and arguments used by proponents of each, and determining which proponent makes the better interpretation of the given evidence and which conclusion is stronger. A support would be to legitimize students' struggle, both cognitively and affectively in adjudicating between competing perspectives.

The student programming board scenario at the beginning of Chapter Eight represents an example of a situation in which a potentially controversial decision must be made. Some students seem to be displaying prereflective thinking by not recognizing uncertainty in relation to the issue of using programming funds to support a special orientation for students of color (for example, "what's right is right, and what's wrong is wrong"). Miriam, as the adviser to the group, could challenge the group by asking board members to supplement their opinions with related rationales and evidence, where possible. At the same time, emotional support could be provided by acknowledging the difficulty and struggle that can accompany the process of trying to understand, present, and evaluate differing views on the issue.

Critique and Future Directions

King and Kitchener have invested a great deal of thought and care in the development of the RJM and the research surrounding it. The culmination of their work, the 1994 book, is well crafted. Although this volume may provide more detail than some readers have an interest in reviewing, the information that elucidates the model, its influences, and its implications for practice is readily available. The chapter devoted to how educational practice in the classroom and beyond can foster reflective judgment is an important ingredient in promoting theory-to-practice connections. At least a fundamental understanding of prereflective, quasi-reflective, and reflective thinking, along with a grasp of how to challenge and support students demonstrating such processes, would have value for both faculty and student affairs practitioners.

As Liddell (1995) noted, the issue of gender differences and the RJM merits further attention. Based on the research providing information along gender lines, Liddell raised the possibility of qualitative differences related to gender and called for further exploration. Her suggestion deserves serious consideration. Research exploring possible relationships between race and ethnicity and reflective judgment could also be valuable.

CHAPTER TEN

KOHLBERG'S THEORY OF MORAL DEVELOPMENT

Dave is a resident assistant on a floor of fifty-five men in a large residence hall housing mainly first- and second-year students. He has called a floor meeting because of several instances of vandalism and harassment targeted at the residents of Room 206, whom other men on the floor assume to be gay. Dave is committed to creating a positive community for all the residents of his floor and hopes that a discussion of the situation will help the men see that their actions of intolerance are hurting everyone. He would like the floor residents to establish a floor policy regarding civility and fair treatment of all residents. He proposes the development of such a policy and asks for reactions. Mark, a first-year resident, protests. "What's in it for me?" he asks. Jim, also a first-year student, is part of the group that has been harassing Randy and Michael, the residents of Room 206. Jim has nothing against them personally, but he wants to get in good with two upperclass students, Bob and Jeff, who think it is cool to give "the fags" a hard time. When asked for his opinion, Jim just shrugs and says that he will go along with whatever the other guys want. A few of the men want to know if the university has a specific policy about civility to which they are supposed to adhere. Dave admits that there is no formal policy on this issue but stresses that as a floor, they can adopt such a policy for themselves. The men look at him blankly; they just don't "get it." Dave is discouraged and frustrated at his inability to reach these guys.

The situation Dave is trying to address is a moral dilemma, an issue in which values conflict. In this case, the right of Randy and Michael, the residents of Room 206, to live in an environment free from fear and harassment conflicts with the rights of the other residents to free speech. Many such dilemmas exist on college campuses. As a result, the college environment serves as an excellent laboratory for moral development, the focus of the theory presented by Lawrence Kohlberg and his associates.

Kohlberg's theory is confined to an examination of moral reasoning, the cognitive component of moral behavior. James Rest (1986b) stressed that moral behavior consists of three additional components: *moral sensitivity,* interpreting a situation involving the welfare of another as a moral problem and identifying possible alternatives; *moral motivation,* deciding to follow the moral path; and *moral action,* implementing and carrying out a moral plan. Rest asserted that to understand moral behavior more completely, each component and the interactions among the components must be investigated. Rest and his colleagues are pursuing such a research program (see Rest, 1986b).

Kohlberg and Candee (1984) argued, however, that moral reasoning is the most important determinant of moral behavior and cited research to back up their claim. Other reviews of research have verified the correlation between moral judgment and moral action (Blasi, 1980; Rest, 1986b). Since encouraging moral behavior is an important developmental goal of higher education (Evans, 1987), understanding and being able to facilitate the development of moral reasoning is an important first step. In this chapter we will review the work of Lawrence Kohlberg and his colleagues as well as that of James Rest and his associates. Rest has developed a modified theory of moral development based on Kohlberg's ideas.

Historical Overview

Kohlberg's involvement with the study of moral development began with his dissertation research at the University of Chicago. In this study, Kohlberg (1958) examined the moral reasoning of adolescent boys, using the assumptions and methodology from Piaget's investigation of the moral development of children (1932/1977).

The data Kohlberg obtained convinced him, as Piaget (1932/1977) had argued, that the reasoning children used proceeded through invariant and qualitatively different stages. In addition to the three stages of thinking Piaget had found in young children, Kohlberg (1958) identified three more advanced stages among his adolescent boys. He also revised the definitions of the three earlier stages identified by Piaget.

Kohlberg and his colleagues next embarked on a series of studies to validate his theory, focusing on establishing that the content and sequence of his stages could be identified in other cultures (Kohlberg, 1979) and on demonstrating the hierarchical arrangement of stages (Rest, 1969). This validation research served as the basis for the first comprehensive statement of Kohlberg's approach to moral reasoning (Kohlberg, 1969).

Kohlberg and his colleagues next began investigating the utility of the theory for designing moral education programs in schools. His visionary statement on this topic (Kohlberg, 1971) led to the establishment of the Center for Moral Education at Harvard (Kohlberg).

Anomalies in stage sequence found in the longitudinal study of Kohlberg's dissertation sample (Kohlberg & Kramer, 1969) led to a reexamination of the stage definitions and the method of measuring and rating stages (Kohlberg, 1979). At the same time, Rest (1979b) developed an objective measure of moral development (the Defining Issues Test) based on a modification of Kohlberg's theory and began a significant program of research at the University of Minnesota. Distinctions between the two approaches will be addressed later in this chapter.

Kohlberg's later writing focused on responding to critics and modifying his theory on the basis of new research data, including analysis of his twenty–year longitudinal sample (Colby, Kohlberg, Gibbs, & Lieberman, 1983). Kohlberg died in 1987; his theory continues to generate substantial interest and research activity.

Moral Development Theory

Kohlberg's theory is cognitive-developmental, in the tradition of Piaget. His work focused specifically on how people make moral judgments. He saw such judgments as having three qualities: an emphasis on value rather than fact, an effect on a person or persons, and a requirement that an action be taken (Colby, Kohlberg, & Kauffman, 1987b).

Kohlberg viewed moral development as more than gaining increased knowledge of culturally defined values. Rather, he saw moral development as representing "the transformations that occur in a person's form or structure of thought" (Kohlberg & Hersh, 1977, p. 54) with regard to what is viewed as right or necessary. Kohlberg (1972) stated that "the principle central to the development of moral judgment . . . is that of *justice.* Justice, the primary regard for the value and equality of all human beings, and for reciprocity in human relations, is a basic and human standard" (p. 14).

Kohlberg's Stages of Moral Reasoning

At the core of Kohlberg's theory is the claim that moral reasoning develops through a six-stage sequence grouped into three levels (Kohlberg, 1976). Each level is defined by its sociomoral perspective, "the point of view the individual takes in defining both social facts and sociomoral values, or oughts" (p. 33).

Kohlberg suggested that each level represented a different relationship between the self and society's rules and expectations. At Level I (preconventional), individuals have not yet come to understand societal rules and expectations; their perspective is concrete and individually focused. In the scenario at the start of this chapter, Mark's response, "What's in it for me?" is typical of individuals at this level who cannot see beyond their own needs and concerns. Level II (conventional) is called the "member-of-society" perspective. At this level, individuals identify with the rules and expectations of others, especially those of authorities. In our example, Jim, who looks to upperclass students for direction, and the men who want to know about the university policy can be considered conventional reasoners. Level III (postconventional or principled) is labeled the "prior-to-society" perspective. At this level, individuals separate themselves from the rules and expectations of others and base their decisions on self-chosen principles. Our RA, Dave, who wants the floor to establish its own rules based on the principles of equity and fair treatment, is functioning at a postconventional level.

The moral stages outlined by Kohlberg center on judgments of rightness and obligation (Colby et al., 1987b). Kohlberg's stages are defined in the following manner (Colby et al.; Kohlberg, 1976):

Level I: Preconventional. Level I has two stages.

Stage 1: Heteronomous Morality. At this stage, what is right is defined as obeying rules so as not to be punished and refraining from physical harm to persons and property. Individuals justify actions based on avoidance of punishment and the superior power of authorities. They do not consider the rights or concerns of others.

Stage 2: Individualistic, Instrumental Morality. Individuals at this stage follow rules if it is in their interest to do so. They understand that other people have needs and interests that may conflict with their own, so right is defined by what is fair, an equal exchange, or an agreement. They maintain a pragmatic perspective, that of assuring satisfaction of their own needs and wants while minimizing the possibility of negative consequences to themselves.

Level II: Conventional. Level II also has two stages.

Stage 3: Interpersonally Normative Morality. At this stage, right is defined as living up to the expectations of those to whom one is close and carrying out one's social roles (for example, son or friend) in an acceptable way. Concern centers around maintaining one's image as a "good person" and gaining the approval of others. Shared feelings, agreements, and expectations take precedence over individual interests, but a generalized social system perspective does not yet exist.

Stage 4: Social System Morality. Individuals at this stage view the social system as made up of a consistent set of rules and procedures that apply equally to all people. Right is defined as upholding the laws established by society and carrying out the duties to which one has agreed. One does what is right to maintain the system and to fulfill one's obligations.

Level III: Postconventional or Principled. Two stages make up Level III as well.

Stage 5: Human Rights and Social Welfare Morality. At this stage, the rightness of laws and social systems are evaluated on the basis of the extent to which they promote fundamental human rights and values. The social system is understood as a social contract into which individuals freely enter in order to protect rights and ensure the welfare of all people. Moral obligations and social relationships are based on making agreements and being able to depend on them.

Stage 6: Morality of Universalizable, Reversible, and Prescriptive General Ethical Principles. Morality at this final stage involves equal consideration of the points of view of all individuals involved in a moral situation. Decisions are based on universal generalizable principles that apply in all situations—for example, the equality of human rights or care and responsibility for others. The process by which a contract is made is viewed as equally important with the fairness of the procedures that underlie the agreement.

In Kohlberg's later writing (Kohlberg, Levine, & Hewer, 1984a), he indicated that he had not yet been successful in empirically demonstrating the existence of Stage 6 since none of the participants in his longitudinal studies had attained this stage. He maintained, however, that it is a philosophical and theoretical stage necessary to bring his theory to a logical end point. Kohlberg and colleagues noted that the writings on which Kohlberg based his theoretical definition of Stage 6 were drawn from a small sample of individuals, including Martin Luther King Jr., who had formal training in philosophy and who demonstrated a commitment to moral leadership.

Kohlberg et al. (1984a) also identified substages (labeled A and B) within each stage and included them in the final scoring system (Colby, Kohlberg, Speicher, et al., 1987). Substage A reflects a heteronomous orientation (concern for obedience to authority), while Substage B indicates an autonomous orientation (concern for rights and welfare). Kohlberg and Candee (1984) demonstrated that individuals using Substage B reasoning were more likely to engage in moral action than individuals using Substage A reasoning.

Characteristics of Kohlberg's Stages

Kohlberg (1981a) claimed that his stages represented "holistic structures that develop in an invariant sequence and constitute a hierarchy" (Walker, 1988, p. 38). These qualities constitute what Kohlberg et al. (1984a) labeled a "hard" stage model.

Walker (1988) viewed the *structure criterion* as the most fundamental of these three characteristics. Based on this criterion, individuals will be consistent in their thinking. At a given stage, they will exhibit a similar reasoning pattern regardless of the content or situation being discussed. For instance, Mark, the person in the opening scenario who wanted to know how establishing a policy on civility would benefit him, would be expected to approach other situations from this perspective as well.

The *sequence criterion* (see Walker, 1988) indicates that stages will appear in a specific order, regardless of setting or experience. Not all individuals will advance through all stages, nor will they move through the stages at the same rate. However, the sequence of stages is fixed.

Though the men in our residence hall example are at different stages of development, they can be expected to move through the stages in the same order and sequentially. For example, Mark, who is now in Stage 2, will move on to Stage 3 given appropriate challenges to his thinking (a topic to be discussed later in the chapter). Jim, at Stage 3, can be expected to move to Stage 4, and on so.

The final stage characteristic, Walker (1988) noted, is the *hierarchy criterion*. This criterion states that each successive stage is more highly developed than the previous one because it incorporates aspects of all of the earlier stages. Individuals will understand and be able to use all stages of thinking below the stage at which they are currently functioning. However, they will not exhibit reasoning at higher stages. For instance, Jim, at Stage 3, would be able to use Mark's Stage 2 reasoning process but not Dave's Stage 5 reasoning.

Rest's Modifications of Kohlberg's Moral Development Model

The core aspects of Rest's moral development stages are borrowed directly from Kohlberg. Rest (1979a) examined two elements in a person's thinking: how expectations about actions (rules) are known and shared and how interests are balanced. He identified the following central concepts for determining moral rights and responsibilities at each stage of moral judgment (pp. 22–23):

Stage 1: Obedience ("Do what you're told.")

Stage 2: Instrumental egoism and simple exchange ("Let's make a deal.")

Stage 3: Interpersonal concordance ("Be considerate, nice, and kind, and you'll get along with people.")

Stage 4: Law and duty to the social order ("Everyone in society is obligated and protected by the law.")

Stage 5: Societal consensus ("You are obligated by whatever arrangements are agreed to by due process procedures.")

Stage 6: Nonarbitrary social cooperation ("How rational and impartial people would organize cooperation is moral.")

Unlike Kohlberg, Rest does not include substages. In addition, his definition of Stage 6 is broader, including reasoning that views the "bases of moral obligation as following from a logical analysis of the requirements of cooperation" (p. 46).

Several other theoretical differences exist between the two approaches. First, Rest (1979a) questioned whether content and structure can be totally separated in moral reasoning, which Kohlberg (1976) advocated. Rest focused on the kind of consideration the individual uses in making a decision, noting that both content and structural elements might be included. He did not assume that the same considerations would be addressed at each stage.

Rest (1979a) rejected Kohlberg's hard stage model and proposed a more complex alternative. He suggested that it is more appropriate to consider what percentage of an individual's reasoning is at a particular stage of development rather than whether a person is "in" a particular stage. He also rejected the idea of step-by-step development through the stages. Rest believes that a person may use or show forward movement in several stages at the same time. Based on his conception of development as a continuous process, Rest and his followers investigate the percentage of thinking an individual demonstrates at each stage rather than labeling a person as "in" the stage at which most of his or her thinking occurs. For instance, they might note that 20 percent of a person's thinking was at Stage 3, 50 percent was at Stage 4, and 30 percent was at Stage 5. They are most concerned with the percentage of thinking at the principled level (Stages 5 and 6).

Prerequisites for Moral Development

Kohlberg (1976) stated that two other domains of cognition are related to moral reasoning: the more general cognitive structures outlined by Piaget (1947/1950) and social perspective taking. Selman (1980) defined perspective taking as the ability to put oneself in another person's place and to understand what he or she is thinking. Kohlberg (1976) hypothesized that perspective taking mediated between cognitive and moral development. Walker's research (1980) supported this hypothesis, demonstrating that both cognitive development and development of perspective taking are necessary, but not sufficient, conditions for moral development. That is, growth in these two domains, while not guaranteeing moral development, appears to create "a state of readiness" for such development (Walker, 1988, p. 53).

Conditions Facilitating Moral Development

Two factors appear to contribute to moral development: exposure to higher-stage thinking and disequilibrium (Walker, 1988). Earlier statements focusing on moral education (for example, Kohlberg, 1972) promoted the use of reasoning one stage above the thinking exhibited by the individual (plus-one reasoning) to enhance development. Theoretically, reasoning more advanced than plus-one would be incomprehensible to the person and therefore have no impact. Based on his review of existing research, however, Walker noted that exposure to thinking at any stage higher than that presented by an individual is sufficient to facilitate development. The kind of discussions that our RA, Dave, held with men on his floor would provide this kind of exposure.

Disequilibrium, or cognitive conflict, occurs when individuals face situations that arouse internal contradictions in their moral reasoning structures or when they find that their reasoning is different from that of significant others (Kohlberg, 1976). Walker (1983), along with other researchers (see Walker, 1988, for a review), has demonstrated that exposure to conflict in both opinions and reasoning leads to moral development. Haan (1985), in a study of university students living in residence halls, found that conflict resulting from exposure to real-life issues, rather than hypothetical situations, was particularly effective in facilitating moral development. The situation before the men on Dave's hall with regard to civility would provide the kind of cognitive conflict that could lead to development of moral reasoning.

Assessment Techniques

Two major instruments exist for measuring moral reasoning: Kohlberg's Moral Judgment Interview (MJI) (Colby et al., 1987) and Rest's Defining Issues Test (DIT) (Rest, 1986a). There are three parallel forms (A, B, and C) of Kohlberg's MJI, each of which has a structured interview format (Colby et al., 1987b). Each version features three hypothetical dilemmas followed by nine to twelve standard probe questions designed to elicit a clear picture (through justification, clarification, and elaboration) of the interviewee's moral reasoning. Two moral issues are in conflict in each dilemma. For instance, the value of preserving life and the value of upholding the law conflict in the famous Heinz dilemma, in which a husband must decide whether to steal a drug to save his wife's life when the druggist is charging more for the drug than the husband can pay. Other conflicts include conscience versus punishment and authority versus contract. The interviews can be conducted verbally or in writing; the verbal interview is preferred because it provides more opportunity for clarification of responses (Colby, Kohlberg, & Kauffman, 1987a).

The Kohlberg scoring system has gone through three revisions (Colby et al., 1987b). The final version, Standard Issue Scoring, is intended to provide more objectivity and reliability by specifying clearer stage criteria and more adequately separating structure from content in the responses. Since no individual in Kohlberg's previous research was found to produce Stage 6 thinking, this version does not provide guidelines for identifying such thinking.

Three different procedures exist for coming up with a final score; the most psychometrically acceptable score is a nine–point global stage score (GSS) that consists of pure and mixed stage scores (Stage 1, 1/2, 2, 2/3, and so on) (Walker, 1988). (However, as Walker pointed out, mixed stage scores do not adhere theoretically to Kohlberg's definitions of stages.)

Colby and Kohlberg (1987) reported very good to excellent test-retest reliability (high .90s), alternate form reliability (.95), and interrater reliability (.98) for the MJI. Walker (1988) and Colby and Kohlberg (1987) have demonstrated construct validity, in the form of invariant stage sequence and consistency of stage usage across moral issues.

The Defining Issues Test (Rest, 1986a) is a paper-and-pencil assessment of moral reasoning. It presents six hypothetical dilemmas similar to those of Kohlberg, each followed by twelve statements that present various interpretations of the dilemmas. Respondents are asked to rate and rank the statements in terms of the importance they should be given in making a decision about the dilemma. These statements correspond to various stages in Rest's model. Using weighted ranks, the percentage of thinking at each stage is computed, as well as the percentage of principled reasoning, or p score (Stages 5 and 6 combined). This p score is the most used and most consistently reliable and valid score obtained from the DIT (Rest, 1986b).

Test-retest reliabilities for the DIT have ranged in the .70s and .80s, as have measures of internal consistency (Rest, 1979a). Because of these modest reliability scores, Rest cautioned against overinterpretation of small changes in repeated measures of the DIT. The DIT and the MJI are moderately correlated (.70s for heterogeneous samples but lower for homogeneous ones). The DIT is also moderately correlated (.40s to .60s) with other measures designed to assess political tolerance, law-and-order attitudes, and comprehension of moral concepts.

An important distinction between the approaches of Rest and Kohlberg has to do with the type of measurement instrument each has developed. The Kohlberg interview (Colby et al., 1987) is a *production* task. Individuals are asked to spontaneously produce verbal responses to a series of questions about a moral dilemma. By contrast, the Defining Issues Test is a *recognition* task. Individuals are presented in writing with a series of standardized moral dilemmas and possible responses to those dilemmas from which they choose the response closest to their thinking. It is much easier to comprehend and agree with a statement of reasoning than it is to verbally generate a response with no prompting (Rest, 1986b). As a result, scores on the DIT are consistently more varied and more sensitive to higher-stage reasoning than those obtained from Kohlberg's Moral Judgment Interview, on which movement through the stages is slow and few individuals score beyond Stage 4, at least until midlife (Bakken & Ellsworth, 1990).

Research

Literally thousands of studies based on Kohlberg's theory of moral development can be found in the research literature. Rest (1986b) reported on more than five hundred using the DIT alone.

Early studies by both Kohlberg's and Rest's research teams focused on validation of the theory and measurement issues related to the respective instruments (Rest, 1979a). As reported earlier in the chapter, both the DIT and the MJI have been found to be valid and reliable. In addition, the basic constructs associated with Kohlberg's theory has been demonstrated (Rest, 1979a, 1986b; Walker, 1988; Walker & Taylor, 1991).

Rest (1986b) summarized later research using the DIT. His categories will be used to examine major findings from research involving both the DIT and the MJI.

Factors Related to the Development of Moral Judgment

Rest's review of the DIT research (1986b) indicates that moral development increases with age and educational level, the latter being the more powerful variable. Pascarella and Terenzini (1991) summarized the research investigating moral development in college, including studies that used the MJI as well as the DIT. They concluded that individuals attending college show a significant increase in the use of principled reasoning (as measured by the DIT), beyond that related just to maturation. This finding holds in other countries as well as the United States (Lind, 1986).

Although education seems to have more influence than age on moral development, studies of middle-aged and elderly adults do indicate that changes in moral reasoning continue throughout a person's life. Bakken and Ellsworth (1990) found that development of principled thinking on Kohlberg's Moral Judgment Interview is likely to occur at midlife and later. Pratt, Golding, and Hunter (1983) found that preference (DIT) and production (MJI) scores were closer in individuals aged sixty to seventy-five than in younger persons, indicating that people may become more reflective as they age. Elderly respondents are also more definitive than younger persons in their moral judgments (Chap, 1985–1986).

Rest (1986b) concluded that becoming more aware of the world in general and one's place in it does more to foster moral development than specific experiences. Pascarella and Terenzini (1991) suggested, for example, that college may foster moral development by providing a variety of social, intellectual, and cultural experiences for students. An introduction to higher-stage thinking provided by upperclass students in residence halls, courses providing conflicting perspectives on various issues, and exposure to divergent ideas resulting from living away from home and interactions with roommates are conditions that have been found to be related to moral development (Whiteley, 1982). The extent to which individuals took advantage of such experiences was the most important factor leading to growth in moral reasoning ability. Rest (1988) suggested that people who seek out learning opportunities, enjoy intellectually stimulating environments, are risk takers, and find environments that reward these qualities are more likely to demonstrate higher levels of moral development.

Kohlberg and Higgins (1984) noted that work experiences after college also influence development of moral reasoning. Employment that requires individuals to consider the perspectives of others, as in medicine or other human service professions, facilitates development.

The Impact of Educational Interventions

Specific interventions designed to foster moral reasoning do seem to have some impact on principled thinking, particularly those that emphasize discussion of moral dilemmas or overall psychological development (Rest, 1986b). Pascarella and Terenzini (1991) suggested, however, that this effect may be conditional; that is, such interventions may work for certain students but not for others. They specifically noted that other areas of student development, such as cognitive development, may affect moral development.

Cultural Differences

Though the rate of development and the stage to which individuals progress vary, the universality of Kohlberg's stage model has been demonstrated in various cultures (Snarey, 1985). Persons from urban and middle-class cultures demonstrate higher-stage thinking, whereas those from rural and working-class cultures do not score above the conventional level. Logan, Snarey, and Schrader (1990) also reported that Israeli adolescents used more Substage B thinking than youth from the United States, Taiwan, Turkey, or the Bahamas, indicating that there may be cultural differences related to autonomous versus heteronomous judgment. These differences seem to reflect the values and socialization of these various cultures.

Individuals' values and the principles on which they base moral judgments (this is, their moral orientation) have been found to vary in different cultures and contexts, with people from Asian cultures demonstrating more altruism and concern for the law and those from Western cultures exhibiting more individualistic values (Iwasa, 1992; Ma, 1989; Miller & Bersoff, 1992). Some researchers, such as Heubner and Garrod (1993), have suggested that Kohlberg's theory may not adequately reflect the range of worldviews and values found in non-Western cultures. Kohlberg's dilemmas, for example, may not be meaningful where concerns such as compassion and karma, rather than justice, are paramount. Mennuti and Creamer (1991) have even questioned whether Kohlberg's theory adequately reflects the orientations used in American society. They identified a "self orientation," defined as "a consideration of the primacy of self-respect in judgments of moral value" (p. 245) used by a sample of community college presidents about real-life professional and personal issues, which took precedence over Kohlberg's justice orientation as well as Gilligan's care orientation. This self orientation was also found in a sample of higher education leaders in Taiwan (Yeh & Creamer, 1995).

Gender Differences

The issue of gender differences in moral reasoning has received significant attention since Gilligan (1982/1993) accused Kohlberg of gender bias. (See Chapter Eleven for a discussion of Gilligan's theory and an extended discussion of these issues.) Two major issues underlie this debate: whether women score lower on the MJI and DIT because of bias in the theory and whether Kohlberg's conception of moral reasoning accurately reflects the moral orientation of care and response. A third issue growing out of this debate involves the use of hypothetical versus real-life dilemmas.

Comprehensive reviews of research using both the MJI and the DIT have found nonsignificant differences between the scores of men and women (Rest, 1986b; Thoma, 1986; Walker, 1984). The existence of two moral orientations, justice and care, has been demonstrated, however (Ford & Lowery, 1986). Women were more likely to use a care orientation in resolving real-life dilemmas, whereas men were more likely to rely on a justice orientation, particularly if they adhered to a traditional male gender role.

These findings indicate that although women score similarly to men on measures of justice reasoning, they tend to prefer a care orientation when they are asked to spontaneously generate and discuss a moral dilemma (Thoma, 1986). However, among Taiwanese leaders in higher education, the context of real-life dilemmas influenced choice of moral orientation more than gender did, with justice reasoning predominating in professional dilemmas and a self orientation being used more in personal dilemmas (Yeh & Creamer, 1995).

Walker (1989) noted that real-life dilemmas were more likely to elicit responses indicating a care orientation and hypothetical dilemmas were more likely to elicit a rights perspective. The content of the dilemma also seems to affect the moral orientation individuals use (Rothbart, Hanley, & Albert, 1986).

Religious Differences

Religious ideology is moderately related to moral development, with individuals who hold a liberal perspective scoring higher (Rest, 1986b). In an attempt to explain this finding, Dirks (1988) suggested that the tenets of evangelical belief systems may foster unquestioning allegiance to a higher authority consistent with conventional rather than postconventional thinking.

Relationship Between Moral Reasoning and Behavior and Attitudes

Moral reasoning has been found to be significantly related to a number of behaviors, including cheating, cooperative behavior, voting preferences, and delinquency (Kohlberg & Candee, 1984; Rest, 1986b). Pascarella and Terenzini (1991) also identified links between principled moral reasoning and moral behaviors such as social activism, adhering to contracts, and helping people in need. They suggested that college indirectly fosters moral behavior by encouraging the development of moral judgment.

Moral judgment scores are also related to liberal versus conservative belief systems, attitudes toward authority, and attitudes toward capital punishment (Kohlberg & Candee, 1984; Rest, 1986b).

Applications

Throughout his career, Kohlberg was committed to creating and evaluating practical applications of his theory. His major efforts were directed toward development of moral education programs and "just communities" for schools and prisons (Kohlberg, 1971, 1972; Reimer, 1981). Kohlberg's early moral education efforts focused on providing students with opportunities to discuss hypothetical moral dilemmas in a classroom setting. The goal was to encourage development by creating cognitive conflict through the presentation of higher-stage thinking. Strategies for conducting such discussions are presented in Galbraith and Jones (1976).

Kohlberg's later just-communities approach was broader in scope. It provided opportunities for members of a school or prison community to be involved in decision making regarding real-life situations they faced (Reimer, 1981). Aspects of the program included creation of a democratic governance system, use of moral discussion principles, regularly scheduled community meetings, and involvement of participants in maintaining agreements made by the group. The goal was to create a moral atmosphere by involving individuals in meaningful moral decision making in which they had to consider the opinions of others, work as a collective, and assume responsibility for the outcomes of decisions. This type of program, with its focus on community, expanded Kohlberg's notion of moral development from the individual to the group level and from cognition to behavior (Kohlberg, 1981b).

Many efforts have been made to adapt Kohlberg's educational programs to college settings (Pascarella & Terenzini, 1991). These efforts have included discussions of moral dilemmas in academic courses (for example, Mustapha & Seybert, 1990) as well as programs that focus on personal development and self-reflection, such as group counseling (for example, Clark & Dobson, 1980).

Whiteley (1982) reported on a curriculum development effort at the University of California in Irvine called the Sierra Project. The goals of this project were to encourage psychological development while challenging students to apply their educational experiences to broader community problems through service activities. This project had many of the characteristics of the just-communities approach. Along with classroom settings, residence hall communities could be strengthened by incorporation of just-communities principles. Penn (1990) argued, and demonstrated, that directly teaching skills in logic, role taking, and moral decision making in an ethics class was more effective than the less direct teaching strategies used in other moral education programs. Role-taking and moral decision-making skills could be taught in orientation courses, leadership courses, or resident assistant training.

Evans (1987) introduced a framework for intentionally designing interventions to foster moral development on college campuses. Her model considers the target of the intervention (individual or institutional), the type of intervention (planned or responsive), and the intervention approach (implicit or explicit). Evans presented policy, programming, and individual approaches based on her model.

Critique and Future Directions

The usefulness and validity of Kohlberg's theory of moral development has been demonstrated in numerous research and evaluation studies. Noteworthy criticisms of the theory have been considered in relevant sections of this chapter. These concerns have centered around Kohlberg's use of a hard stage model, his claim of cultural universality, his focus on cognitive reasoning to the exclusion of other aspects of moral behavior, his use of hypothetical rather than real-life dilemmas, and his exclusive focus on justice issues as the basis of moral reasoning. Kohlberg's response to these criticisms is outlined in Kohlberg, Levine, and Hewer (1984b).

The most persuasive criticism of Kohlberg's work concerns the degree to which he has indeed "mapped" the moral domain (Rest, 1985). Gilligan (1982/1993), Mennuti and Creamer (1991), and others have demonstrated that moral judgments are based on many factors in addition to justice, including care and responsibility and self-respect. Kohlberg himself acknowledged this point (Kohlberg et al., 1984b). Though Kohlberg's stages of justice-based moral reasoning seem to hold for women and people from other cultures, the question remains of whether justice is the primary consideration in non-Western cultures or, indeed, for nondominant groups within American culture. An extensive review of the literature uncovered no research examining any aspect of the moral reasoning of individuals of color within the United States. Such a program of research would be a welcome addition to the knowledge base related to moral development.

Rest (1986b) proposed additional directions for future research, including assessment involving real-life situations rather than hypothetical dilemmas, investigation of the relationships among the four components of moral behavior so as better to predict actual behavior, continued investigations to determine the specific aspects of moral education programs that are effective, further research on the relationship of life experiences to moral development, and further investigations of cultural differences in moral development. Although thousands of studies have been done related to moral development, much additional work is needed before we truly understand all the factors influencing this important component of human development.

Higher education is an important conduit for the transmission of values in society and should be about the business of encouraging the highest level of ethical decision making. Kohlberg's theory is a helpful framework for understanding how moral development takes place and provides direction for fostering the development of moral judgment. The theory can be used to structure our work with individuals, groups, and policy development. The thoroughness with which Kohlberg's theory has been validated, the numerous practical applications that have been based on his work, and the extent of research the theory has generated make Kohlberg's theory one of the most important contributions to our knowledge of student development.

CHAPTER ELEVEN

GILLIGAN'S THEORY OF WOMEN'S MORAL DEVELOPMENT

Tia is a senior and chair of the Commuter Student Organization (CSO) at Soar University. Voted into this prestigious position by the group's seventy undergraduate members, Tia is popular among her peers, and the group serves as her main support system. Vanessa, the younger sister of one of Tia's best friends from high school, has emulated Tia since childhood. Vanessa decides to live at home, attend the university, and join the CSO. Vanessa's sister asks Tia to watch out for Vanessa and help her get acclimated to college, since Vanessa is rather shy and has trouble making friends. Tia wants to help Vanessa experience a sense of belonging on campus, especially knowing that most commuter students who do not get involved in campus activities tend to feel isolated from campus life.

The CSO is known at Soar University for its strong intramural team, which competes weekly against other campus organizations, residence halls, and faculty and staff intramural teams. Sometimes the atmosphere for intramural volleyball is just as intense as competitive collegiate sports. A large traveling trophy is passed to the championship team each semester and is displayed in a glass case in the student center with pictures of the winners. This past year, two women students from the CSO were accepted as walk-ons by the university volleyball team, which has a record of twenty-nine wins and eleven losses.

Tia knows that Vanessa enjoys volleyball but was merely a benchwarmer for her high school team. In fact, Vanessa played a total of only five minutes during her whole high school career. Vanessa confides to Tia that she wants to play volleyball for the CSO. Tia becomes very quiet. She is aware that from the perspective of several CSO members, particularly her best friend Chad's, students need not try out for a spot on the CSO volleyball team unless they are exceptionally talented. They believe that the volleyball team is what gives the CSO status on campus and that continuing to win is vital to the organization's maintaining its visibility and prestige. Privately, Tia wonders how a group of commuter students who formed a social group based on inclusiveness and campus involvement could have become so caught up in exclusivity and competitiveness and why intramurals, which were originally formed for recreational and social purposes, became so intense. Although Tia has a different perspective, she is afraid to voice her opinion knowing that others disagree. Because of the conflict she feels between helping Vanessa and supporting her friends on the team, Tia decides to talk privately with Leah, one of the leading scorers on the team. Leah, too, has had doubts about the "winning is everything" mentality that has evolved in the CSO. Being somewhat shy herself, she empathizes with Vanessa's situation. When Chad remarks on Vanessa's lack of coordination during an informal volleyball practice, a heated discussion erupts between Leah and Chad. At a CSO meeting later that evening, Leah raises the issue of membership requirements for the volleyball team, arguing that the needs of the members of the CSO to feel a part of the group are just as important as winning volleyball games. Conflicts about care (in this case, friendship and concern for new members) and justice (who is qualified to be on the team) last for several hours, with members of the organization taking sides on the issue.

This dilemma, not unlike Dave's situation in Chapter Ten, presents an obvious conflict of values. In this case, however, both university women and men find themselves in the midst of a moral conflict. Carol Gilligan contends that women view the world differently than men and emphasize relationships between people in a specific context rather than abide by an abstract universal justice. Although students' sex does not necessarily determine how the dilemma is resolved, the conflict between the concern that Tia and Leah have for Vanessa's well-being and Chad's demand that Vanessa be evaluated using the same criteria as other players shows how students can approach moral dilemmas differently. Chad represents a justice orientation as he pleads for an impartial evaluation of Vanessa's abilities as a volleyball player. Conversely, Leah's plea for the CSO to include Vanessa to help her adjust to college represents a moral orientation of care.

Gilligan was one of the first to recognize and document what she perceived as two different moral orientations (Gilligan, 1977, 1982/1993). Over the past twenty years, her research has received praise and stirred controversy in academe and the general public over the moral orientations of women and men.

Historical Overview

Several theorists in the twentieth century singled out women as a group and portrayed women's experience as inferior and qualitatively different from that of men. Prior to the popular and scholarly success of Gilligan's *In a Different Voice* (1982/1993), human development theorists, for the most part, did not see women as a group worthy of psychological study. In fact, since Freud (1905/1965) neglected to include women in the Oedipal theory, women have been characterized as deficient and dysfunctional (Gilligan, 1977). Freud's work began a snowball "portrayal of women as deviants" (Kuk, 1992, p. 26) and set men as the standard by which to judge what was normal.

In keeping with this tradition, research on moral development conducted by Kohlberg (1969) did not include women as subjects. However, Kohlberg generalized his research findings to both women and men (Gilligan, 1982/1993). Using a theory based solely on male subjects, Kohlberg (1981a) concluded that women are unable to reach the same developmental pinnacle as their male counterparts. Although Kohlberg eventually began to include women as subjects in his research, he continued to compare women to the same norms as men and continued to find them "underdeveloped" (Gelwick, 1985, p. 29).

Both psychological and cognitive-structural theorists influenced Carol Gilligan's research on the moral development of women. For example, Freud (1905/1965) recognized that women experience ethics differently than men and that unlike men, women's experience is influenced by feelings and emotions. Piaget (1952) uncovered sex differences in children's play. He found that girls were less structured than boys when setting game rules. Erikson (1964) revealed the inadequacy of separation as "the model and the measure of growth" (Gilligan, 1982/1993, p. 98). He also helped Gilligan understand the intricate bonds between people and their history and how psychology and politics intertwine with social history and life history to enlarge our understanding of what makes us human (Gilligan, 1982/1993).

A more contemporary influence on Gilligan's research was Jean Baker Miller, one of the first women to argue for a gender-based developmental perspective. Miller (1976) legitimized women's experience by couching the relational aspects of women's lives in a positive psychological frame. Paradoxically, at the same time, she revealed that women "keep a large part of themselves out of relationship" (Gilligan, 1982/1993, p. xxiv) in order to maintain connection with others.

Soon thereafter, Nancy Chodorow (1978) asserted that children, especially those under six, are dependent on their mothers to be their primary caretaker. Both girls and boys identify with their mother and attach to her early in life. Ultimately, boys psychologically separate from their mothers, but girls continue to identify with them.

As they grow older, boys and girls appear to play out different identity formation scenarios. Young girls develop identity by connecting to others; their identity is threatened by separation. Young boys develop identity by acting autonomously from others and are threatened by intimacy. Thus Chodorow (1978) concluded that children experience sex differences in their dependent and independent relationships with others. Each of these psychologists built increasing evidence for Gilligan that although women are measured by a male norm, their differences made them different, not deficient.

Lawrence Kohlberg, a cognitive psychologist and Gilligan's professor at Harvard, was primary among those who influenced her research (see Chapter Ten). In the early 1970s, as a doctoral student at Harvard, she was his research assistant. As Gilligan began to study the relationships between moral reason and action, "she discovered a form of moral reasoning that she believed to be different from the reasoning described by Kohlberg" (Rodgers, 1990b, p. 36). Using Kohlberg's language, Gilligan (1982/1993) called the pattern of reasoning identified by him as the "justice voice" and named the moral orientation revealed through stories of women contemplating abortion as having a "care voice."

Kohlberg's rejection of both ethical neutrality and cultural relativism was grounded in his experience of the Holocaust (Gilligan, 1982/1993). While first studying at Harvard, Gilligan found his argument a potent one. Eventually she came to believe that Kohlberg and others generalized their findings because of their lack of awareness of the patriarchal hegemony embedded in their philosophy and assumptions. Derived from "a so-called objective stance" of traditional social science research, Gilligan concluded that their research "was blind to the peculiarities of voice and the inevitable constructions that constitute point of view" (p. xvii). This insight led her to attempt to shift the discourse on moral development from objective individualism to relationship. For two decades now, her voice has been heard in continuing debates in psychology, political theory, law, and ethics (Gilligan, 1995) around the paradigm shift from the struggle of the individual as an autonomous moral agent (engaged with or against society) to the struggle of the individual as a connected moral agent (engaged in affiliation with members of a society).

In her seminal 1982 work *In a Different Voice*, Gilligan presented her research findings and articulated her conclusions about the moral development of women. She also disputed the previous models of human growth that did not fit women's experience. The different voice she delineated is not distinguished by gender but by the themes of care and justice.

In a break from tradition, Gilligan interviewed both women and men to trace the two themes of care and justice. Seeking a space to hear the silenced voices of women, Gilligan contrasted female and male voices by empirical observation to pinpoint "a distinction between two modes of thought and to focus a problem of interpretation rather than to represent a generalization about either sex" (1982/1993, p. 2).

In a Different Voice presented research from three studies: one explored identity and moral development of college students (Gilligan, 1981), another emphasized how women make decisions about abortion (Gilligan & Belenky, 1980), and a rights and responsibilities study examined different ways of moral thinking and their relationship to different ways of thinking about the self (Gilligan & Murphy, 1979). Each study employed similar qualitative methods to reveal how different voices (that is, care and justice) reflect moral life. No quantitative results are reported; data are framed using interview excerpts accompanied by Gilligan's interpretations (Brabeck, 1983).

In the longitudinal study of college students' identity and moral development, Murphy and Gilligan (1980) and Gilligan (1981) reported on interviews with twenty-six undergraduate students at Harvard in their senior year and then again five years after graduation. Ironically, the students chosen were enrolled in a moral and political philosophy course taught by Kohlberg. The intensive interviews were conducted toward the end of the senior year when students typically ask themselves about commitment and choice. Since identity is directly related to moral decision making, the interviews were designed to address these issues by asking students "to discuss their experience of moral conflict and choice, their thinking about commitments, made and foreseen, and their sense of themselves" (Gilligan, 1981, p. 153.) In addition, their moral development was measured using Kohlberg's standard assessment procedures.

The abortion decision study (Gilligan & Belenky, 1980) examined the relationship between personal experience and thought, taking a particularly close look at the role of conflict in moral development. Interviews were conducted with twenty-nine women diverse in age (fifteen to thirty-three), ethnicity, social class, and marital status who were considering an abortion in their first trimester. Rather than presenting participants with a hypothetical problem needing a solution, they were asked to define their real-life moral problems and explain how they decide among alternatives.

Finally, the rights and responsibilities study (Gilligan & Murphy, 1979; Murphy & Gilligan, 1980) included an interview sample of 144 females and males matched for age, intelligence, occupation, and social status at nine points across the life span: ages 6–9, 11, 15, 19, 22, 25–27, 35, 45, and 60 (eight females and eight males at each age). Drawing from earlier works, Gilligan and Murphy collected data on individuals' "conceptions of self and morality, experiences of moral conflict and choice, and judgments of hypothetical dilemmas" (Gilligan, 1982/1993, p. 3).

Gilligan's Theory

Gilligan and Kohlberg believed that people made meaning of their world in two very different ways. Kohlberg's justice orientation (1969) focused morality on understanding rights and rules. His six-stage hierarchy reflects a progression from lower-order to higher-order moral thinking in which autonomy is prized and universal justice is the goal (Romer, 1991). In contrast, Gilligan (1986) observed "in women's thinking the lines of a different conception, grounded in different images of relationship and implying a different interpretive framework" (p. 326). Thus the central focus of Gilligan's care orientation is attachment to others. She made it clear that relationships with others must carry equal weight with self-care when making moral decisions, a fact overlooked by some critics.

In recent defense of her research, Gilligan (1995) referred to the justice voice (based on equality, fairness, and reciprocity) as "patriarchal," treating the individual as separate, autonomous, and independent. In contrast, she "depicts the care voice as derived from a conception of the self that is relational and a view of self and others as connected and interdependent" (Perreault, 1996, p. 34).

Gilligan (1977, 1982/1993) demonstrated that women identified care and responsibility as the central theme behind women's moral compass. Derived from responses of twenty-nine women facing an abortion decision, Gilligan (1977) "formed the basis for describing a developmental sequence that traces progressive differentiations" in how women understand and judge "conflicts between self and others" (p. 482). She proposed that women's moral development proceeds through a sequence of three levels and two transition periods. Each level identifies a more intricate relationship between self and others. Each transition represents the achievement of a more sophisticated understanding between selfishness and responsibility.

Level I: Orientation to Individual Survival

At the first level, the individual is self-centered and preoccupied with survival. Individuals are unable to distinguish between what "should" occur (necessity) and what "would" occur (wish). For instance, one eighteen-year-old respondent in Gilligan's study affirmed that "there was no right decision" when it came to her abortion because she did not want to be pregnant. For this young woman, "the question of [what constitutes a] right decision would emerge only if her own needs were in conflict" (Gilligan, 1977, p. 493). At that point, growth and transition have potential to occur if her dilemma compelled her to seek another moral option.

For most women at this level, relationships do not meet their expectations. In some circumstances, women intentionally isolate themselves as protection against the pain associated with unfulfilled intimacy. For example, when one young woman participating in Gilligan's research was asked how she would describe herself to herself, she responded, "I am a loner in life. I prefer to be by myself than around anybody else. I manage to keep my friends at a limited number with the point that I have very few friends" (1977, p. 493).

The goal at this level is to fulfill individual desires and needs for the purpose of preserving the self. In the hypothetical case discussed at the beginning of the chapter, Chad is typical of individuals at this level in that he is motivated by his own self-interest (to have a winning team) and is unable to understand other members' desire to be inclusive.

First Transition: From Selfishness to Responsibility

In this transition, the most poignant issue is one of attachment and connection to others. In effect, the criterion used for judging shifts from independence and selfishness to connection and responsibility. The conflict between "should" and "would" is distinguishable, giving the individual more choices for moral judgment. Questioning their self-concept, individuals moving through this transition consider the opportunity for doing the right thing. Gilligan (1977) described the right thing as "the ability to see in oneself the potential for social acceptance" (p. 495). On the whole, during this transition, the individual integrates responsibility and care into her repertoire of moral decision-making patterns.

Level II: Goodness as Self-Sacrifice

As the individual moves from a self-centered, independent view of the world to one of greater engagement with and reliance on others, survival becomes social acceptance. Seeking the paradox of self-definition and care for others, individuals at this level reflect conventional feminine values. In fact, at this level, an individual may give up her own judgment in order to achieve consensus and remain in connection with others. Thus disequilibrium arises over the issue of hurting others. Although conflict exists, it is typically voiced not in public but in private. Although Tia privately thinks that her friend, Vanessa, should be allowed to play on the volleyball team, staying in connection with other members of the CSO who feel differently is more important to Tia than standing up for her own beliefs.

Second Transition: From Goodness to Truth

In the second transition, the individual questions why she continues to put others first at her own expense. During this time of doubt, the individual examines her own needs to determine if they can be included within the realm of responsibility. However, the struggle "to reconcile the disparity between hurt and care" (Gilligan, 1977, p.498) continues. At this time, the individual makes a moral judgment shift from deciding in accordance with those around her to deciding by inclusion of her own needs on a par with those of others.

For the first time, the individual views examination of her needs as truth, not selfishness. As with the first transition, the second one is linked to self-concept. Taking responsibility for the decisions one makes comes as a result of being honest with oneself. At this potentially vulnerable time, a transitional impasse can catch a person between selfishness and responsibility—in other words, torn between survival and morality.

Level III: The Morality of Nonviolence

The individual raises nonviolence, a moral mandate to avoid hurt, to the overriding principle that governs moral judgment and action. At this level, the individual is elevated to the principle of care by a "transformed understanding of self and a corresponding redefinition of morality" (Gilligan, 1977, p. 504). Through this second transformation, which now includes respect for the self, the dichotomization of selfishness and responsibility disappears. This reconciliation opens the door for the individual to recognize her power to select among competing choices and to keep her needs within the mix of moral alternatives. In opening this door, the individual recognizes the "moral equality between self and other" (p. 504).

Leah is an example of a student who has moved beyond her individual desire. She chooses to speak out in favor of accepting Vanessa onto the volleyball team at the risk of other members' rejection. Leah rejects the unstated criteria for membership on the volleyball team, which members like Chad adhere to, and makes a strong appeal to disregard them and include Vanessa on the team.

Assessment Techniques

Several formal assessment tools exist to identify and measure the moral orientation of care. Assessment approaches have ranged from formal interviews with elaborate scoring protocols to pencil-and-paper tests. Nona Lyons (1983), one of Gilligan's students at Harvard, was the first scholar to empirically test Gilligan's findings in a systematic way. In doing so, Lyons developed reliable, measurable criteria to examine the relationship between self-perception and moral ways to reason (Skoe & Marcia, 1991).

The Ethic of Care Interview (ECI) was developed to measure moral reasoning in terms of the levels and transitions of Gilligan's theory (Skoe & Marcia, 1991). Using a structured interview format, participants are asked to describe their response to one real-life dilemma and three hypothetical dilemmas. Responses to each dilemma are scored 1 to 5 (or 1 to 3 in half-point increments), reflecting Gilligan's three levels and two intermediate transitions. Assignment of a score is based on the reasons given and the relative importance of concern for self and others, rather than the action taken.

The original validation study (Skoe & Marcia, 1991) involved interviews with eighty-six single female undergraduate volunteer students (the majority of whom were psychology majors). Using one untrained and two trained independent female raters, interrater reliabilities ranged from .78 to .96 and kappas ranged from .63 to .94. To examine the relationship between moral reasoning and identity in development, responses to the ECI were compared to Marcia's four levels of identity development (1966, 1980): diffusion, foreclosure, moratorium, and achievement. As predicted, scores on the ECI increased with age ($F = 83.55$, df $= 1/81$, $p < .0001$), and women who scored high on the ECI had higher identity status ($F = 90.62$, df $= 3/81$, $p < .0001$).

In 1994, Skoe and Diessner expanded the investigation of the relationship between identity and moral reasoning, using both women and men and using measures based on both Gilligan's and Kohlberg's theories. The Ethic of Care Interview (ECI), Kohlberg's Moral Judgment Interview (MJI) Form A, and Marcia's Measure of Ego Identity Status (1966, 1980) were administered to seventy-six female and fifty-eight male volunteers ranging in age from seventeen to thirty, 97 percent of whom were white and all of whom were attending Boston area universities and high schools. The researchers found that care-based morality is related to "age, ego identity, and justice-based morality for both women and men" (Skoe & Diessner, p. 282). In this study, identity status was superior to chronological age as a predictor of ECI and MJI scores for women and men. Moreover, the finding that the relationship between identity and the ECI is stronger for women than for men supports Gilligan's hypothesis that "care-based morality has particular relevance for women's personality development" (p. 283).

The Measure of Moral Orientation (MMO) (Liddell, 1990; Liddell & Davis, 1996; Liddell, Halpin, & Halpin, 1992) is the only paper-and-pencil instrument designed to measure care and justice. It was designed to be easy to administer and score and is intended for use with traditional-aged college students. The instrument has recently been revised to improve its psychometric properties. One moral dilemma was deleted. The instrument measures preference for care or justice responses to moral problems through a series of nine moral dilemmas. Each dilemma includes an option to choose a care or justice orientation. Participants choose from a four–point Likert scale (strongly agree, somewhat agree, somewhat disagree, strongly disagree) in response to each option. The instrument also measures "respondent's perception of himself or herself as caring or just" (Liddell et al., 1992, p. 327) through a twelve–item self-description questionnaire.

The sample used to validate the revised instrument included 381 students at a large public midwestern university. Respondents most frequently indicated intended careers in education (53 percent), the fine or performing arts (9 percent), business (7 percent), medicine (7 percent), and science or research (6 percent). Students were administered the World View Questionnaire (WVQ) (Stander & Jensen, 1993) and the Defining Issues Test (DIT) (Rest, 1986a) in addition to the MMO.

Liddell and Davis (1996) concluded that the MMO was a reliable measure of moral sensitivity (how an individual interprets a situation), whereas the DIT measures action-oriented moral judgment. Evidence of convergent validity of the MMO included significant correlations between justice and self-justice ($r = .39$) and between care and self-care ($r = .50$). Discriminant validity was verified by an intercorrelation between justice and care ($r = .28$) and between self-description of justice and care ($r = -.20$) that are low enough to confirm that the instrument measured the two constructs.

Liddell and Davis (1996) recommended use of the MMO to assist college students in developing "a moral language that encompasses both an ethic of care and an ethic of justice" (p. 492). They also cautioned against using the MMO to measure moral development, since items were not designed to measure developmental stages according to either Gilligan's or Kohlberg's model.

Research

There is no doubt that Gilligan's prolific research and publication record in the past two decades (Brown & Gilligan, 1991, 1992; Gilligan, 1977, 1981, 1982/1993, 1987a, 1987b, 1991, 1996; Gilligan, Lyons, & Hanmer, 1990; Gilligan, Ward & Taylor, 1988; Gilligan & Wiggins, 1987; Taylor, Gilligan, & Sullivan, 1995) has had a strong influence on the attention paid to relational aspects of moral reasoning. Continuing to modify and extend her original work, Gilligan has moved from examination of primarily white, privileged women's moral development to a more inclusive examination of women and girls' relationships and how cultural differences influence these relationships and their development (Taylor et al.). Besides Gilligan, others have contributed to a better understanding of the nature of the care ethic through their research. However, others' findings on gender-related moral orientation are not always consistent.

Gender Differences

Lyons (1983) confirmed Gilligan's hypotheses that women and men use two distinct types of moral judgment—care and justice—in their thinking and that these two patterns are gender-related and may be related to self-concept. Although Lyons could not and did not claim a causal relationship, she did identify the existence of an important relationship between ways individuals make moral choices and ways individuals define themselves. Lyons found that regardless of sex, individuals who indicate connectedness to others "more frequently used care considerations of response in constructing and resolving real-life moral conflicts" (p. 141). In contrast, individuals who define themselves in terms of separation from others more frequently used a rights orientation to moral dilemmas. Further research with adolescent girls (Lyons, 1987) indicated that relationships do play a central role in how individuals perceive the ever-changing self and how they make moral choices.

Building on Gilligan's and Lyons's research, Stiller and Forrest (1990) examined differences between female and male undergraduate residence hall students at a large midwestern university to determine differences in how they self-identify and morally reason. The results supported Gilligan's and Lyons's theoretical constructs. Although the study was limited by a low return rate, the authors found that women showed more diversity than men in their descriptions of themselves and in their choice of moral reasoning. Men, by contrast, displayed "almost exclusively" a preference for a separate or objective self and a rights orientation.

Finding a strong relationship between moral orientation and gender in adolescent reasoning, Wingfield and Haste (1987) argued that conflict resolution differed with the orientation favored by participants. Those who favored connection were likely to focus on negotiation with an attempt to integrate all points of view, and those who favored separation were likely to focus on adherence to rules. Wingfield and Haste advocated use of both orientations, the choice of one over the other depending on the context of the moral conflict.

In addition, a qualitative study of community college presidents (Mennuti & Creamer, 1991) found some gender differences in moral decision making. Mennuti and Creamer offered convincing evidence that "the moral reasoning process for women may indeed be different from, but not inferior to, that of men" (p. 247). Women's process of reasoning was based on principles of fairness, whereas men focused more on justice principles. The researchers found no evidence to suggest differences related to the nature of the moral dilemma in the bases for decision making.

Others have examined gender differences in moral reasoning with different results. Ford and Lowery (1986) found few significant differences in the two moral orientations used by 202 female and male college students. Using a self-report questionnaire on real-life dilemmas experienced by participants, the researchers learned that females were more consistent in their use of a care orientation and males were more consistent in their justice orientation.

In research on parenting dilemmas to determine whether the dilemma or the approach to moral problems differed by gender, Clopton and Sorell (1993) concluded that "differences in moral orientation result from differences in current life situations rather than stable gender characteristics" (p. 85). As suggested by others (Hare-Mustin & Marcek, 1988; Mednick, 1989), they argued that women and men who encounter similar problems in their daily lives reason similarly, thus adding evidence to the assertion that differences in moral problems, not differences in gender, influence moral reasoning.

Cultural Differences

The authors of one study (Stimpson, Jensen, & Neff, 1992) reported gender differences in moral orientation and found differences recognizable across cultures. Using an empirically tested scale derived from Bem's Sex Role Inventory (1974), an instrument used to measure feminine and masculine attributes that were considered culturally appropriate by gender in the United States in the 1970s, a questionnaire was administered by professors during class to female and male college students in Korea, Thailand, the People's Republic of China, and the United States. In all four countries, women showed a preference for an ethic of care.

In her research on the moral orientation of American Indian college students, Arvizu (1995) used the MMO (Liddell, 1995), along with four additional survey questions, to identify objectively the moral orientations of students from three tribal colleges (Little Big Horn College, Kootenai College, and Southwest Indian Polytechnic Institute). The findings contrasted with the literature regarding women's care and justice scores. Arvizu found that female American Indian students score "higher on justice than either American Indian men or the Euro-American men in these studies" (p. 11).

A qualitative study of American Indian high schools students (McCartney, Steffens, Imbra, & Slack, 1992) contradicts this evidence, however. The study revealed that female adolescents from the Turtle Mountain Community Middle School on the Ojibwa Indian Reservation in Belcourt, North Dakota, must choose between staying culturally connected to their families and community (care) or being culturally separated from those they have known all their lives (justice). For a girl from this reservation to separate means that "she must leave behind her culture by 'becoming white' or 'becoming one of them' in order to fit in or survive a predominantly Eurocentric environment" (p. 19). These researchers found that the resolution of Native American girls' personal career journey is a path that leads most of them to reject the dominant culture and remain in connection with their own.

The enigma remains regarding why more women than men from various cultures primarily adhere to the ethic of care. Some theorists speculate that the complex answer is linked to historical social roles of women, their lack of diverse experience, and limited representation in positions of social power (Kohlberg, 1984; Liddell, 1990). Conceivably, the high justice scores of the women college students from Arvizu's research (1995) may support this speculation and reflect tribal values for women and women's positions of power within their tribes, thus setting them apart from other cultures. Moreover, care and justice constructs do not have to be polar opposites (Guido-DiBrito, Noteboom, Nathan, & Fenty, 1996). Perhaps care and justice orientations can, and should be, interdependent constructs of a holistic moral fabric (Gilligan, 1982/1993; Liddell et al., 1992).

Applications

The popularity of Gilligan's theory of women's moral development has led to its application in such fields and disciplines as student affairs, teaching, social work, developmental psychology, and moral and political philosophy.

Student Affairs

For most student affairs professionals, the ethic of care is embedded within their personal value system and translated daily into professional practice. Since the profession is premised on a long history of support and care of students (see Chapter One), a long-standing relationship exists between moral reasoning based on care and practice in student affairs (Canon & Brown, 1985).

Delworth and Seeman (1984), in a feature article in the *Journal of College Student Personnel,* highlighted Gilligan's ethic of care and its implications for the student affairs profession. They suggested helpful ways of integrating moral theory and practice. For example, institutional policies and organizational structures should be examined for their underlying assumptions about care and justice. Furthermore, the intensely close family ties of some ethnic groups (for example, Native Americans, Asian Americans) may be representative of the ethic of care. If so, should students with a predominant care mode be treated differently than those who follow the dominant justice mode?

Likewise, Gilligan's ideas concerning ethics of care and justice have been applied to counseling (Enns, 1991; Hotelling & Forrest, 1985), residence life (Picard & Guido-DiBrito, 1993; Porterfield & Pressprich, 1988), career planning (Stonewater, 1989), and leadership development (Fried, 1994; Picard & Guido-DiBrito, 1993). This literature offers insight and practical suggestions for student affairs professionals who want to understand how gender differences may influence students' moral development. For example, Enns described five relationship models, including Gilligan's, and suggested links to the role of the counselor. She advocated using Gilligan's model as a way to understand the positive aspects of the ethic of care and how to apply care in relationship to the self. Hotelling and Forrest emphasized that when care and connection are viewed as a strength in human relationships, "both counselors and clients are less likely to view embeddedness in relationships as dependency, and are more likely to convey that intimacy and closeness may lead to more complete self-definitions in both men and women" (Enns, 1991, p. 210). Given that men have a proclivity to a morality of justice, it is suggested that counselors integrate both moral orientations of care and justice and "reinforce that part of the male client heretofore undeveloped" (Hotelling & Forrest, 1985, p. 185).

In residence life, writers warn of the danger of emphasizing one moral orientation over the other when training residence life staff (Porterfield & Pressprich, 1988). Instead, these scholars encourage resident assistants to understand the differences between justice and care and seek balance in realizing both orientations. Using female and male voices to demonstrate the interaction processes between students and resident assistants, Porterfield and Pressprich apply Gilligan's theory in the contexts of community development, policy enforcement and dealing with conflict, and team and relationship building. For example, conflict between female roommates might best be resolved through sensitive negotiation that benefits both parties, while male roommates might best resolve conflict in a sports contest where rules are followed and a clear winner is decipherable (Picard & Guido-DiBrito, 1993).

Gilligan's theory is also applied in ways that give student leaders and student affairs professionals a better understanding of how care and justice shape their role (Fried, 1994; Komives, 1994; Picard & Guido-DiBrito, 1993). For instance, the justice voice emphasizes power, domination, assertiveness, strength, ability to remain cool, control of emotions, and independence in leader roles. Yet values characteristic of the care voice, such as involvement, interdependence, concern for relationships and process, sharing information, and developing a web of inclusion (Helgesen, 1995; Rogers, 1989), must also be developed if leaders are to be effective in our rapidly changing organizations. Ultimately, advisers to student organizations "can serve students best by understanding, modeling, and teaching how the voice of care and the voice of justice influence group members" (Picard & Guido-DiBrito, 1993, p. 30).

Teaching, Social Work, and Developmental Psychology

Gilligan's ethic of care also has been examined and related to applied academic disciplines like arts therapy (Wadeson, 1989), educational technology (Damarin, 1994), journalism (Elliott, 1991), nursing (Peter & Gallop, 1994), social work (Freedburg, 1993; Rhodes, 1985), developmental psychology (Twohey & Ewing, 1995; Will, 1994), and cognitive psychology (Baxter Magolda, 1992; Belenky, Clinchy, Goldberger, & Tarule, 1986; King & Kitchener, 1994). Although this list is by no means exhaustive and addressing it in its entirety is beyond the scope of this chapter, it gives some notion of the breadth of Gilligan's influence. Application of the care orientation in classroom interaction in the various academic disciplines calls for a reevaluation of the methods used to teach college students. Much of the recent literature on moral and cognitive development questions the value of traditional models (with their focus on rules and objectivity) in applied fields and stresses the application of emerging models (with their focus on care and connection).

Student affairs practitioners can develop links with their colleagues in the classroom by understanding and demonstrating for faculty how student learning is manifested differently in care and justice moral orientations. For example, faculty may want to think about whether to learn best, students in their classes need to be in relationship with other students or autonomous. However, before this process can begin, student affairs professionals can assist faculty in identifying how their own moral orientation is reflected in their teaching. Student affairs practitioners can offer assistance to faculty who want to apply morality to the "what" and "how" of their teaching.

Moral and Political Philosophy

Political philosophy (Deveaux, 1995; Tronto, 1993), moral philosophy and feminist ethics (Callan, 1992; Heckman, 1995; Hepburn, 1994; Pitt, 1991; Ruddick, 1989/1995; Sichel, 1985; Vreeke, 1991), and interdisciplinary feminist studies (Friedman, 1993; Larrabee, 1993; Thayer-Bacon, 1993) contain the heaviest concentrations of discourse on the role of care in moral life. In some way, each addresses the differences between care and justice as conceived by Kohlberg and Gilligan. Critics of a care orientation for women object primarily to its implied subservience and oppression, derived from the social roles of women in history.

The moral philosophical debate is too complex to discuss in depth here. Yet the argument can be framed with two examples. Most experts agree to some extent with Gilligan that integration of care and justice are necessary for a fulfilled moral life. One notable exception to this perspective is Noddings (1984). She contended that care and justice are incompatible and originate from two different ethical positions. Tronto (1993), by contrast, argued that by transforming our traditional conceptions of human relationships and moral boundaries, "the relationship between justice and care can be a relationship of compatibility rather than hostility" (p. 167). In Tronto's opinion, feminist moral thinkers neglect the political context of care and in doing so give a distorted picture of its historical and empirical roots. Making a case for care as a central activity of human life, she warned of our society's denigration of nurturance that keeps the privileged in power and demeans individuals who embody the care ethos.

Critique of Theory and Future Directions

As is not uncommon in the history of science, new methodologies and bold ideas often receive both critical acclaim and careful scrutiny. One feminist moral philosopher proclaimed *In a Different Voice* "one of the most influential books of the 1980s" (Heckman, 1995, p. 1). Although Gilligan's hypotheses are no strangers to criticism, her research has forever changed the examination of moral theory in that it opened up the patriarchal doors to lively discussion and debate of morality's orientation and gender-relatedness.

Gilligan's critics come from many corners of the academy. Most are scattered throughout the feminist literature, particularly in psychology and moral philosophy. The concept of a different voice has become so popular that one psychologist warns of the "bandwagon" effect (Mednick, 1989). Mednick claimed that individuals psychologically construct a simplified version of the world. She sees this manifested in the popularity of Gilligan's different voice, which has "intuitive appeal and easy connection to personal experiences" (p. 1121). In Mednick's widely cited critique of Gilligan's research, she "raises concerns about arguments from feminists on the superiority of women that would be roundly rejected if the genders were switched" (Romer, 1991, p. 22). She warned of the dangers and implications of stereotyping women in their traditional social roles and judging women by male standards.

Others have joined the debate about whether moral development is influenced by biology (nature) or society (nurture). Pitt (1991) claimed that although Gilligan applied her theory to both women and men, historically, men are considered "inherently superior to women" in moral objectivity and rational thought. Mednick (1989) contended that the ethic of care resonates with stereotyped expectations about gender socialization. Romer (1991) added that Gilligan is part of a group of feminists who want to "glorify women" to prove that women are better than men. In a cross-disciplinary symposium published in *Signs: Journal of Women in Culture and Society*, feminist scholars debated these and other issues around sex differences related to female and male moral development (Kerber et al., 1986).

In response to her critics' questions about the derivation of gender differences, Gilligan (1982/1993) pointed out the limitation of their worldview: "I find the question of whether gender differences are biologically determined or socially constructed to be deeply disturbing. This way of posing the question implies that people, women and men alike, are either genetically determined or a product of socialization—there is no voice—and without voice, there is no possibility for resistance, for creativity, or for a change whose wellsprings are psychological" (p. xix).

It is not surprising that Gilligan's research has been the target of controversy, given its widespread popularity with scholars and the press alike. Nevertheless, examining moral development through a different lens lends richness to morality not found in the singular, objective reality of the traditional paradigm.

Much of the research on moral development suggests that learning to recognize and practice both care and justice morality is a goal worthy of individual pursuit. Friedman (1993) advocated a balance between the competing interests of individual responsibility to others and a universal, abstract justice. More research is needed to examine how to work best with students, faculty, and staff who practice a preference for one moral orientation over the other. A careful examination of our own moral decision-making preference and how to practice the art of care and justice is a good start. Student affairs professionals, particularly senior student affairs officers, should understand how care and justice, connection and autonomy, interdependence and independence, relationship and individuality are fostered or hindered by the organizational culture. As individuals, a preference is exhibited for one over the other, but our ever-changing organizations need both.

There are many opportunities on our campuses in and out of the classroom to observe and examine gender-related morality. Yet if student affairs professionals are to create positive learning environments, more must be known about the moral development of students like Tia, Vanessa, Leah, and Chad. Scholars have begun to examine the many variations of care and to deconstruct its many parts (Weinberger, Yacker, Orenstein, & DeSarbo, 1993). But much more research is needed. We need to be able to answer the following questions: Why was Leah willing to risk rejection by supporting Vanessa's membership on the volleyball team? What kind of environment would offer the most growth for students like Vanessa and Chad? What can student affairs professionals do to help students on their campus understand how faculty and staffs' justice and care orientations either alienate them from students or connect them with students? How do university policies reflect the morality of care and justice? How can a student affairs division create an environment where Tia, Vanessa, Leah, and Chad all feel supported and challenged in their moral development? Finding a balance between care and justice will not be easy.

PART FOUR

TYPOLOGY THEORIES

Maryann, a first-year student, has just met her roommate, Ellen. Since they are both from small towns and planning to major in English, Maryann is sure that they will get along. In letters they exchanged over the summer, they shared their apprehensions about whether they would "make it" in college, their concern about leaving home for the first time, and their worries about making new friends. They seemed to have a lot in common.

A week later, Maryann approaches her resident assistant about a room change. She has discovered that she was completely wrong about Ellen. Despite her initial impression, she now believes that there is no way that she and Ellen will ever get along. Ellen always seems to need to be surrounded by people and is constantly looking for a party, whereas Maryann prefers to talk quietly with one or two people when she socializes and likes to have time alone to regroup and think about her day. Ellen never seems to plan anything and leaves the room a mess; Maryann likes to schedule her activities and needs order in her living space. Ellen always seems to be arguing and debating points; Maryann needs harmony and wants a roommate who shows some concern for her feelings.

The RA, who learned about Myers-Briggs personality types in staff development, quickly determines that Maryann and Ellen have very different personality types. She decides that it might be helpful for the women to discuss their differences using this theoretical framework, with the goal of helping them come to appreciate the strengths of each of their types and discover what positive attributes they each bring to their living situation.

Typology theories reflect individual stylistic differences in how students approach their worlds. Unlike the psychosocial and cognitive-structural theories, they are not truly developmental in that they do not consist of stages through which individuals progress.

Carl Jung (1923/1971), a typology pioneer, suggested that human behavior does not vary by chance but rather is caused by innate differences in mental functioning. These differences appear in many aspects of life, such as how persons take in and process information, how they learn best, or the types of activities that interest them and in which they prefer to spend their time.

Typology theorists identify factors that create consistent ways of coping with change and the demands of life. When faced with similar developmental challenges, environmental factors, or living situations, people will respond differently, depending on their type. Maryann and Ellen, for example, were both concerned about their adjustment to college and both faced the pressures of being in an unfamiliar college setting. They reacted differently to these challenges, however, in part because of their different personality types.

Typology, then, serves as a framework within which psychosocial and cognitive-structural development takes place, and it influences the manner in which students address development in these aspects of their lives. Ellen, for example, chooses to deal with her concerns about establishing herself socially (the interpersonal aspect of Chickering's first vector, Developing Competence) by surrounding herself with people and going to parties every weekend, while Maryann addresses the same issue by choosing to spend time with one or two individuals on her floor with whom she is able to have meaningful conversations.

Typology theories also give us important information about sources of support and challenge for students who are otherwise developmentally similar. Ellen thrives on spontaneous activity and the freedom to "do her own thing," while Maryann does better when she can plan ahead and has a structured outline from which to work.

Typology theories are nonevaluative. Various types are viewed and discussed as being different but not "good" or "bad." Each type is seen as contributing something positive and unique to any situation. As the RA in our scenario hoped would happen for Ellen and Maryann, learning about the various types or styles described by these theories can lead to acceptance and appreciation, not only of one's own type or style of adaptation, but also of other types.

Typology theories are particularly helpful in providing guidance concerning the design of classes, workshops, training sessions, and other structured educational experiences. Certainly Maryann would feel more support, and perhaps do better, in a class in which the instructor provided a detailed syllabus and clearly outlined assignments, whereas Ellen might feel constrained by so much structure and prefer a looser classroom atmosphere.

Typology theories also help explain interpersonal interactions and provide guidance in working through conflicts, as they did for our RA. In the same way, group interactions can be analyzed using typology theory, and team-building activities can be developed to improve group functioning and cohesion.

Finally, typology theories can be of great utility in making effective work assignments. Maryann would be very effective if given a task requiring precision and organization, while Ellen would be a wonderful "idea" person. Positive work environments can be created when individuals' strengths are recognized and used and people learn to value what each individual brings to the work setting.

As with cognitive-structural theories, little research has investigated the applicability of these theories to members of various racial and cultural populations. The minimal research that does exist indicates some differences in type related to racial and cultural background (Hammer & Mitchell, 1996; Hansen, 1987). Gender differences have also been noted (Hammer & Mitchell; Holland, Powell, & Fritzsche, 1994). These racial, cultural, and gender differences may be due to socialization (Hansen, 1987; Holland, Powell, & Fritzsche).

In Part Four we examine three of the best-known and most extensively used typology theories: Kolb's theory of learning styles (1984), which proposes that we all have preferred ways of learning; Holland's theory of vocational interest (1985/1992), which presents typologies of both the person and environment and examines their interaction and its effects on behavior; and the Myers-Briggs adaptation of Jung's theory of personality type (Myers, 1980).

CHAPTER TWELVE

KOLB'S THEORY OF EXPERIENTIAL LEARNING

April is a first-generation African American college student who has recently begun her first semester of school. Because she would like to major in business, she enrolled in the math course that is a prerequisite. April is concerned about her performance on the first two quizzes given in this course. Her grades of C and D reflect both her difficulty in understanding the mathematical concepts and the bell-shaped curve that her professor uses to grade test results. April considers her professor very intelligent but rather intimidating. The professor has told the class that her job is to teach and their job is to learn. Relatedly, April is scared to ask for help. She's afraid her professor will think that she is not very smart or is just not working hard enough. By contrast, April really enjoys her introductory sociology class. She finds the instructor friendly. He usually comes to class early and walks through the lecture hall talking to the students. He also frequently encourages the students to come and talk with him if they have any questions. April also likes the assignments he gives. For example, she enjoys reviewing the newspaper to find examples of articles that demonstrate concepts presented in the professor's lectures, and she is looking forward to the field trip planned later in the semester. The members of her small group have already met a few times to begin work on the research project that they will conduct and present to the class. April feels she is learning a lot from this opportunity to discuss the course material with other students, and she is enjoying getting to know these students better.

Alex is a junior and a philosophy major. He has recently become a resident assistant. He was disappointed in the training he received to start off the semester. As a person who likes to think about issues and strategies and consider the possibilities, he found his training to consist almost entirely of "nuts and bolts." He felt that he spent a lot of time listening to others tell him what to do. He wanted to understand more about the rationales for the policies he was responsible for enforcing. When he went to speak with his supervisor about his concerns, the hall director told him that he really didn't know what the reasons were for some of the policies, but what was really important, anyway, was to get the job done. Alex feels increasingly frustrated with his job. The one bright spot for him is his programming responsibilities, which have permitted the opportunity to use his creativity and form meaningful connections with the residents on his floor. The hall director has heard that Alex is doing a good job with programming, but he considers Alex's constant challenging of policies and procedures a "pain in the butt." Lately he has been wondering if perhaps Alex wasn't such a good choice for RA.

Given the diversity of today's student population, the importance of understanding and being able to work with student differences effectively both in the classroom and beyond must be emphasized. David Kolb's theory of experiential learning provides much information that can be useful in gaining insight into and responding effectively to style differences, thereby enhancing our ability to provide appropriate challenge and support in the various environments in which student learning and development can occur.

Although Kolb's theory is probably best known for its learning style component, it is conceptually much more broadly based. In fact, Kolb (1984) described his theory as one of adult development. In relation to the body of student development theory, it may be most helpful to classify Kolb's theory as a typology theory.

Historical Overview

In the preface to his 1984 book, Kolb noted that it had been seventeen years since he began his work with experiential learning theory. At that earlier time, Kolb was a faculty member at the Massachusetts Institute of Technology. During this period, as he described in his chapter in *The Modern American College* (1981), Kolb became interested in academic cultures and the issue of fit for individual students. This interest and related observations evolved into his theory of experiential learning, which is presented most fully in his book *Experiential Learning: Experience as the Source of Learning and Development* (1984).

Kolb (1984) chose the expression "experiential learning" to link his ideas to their roots in the work of Dewey (1958), Lewin (1951), and Piaget (1971) and to underscore the role of experience in the learning process. He also acknowledged the influences on the development of his theory of the "therapeutic psychologies" (Kolb, p. 15), especially the work of Jung (1960); the "radical educators" (p. 16),

Freire (1973, 1974) and Illich (1972); brain research, particularly left brain/right brain discoveries; and the philosophical literature concerned with metaphysics and epistemology. Clearly, Kolb's theory has a strong intellectual foundation and a sophistication that transcends the simplicity of the learning style component if the latter is considered only in isolation. Kolb's 1984 book is intricately crafted and conceptually complex. Student affairs practitioners and faculty wishing to focus on a more basic understanding of Kolb's theory may find *The Modern American College* chapter (1981) more helpful for an initial exposure to the author's own words.

The Theory

Let us examine Kolb's ideas about learning styles, the relationship between learning and development, and implications of learning style for higher education.

Learning Styles

Kolb (1984) defined learning as "the process whereby knowledge is created through the transformation of experience" (p. 38). Kolb (1981, 1985) regarded learning as a four-stage cycle consisting of *concrete experience* (CE), a feeling dimension; *reflective observation* (RO), a watching dimension; *abstract conceptualization* (AC), a thinking dimension; and *active experimentation* (AE), a doing dimension. Although Kolb used the term *stage* in describing the learning cycle, what he was actually referring to is a series of steps rather than developmental stages per se. Each step provides a foundation for the succeeding one. Concrete experience (CE) forms the basis of observation and reflection (RO). These observations are in turn used to develop one's ideas, including generalizations and theories (AC). From this development of ideas, new implications for action can be discerned (AE). To be effective, learners need the abilities represented by each of these four components of the learning cycle. They need to be able to involve themselves fully and without bias in learning experiences (CE), observe and reflect on these experiences from multiple perspectives (RO), formulate concepts that integrate their observations into theories (AC), and put such theories to use in making decisions and solving problems (AE). (See Figure 12.1.)

Mastery of all four components, or adaptive modes, is complicated by Kolb's additional observation that learning requires abilities that are polar opposites. CE and AC compose a prehending or grasping dimension—how one takes in information. AE and RO form a transforming or processing dimension—how one makes information meaningful. Learners must therefore choose which learning abilities (CE or AC, AE or RO) they will use each time they encounter a learning situation.

FIGURE 12.1. KOLB'S CYCLE OF LEARNING.

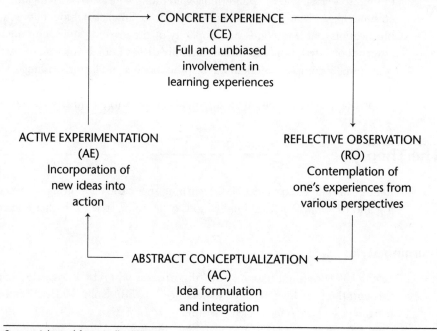

Source: Adapted from Kolb, 1981.

Based on individual preferences for one of the polar opposites in each of these processes, four individual learning styles emerge (see Figure 12.2). Kolb (1981) defined a learning style as a habitual way of responding to a learning environment. Kolb (1984) has offered detailed descriptions of each of the styles. Briefly, *convergers (AC and AE)* are inclined to be good problem solvers and decision makers. They are effective at applying ideas to practical situations. They excel at tasks involving identification of the single best answer when there is only one (for example, conventional intelligence tests) and display deductive reasoning. Convergers would rather deal with technical tasks and problems than social and interpersonal concerns. *Divergers (CE and RO)*, in many ways the opposite of convergers, tend to be imaginative and aware of meaning and values. They can view situations from many perspectives and excel at coming up with alternatives and implications. Divergers display an interest in people and are feeling-oriented. *Assimilators (AC and RO)* excel at inductive reasoning and display an ability to create theories by integrating disparate ideas. Ideas are valued for their logical soundness more than for their practical value. Assimilators prefer to focus on ideas and concepts more than on people. Finally, *accommodators (CE and AE)* are doers. They implement plans,

FIGURE 12.2. KOLB'S LEARNING STYLE MODEL.

CONCRETE EXPERIENCE (CE)
(feeling)*

	Accommodator	**Diverger**	
	• Is action-oriented and at ease with people, prefers trial-and-error problem solving	• Is people- and feeling-oriented	
	• Is good at carrying out plans, is open to new experiences, adapts easily to change	• Has imagination and is aware of meaning and values, is good at generating and analyzing alternatives	

ACTIVE EXPERIMENTATION (AE) (doing)† ...... REFLECTIVE OBSERVATION (RO) (watching)†

	Converger	**Assimilator**	
	• Prefers technical tasks over social or interpersonal settings	• Emphasizes ideas rather than people	
	• Excels at problem solving, decision making, and practical applications	• Is good at inductive reasoning, creating theoretical models, and integrating observations	

ABSTRACT CONCEPTUALIZATION (AC)
(thinking)*

*Grasping dimension

†Processing dimension

Source: Grid idea adapted from Kolb, 1985; text from Kolb, 1984. *Experiential Learning,* by Kolb, © 1984. Adapted by permission of Prentice-Hall, Inc., Upper Saddle River, NJ. Also, © Experience-Based Learning Systems, Inc., 1981, revised 1985. Developed by David A. Kolb. Reproduced with permission from McBer and Company, Inc., 116 Huntington Avenue, Boston, MA, 02116.

complete tasks, and are open to new experiences. Accommodators are willing to take risks and tend to be good at adapting to changing circumstances. They prefer a trial-and-error approach to problem solving over using analytical ability. Accommodators are comfortable with people.

As Smith and Kolb (1986) noted, learning styles also contain weaknesses. Individuals who are too embedded in their styles are likely to display various shortcomings. Convergers are prone to premature decision making and solving the wrong problem, divergers can be indecisive and overwhelmed by alternatives, assimilators may be impractical and seem lost in the clouds, and accommodators can get caught up in activity for activity's sake, engaged in insignificant efforts. The lack of adequate skills represented by each of the four styles can result further in limitations for the individual. Too little convergence can result in a lack of focus and a failure to test out ideas; too little divergence can result in an absence of both creativity and the ability to recognize opportunities and problems; too little assimilation can result in an unsystematic approach and an inability to learn from mistakes; too little accommodation can result in impractical plans and a failure to complete work on time. Because Kolb (1984) views learning as essentially a person-environment transaction, what the individual needs is not a "balanced" learning style per se but rather flexibility in style to have the competencies needed to be contextually adaptive.

Learning styles are influenced by heredity, past life experiences, and the demands of the present environment. In the environment, Kolb (1984) especially acknowledged the influence of one's undergraduate specialization, career choice, current job, and current tasks on the job. Learning styles are therefore viewed not as fixed traits but as stable states.

Learning and Development

Kolb views learning as a central life task. "How one learns," he points out, "becomes a major determinant of the course of personal development" (1981, p. 248). Development in turn consists of three stages: (1) *acquisition,* in which basic learning abilities and cognitive structures develop and which occurs from birth until adolescence; (2) *specialization,* in which social, educational, and organizational socialization forces shape the development of a particular learning style and which extends through formal schooling or career training and the early experiences of adulthood, both work-related and personal; and (3) *integration,* in which the person emphasizes the expression of his or her nondominant adaptive modes (learning cycle components) or learning styles in work and personal contexts and which is likely to begin at midcareer, though much individual variability characterizes the timing of this transition (Kolb, 1981, 1984).

Kolb (1981, 1984) posited that development through these stages is characterized by increasing complexity and relativism in dealing with the world and by increased integration of the dialectical conflicts between concrete experience (CE) and abstract conceptualization (AC) and between active experimentation (AE) and reflective observation (RO). Each of these four adaptive modes or learning cycle components is associated with a major facet of personal growth. Development in the adaptive mode results in increased complexity in the specified facet. More specifically, development in the mode of concrete experience increases one's affective complexity (feelings), development in reflective observation increases perceptual complexity (observations), development in abstract conceptualization increases symbolic complexity (thoughts), and development in active experimentation increases behavioral complexity (actions). Integrative development, or the ability to adapt by using nondominant modes, is considered by Kolb to be important not only for personal fulfillment but also for cultural development.

Higher Education and Learning Styles

Kolb's theory has many implications for higher education and the environments represented both in and beyond the classroom. His discussion of disciplinary cultures is especially relevant to academic programs, including graduate preparation in student affairs. Kolb (1981) observed that different academic disciplines are inclined to impose different kinds of learning demands, as is evidenced in "the variations among their primary tasks, technologies and products, criteria for academic excellence and productivity, teaching methods, research methods, and methods for recording and portraying knowledge" (p. 233). In addition, disciplines demonstrate sociocultural variation, including differences in faculty and student demographics, personality and aptitudes, values, and group norms. From Kolb's perspective, therefore, education in an academic discipline represents for the individual student a process of socialization to the norms in that field. These norms are related not only to "truth"—what it is, how it is communicated and used, and so forth—but also to personal styles, attitudes, and social relationships. Kolb added that over time, an "increasingly impermeable and homogeneous disciplinary culture" is produced, along with "a specialized student orientation to learning" (p. 234). In other words, norms within the academic discipline can become exclusionary, and one learning style may be favored.

In relation to the four learning styles, Kolb (1981) indicated, for example, that convergers are often found in the physical sciences and engineering, divergers in the humanities and liberal arts, assimilators in the basic sciences and mathematics, and accommodators in practical fields such as business. Kolb also reported a positive relationship between student-discipline learning style congruence and academic performance, social adaptation, and career commitment; students whose style matched the dominant one were more successful in these areas.

If academic disciplines are to be accessible to students with diverse learning styles, efforts must be made to provide varied methods of instruction and evaluation. Such methods, to provide both support to aid students in connecting with subject matter and challenge to assist them in developing the nondominant aspects of their preferred styles so that they can achieve the level of flexibility needed to respond to differing environmental demands, need to include activities that match as well as mismatch each of the four learning styles. Smith and Kolb (1986) provided examples of preferred learning situations for those with strengths in each of the four components of the learning cycle. For example, those with strengths in concrete experience (CE) would value methods such as games, role plays, peer discussion and feedback, and personalized counseling; students strong in reflective observation (RO) would value lectures, observing, seeing different perspectives, and tests of their knowledge; individuals who favor abstract conceptualization (AC) would value theory readings, studying alone, and well-organized presentations of ideas; and those inclined toward active experimentation (AE) would value opportunities to practice with feedback, small group discussions, and individualized learning activities. Because individuals prefer either CE or AC and either RO or AE, activities associated with the nonpreferred component can be considered challenging for an individual. Each of the four components also represents a different preference for the role of the instructor, with CE seeing the teacher as a coach or helper, RO as a guide or taskmaster, AC as a communicator of information, and AE as a role model for how to do something.

Returning to the introductory scenario, April's positive regard for small group work, finding actual examples of concepts in the newspaper, and a proposed field trip seems to indicate a preference for CE and AE components, a "hands-on" orientation. By contrast, she is having difficulty with the abstraction of mathematical concepts, an AC component. Her valuing of the instructor who seems to take on the coach or helper role provides another indication that her learning style is probably that of an accommodator.

Alex's situation as an RA exemplifies how learning style is relevant to learning environments outside the classroom. Alex's interest in exploring ideas and rationales and his contrasting disregard for "nuts and bolts" implies some valuing of both AC and RO dimensions. At the same time, Alex's interest in having meaningful relations with his residents and his valuing of creativity represent a connection to CE aspects. Though he articulates preferences typical of a thinker, Alex is also a doer in relation to his programming role, reflecting the AE aspect. Thus while Alex is likely to be a diverger, on the basis of the information given, his profile also shows that all four dimensions can be present to some degree in any individual.

Assessment Techniques

Kolb presented the first version of his Learning Style Inventory (LSI) in 1976 and a revised version in 1985. The revision contains twelve items related to learning, for example:

I learn best from

____ personal relationships.

____ observation.

____ rational theories.

____ a chance to try out and practice.

For each item, respondents are asked to rank the four responses based on how they think they learn best (4 = "most like you" to 1 = "least like you"). Each of the four responses corresponds to one of the components of learning (CE, RO, AC, and AE). Scores for each learning component are determined by adding the numerical ratings produced in each column. The LSI is designed to be self-scored.

Kolb (1985) reported that the norm group for the 1985 edition of the LSI consisted of 1,446 adults, ranging in age from eighteen to sixty. The group was described as ethnically diverse, including slightly more women that men, possessing an average of two years of education beyond high school, and representing a wide range of occupations and educational backgrounds.

Kolb (1984) provided evidence for his two-dimensional structure of learning by citing studies that used the original version of the LSI and reinforced the dialectically opposed natures of the abstract-concrete and active-reflective dimensions by reporting a negative correlation between the variables in each pairing (Certo & Lamb, 1979; Gypen, 1980; Kolb, 1976). Ferrell (1983) conducted a factor-analytic comparison of four learning style instruments and found that a match existed between factors and learning styles only for the original LSI, thereby contributing to construct validity. Merritt and Marshall (1984) studied reliability and construct validity of both ipsative and normative forms of the original LSI and reported similar results for both versions. Construct and concurrent validity received endorsement, and moderate scale reliability was reported. For the 1985 revision of the LSI, Smith and Kolb (1986) reported reliability coefficients (Cronbach's alpha) for each of the scales, with a range of .73 to .88. Finally, Sims, Veres, Watson, and Bruckner (1986) noted improved reliability from the earlier version, reporting coefficients ranging from .76 to .85.

Other studies have raised concerns about the 1985 LSI. Some authors have cited evidence that questions Kolb's two-dimensional, bipolar structure of learning (Geiger, Boyle, & Pinto, 1992; Ruble & Stout, 1990). Several authors (Geiger & Pinto, 1991; Ruble & Stout, 1991, 1992; Veres, Sims, & Shake, 1987) have expressed concern about the potential for response sets, based on the single learning mode per column format of the 1985 version, and the possibility that such response sets can produce inflated internal consistency coefficients. Yet despite conflicting reports related to the psychometric properties of the LSI, even some of its critics caution against dismissing the instrument (Geiger & Pinto, 1991) and maintain that useful information can be provided by it (Veres et al., 1987).

To address the criticism of the potential for response sets, Kolb (1993) issued a version of the LSI called the LSI-IIA. All items and response options remain the same as in the 1985 version. However, the response options for each of the twelve items have been reordered so that the responses are scrambled and no longer result in all CE responses being in column one, all RO responses in column two, and so on.

Claxton and Murrell (1987) have stated that when the LSI is used for dialogic purposes, it is extremely useful. This type of usage is consistent with Smith and Kolb's recommendation that the instrument be used for "self-exploration, self-understanding, and self-development" (1986, p. 8).

Both the 1985 revision of the LSI and the LSI-IIA are available in a research version as well as the more extended versions. The inventories themselves are the same in both versions; only the amount of supplemental material differs. Some additional explanatory information related to scoring may be needed if the research versions are used.

Two other assessment techniques related to Kolb's theory are also available: the Adaptive Style Inventory (ASI) (Boyatzis & Kolb, 1993a) and the Learning Skills Profile (LSP) (Boyatzis & Kolb, 1991, 1993b). The ASI is designed to assess an individual's ability to adapt to different learning situations. The four learning style components of concrete experience, reflective observation, abstract conceptualization, and active experimentation form the basis for the inventory. No reliability or validity information is provided in the scoring instructions and interpretive notes. The LSP provides individuals with a means of assessing their personal learning skills and comparing them to important skills required in a job. The LSP involves card sorts and follow-up workbook exercises. Cronbach alpha reliability coefficients ranging from .62 to .92 were reported for the LSP scales (Boyatzis & Kolb, 1991). Some preliminary evidence for relational, criterion, and construct validity was also reported, but the need for further validation studies remains (Boyatzis & Kolb, 1991).

An informal assessment of learning styles can be done by presenting individuals with written descriptions of the styles and having them select the one that seems most like them or having them underline aspects in any of the descriptions that sound like them. Informal assessments may also be done by asking probing questions about how individuals approached sample learning tasks (learning to drive, finding one's way around campus, and so forth).

Research

Kolb maintains and periodically updates a bibliography of research on experiential learning theory and the Learning Style Inventory (Kolb, 1994). This listing reflects a wide array of research based on Kolb's work. In relation to higher education, the learning styles of several student populations have been researched. These populations include but are not limited to nursing students, accounting students, adult learners, and community college students. Forney (1994) studied a national sample of master's students in student affairs and found the most frequently represented learning style to be that of accommodator and the least frequently represented to be that of assimilator. One implication is the need for program faculty to underscore the relationship between the academic and experiential aspects of the field seeing that the traditional classroom experience (lecturing and note taking) is inconsistent with the accommodators' more active preferred modes of learning.

Holley and Jenkins (1993), in a study of accounting students, found some relationships between learning style preferences and performance on different test question formats (for example, multiple-choice, open-ended). The potential for different forms of measurement to favor certain learning styles is an issue that can be extrapolated from this study. This issue can in turn have implications for how learning is measured across academic disciplines.

Exploring linkages between different aspects of development, Baxter Magolda (1989) studied learning styles and cognitive complexity among first-year college students. Considering gender, Baxter Magolda found that the percentage of men and women preferring each of Kolb's learning styles was almost equal. More women preferred concrete experience over abstract conceptualization (the grasping dimension), while men were evenly divided, and more men and women preferred reflective observation over active experimentation (the transforming dimension), though none of these findings based on gender was statistically significant. Baxter Magolda also found that different cognitive structures were accompanied by different learning orientations on the grasping dimension. Using the Measure of Epistemological Reflection, with positions corresponding to the first five Perry positions, as well as an interview to assess cognitive development, she found that Position 2 (Multiplicity Prelegitimate) students preferred abstract conceptualization, while Position 3 (Multiplicity Legitimate but Subordinate) students preferred concrete experience, a result that was statistically significant for women. Baxter Magolda interpreted these findings with caution, in light of the limitations of a sample composed only of first-year students.

In conclusion, although a substantial body of research based on Kolb's work exists, much of it addresses the classroom or populations outside of higher education. Learning style research conducted in traditional student affairs functional areas represents a potentially valuable and unexplored direction.

Applications

The most direct application of Kolb's theory may be in the use of the information on learning styles as an empathy and design tool in responding to the increasing diversity represented among the student population as we seek to provide both challenge and support in learning experiences in the classroom and beyond and in the modes we use to deliver our services to students.

In most groups, it is likely that all learning styles are present. Therefore, particularly in relation to group-based application activities based on Kolb's theory, it is not necessary to know the learning style composition. Using techniques that reflect all four learning cycle components has the potential to form some connection for each participant, as well as to introduce some challenging elements for each.

Student Affairs Programmatic Applications

Claxton and Murrell (1987) cited the use of learning style information in orientation to aid students in understanding their preferences and strengths in learning and to stimulate the development of new ways of learning so as to be successful in the classroom. These authors also noted similar advantages in using learning style information in both academic advising and study skills assistance. Chickering and Schlossberg (1995), in their guide to succeeding in college, included activities designed to help students analyze courses and interview faculty to determine how different learning style components may be addressed.

Sugarman (1985) has found links between Kolb's cycle of learning and the implementation of the counseling process. The symbols for the learning style components have been inserted to show the connection. Sugarman stated, "As a counselor, I aspire to approach each client in an open minded way and attempt to involve myself fully and without bias in the experience [CE] . . . I must, however, remain separate from the experience so that I can observe and reflect on it [RO] . . . On the basis of these observations, I develop a theory or hypothesis of how best to intervene next [AC] . . . Finally, I test out my hypothesis by intervening or not intervening [AE] . . . As I experience and reflect on the consequences of the intervention, the learning cycle begins to repeat itself" (p. 267). Sugarman also noted that counselors can use Kolb's model to reflect on their own counseling styles. For example, convergers can consider whether they may tend to be too dominant in the relationship, and divergers may find that they are sometimes too reluctant to share their own views.

Atkinson and Murrell (1988) demonstrated how Kolb's model can be applied to career counseling to aid in providing variety in the kinds of techniques that are offered to help individuals learn more about both themselves and the world of work. Self-exploration activities can be designed to correspond to each of the four learning style components. For example, talking with a counselor about personal values, wants, needs, and interests corresponds to CE; identifying patterns in past life and career decisions corresponds to RO; completing and receiving interpretations of career inventories corresponds to AC; and interviewing individuals in careers of interest corresponds to AE. In relation to the world of work, shadowing represents CE, a group-based discussion of personal reactions to careers explored reflects RO, researching careers through print and other resources corresponds to AC, and role playing as a preparation for job interviews represents AE.

Forney (1991a, 1991b) explained how career centers can use learning style information as a support in providing services that are responsive to a diverse student clientele. Diversifying the modes by which a given service is made available represents one alternative. For example, students could learn about the process of writing a résumé via a handout, a computer program, a workshop involving both information and group discussion, or an individual critique with a staff member. Such a variety of options gives students access to the service and the information involved in different ways. Assimilators would probably value the printed information, information shared by a staff member, and the opportunity to raise questions about their own ideas. Accommodators are likely to appreciate personal contact, the chance to focus on nuts and bolts, and receiving feedback on their own drafts. Convergers may prefer accessing information on the computer and also wish to discuss the best approach for their own résumés, including receiving answers to specific questions. Divergers would generally appreciate the opportunity to read and reflect on printed materials and follow up with personal contact, individually or in a group.

Forney (1991b) also discussed how meaningful activities for each learning style can be incorporated into a single instructional session, such as a job-hunting workshop. For example, a staff member's providing information on available resources, suggested job-hunting strategies, and considerations to think about, along with an opportunity for students to receive feedback on some of their own ideas and plans, supports assimilators. A group discussion on putting the information to use in relation to personal situations, with accompanying attention to individual questions and concerns, supports accommodators by giving attention to action, convergers by addressing questions about individual situations, and divergers via group involvement. Actually showing participants the career library or computerized job vacancy services and how to use them could connect with the accommodators' desire for hands-on experience and the convergers' inquisitiveness. Divergers and assimilators are likely to value knowing that they can schedule a follow-up appointment after they've had more time to think about the job-hunting process.

Although the preceding examples focus primarily on career development, it is important to recognize that any educational function (for example, programming, counseling, and teaching or training) that student affairs departments perform can be rendered more or less accessible to a diverse student clientele by nature of the degree to which learning styles are addressed. Moreover, Lea and Leibowitz (1986) maintained that programmers need all four learning style components to be effective in different stages of the program development process.

The process of helping students (and others) better understand the concept of learning styles can be aided by Hagberg and Leider's work (1982). Producing their own adaptation of Kolb's theory, they discuss four styles—imaginative (diverger), logical (assimilator), practical (converger), and enthusiastic (accommodator)—and provide helpful examples in language that is less academic than Kolb's. Their material can aid in translating Kolb's important ideas to students in general, such as entering students, as well as to students who occupy leadership positions in which helping others learn is a primary responsibility—for example, peer educators and sorority and fraternity scholarship chairs.

Classroom Applications

Smith and Kolb's efforts (1986) to provide examples of learning activities that correspond to the four components of the learning cycle are complemented by the work of Murrell and Claxton (1987), Svinicki and Dixon (1987), and Anderson and Adams (1992). All these authors provided helpful resources for designing classroom environments and activities that can both challenge and support students with different learning styles. For example, Svinicki and Dixon listed the following learning activities as being supportive of each of the four learning style components: for CE, laboratory observations, primary text reading, simulations and games, fieldwork, trigger films, readings, problem sets, and examples; for RO, logs, journals, discussion, brainstorming, thought questions, and rhetorical questions; for AC, lectures, papers, model building, projects, and analogies; and for AE, simulations, case study, laboratory, fieldwork, projects, and homework. Anderson and Adams included information that addresses the potential impact of ethnicity and gender on learning styles. For example, considering African American, Hispanic, and Native American students, they stated, "Generally, the pattern that emerges is that these students demonstrate competence in social interactions and peer cooperation, performance, visual perception, symbolic expression, and narrative and therefore are less comfortable with tasks that require independence, competition, or verbal skills" (1992, p. 21). Regarding gender, one example of potential learning style differences is the tendency of white females and African American, Native American, and Hispanic males and females to prefer a relational rather than an analytical style.

The relationships that Kolb (1981) reported between learning styles and academic majors and Smith and Kolb (1986) reported between learning styles and career choice have implications for the classroom. Kolb (1981) cited a tendency for academic disciplines to have a dominant learning style evidenced among student majors (for example, English includes many divergers; mathematics, many assimilators; engineering, many convergers; and education, many accommodators). Smith and Kolb described a relationship between learning styles and the careers individuals choose (for example, divergers choose arts and entertainment and service; assimilators, information careers and science; convergers, technological and specialist careers; and accommodators, business and organizational careers). Although, as Kolb (1981) indicated, types should not become stereotypes, these tendencies have implications for students whose learning styles deviate from the norm for that discipline or for their chosen career. For example, learning may be more difficult, and feelings of not fitting in may exist. Instructional methods that attempt to address learning style differences can serve as an "equalizer" for students, as can helping all students understand their own learning styles and potential supports and challenges.

Considering again the scenario of April, one might conclude that she should switch her major from business to sociology to avoid her current difficulties with math. This possible solution maintains the status quo in the math classroom, an environment that is likely unintentionally, yet systematically, to exclude other students like April. Such a classroom, however, could be modified to include tutorial assistance, encouragement of study groups, and efforts to render the abstract concepts more concrete through the use of examples and simplified language in explanations. A more personalized style on the part of the instructor could also be implemented. If such modifications are made, April may become successful, especially since no indication is given that she is not "bright enough" to master math. Even if the environment remains unchanged, April, if she understood more about her own learning style, could potentially seek out outside supports, such as tutorial assistance or the use of a study group, on her own.

As Kolb (1981) stated, "Rather than being a cause of successful academic performance, motivation to learn may well be a result of learning climates that match learning styles and thereby produce successful learning experiences" (p. 248).

Staffing Applications

Undergraduate staff training represents another area where learning style information can be useful. In a discussion of Kolb's theory in a graduate course, a student claimed an "aha" experience when she came to the realization that the department in which she had her graduate assistantship tended to conduct training sessions as though everyone learned in the same way. In the example of Alex, one can see the evidence of unmet needs and a developing alienation stemming from a training experience in which no connection seemed to be formed. The RA experienced a mismatch: lots of nuts and bolts but no opportunity to explore the more abstract—the ideas and rationales behind the policies and expectations. The hall director's dismissal of Alex's concern in favor of getting the job done tends to reinforce the stereotype of student affairs professionals being doers more than thinkers (Winston & McCaffrey, 1983). Providing work environments that both challenge and support a diverse group of individuals is important if we seek to attract and retain a diverse staff.

Kolb's theory can also supply insight into staff dynamics, with implications for both the individual and the organization. Claxton and Murrell (1987) maintained that how we work together in the future will be increasingly influenced by our particular personality and learning orientation. Hagberg and Leider (1982) provided examples of how work tasks may be approached differently, based on learning styles. For example, in relation to turning in reports, accommodators ("enthusiastic" in Hagberg and Leider's adaptation of Kolb) are likely to hate long, detailed writing and prefer verbal reporting; divergers ("imaginative") appreciate having a lot of notice and are likely to embellish their work with analogies and charts; assimilators ("logical") appreciate clear expectations and are likely to be well organized but tend to write volumes; finally, convergers ("practical") are likely to want to know the rationale for doing the report and will produce a concise, well-documented piece.

Kolb (1984) has noted that individuals with different learning styles display different strengths in relation to their adaptive competencies. Divergers are likely to excel in valuing skills (for example, being sensitive to people and listening with an open mind), assimilators in thinking skills (for example, organizing information and conceptualizing), convergers in deciding skills (for example, choosing the best solutions and experimenting with new ideas), and accommodators in acting skills (for example, committing to objectives and influencing and leading others). In turn, these differing strengths can result in differing contributions that can be made to the process of problem solving. Relatedly, because of differing strengths in adaptive competencies, some tasks may be best carried out by a homogeneous group (for example, brainstorming by divergers) and some by a heterogeneous group (for example, complex problem solving). It may also be helpful to consider adaptive competencies when making work assignments to individuals. Drawing on individual strengths as well as helping individuals develop nondominant aspects could both be considerations.

Finally, Abbey, Hunt, and Weiser (1985) maintained that supervisors function best when they can draw on all four learning or adaptive modes. In short, learning style information can provide a systematic way of looking at and dealing with individual differences among staff.

Critique and Future Directions

The learning style component of Kolb's theory provides support both in conceptualizing how students learn and in designing experiences that respond to individual differences. Kolb's work aids in understanding that in any classroom or any other learning environment, students represent multiple realities regarding what it is like to be a learner in that context, what instructional techniques offer challenge and support, and many other aspects of learning. Some questions remain unanswered, however. For example, what role does intelligence or cognitive complexity play in the evolution of one's learning style? In addition, more research is needed to expand the knowledge base dealing with possible relationships between gender, race, and culture and learning styles.

Looking at Kolb's experiential learning theory as a whole also prompts some questions. If one considers Kolb's theory a theory of development, a question must be raised as to how adequately he addresses the personal aspects. Is it more accurate to regard Kolb's theory as a learning theory or a typology theory rather than a more full-blown theory of adult development? Also, because of the heavy emphasis in Kolb's theory on formal education and traditional careers, how do individual differences affect the nature of adult development? For example, how well does the theory incorporate populations that are not white-collar or individuals who are "off time," such as adult learners? Such questions may be of less concern if one is dealing only with the traditional college student population or if one is drawing primarily on the learning style dimensions of the theory.

In relation to student affairs programs and services, the classroom, and staffing, issues related to alienation and limited performance of the persons involved can undercut success for the individual as well as for the organization. Learning style information can assist us in providing support by demonstrating our understanding, fostering feelings of connectedness, and building on individual strengths. Learning style information can assist us in providing challenge by supplying developmental mismatches to aid in overcoming weaknesses and by helping individuals to value differences in others. In constructing short-term learning experiences such as a one-shot program, providing connections for all learning styles is important so that learning can occur relatively quickly. In teaching a semesterlong course, matches as well as mismatches to promote further development of nondominant learning style components are appropriate.

Hagberg and Leider (1982) noted that individuals with different learning styles approach the process of growth and change differently. An awareness of this concept seems important in fulfilling our student development function. Moreover, Claxton and Murrell (1987) asserted, "Consideration of styles is one way to help faculty and administrators think more deeply about their roles and the organizational culture in which they carry out their work" (p. 1).

In conclusion, Kolb presents a theory that can be very useful in understanding ourselves as learners, service providers, staff members, supervisors, and faculty. It can also help students gain a level of self-awareness that can support their success in the learning environments of higher education as well as in environments they will encounter in their careers. Kolb's theory also provides the design tools necessary to create inclusive learning environments for both challenging and supporting all participants. We seek to respond as a profession to the increasing diversity of the student population and to have that diversity represented among student leaders, student staff, graduate students in professional preparation programs, and professional staff. To make progress toward such goals, we need to provide services that meet the needs of a variety of students, and we need to provide educational and work environments that both challenge and support a diverse group of individuals. Kolb's theory can aid us in doing so.

CHAPTER THIRTEEN

HOLLAND'S THEORY OF VOCATIONAL PERSONALITIES AND ENVIRONMENTS

A meeting of the planning committee for the student government orientation is about to begin. The group's agenda is determining how to proceed. Sherry is the first to speak; she suggests that the usual way of doing orientation be scrapped. She wants to try out some new and creative approaches this year. Jeff disagrees; he does not want to change anything. He argues that if the group sticks with what was done last year, the schedule can be followed just as it is outlined in last year's report. Michele suggests that the group look into how other schools organize their orientation programs. She would also like to do a formal survey of new officers' needs and interests to obtain some hard data on which to base the program. Scott indicates that he is willing to try some new ideas, but he is concerned with an issue that he thinks is more important. He believes that the planning team members should be paid for the work they are putting in or at the very least receive academic credit for organizing the orientation program. Susan is not too crazy about being part of this planning team in the first place, but when asked what she thinks they should do, she states that she would like to see some "action" types of activities added, like a volleyball game or a "teams challenge course." Bethany suggests that more social events are needed to allow people to get to know each other better. Everyone seems to have a personal agenda, and as the meeting goes on, people become frustrated because no one seems willing to compromise and no progress occurs.

The original idea for the opening scenario in this chapter was provided by Dr. Carney Strange, professor of higher education and student affairs, Bowling Green State University, Bowling Green, Ohio.

Down the hall, another group is meeting to plan the orientation for the new student activities fee allocation board. Kelli isn't quite sure how she got on this committee because she has no background in accounting, but she is creative and figures that she can offer some really innovative and interesting suggestions for livening up the orientation program. She suggests to the committee that they pitch last year's program and start over. Tammy is appalled; she notes that last year's group worked hard on the program and that since it went well, nothing should be changed. Diane agrees, pointing out that all the leftover handouts could be used to save time and paper. Joe offers that following last year's schedule will make assigning responsibilities easier. Alicia adds that if the old schedule is followed, all the committee members will know what they are supposed to do and deadlines can be set for completing each assignment. Jennifer chimes in that she has only so much time to devote to this committee and that sticking to the old plan will be more efficient. Poor Kelli; she feels like she is on another planet. No one is listening to her new ideas. Her enthusiasm and desire to make a contribution are rapidly disappearing. She can't wait to get out of the room and is having serious doubts about continuing her involvement on this committee.

T he group dynamics in the two situations described in the scenario can be explained using a theory outlined by John Holland. Holland's theory of vocational personalities and work environments can be categorized as both a typology theory and a theory of person-environment fit. Holland (1985/1992) identified six basic personality types and six corresponding types of environments. He hypothesized that satisfaction, achievement, and persistence can be predicted by the degree of "fit" between persons and the environments in which they find themselves. Although Holland's main purpose in developing his theory was to explain vocational behavior, the concepts he introduced are also useful in explaining behavior in social and educational settings.

Holland's theory has been identified as the most popular and influential theory of career development (Hackett, Lent, & Greenhaus, 1991). It has generated extensive research, a number of assessment instruments, and practical strategies for assisting people with career decision making. The major tenets of Holland's theory will be presented in this chapter, and research and applications related to it will be reviewed.

Historical Overview

Holland's ideas about vocational behavior grew out of his work as a vocational counselor in educational, military, and clinical settings (Holland, 1985/1992). He observed that people seemed to fall into broad categories with regard to interests, personality traits, and behavior. His observations corresponded to the ideas of several early psychologists who proposed both occupational stereotypes (Darley, 1938) and patterns of interests (Guilford, Christensen, Bond, & Sutton, 1954). Holland used his ideas about type to develop the six scales of the Vocational Preference Inventory (Holland, 1958). Further refinement of his theory was based on research using this instrument.

Holland built on the work of Linton (1945) in developing his idea that environments are transmitted through the collection of people who compose them. Following Lewin (1935), Holland hypothesized that behavioral outcomes result from the interaction of the person and the environment.

Holland has continually revised his theory, drawing on research conducted and critiques published since his original statement in 1959. Holland's descriptions of personality and environmental types have remained constant, while concepts addressing how types interact have been added and modified (Weinrach & Srebalus, 1990). Super (1985) noted that the current version of Holland's theory is more developmentally oriented than earlier statements and does a better job of taking into account social context and historical time.

Holland's ideas were slow to gain popularity with psychologists, who are generally wary of typology theories (Hackett et al., 1991). However, after the publication of the Self-Directed Search (Holland, 1971) and other easy-to-use assessment instruments, extensive study was undertaken of the personality types of individuals in various occupations, the key constructs of Holland's theory, and the validity of assessment tools designed for use in career counseling (Hackett et al.). Study of person-environment congruence was popular in the 1980s (Spokane, 1985). Recent work has explored the validity of Holland's theory with diverse populations and examined possible gender bias (Weinrach & Srebalus, 1990).

The Theory

Holland's theory begins with four assumptions. First, Holland (1985/1992) proposed that to varying degrees, people resemble each of six personality types. The more similar they are to a particular type, the more they exhibit the behaviors and attitudes associated with it. Similarly, there are six model environments that parallel each of the personality types with regard to qualities and attributes. This parallel structure exists because "environments are characterized by the people who occupy them" (Weinrach & Srebalus, 1990, p. 40). Third, Holland suggested that people seek out environments that provide them with opportunities to use their talents and express their values and attitudes. That is, people seek out environments made up of individuals similar to themselves. Finally, Holland restated

Lewin's hypothesis (1935) that behavior results from the interaction of the person and the environment.

Type Development

Holland has often been criticized for not explaining how individual types develop (see, for example, Brown, 1987). In the latest iteration of his theory, however, Holland (1985/1992) discussed the role of environment in shaping development. In particular, Holland sees the personality types of parents playing an important role in determining the type of opportunities provided for their children and the kinds of activities and attitudes that are reinforced. Holland also believes that children inherit a biological predisposition to certain characteristics.

As children's preferences for certain activities are reinforced, the preferences become more strongly defined interests and skills (Holland, 1985/1992). Children come to value particular activities they are good at and for which they are rewarded, and they build their self-concepts around these activities. Changes in personality are less likely to occur as the person ages because of the cumulative effect of learning and experience. Environments are also less likely to allow people to change the longer persons have been engaging in particular kinds of activities. For example, a woman who has been in one career for an extensive period of time is likely to find that people will have trouble accepting that she wants to change fields.

The Six Types

Holland's six personality types are defined by specific interests, behaviors, and attitudes. The environmental types provide opportunities to engage in the activities and reward behaviors that each type values. The types are defined as follows.

Realistic. Realistic people tend to be interested in and prefer activities that involve working with objects, tools, machines, and animals. They are competent in manual, mechanical, agricultural, and technical areas. They value concrete things like money and personal qualities such as power and status. Realistic people tend to be frank, practical, inflexible, uninsightful, and uninvolved. In the first planning meeting in the opening scenario, Susan could be described as Realistic; she wasn't crazy about being part of a group, and the types of activities she preferred involved physical, outdoor activity.

Investigative. Investigative types prefer activities that call for systematic investigation designed to understand and control physical, biological, or cultural phenomena. They are competent in scientific and mathematical areas. They value science and can be described as analytical, intellectual, precise, reserved, and cautious. Michele was the Investigative type in the first planning meeting. She wanted to investigate what other schools did for orientation, and she favored a survey of students.

Artistic. Artistic people prefer spontaneous, creative, unregulated activities that lead to the creation of various art forms. They are competent in artistic areas such as language, art, music, drama, and writing. They value aesthetic qualities and tend to be emotional, expressive, original, imaginative, and impulsive. In our student government planning group, Sherry would be described as Artistic. She wanted to see some new, creative ideas and was the first to express her opinions.

Social. Social individuals prefer activities that involve working with others in ways that educate, inform, cure, or enlighten. They possess interpersonal and educational competencies. They value helping others and engaging in social activities. Social types can be described as cooperative, friendly, helpful, empathic, and tactful. Bethany was the Social member of the planning committee. She was interested in making sure that social activities were included in the orientation and that everyone had a chance to get to know each other.

Enterprising. Enterprising types prefer working with other people to achieve organizational goals or material outcomes. They possess skills in leadership and persuasion. They value political and economic achievement and tend to be domineering, extraverted, self-confident, talkative, and adventurous. Scott, the entrepreneur who wanted to be sure he was getting something in return for his involvement, was the Enterprising member of the planning team.

Conventional. Conventional types like activities that involve working with data in systematic, orderly, and explicit ways. They are competent at clerical and computational tasks. They value business and monetary achievement and can be described as conforming, efficient, inflexible, practical, and unimaginative. Jeff represented the Conventional type in the first group. He was interested in doing things efficiently by using existing materials and saw no need for new ideas.

Personality Patterns and Subtypes

Originally, Holland (1966) suggested that a person could be identified as belonging to a single type. In his later writings (Holland, 1985/1992), however, he proposed the concept of personality profiles or subtypes. Subtypes may include two to six types but have typically consisted of three. The dominant type is listed first, the second most dominant appears second, and so forth.

Subtypes are used to categorize both people and environments. For the sake of simplicity we have identified the students in the first planning group by their dominant type only. In all likelihood, however, they each have a mix of interests. Although Sherry may most closely resemble the Artistic type, she could also have secondary interests in Social activities and concerns as well as some Investigative interests. Her subtype, then, would be "ASI."

Environmental subtypes can be illustrated by the second planning group in the opening scenario, which consisted of five Conventional types and one Artistic type. This group's subtype would be "CA_" (the blank denotes the absence of a third type).

Secondary Assumptions

Holland (1985/1992) offered several secondary assumptions that apply to both personality types and environments. These assumptions help explain how people and environments interact and how types influence behavior.

Calculus. The relationships among types can be illustrated by using a hexagonal model (Holland, 1985/1992) (see Figure 13.1). Types are located on the points of a hexagon in the following order: R-I-A-S-E-C. Types that are similar are closer together on the hexagon; those that are different are further apart.

Consistency. Consistency refers to the degree to which pairs of types are related. Holland hypothesized that some types are more similar to each other than they are to other types. For example, a Social type has more in common with an Enterprising type than with an Investigative type. Social and Enterprising types both like to interact with others and work with people, whereas an Investigative type prefers working with data and ideas and doesn't feel comfortable in social situations. Therefore, a person with Social and Enterprising qualities would be labeled as having a consistent personality subtype, while a person with Social and Investigative qualities would have an inconsistent subtype. Likewise, environments can be considered consistent or inconsistent. The second planning team, made up of Conventional and Artistic people, types that have almost nothing in common, would be considered highly inconsistent.

Holland (1985/1992) suggested that consistent people are more predictable and harder to influence than inconsistent people. Consistent environments tend to exert more influence on the people in them than inconsistent environments.

Differentiation. Differentiation refers to the extent to which a particular type describes a person or an environment. A differentiated person has interests that are characteristic of mainly one type (for example, interests that are associated only with

FIGURE 13.1. HEXAGONAL MODEL FOR DEFINING PSYCHOLOGICAL RESEMBLANCES AMONG PERSONALITY TYPES AND ENVIRONMENTS AND THEIR INTERACTIONS.

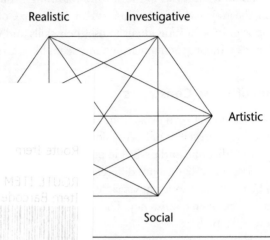

erentiated person has a variety of interests for example, some interests associated with ial type, and still others with the Enterpris- by subtracting the person's lowest type score whatever Holland assessment instrument is ne more differentiated the person is.

ated include a predominance of people of g group, which is a differentiated Conven- tional environment. Our first planning group, in contrast, is undifferentiated be- cause it includes one person of each type. Degree of differentiation is determined by counting the number of people of each type and subtracting the lowest num- ber from the highest. Like consistency, differentiation is associated with pre- dictability. Hypothesized behaviors are more likely to occur and are likely to be of greater strength in differentiated people and environments.

Identity. Identity is a concept that Holland added in later iterations of his theory (1985/1992). It refers to the "clarity and stability" of the person's goals, interests, and abilities or, in an environment, the degree to which goals, tasks, and rewards are stable over time (p. 5).

Congruence. Congruence refers to the degree of "match" between a person and an environment. Perfect congruence occurs, for example, when a Conventional person finds herself in a Conventional environment, as Tammy and her Conventional friends did in the second planning group. For Kelli, the Artistic person, the group was highly incongruent, however. Congruent environments provide opportunities for individuals to use their skills and interests and reward them for doing so. Incongruent environments seem like "foreign territory."

Interaction of These Constructs

Interactions between persons and environments involving varying degrees of congruence, consistency, differentiation, and identity will lead to different results. The most predictable and desirable outcomes result when people and environments are congruent, consistent, differentiated, and high in identity. Congruence seems to be the most important variable in determining outcome, followed by differentiation and then consistency. The role of identity is still unclear, as it is a relatively new concept.

Holland (1985/1992) pointed out that differentiation, consistency, and identity are really three ways of describing the clarity, focus, and definition of a person or an environment. He suggested that in reality, they may be three techniques for defining what is essentially the same concept.

Assessment Techniques

Holland and his colleagues have developed a number of instruments to assess both vocational personality types and environmental types. We will review only the most important of these instruments; numerous others are listed in *The Self-Directed Search Professional User's Guide* (Holland, Powell, & Fritzsche, 1994). A number of instruments developed by other researchers are also based on Holland's theory (see Chartrand, Strong, & Weitzman, 1995). Of particular note, the Strong Interest Inventory (SII) assesses Holland's personality types using the General Occupational Theme Scales. The SII manual (Harmon, Hansen, Borgen, & Hammer, 1994) provides information concerning these scales and their development.

The Vocational Preference Inventory

The Vocational Preference Inventory (VPI) (Holland, 1985) was the first instrument developed by Holland to measure personality type. It consists of a list of 160 occupational titles that persons completing the instrument indicate they either like or dislike. Items related to each of the six personality types are totaled, and a profile ranked from highest to lowest is developed, with the highest score representing the type the person most resembles. Differences of four or five points between scales are meaningful, based on standard errors of estimate. To provide additional data about the test taker's personality, the VPI includes scales labeled Self-Control, Masculinity-Femininity, Status, Infrequency (of response), and Acquiescence in addition to the six type scales. The instrument has been revised many times to enhance its reliability and gender fairness (Weinrach & Srebalus, 1990).

Holland (1985) reported that the internal consistency of the scales measuring each of the six personality types ranged from .85 to .91 on the 1977 version of the VPI for samples of employed men and women and college students. Test-retest reliabilities of the six personality type scales based on a sample of college seniors tested over a six-week interval ranged from .74 to .92. A sample of college freshmen tested over an interval of one year resulted in test-retest reliabilities of .61 to .86 for the type scales. Holland reported that the remaining VPI scales (Acquiescence, Status, and so on) have only moderate reliability.

Many correlational studies have examined the relationship of VPI types to measures of personality, such as the Sixteen Personality Factors Questionnaire (16PF) and the California Psychological Inventory, and have found that Holland's types are moderately related to personality variables the theory would predict (for example, the correlation of the Sociability scale of the 16PF and the Social scale of the VPI is .49) (Holland, 1985). The VPI correlates moderately with other interest tests, such as the Kuder Occupational Interest Inventory and various iterations of the Strong Interest Inventory. It also correlates moderately with self-reports of competencies and values. The VPI scales are able to discriminate among a range of criterion groups, such as persons employed in specific fields and students in different majors. They also predict choice of major and occupation with 35 to 60 percent accuracy. The VPI has been translated into twenty languages, and use of the instrument in different countries has resulted in consistent findings (Holland & Gottfredson, 1992). Extensive validity studies are reported in the VPI manual (Holland, 1985) as well as in *Making Vocational Choices* (Holland, 1985/1992).

The Self-Directed Search

In 1971, Holland introduced the Self-Directed Search (SDS). The SDS (Holland, 1994) is a self-administered and self-scored instrument designed for individuals to use independently, although some reviewers have suggested that it is more effective if reviewed with a counselor (Krieshok, 1987; Super, 1985). It consists of two booklets: an assessment booklet and an occupational classification booklet. The SDS assesses type more broadly than the VPI by having individuals report on their activities, competencies, occupations, and self-estimates (Holland, Fritzsche, & Powell, 1994). Six summary scores form the person's profile, from which is derived a three-letter Holland Occupational Code (HOC), made up of the three highest scores, in descending order. Based on the standard error of measurement, differences of eight points or greater between scores on the type scales are considered meaningful. The HOC is used to identify congruent careers using the Occupations Finder, the occupational classification booklet that contains 1,335 occupational titles arranged according to Holland code.

Like the VPI, the SDS has been revised several times (Holland, Fritzsche, & Powell, 1994). It is available for several different ages groups, including adults in transition, adults and students with limited reading ability, and junior high school students (Holland, Powell, & Fritzsche, 1994). A computerized version has also been developed (Reardon, Psychological Assessment Resources, & Holland, 1985).

Holland, Fritzsche, and Powell (1994) reported internal consistency reliabilities (KR 20) ranging from .90 to .93 for the summary scales based on a college sample including both men and women. Test-retest reliabilities over four- to twelve-week intervals for the six summary scales ranged from .76 to .89 for high school, college, and adult samples.

For the 1994 version of the SDS, summary scale intercorrelations for different age groups by gender were similar across samples and approximated the hexagonal model (Holland, Fritzsche, & Powell, 1994). Tests of concurrent validity demonstrate that the high-point Holland code and vocational aspiration, current occupation, or college major agree an average of 55 percent of the time, a figure that is high for interest inventories. Like the VPI, the SDS has been translated into twenty languages and has been found to produce similar results in a variety of countries (Holland & Gottfredson, 1992). The manual for the SDS (Holland, Fritzsche, & Powell, 1994) provides extensive information about construct, concurrent, and predictive validity of the instrument.

In his review of the 1985 version of the SDS, Krieshok (1987) stated, "When compared to other interventions on cost, reactions of test takers, time, research support, and usefulness, the SDS, in my opinion, is in a class by itself" (p. 514).

Comparison of Instruments Measuring Vocational Personality

Spokane (1985) reported the results of several studies comparing earlier versions of the Vocational Preference Inventory, the Self-Directed Search, and the General Occupational Themes of the Strong Vocational Interest Blank (SVIB). He noted that intercorrelations were "reasonably high" and suggested that the three measurement tools could probably be used interchangeably to measure personality type (p. 308). Holland, Powell, and Fritzsche (1994) also reported studies that indicate that the VPI and the SDS measure similar domains.

Occupational Classification

Holland developed a classification system for occupations based on the personality types of workers found in each. While not really an assessment instrument, the Occupational Classification can be used to organize occupational information, analyze work histories, and assist clients in planning career exploration (Helms, 1973). The preliminary version of the classification system was based on the VPI scores of students planning to enter particular occupations (Holland, 1985/1992). Using a variety of research techniques, Holland and his colleagues then extended the system to all common occupations in the United States and have recently updated it to include newer occupations (Holland, Fritzsche, & Powell, 1994).

Two versions of the classification exist. The first is the Occupational Finder, used with the Self-Directed Search (Holland, 1994). The Occupational Finder contains 1,335 occupational titles, their Holland Occupational Codes, educational requirements, and numbers from the *Dictionary of Occupational Titles* (DOT) (U.S. Department of Labor, 1977). A more extensive version is the *Dictionary of Holland Occupational Codes* (DHOC) (Gottfredson & Holland, 1989), which lists 12,860 coded occupations arranged according to Holland's hexagonal model and educational level.

Holland (1985/1992) reported evidence of the validity of his occupational classification. Studies demonstrate that the classification is able to predict aspirations and work histories. The system is also similar to other classification systems used by the government and sociologists. Studies also indicate that occupational codes for workers or students in a particular occupational category were similar and that occupations belonging to the same category have similar characteristics.

The Environmental Assessment Technique

Based on the assumption that environment is transported through people, Astin and Holland (1961) developed the Environmental Assessment Technique (EAT). The first version of the EAT identified preferences of students tabulated for each of Holland's six environmental types, resulting in a six-variable profile. The absolute numbers for each type were then converted into percentages of the total population in the environment being studied. Later, Richards, Seligman, and Jones (1970) expanded the technique by examining the number of course offerings related to each type, as well as the number of faculty in each area of study and the number of students graduating in each field.

Reliability coefficients for the EAT over one to six years ranged from .54 to .97, with a median of .93 (Astin & Holland, 1961). Percentages of the six student types identified by the EAT predicted student descriptions of colleges on the College Characteristics Index (Astin & Holland, 1961). Other studies suggest that the EAT variables are related in predicted ways to numerous subjective and objective aspects of the environment, such as characteristics of entering freshmen (Astin, 1964), popularity and selectivity of colleges (Astin, 1965b), and classroom environments in various fields of study (Astin, 1965a).

Richards et al. (1970) found that faculty, curriculum, and student assessments of the curriculum were significantly intercorrelated, indicating that the three methods produce similar findings. Curriculum and faculty profiles were also related in predicted ways to measures of campus climate.

Research

Research based on Holland's theory has been extensive. Much of it has been conducted to validate aspects of the theory itself, as well as the instruments reviewed in the preceding section. Other studies have investigated outcomes associated with Holland's concepts, particularly those related to congruence. Recently, a number of studies have been conducted to determine the validity of Holland's constructs for women and racial and cultural groups. This necessarily brief review will concentrate on studies that focus on college students.

Personality Types

The first studies of Holland's theory sought to validate the existence of the six distinctive personality types he proposed. Holland (1985/1992) reported extensive research suggesting that the Holland types are related to characteristics the types suggest. Later studies (see Fouad, 1994) have supported these earlier findings. Personality type has been found to correlate with academic ability, self-ratings of personality characteristics, involvement in activities, academic interests, personal achievements, and personality traits.

Development of Personality Types

Holland (1985/1992) presented research evidence supporting his belief that different types have different life histories because of their family backgrounds and the different environments to which they are exposed. Several studies have indicated that college students' types can be predicted from their parents' occupations.

A study involving biological and adopted children (Grotevant, Scarr, & Weinberg, 1977) also suggested that personality type has an inherited component.

Differentiation, Consistency, and Identity

Holland (1985/1992) and others have reported mixed results from studies examining personality patterns. A few studies suggest that differentiation is related to stability of career choice, but more have resulted in negative findings. Many of these latter studies are methodologically weak, however.

Studies of the relationship of consistency and stability have also produced contradictory results. Holland (1985/1992) pointed out, however, that well-designed studies have shown a strong relationship between consistency and stability of career aspiration for college students. Strahan (1987) critiqued earlier measures of consistency and introduced more complex statistical procedures for assessing this construct that he believed would contribute to more productive research.

Weinrach and Srebalus (1990) reported that identity is related to occupational commitment. Fouad (1994) noted, though, that no relationship has been found between identity and achievement, consistency, or differentiation in recent studies.

Congruence

Holland (1985/1992) and Weinrach and Srebalus (1990) reported support for the congruence hypothesis with regard to the vocational choices of college students. Career aspirations tended to remain stable when their environments were dominated by students whose career choices were similar. Other studies indicate that congruence of type and field of study is correlated with persistence and academic adjustment (Spokane, 1985).

Many studies suggest that satisfaction is related to congruence in educational environments (Fouad, 1994; Weinrach & Srebalus, 1990). However, the results of a recent meta-analysis (Tranberg, Slane, & Ekeberg, 1993) failed to support this conclusion. The authors of this study were quite critical of the quality of research in this area, however, suggesting that better measures of the constructs might produce different results.

Early studies of the relationship between congruence and academic achievement were positive (Spokane, 1985). Assouline and Meir (1987), however, found a nonsignificant relationship between congruence and achievement in their meta-analysis. Schwartz (1991) suggested that the relationship between academic achievement and congruence found in some studies is confounded because Investigative students tend to be high achievers and Realistic types to be low achievers.

Typological Structure

Holland (1985/1992) noted that the hexagonal model has received substantial research support. Although the sides of the hexagon are not necessarily equidistant,
the ordering of the scales is usually the same. Rounds, Tracey, and Hubert (1992)
reviewed studies examining the hexagonal structure of Holland's theory and found
conflicting results. They criticized the various methods used to test structure and
presented alternative tests they believe would yield more precise results. Based on
a reanalysis of earlier data, Rounds (1995) reported that Holland's calculus assumption does hold (that is, adjacent types on the hexagon are most related, opposite types are least related, and alternating types fall in between), but the sides of
the hexagon are not equidistant.

Educational Environments

Much less research has investigated environments than personality types. The research that exists indicates that the college environment is defined, at least in part,
by the proportion of students and faculty in different academic areas (Holland,
1985/1992). For example, residence hall climate, as measured by the University
Residence Environment Scales, seems to be related to the mix of personality types
living in the hall (Hearn & Moos, 1976).

Gender and Sexual Orientation

Gender differences exist with regard to frequency of type (Holland, Powell, &
Fritzsche, 1994). In particular, women are more likely to be Social types and less
likely to be Realistic types. Holland argued that differences between men and
women found when types are assessed are due to socialization. He stated, "Tests
do not 'slot' people; people incorporate values, goals, and competencies from the
culture and 'slot' themselves" (Holland, Powell, & Fritzsche, p. 53).

The hexagonal structure of interests does seem to fit men better than
women, however (Hansen, Collins, Swanson, & Fouad, 1993). Women seem to
discriminate less between Realistic and Investigative items than men, and Social
items seem to have more importance for women. The authors suggested that socialization and occupational opportunity may contribute to these differences.
Mobley and Slaney (1996) suggested that congruence of personality type and occupational choice may not be as salient for lesbians and gay men as for heterosexual individuals. They hypothesized that environmental conditions such as
acceptance and support for gay men and lesbians in occupational fields may be
a more important factor in career choice than congruence of type for this pop-

ulation. They also suggested that stage of gay or lesbian identity development may influence career decisions.

Race and Culture

Based on their research review, Weinrach and Srebalus (1990) concluded that Holland's theory is useful with diverse racial groups. Hansen's review (1987) calls into question whether VPI and SDS types accurately predict the occupations of African Americans. It is important to note, however, that the majority of studies she discussed involved non-college-educated participants. Leong and Brown (1995) suggested that the lower congruence between type and occupation found for some ethnic groups may be related to real and perceived employment barriers.

Holland, Powell, and Fritzsche (1994) reported that the SDS has been used successfully in diverse nations, including Australia, Hong Kong, Israel, the Netherlands, Nigeria, and Pakistan, demonstrating its relevance in many cultures.

A number of studies examining Holland's structural hypotheses for different races and cultures have generally supported the ordering of types around the hexagon but not the idea that they are equidistant (Fouad, 1994; Hansen, 1987). As noted earlier in this section, examination of studies based on white samples led to similar conclusions. However, a recent meta-analysis by Rounds and Tracey (1996) that included data from eighteen countries as well as ethnic groups in the United States, indicated that Holland's hexagon was a good fit for only two countries, Iceland and Israel. They cautioned against applying Holland's theory cross-culturally.

Some differences have been found in distributions of personality types and occupational preferences of different groups (Hansen, 1987). For example, Asian American students are more likely than white students to aspire to Investigative occupations and less likely to consider Enterprising and Conventional occupations (Leung, Ivey, & Suzuki, 1994). Such differences are hypothesized to be related to socioeconomic differences and cultural differences regarding values, gender appropriateness of various occupations, and prestige associated with certain fields (Hansen, 1987; Leung et al., 1994).

Applications

Holland's theory has applicability in many areas of student affairs. Since it is a theory of vocational development, its use in career development is readily apparent. Applications in counseling, orientation, advising, residence life, and student activities have also been cited in the literature.

Career Development

The most common applications of Holland's theory have been in the area of career development. For instance, Reardon and Minor (1975) developed a career information service tied to curriculum in which the Self-Directed Search was included as a module that students could take independently. Career orientation programs for freshmen have also been based on Holland's theory (for example, Calliotte, Helms, & Wells, 1975). Holland, Powell, and Fritzsche (1994) provide many suggestions for using Holland's theory in college career counseling centers.

Counseling

Knowledge of vocational personality type can be useful in understanding clients' needs and reactions in personal counseling situations. Bruch (1978) pointed out that most counselors are Social types and suggested that the counseling environment they create may not be effective with other types. Lowman (1987) provided an analysis of how each of Holland's six types would approach therapy and suggested ways that counselors could structure the therapeutic relationship to work most effectively with each type. For instance, a structured behavioral approach might be more effective with a Realistic client than a client-centered approach.

Orientation and Advising

Jacoby, Rue, and Allen (1984) used Holland's theory to design a series of guides to academic, vocational, and cocurricular activities targeted at specific types of students. Called UMaps, the guides took the form of posters displayed around campus and brochures distributed by advisers. After students completed a short assessment of Holland type, UMaps were used in orientation programming to help students locate classes, programs, and activities compatible with their types. Advisers used the UMaps to help students connect activities and interests to career possibilities.

Residence Life

Williams (1967) found that personality type of roommates influenced their ability to get along. Incongruent pairs of freshmen male roommates were more likely to experience conflict than congruent pairs. Placing students in congruent residence hall environments based on majority type has also been shown to be related to academic achievement, at least for Realistic men (Snead & Caple, 1971).

Positive outcomes associated with Holland's concept of congruence can be used as support for creating interest houses or floors, since students opting for such units are likely to have similar Holland types. Understanding the dynamics associated with congruence can also help staff work with students who may not "fit" with the predominant type in a unit.

Student Activities

Sergent and Sedlacek (1990) found that student volunteers in different organizations were different types who had different motivations for joining. Volunteers involved in recruitment of new students for the Admissions Office, for instance, were likely to be Enterprising types motivated by needs for autonomy, affiliation, and achievement. Knowledge of the personality types of student organization members and their needs can be useful when recruiting, training, and advising student volunteers.

As indicated in the opening scenarios, understanding the group dynamics resulting from various combinations of Holland personality types working together can be very useful. Advisers could use such information in organizational and leadership development activities as well as individual advising sessions.

Critique and Future Directions

Holland's theory of personality type and vocational environments is one of the best-known theories in the fields of counseling and student affairs. A major reason for the popularity of Holland's theory is its simplicity. The theory is easy to use and understand (Borgen, 1991; Carson, 1994; Hackett et al., 1991). Concepts are clearly defined, and hypotheses are well delineated (Brown, 1987).

Holland's theory is very practical (Brown, 1987). As noted earlier, it has applicability not only to vocational decision making but also to many other areas, such as group interaction, design of programming, and structuring of effective work and living environments. Individuals quickly grasp Holland's concepts and see their utility.

Holland has developed instrumentation that is easy to use as well as reliable and valid (Osipow, 1990; Walsh & Holland, 1992). In part because of the readily available assessment tools, Holland's theory has generated extensive research, and Holland has used research findings and criticism to modify and improve his theory (Borgen, 1991; Brown, 1987; Hackett et al., 1991). Holland has encouraged and worked collaboratively with other researchers in addition to conducting his own investigations.

A theory as well known and popular as Holland's is certain to draw criticism. Much of the criticism of Holland's theory has centered around his hexagon model and the hypotheses concerning consistency, differentiation, and congruence that grow out of it. As noted in the research section of this chapter, findings have been mixed regarding the validity of these concepts. Some reviewers have discounted Holland's theory because of these findings (Schwartz, 1992), while more moderate voices have called for modification of the hypotheses to create a more universally valid model (Hansen, 1992). The concept of identity has also come under attack because of its lack of conceptual clarity and research support (Brown, 1987). In addition, Dawis (1992) was critical of Holland for limiting his theory to a consideration of vocational interests rather than also including other vocationally related variables, such as ability.

Chartrand et al. (1995) pointed out that research related to Holland's theory has failed to adequately delineate the environment, the individual's position in the environment, and the meaning of person-environment fit. Holland (1985/1992) acknowledged that the role played by environmental factors, such as status and distribution of influence, is not taken into account by the theory. Carson (1994) also noted that when economic or political conditions are unstable, job satisfaction may have less to do with congruence than with security and meeting basic needs. More research is needed to address these concerns.

Leong and Brown (1995) took Holland to task for not adequately considering the role of culture in creating and maintaining environments. While acknowledging that some research exists using African American samples, they noted the lack of studies examining the applicability of Holland's theory for other ethnic groups. Further studies using more varied samples are needed to illuminate the role of race, ethnicity, and culture in the development of personality type.

Subich (1992) is also critical of researchers investigating Holland's hypotheses for not specifically defining their variables. For example, Subich pointed out that there are many types of congruence, including congruence with supervisors, with coworkers, and with job tasks. Each will differentially influence outcomes.

Although Holland's theory will continue to generate controversy, its appeal and utility are beyond question. At a time when career decision making is becoming a much more challenging process for many people because of the increasing complexity of society, Holland provides a tool for simplifying and understanding some of the many factors involved. Holland's theory also helps us understand individual behavior and interpersonal interactions in a variety of settings. His work is an important addition to the student affairs field.

CHAPTER FOURTEEN

THE MYERS-BRIGGS ADAPTATION OF JUNG'S THEORY OF PERSONALITY TYPE

Kiersten and Kelly have been assigned to work together on a presentation for their Leadership Development class. Their topic is effective time management. In their first meeting, it becomes evident that the two women have very different approaches to the project. Kiersten wants to do something that is lively, fun, and creative. She wants to involve the whole class in some type of experiential activity and then process whatever happens. Kelly is more interested in making sure that their presentation is educational and includes information that the students can use. She thinks a more straightforward, structured presentation involving lecture and a lot of handouts will be more successful. Kelly believes that it is essential for the two of them to do a lot of background research on time management to make sure that they are covering all the important concepts. Kiersten disagrees; to her, people's personal approaches to time management are what is important. She doesn't think the concept can really be "taught" objectively. Kelly thinks it is necessary to plan every detail of the presentation and to rehearse and time it to make sure that they know exactly what they will each be doing. Kiersten thinks this idea is ridiculous. She favors a spontaneous, free-flowing approach that will be more "natural." Obviously, these two students view learning very differently.

The Myers-Briggs adaptation of Jung's classic theory of personality types (1923/1971) can help explain the differences in how Kiersten and Kelly would address their assignment. This theoretical approach identifies individual differences in the ways in which people prefer to take in and process information, that is, how they perceive their environments (become aware of people, things, events, and ideas) and how they make judgments, or reach conclusions, about the information they take in. Because this approach categorizes people on the basis of individual preferences, it is considered a typology theory.

Jung's work related to personality development has many implications for student affairs practice (Salter, 1997). Because of space considerations, we have chosen to limit our discussion to a review of his ideas concerning personality type (Jung, 1923/1971), particularly as interpreted and modified by Isabel Briggs Myers (1980). Because of its extensive use in assessing personality type, the Myers-Briggs Type Indicator (Myers & McCaulley, 1985) will be discussed in some detail. The related work of Keirsey and Bates (personality temperament) will also be noted.

Historical Overview

Personality type and temperament has been a topic of interest to scholars throughout history. Brownsword (1987) noted that a number of German scholars in the late nineteenth and early twentieth centuries attempted to explain differences they saw in people's personalities. These "theories," however, were not based on any systematic research.

In the early 1900s, Carl Jung, a Swiss psychoanalyst, became interested in determining if people differed in any consistent way across time and culture (Spoto, 1989). After extensive clinical observation, analysis of social interaction, and self-reflection, Jung (1923/1971) suggested that such differences did exist and that they helped explain "the relationship of the individual to the world, to people and things" (p. v). His theory examined the "conscious use of the functions of perception and decision making and the areas of life in which these functions are used" (McCaulley, 1990, p. 181). Though Jung is best known for his theory of personality type, it is only a small part of his contribution to the study of personality development (Hopcke, 1989).

Jung's work intrigued Katherine Briggs and her daughter, Isabel Briggs Myers, who together studied it for over twenty years (McCaulley, 1990). During World War II, they noticed that many people were taking jobs that seemed inappropriate for their personality types. Convinced that an understanding of personality type could help people learn more about themselves and result in better matches of personality and jobs to bring the war effort to a successful conclusion, they decided to develop an instrument based on Jung's theory. Development of the Myers-Briggs Type Indicator (MBTI) became Isabel Myers's lifework (Spoto, 1989).

Although she had no formal training in research or psychology and no academic affiliation, Myers developed an instrument to measure the attitudes and behaviors associated with the different psychological types presented by Jung, as clarified and modified by Myers and Briggs. Persuading family and friends to assist her in finding individuals to take the instrument, she worked on validating the MBTI from 1942 until 1957 (McCaulley, 1990). Because she lacked the "proper" academic credentials, most of organized psychology did not take Myers's work seriously (Black, 1980).

In 1957, however, the Educational Testing Service (ETS) offered to distribute the MBTI as a research instrument and began to conduct more extensive research to evaluate the instrument (Pittenger, 1993). Although the ETS published a manual for the MBTI in 1962, an unfavorable internal review of the instrument (Strickler & Ross, 1962) resulted in their discontinuing its publication (Pittenger, 1993).

A few scholars, including Mary McCaulley at the University of Florida, Cecil Williams at Michigan State, Harold Grant at Auburn, and Donald McKinnon at the University of California, did find merit in the instrument, and their research added to its credibility in academic circles (McCaulley, 1990). In 1975, Consulting Psychologists Press began to publish the MBTI for applied use.

To encourage further research and training, Mary McCaulley and Isabel Myers established the Center for Applications of Psychological Type in 1976 (McCaulley, 1990). A professional organization for individuals interested in psychological type, the Association for Psychological Type, was formed in 1979. In addition, a refereed journal, the *Journal of Psychological Type*, was started in 1977 by Thomas Carskadon at Mississippi State University.

Isabel Myers's definitive statement of her work and theory of psychological type, *Gifts Differing*, was published in 1980, the year of her death. In 1985, a revised edition of the MBTI manual was published by Consulting Psychologists Press (Myers & McCaulley, 1985).

Following its publication by Consulting Psychologists Press in 1976, the Myers-Briggs Type Indicator gained enormous popularity. Pittenger (1993) reported that over two million copies of the MBTI are sold annually. The test is used in a wide variety of educational, business, and counseling settings.

Controversy continues, however, over the validity of the instrument and the appropriateness of its use in various settings (for example, Carlson, 1989; Healy, 1989; Pittenger, 1993). Keirsey and Bates (1984) and Salter (1995b) have extended the work of Jung and Myers to explore temperament and environment, respectively.

The Theory

Personality type theory focuses on how people use perception and judgment. Myers (1980) stated: "Together, perception and judgment, which make up a large portion of people's total mental activity, govern much of their outer behavior, because perception—by definition—determines what people see in a situation and their judgment determines what they decide to do about it" (p. 1).

Myers (1980) believed that each individual demonstrates a preference for either perception or judgment when dealing with the outside environment. Agreeing with Jung (1923/1971), Myers also hypothesized that people differ in their relative interest in the outer world of people and things (extraversion) versus the inner world of ideas and concepts (introversion).

Personality type theory as proposed by Jung (1923/1971) and further developed by Myers (1980) suggests that there are eight preferences arranged along four bipolar dimensions: extraversion–introversion (EI), sensing–intuition (SN), thinking–feeling (TF), and judging–perception (JP). These preferences can be organized into sixteen different types (ISTJ, ISFJ, ENTP, ENTJ, and so forth). Individuals will differ from others in ways that are representative of their types. Myers and McCaulley (1985) suggest that "people may reasonably be expected to develop greater skill with the processes they prefer to use and with the attitudes (extraversion or introversion) in which they prefer to use these processes" (p. 3).

Attitudes and Functions

Jung (1923/1971) hypothesized that people exhibit biologically based, naturally preferred behaviors that can be classified according to attitude type and function type. Attitude type refers to the person's response to his or her environment; introverts focus their energy inward, whereas extraverts direct their energy toward objects in the outer world (Hopcke, 1989). For introverts, interacting with the external world is draining; they tend to be reflective and enjoy solitude since they are stimulated by the subjective world of ideas and concepts (Spoto, 1989). Extraverts, by contrast, are stimulated by the world around them; they enjoy social interaction and activity. After a busy day at work, for example, an introvert would be rejuvenated by some quiet time at home reading, whereas an extravert would be refreshed by socializing with friends at a party. In the example that opened this chapter, Kiersten could probably be considered an extravert; she wants lots of interaction and discussion in the program she and Kelly are developing. Kelly, however, is more likely to be an introvert. She would prefer to present information without as much participant involvement.

Jung described four function types, two "irrational" and two "rational," that "direct conscious mental activity toward different goals" (Myers & McCaulley, 1985, p. 13). He further stated that one of these functions would be dominant, or superior, in that it is the most differentiated or "strongest" preference used by the individual.

The irrational, or perceiving, functions are used to take in information and experience events. Intuition consists of perceiving information based on unconscious processes, relying on symbols, imagination, connections, possibilities, and inferred relationships. Sensing involves taking in information directly by way of the five senses and concretely observing details and facts. When asked to observe and think about an apple, for example, a person using her intuitive function might think about the wicked witch who tried to poison Snow White with a poisoned apple, William Tell shooting an apple off his son's head, and so forth. When using the sensing function, in contrast, a person might describe the characteristics of an apple: red, round, shiny, and sweet. Referring again to our example, one might guess that Kiersten prefers the intuitive function since she wants the presentation to be creative, fun, and interesting. Kelly, however, prefers a more straightforward sensing approach; she would rather present data and strategies taken directly from the time management literature.

The rational, or judging, functions are used to organize information and make decisions (Hopcke, 1989). They consist of thinking and feeling. When using the thinking function, a person organizes information and makes decisions based on facts, evidence, and logic. When relying on the feeling function, a person focuses on subjective values, likes and dislikes, and individual worth. Kelly was using her thinking function when she suggested to Kiersten that it would be important to research their topic thoroughly and present the best-documented theories about time management. Kiersten, by contrast, was approaching the project from a feeling perspective: she wanted to discover what was most important to the people in the audience.

Jung (1923/1971) did not explicitly discuss the importance of judgment and perception. Myers, however, saw the JP preference as having two uses: (1) describing "identifiable attitudes and behaviors to the outside world" (Myers & McCaulley, 1985, p. 13) and (2) identifying, in combination with EI, the dominant (strongest) and auxiliary (second strongest) functions. Myers and McCaulley (1985) stated that the JP preference indicates the person's orientation to the *outer* world. Perceptive types tend to spend more time observing and taking in information, whereas judging types take in information more quickly and focus on drawing conclusions and making decisions.

Type Dynamics

Jung (1923/1971) suggested, but did not elaborate on, the need for an auxiliary function to balance the dominant function. Myers and Briggs developed these ideas for use in the Myers-Briggs Type Indicator (Myers & McCaulley, 1985, p. 15). They assumed that each person has one dominant function that is used in the favorite attitude (introversion or extraversion) and a second or auxiliary function that provides balance and is used in the opposite attitude. For example, an extraverted person might have sensing as his or her strongest function. The person's second strongest (auxiliary) function, thinking, would then be directed inward.

An introvert, it should be noted, shows only her or his second strongest function to the external world because the dominant function is directed inward, while an extravert shows his or her best function to others. This dynamic is often responsible for the feeling people sometimes have of "not really knowing" an introverted person.

If the dominant function is perceptive (S or N), the auxiliary function will be judging (T or F), and vice versa. The function opposite the dominant is the weakest, least developed function. It is called the inferior or shadow function.

Sixteen distinct personality types result from the various combinations of attitudes and functions (Myers, 1980). Each is a result of its dominant function, either directed outward (extraverted) or inward (introverted), and modified by its auxiliary directed toward the opposite attitude. The auxiliary is particularly important in introverts because it is responsible for their outward behavior. Myers provides descriptions for each of the sixteen types.

Type Development

Jung believed that every individual is capable of using each of these attitudes and functions but is born naturally preferring one of each pair over the other (McCaulley, 1990). The environment is important in influencing the development of type. Environmental conditions can either support and reinforce the development of the individual's natural preferences or retard such development by forcing the individual to use less preferred functions, leading to "falsification" of type (Myers & McCaulley, 1985, p. 15). For instance, an intuitive child in a family of sensors might be discouraged from creative activities and pushed to become involved in sports and other concrete, sensing-oriented activities. He or she would learn to rely on his or her senses, but at the cost of feeling uncomfortable and incompetent.

Myers and McCaulley (1985) see type development as an ongoing process of gaining competence in the use of the four functions. Such development is part of the process of individuation, defined as achieving balance or "rounding out" the self by developing skills not previously possessed. During youth, individuals work to achieve a high level of accomplishment with regard to the two preferred functions. In later life, once the preferred functions are well developed, individuals turn their attention to achieving at least an adequate competency level in the two least preferred functions.

Keirsey's Temperament Theory

Keirsey and Bates (1984) suggested that the Myers-Briggs preferences can be grouped into four temperaments that they believe do a better job of explaining people's behavior than the MBTI types do. They defined temperament as a coming together of opposing forces that result in a consistency in behavior. Though unwilling to say that temperament is inborn, they did note that it could be observed early in life. In contrast to Myers, Keirsey and Bates see temperament as developing as a result of differentiation rather than by combining functions. Keirsey (1987) saw little difference between extraverts and introverts and did not use these attitudes in his theory. Keirsey and Bates (1984) did use the other three preference pairs to define their temperaments. First drawing on Greek mythology for labels, Keirsey (1987) later changed the temperament labels to better reflect the characteristics of each temperament. The four temperaments are as follows:

Dionysian or Artisan (SP). People with this temperament place importance on freedom and action. They are impulsive and present-oriented.

Epimethean or Guardian (SJ). These individuals are other-oriented, like to be useful, often display judgmental attitudes, have a strong work ethic and sense of responsibility, and are often pessimistic.

Promethean or Rational (NT). Prometheans are driven individuals who live for their work, are future-oriented, are self-critical, have high standards, and thrive on knowledge and power.

Apollonian or Idealist (NF). These people are inwardly directed, search for the meaning in life, tend to be perfectionistic, and value integrity.

Little research has examined the premises of Keirsey's theory (1987). Therefore these concepts should be used with caution when working with students and staff.

Assessment Techniques

Two well-known instruments have been used to measure personality type: the Myers-Briggs Type Indicator and the Keirsey Temperament Sorter.

The Myers-Briggs Type Indicator

The Myers-Briggs Type Indicator is the most extensively used instrument for assessing personality type. It is a forced-choice instrument that is appropriate for use with high school students and adults (Myers & McCaulley, 1985). The standard form G has 126 items, some of which are experimental and are therefore not scored. Versions of the MBTI for research and for use with children also exist.

Each item on the MBTI is related to one of the four preference scales: extraversion–introversion (EI), sensing–intuition (SN), thinking–feeling (TF), or judging–perception (JP). The test taker is presented with two choices on each item, each representing one of the two preferences on that scale. For instance, an item on the EI scale asks: "Are you usually (a) a 'good mixer' or (b) rather quiet and reserved?"

The MBTI is scored by tallying the number of times each of the eight preferences is selected. Answers are weighted 0, 1, and 2, based on the relative popularity of each answer, thus taking social desirability into account (McCaulley, 1990). These point scores are then converted into preference scores consisting of a letter denoting the direction of the preference and a number indicating the strength of the preference. For instance, a person might obtain the following scores on the MBTI: I–14, E–12; S–5, N–25; T–0, F–24; and J–20, P–10. The higher score on each scale would indicate the person's preference on that scale, and these four letters would form the person's type: INFJ. Point scores are then determined by subtracting the lower score from the higher score on each scale and referring to a table to identify the equivalent preference score. Bayne (1995) cautioned that preference scores "only measure how clearly someone has voted; they do not measure how much of the preference someone has, how good they are at it, or type development" (p. 90). All that can really be said is that the higher the preference score, the greater the certainty that the MBTI is accurately reflecting the person's true preference. Scores of 41 or higher (31 for F) indicate very clear preferences; scores of 21 to 39 (29 for F), clear preferences; 11 to 19, moderate preferences; and 1 to 9, slight preferences (Myers & McCaulley, 1985).

Preference scores are sometimes converted to continuous scores for statistical analysis. However, McCaulley (1990) cautioned that type theory assumes that preferences are dichotomous and that researchers who use continuous scores are violating assumptions of the theory.

McCaulley (1990) stressed that the person's four-letter type rather than individual preference scores should be the unit of analysis, and interpretation of the MBTI should be based on this type. Descriptions of each of the sixteen MBTI types are provided in Myers (1987). Extended discussion of the types can be found in Myers (1980).

McCaulley (1990) urges individuals using the MBTI for counseling and other purposes to first verify the accuracy of the obtained personality type with the tested individual. Strategies for verification are included in the MBTI Manual (Myers & McCaulley, 1985) and in Bayne (1995).

The reliability and validity of the MBTI have been extensively studied and argued from its inception (Pittenger, 1993). Researchers do not seem to be able to come to an agreement concerning the merits of this instrument for use in applied settings (Carlson, 1989; Healy, 1989) or whether it accurately measures Jungian theory (McCaulley, 1990, 1991; Merenda, 1991).

Factor-analytic studies have been conducted to determine the construct validity of the MBTI, that is, whether the MBTI accurately measures the preferences outlined in personality type theory. After critiquing previous studies and conducting a large-sample study of his own, Tischler (1994) contended that the MBTI items do indeed measure the four MBTI scales effectively. Pittenger (1993) countered with evidence that the MBTI factors are not independent; in particular, the JP and SN scales have been found to correlate.

Wiggins (1989) noted that the principal concern about validity on the MBTI lies in its failure to demonstrate that the four scales are dichotomous. He argues that validity data obtained from use of continuous scores is much more extensive. After reviewing the MBTI literature, Pittenger (1993) also failed to find evidence supporting the bimodality of scales.

The MBTI manual (Myers & McCaulley, 1985) includes data showing that MBTI scores are related to other variables with which one would expect them to correlate: various personality assessments, academic performance, test-taking ability, and career preferences. The MBTI also correlates with other measures of Jungian theory. Self-ratings of type and the type assessments of significant others have been found to correlate significantly with MBTI scores (Carlson, 1989; Thorne & Gough, 1991). Carlson (1989), while noting the somewhat haphazard study of criterion validity, did conclude that MBTI type does generally predict behavior hypothesized to be associated with the type. Pittenger (1993) cautioned, however, that correlations between MBTI scores and various personality traits and behaviors are only moderate.

Devito (1985) reported that test-retest reliability coefficients from various studies are good, ranging from .48 to .87. He indicated that the TF scale for males appears to be the least stable. Pittenger (1993) pointed out, however, that type profiles, which Myers claimed should be stable over time, often do change. McCarley and Carskadon (1983) found that over a five-week period, 50 percent of individuals in their study were reclassified on one or more of the MBTI scales. Pittenger (1993) also noted that preferences scored in the 0 to 15 range often change and cannot be considered reliable.

Many Jungian psychologists have criticized the MBTI for not being a true representation of Jung's ideas about personality type (see Bayne, 1995). It is important to remember that the MBTI is a reflection of *Myers's* version of the theory, which is a modification of Jung's original ideas. The MBTI very consistently measures the concepts outlined by Myers (1980).

Despite these mixed results, evidence suggests that the MBTI is a popular and helpful personality measure (Zemke, 1992). A study conducted by the National Research Council Committee on Techniques for the Enhancement of Human Performance (cited in Zemke) found that people who completed the MBTI remembered it more than any other instrument and that 84 percent of the test takers found the information they received about their type accurate and helpful. Eighty percent of these individuals felt that taking the MBTI had an impact on their behavior, and 74 percent noted that they related to others differently after taking the MBTI. In conclusion, perhaps it is the face validity of the MBTI that has made it the most popular personality measure in use today despite conflicting research results concerning its true validity (Zemke).

The Keirsey Temperament Sorter

The Keirsey Temperament Sorter (Keirsey & Bates, 1984), derived from the MBTI, can be used to identify temperament. It has been shown to correlate significantly with the MBTI (Quinn, Lewis, & Fischer, 1992). Because this instrument is shorter than the MBTI and more readily available, it is often used in training workshops. Users are cautioned, however, that little validity information is available on the Temperament Sorter and that its results should be interpreted with even more caution than those obtained from the MBTI.

Research

As noted, the MBTI manual (Myers & McCaulley, 1985) presents a comprehensive overview of research validating the MBTI. Other studies have investigated the relationship of personality type to variables of particular interest in higher education.

Racial and Cultural Differences in Personality Type

Only a few studies have explored personality type among nonwhite populations. These few studies have consistently found that African American college students are more likely than white students to be categorized as sensing (Hill & Clark, 1993; Levy, Murphy, & Carlson, 1972; Levy & Ridley, 1987).

A recent large-scale study (Hammer & Mitchell, 1996) based on a national sample of 1,267 adults stratified by gender, ethnicity, and geographical region, found that African Americans were more likely than the total sample (70 percent S and 53 percent T) to prefer sensing (81 percent) and thinking (70 percent). Based on data from this study, the modal type for African American students is ISTJ (22 percent), as it is for the total sample (15 percent). Hispanic adults were more likely to be feeling types (54 percent) and extraverts (54 percent) than the total sample (47 percent F and 46 percent E). The modal type for Hispanics was also ISTJ (15 percent), but ISFJ and ESFJ were close seconds with 13 percent each. In another comparison study of African American, Hispanic, and Caucasian adolescents and adults, more thinking types were found among African Americans. No other differences were evident (Kaufman, 1993).

Two studies of American Indian students have also found more sensing types than appear in Caucasian student populations (Huitt, 1988; Simmons & Barrineau, 1994). Finally, a study comparing personality type among mainland Chinese, American, and Canadian Francophone students found that the Chinese students were more likely to exhibit a preference for T and TJ than students from the United States or Canada (Williams, Williams, Xu, & Li, 1992).

More research is needed to determine if the racial and ethnic differences found in these studies indicate real differences or are the result of cultural bias in the MBTI. These studies do, however, underscore the importance of considering type when working with students of different racial and cultural backgrounds.

Gender Differences in Personality Type

The MBTI manual (Myers & McCaulley, 1985) reports a gender difference on the TF scale, with 60 percent of men preferring thinking and 65 percent of the women preferring feeling. In the MBTI Form G data bank maintained by the Center for Applications of Psychological Type (cited in Hammer & Mitchell, 1996), which includes data from 232,557 individuals, 70 percent of the men preferred T and 58 percent of the women preferred F. The national study conducted by Hammer and Mitchell (1996) also examined gender differences in personality type. Like the earlier studies, they found that women were more likely to prefer feeling (61 percent) than men (31 percent). Women were also slightly more likely to prefer sensing (71 percent) and judging (61 percent) than men were (64 percent S and 55 percent J). The modal type for women was ISFJ (16 percent), with ESFJ next most common (14 percent). For men, the modal type was ISTJ (19 percent).

As with the studies cited involving members of different racial and ethnic groups, the studies examining gender differences must not be overinterpreted. Certainly, responses to questions on the MBTI are subject to influence by societal norms concerning the expected behavior and attitudes of women. In addition, gender bias in the instrument is a possible cause of the differences found in this research.

Relationship of Personality Type and Other Aspects of Development

A few researchers have examined the relationship of personality type and other aspects of development, notably psychosocial development, learning style, and conceptual level. Anchors and Robinson (1992) found several correlations between

MBTI preferences and scales on the Student Development Task Inventory–2, a measure of several of Chickering's vectors, indicating that personality type plays a role in accomplishment of developmental tasks. Carter (1990) explored the relationship of MBTI type and learning style (as defined by Belenky, Clinchy, Goldberger, & Tarule, 1986; see Chapter Nine) used by nontraditional women students. Separate knowers more often preferred intuition over sensing and perceiving over judging, whereas connected knowers preferred extraversion over introversion and feeling over thinking.

Brown and DeCoster (1991) found that higher scores on intuition predicted higher conceptual level, defined by Harvey, Hunt, and Schroeder (1961) as increased cognitive complexity demonstrated by movement from concrete to abstract thinking.

Personality Type in Student Affairs Settings

Many researchers have investigated personality type dynamics in various functional areas of student affairs. Some of the major studies have been conducted in residence life, discipline, counseling, advising, and career development settings.

Residence Life. A number of studies have examined the impact of pairing roommates on the basis of personality type (Kalsbeek, Rodgers, Marshall, Denny, & Nicholls, 1982; Schroeder, 1976; Schroeder, Warner, & Malone, 1980). Generally, results indicate that damages decrease, retention in the residence halls increases, and community is strengthened when students with similar types live together. However, one study failed to find a relationship between similar personality type and roommate satisfaction for men (Carey, Hamilton, & Shanklin, 1986); the authors suggested that there may be a gender effect on this dimension.

Discipline. A study by Griffin and Salter (1993) found that students involved in university disciplinary cases are statistically more likely to be E_TP types rather than any other type. Similarly, another study (Anchors & Dana, 1992) found that students referred to a university conduct office for minor alcohol violations were more likely to prefer extraversion, intuition, thinking, and perception than the university population as a whole. This information can be used to train resident assistants to design disciplinary interventions appropriate for such students and to plan alternative activities designed to appeal to these types.

Williams and Nelson (1986) examined interventions made by residence hall staff in disciplinary situations. They found that EST_ types gave more nonassertive responses in disciplinary situations than other types. Individuals with this type may need more training and supervision than other types who demonstrated more assertive responses.

Counseling. A rather dated review of fifty studies of uses of the MBTI in counseling (Carskadon, 1979) found that counselors are predominately NFs. University counseling center clients are more likely to be NPs than the general university population. Moderate similarity between counselor and client seemed to lead to better outcomes.

Counselors who are Ts tended to prefer cognitive counseling approaches, while Fs were more equally divided in their preference for cognitive and affective approaches in one study (McBride & Martin, 1988) but preferred affective approaches in another (Erickson, 1993).

Advising. Crockett and Crawford (1989) examined the advising style preferences of students. Sensing students preferred advising that addressed the practical details of course registration and academic planning, whereas intuitive students were more interested in developmental advising that examined their experiences and goals more broadly. Feeling students, more so than thinking students, also preferred a developmental advising model that focused more on creating a close working relationship with their adviser.

Career Development. Significant relationships between personality type as measured by the MBTI and Holland's typology as measured by the Strong-Campbell Interest Inventory (an earlier version of the Strong Interest Inventory) have been identified (Dillon & Weissman, 1987), indicating some overlap between the two typologies. In particular, intuitive students tend to exhibit strong artistic and investigative career interests (Apostal, 1991).

Influence of Personality Type on Learning and on Teaching

In addition to research conducted in student affairs settings, the influence of personality type has also been investigated in academic arenas.

Learning Styles. Studies have demonstrated that personality type is related to learning style (Lawrence, 1993). Extraverts learn best through discussion and group activity, whereas introverts need time to process information and prefer reading and working individually. Sensors need step-by-step instruction and do best on practical tasks that require remembering facts and observing specifics. Intuitives prefer independent learning and tasks that call for imagination, seeing relationships, and grasping general concepts. Thinking types value organization, objective material to study, and depth and accuracy of content. Feeling types value rapport with the teacher, learning through relationships, and personal connection to content. Judging students work in a steady, orderly manner and prefer outlined tasks and formalized instruction. They have a need for closure. Perceptive types work in spurts and follow impulses. They prefer informal learning and discovery tasks.

Reviewing fifteen years of data, Schroeder (1993) reported that 60 percent of the students in higher education are sensing types. Fifty percent of all high school seniors are extraverted sensors with concrete active learning styles. Schroeder noted that a similar distribution can be found among college students.

Teaching Styles. Lawrence (1993) reported that NTs are overrepresented in higher education faculty roles. He suggested that they are drawn to the impersonal curriculum and abstract subjects found at the postsecondary level. Lawrence stated that the modal personality type for university professors is ISTJ, followed by INTJ. Specific styles are associated with these modal types.

Introverted teachers are more likely to structure learning activities, need control, and be focused on the ideas they are teaching. Sensing types focus on facts, concrete skills, and practical information, whereas intuitive teachers provide more choices, use small groups, and expect independent and creative work. Thinking teachers provide relatively little feedback, most often in the form of objective comments, and prefer that students focus on information the teacher is conveying. Judging teachers are orderly and adhere to schedules and routine.

Classroom Environment. Salter (1995b) has developed an environmental measure of the MBTI and used it to examine classroom environments. He has found that regardless of their personality types, students report that they perform better in environments that can be characterized as extraverted, intuitive, and feeling (Salter, 1994). By contrast, 61 percent of the classrooms in which students reported that they performed poorly have an ISTJ environmental profile characterized by low classroom interaction, lecture and demonstration, independent work, and a competitive atmosphere (Salter, 1995a). The astute reader will note that the modal teaching style found in the research previously cited was ISTJ.

Retention. Provost (1985) found that students who were most likely to leave college before graduation were SPs who reported difficulty becoming involved and feeling connected to the university. Students most likely to persist were extraverts who indicated that they were highly involved in campus activities. However, Spann, Newman, and Matthews (1991) found that among a group of students who did not meet regular admissions criteria, ISs were the most likely to persist. They noted that tenacity and perseverance are qualities associated with this type combination. Schurr and Ruble (1988) reported that students' choice of major in relation to MBTI type was also related to retention. Extraverts in majors dominated by introverts and vice versa were more likely to drop out of college than students in majors dominated by their own type.

Applications

Myers's work has been extremely successful, largely because of its practical utility. It has been used extensively in business and industry, religion, and mental health as well as educational settings. Personality type concepts can be helpful when working with groups and organizations as well as individuals.

Many writers have discussed the utility of personality type in organizational development (for example, Barr & Barr, 1989; Hirsh & Kummerow, 1990). In student affairs, Myers's concepts have been used in staff development and team-building workshops designed to help individuals understand each other and appreciate the different approaches each person brings to the organization (McNickle & Veltman, 1988; Rideout & Richardson, 1989). In a similar fashion, information about personality type can be presented to student groups, such as student government or Greek organizations, to assist them in working together more effectively.

Since the strengths and weaknesses of individual staff members vary according to personality type, knowledge of Myers's theory can also be useful to supervisors who wish to facilitate personal and professional growth among their staff (Ricci, Porterfield, & Piper, 1987) and to student organization advisers in their work with student leaders. Personality type concepts can be effectively introduced in leadership development classes or workshops.

As reported earlier, MBTI profiles have been used successfully by a number of university residence life divisions to place students so as to create floors with unique characteristics (Schroeder & Jackson, 1987). Although pairing roommates and suitemates by type is logistically difficult, greater student satisfaction and improved residence hall retention rates may be worth the effort. Personality type concepts have also been used to help resolve conflicts between roommates.

As noted, research has also demonstrated that personality type is reflected in learning and teaching styles. Lawrence (1993) and Carskadon (1994) offer many suggestions for structuring learning environments to provide appropriate supports and challenges for students with varying personality types. For example, Schroeder (1993) suggested that experiential activities including case studies and the use of small groups are particularly effective with the large numbers of extraverted sensors found in higher education today.

Jensen and DiTiberio (1984) specifically examined the writing strategies that are most effective for various personality types. For instance, intuitives write best when given a general assignment that allows them freedom to develop their own ideas, whereas sensing types respond better to an assignment with step-by-step instructions.

Understanding personality type is particularly important for academic advisers, both in structuring their work with individual students and in helping students make decisions about specific courses and majors in which they will be happy and successful (Anchors, 1987). Such information can also be useful in helping students develop effective study skills and time management techniques in line with their personality types.

Personality type is related to career choice (Myers, 1980; Myers & McCaulley, 1985). The MBTI has been used to help students understand themselves better when considering career options (Golden & Provost, 1987; McCaulley, 1990; Pinkney, 1983). Personal counselors have also used the MBTI to gain insight into their clients and to develop appropriate strategies for working effectively with them (McCaulley, 1990; Provost, 1987). Cairo (1992) suggested that the MBTI can be a particularly helpful tool in working with returning adult students to help them deal with the transitions they are facing in their lives.

Critique and Future Directions

Bayne (1995) presented a summary of the major criticisms of type theory and added his responses to them. Criticisms of the MBTI as a measurement tool have already been addressed.

Many people believe that personality type theory "puts people in boxes" and does not acknowledge individual variations in personality. It is possible to use the MBTI inappropriately to categorize and stereotype people. However, the intent of personality type theory is to "offer a broad framework which helps people move towards appreciating individuality" (Bayne, 1995, p. 77).

Others argue that behavior changes with the situation. Research has demonstrated that although situations have some effect, behavior is generally consistent over time. Bayne (1995) stated that if we know individuals' preferences "(in the MBTI sense) we can predict much of their experience and behavior most of the time" (p. 78).

Some people have criticized the type descriptions as either too vague or too positive. It is true that the type descriptions focus on broad themes, but individuals do seem to recognize themselves in the descriptions. For example, Carskadon (1982) asked individuals who had taken the MBTI to identify from descriptions of the sixteen types the one that best described them. Individuals were more likely to pick out the description that matched their tested type than any of the other descriptions. Bayne (1995) also noted that the positive nature of the type profiles is a strength in that people are not threatened by them.

Additional research is needed to validate the MBTI, particularly with regard to type dynamics and type development. Evaluation of the effectiveness of interventions using the MBTI in higher education settings is also needed. Too much of the research using the MBTI is of a descriptive nature. Although it may be interesting to know the distribution of personality types in certain occupations or organizations, the implications of such data are somewhat questionable since in any setting a wide range of types is always present and must be considered.

Personality type theory makes an important contribution to our understanding of individual difference. It stresses the positive contributions made by all types of people and provides helpful strategies for understanding and working effectively with others. The enormous popularity of Myers's approach in training, organizational development, classroom applications, and individual counseling and advising is a testament to its utility and importance in higher education.

PART FIVE

REFLECTING ON THEORY IN PRACTICE

Regina has come to the end of her course on student development theory. Throughout the semester, she has studied a number of psychosocial theories, cognitive-structural theories, and typology theories. She read Perry's original work and wrote a critique paper of his book. She has considered the implications of each theory for diverse student populations and has interviewed several Asian American students to determine if the theories "fit" their experiences. She has examined research related to each theory and has even designed a study to investigate whether lesbian identity development is similar for African American and Caucasian women. She has considered how theory can be used in practice and has designed an orientation program for transfer students based on Schlossberg's transition theory. As she reflects on the course, Regina is unsettled. She has been exposed to a lot of material and experiences designed to provide her with a comprehensive background in student development theory and its uses in practice. But somehow it isn't all coming together. Maybe the final take-home exam will help. It requires that she analyze a scenario and discuss ways in which various theories can be used in combination to understand and intervene in the situation. In addition, she is asked to critique the knowledge base with regard to student development theory and make recommendations concerning future directions. The exam is due in a week. Regina decides she better get busy!

As with Regina, our work is drawing to a close. In Parts One through Four we have considered the concept of student development, reviewed the historical and philosophical underpinnings of the student development movement, discussed the uses of student development in practice, and reviewed the major psychosocial, cognitive-structural, and typology theories. Now we must step back from the details and look at the big picture. How do these ideas and theories come together to guide educational practice? What do we gain from all this knowledge?

In many respects, student development theories are like a kaleidoscope. When you turn the kaleidoscope, the design changes. Likewise, when you use different theories to interpret the same situation, the results of your analysis vary. Thinking about situations through the many different theoretical lenses helps provide a more comprehensive understanding of what is going on and points to a variety of possible strategies for addressing issues. Depending on the particular situation, some theories will fit better than others. Having a repertoire of theories to consider is helpful in finding the ones that are of most value.

Nor can theory always lead us to the best solution. In some instances, theory just isn't sophisticated enough to be of much assistance. In other cases, it doesn't apply to the particular population under consideration. Sometimes it helps us describe the situation but doesn't provide guidance in terms of how to proceed. We must recognize the limitations of theory as well as the positive contributions it has made to educational practice.

All professionals are obligated to reflect on the current state of their profession and the knowledge base that underpins it. Further, they must challenge themselves and their colleagues to test, refine, and extend that knowledge base. As educators, it is particularly important that we critically examine student development theory and constantly seek out opportunities to add to the information we already have about how students change and grow during the college years. For it is through such efforts that educational practice is improved, and society, in the long run, is benefited.

In the final two chapters that make up Part Five, we take on the tasks outlined in Regina's final exam. In Chapter Fifteen, we explore ways in which theories can be used in combination to understand and address issues on college campuses. Three scenarios are discussed. In the first situation, a student's dilemma concerning the future is presented and ways of thinking about the situation are reviewed through various theoretical lenses. In the second situation, an instructor uses Knefelkamp, Golec, and Wells's PTP model (1985) to redesign a class for peer counselors. In the final example, student development theory is used to inform a student affairs divisional initiative based on the Student Learning Imperative ("Student Learning Imperative," 1996). The chapter concludes with a discussion of responsible use of theory in practice.

The final chapter presents our concluding thoughts and recommendations for future work related to student development. We begin with a review of the current status of developmental theory, research, and practice, looking at its accomplishments and also at its limitations. We then provide a list of recommendations that we believe will extend our knowledge base and improve our work with students. Finally, we reflect on some recent criticisms of student development as a philosophical and theoretical base for the student affairs profession.

CHAPTER FIFTEEN

USING THEORIES IN COMBINATION

Rarely is an issue in student affairs so straightforward that one theory will adequately explain it or provide sufficient guidance to address it. Looking at concerns from a variety of perspectives can help practitioners understand the dynamics involved in situations they face and come up with a number of possible strategies to consider. In this chapter we present three scenarios that demonstrate the use of theories in combination. The first example focuses on an individual student's dilemma, the second situation involves the redesign of an academic course, and the third scenario revolves around an institutional initiative.

Advising a Student

A senior student, Pat, comes to talk with the hall director near the conclusion of the final semester. Pat shares the following: "I have a lot of decisions that I feel I have to make soon. You've known me for the past three years that I've been living in the hall. I thought maybe you could help me sort things out. For quite a while now, I've wanted to go into the ministry. My father is a minister. But there are some things going on with me personally that are making me wonder if I should forget about going to the seminary. This is kind of hard to talk about, but for the past six months I've been in a relationship that has become very important to me. Chris and I have become very close. I've never been in a homosexual relationship before, but this relationship just feels right—much better than the relationship I had with Terry, even though Terry and I almost became engaged.

"Anyway, my church teaches that homosexuality is wrong. So I don't know what to do about the seminary. I have my interview next week. I don't know whether to be open about my sexual orientation or not. Chris thinks I should be honest and tell. Chris may be right. On the one hand, I hate the idea of not being who I am. On the other hand, if I am open about my homosexuality, I think my chances of being admitted are zip! And what if my parents find out? They would be so hurt and disappointed in me. I feel caught between people that I care about very much. If I'm open about who I am, I hurt my parents; If I'm not open, I hurt Chris. I don't want to harm anyone.

"And if I don't get to go into the ministry, what will I do? Some of my professors in my major department, English, have been pushing grad school in that area, but that idea just doesn't feel right. Besides, I've been a good student, but not a great one in terms of my grades. I don't think I'd really like being an 'egghead' professor. I love the theater and I've done some acting on campus, but I don't think I have anywhere near enough talent to be a professional. Why can't I be who I am and be a minister in my church too? I am so frustrated! It seems so unfair!

"Sometimes I just wish the semester would never end. I feel comfortable here. The pressure about what to do next feels overwhelming. Sometimes I think I'd just like to disappear, to get away from all the stress for a while, but I guess that would be too irresponsible. Sometimes I feel like I can't even think straight. Please help me."

Clearly, Pat is facing a number of challenges. Several developmental theories, used in combination, can be helpful in understanding and responding to Pat. First, psychosocial theories can serve as a useful resource. For example, Pat is struggling simultaneously with several of the developmental issues described in Chickering's vectors (Chickering & Reisser, 1993). Identity concerns are paramount, particularly in relation to sexual orientation. The question of "Who am I?" and the resulting ramifications of the response represent a complex process of struggling and coming to terms for Pat. These identity issues also have an impact on Pat's ability to resolve aspects of developing purpose. Interpersonal and career aspects are somewhat at odds because of the conflict between who Pat seems to be and the lack of acceptance in the church's values. In addition, congruence issues arise for Pat in regard to developing integrity. Pat could be at a point of desperation. The fact that Pat has chosen to come talk with the hall director demonstrates the value of one of the Chickering's key influences, student developmental programs and services. Over a three-year period, the hall director has formed a relationship that gives Pat an important environmental support in a time of personal crisis and difficult decision making.

Pat's self-identification with homosexuality makes clear the potential value of both the Cass (1979) and D'Augelli (1994a) models. Pat may be in the middle stages of developing a homosexual identity. Characterizing involvement in a same-sex relationship as a new experience, Pat also expresses the desire to "be who I am," as well as frustration of having to deal with others (for example, church leaders) who render the identity illegitimate and consider it a basis for denying the opportunity to pursue a career in the church. Coming-out issues for Pat can become even more difficult because of the career goal of becoming a minister in a church not supportive of Pat's identity. From the perspective of D'Augelli's model, while Pat seems to have established an intimacy status, the process of "becoming a lesbian/gay/bisexual offspring" remains. That Pat views the hall director as an individual who can be trusted to hear and not judge the concern is a plus. The hall director also needs to display sensitivity to the challenges inherent in the decisions related to coming out with parents and with seminary personnel and the related impact of such decisions on Pat's relationship with Chris.

Pat's gender and race are not specified in this scenario. Both these characteristics are relevant, and psychosocial theory could be helpful here as well. For example, if Pat is African American, multiple issues of oppression are likely to exist (Wall & Washington, 1991). The role of the family and of the church may also take on heightened importance. Gender has implications for sexual identity development because the process can differ for gay men and lesbians (Levine & Evans, 1991).

Schlossberg's theory (Schlossberg, Waters, & Goodman, 1995) provides insight related to the transition issues that Pat is experiencing. For example, the shift in sexual identity for Pat and the upcoming graduation both represent major transitions. In relation to the 4 *S*'s and the first variable, "situation," these events combine to form multiple transitions that are producing a great deal of stress for Pat. Major role changes are involved: view of self as heterosexual to view of self as homosexual, and shift from the role of undergraduate student to an unknown role in terms of education or career. The fact that graduation is approaching puts pressure on Pat to figure out where to go and what to do next. The need to address sexual identity matters must take place in the context of an environment that must soon be vacated.

Descriptive information related to the "self" aspect of the 4 *S*'s is limited. Identifying as a member of a minority may be a new experience if Pat has not previously done so in regard to other personal or demographic characteristics. If Pat is African American, for example, increased feelings of marginalization (Schlossberg, 1989b) could occur, based on the reality of multiple issues of oppression.

Support, the third of the 4 *S*'s, could be a difficult aspect for Pat since the intimate relationship with Chris has the potential to conflict with the possibility of receiving support from family. For now, Pat has the opportunity to use the hall director as a source of institutional support. Since the semester will soon end, Pat is likely to lose this resource in the very near future.

For strategies, the last of the 4 *S*'s, Pat could benefit from assistance in developing all three types: modifying the situation where possible, controlling the meaning of the situation, and managing related stress.

Cognitive-structural theories also provide insight into how Pat is making meaning and what types of approaches may be useful. Early on in the conversation with the hall director, Pat asks for help in sorting things out. This request, quite different from asking to be told what to do, would seem to imply a level of cognitive complexity beyond the basic. Issues of connection, found in Belenky, Clinchy, Goldberger, and Tarule's model (1986), as well as in Baxter Magolda's model (1992), seem to be reflected in Pat's meaning making. Gilligan's care voice (1977, 1982/1993) can be heard in Pat's desire to avoid doing harm to anyone—parents or Chris. Kohlberg's justice voice (1976) can also be heard in Pat's challenging the fairness of not being able to be both oneself and a minister. Pat's wish for the semester never to end and the desire to disappear may signal the need for one of the deflections that Perry (1968) described. Pat is snared in a web of dilemmas, and coming to conclusions seems like an overwhelming task. Pat may genuinely need to take some time out.

Typology theories may be of limited use, given the information provided. They could become more helpful if additional information is gathered about Pat. Yet typology theories do have some relevance, even in the context of the brief scenario. Person-environment fit issues, as discussed by Holland (1985/1992), underlie Pat's consideration of careers. Homosexuality and the church form the most blatant conflict. Kolb's discussion of fit with academic cultures (1981) seems to apply to Pat's reluctance to consider going to graduate school in English to become a professor. More typology information, such as might be gathered by instruments used to conduct assessments related to the theories of Holland (1985/1992), Kolb (1981), or Myers (1980) might give Pat greater insight into options currently under consideration as well as additional possibilities for meaningful work.

A focus on Pat's situation reinforces the value of using multiple theoretical filters to aid in understanding and attempting to provide assistance. As described in the foregoing analysis, the hall director can provide various forms of support, such as serving as a sounding board for exploration of identity issues, including aiding Pat with decision making and planning regarding communicating with others about these issues. The hall director can also serve as a helper who can collaborate in analyzing Pat's transitions and in developing an approach to using and enhancing current coping strategies. The staff member's understanding of cognitive development can be used to discuss with Pat the possibility of taking a "timeout" to sort through what is happening and to consider future alternatives more fully. As a final example from the scenario, the hall director can act as a referral agent for more information gathering, as through use of the typology instruments and perhaps more in-depth counseling. Rarely is a single theory likely to be sufficient in making meaning of students' experiences and supplying appropriate challenges and supports. Practice can be enhanced by drawing on a combination of theories.

Using the PTP Model

The PTP model (Knefelkamp, Golec, & Wells, 1985), discussed in Chapter Two, can provide a more structured approach to using developmental theory to provide insight and possible guidelines for action. An example of redesign in a classroom setting will be used to demonstrate how the PTP model can provide support.

An instructor is concerned about addressing two issues in an undergraduate counseling course. First, although the course is described as being a peer counseling course, the texts are geared to a professional audience, particularly the case examples used. Second, the instructor wants to help students value and respond to individual differences while also being able to see commonalities shared with others. The design of the course, however, seems to emphasize the difference aspect to the extent that students lack connection to others who were in some ways different and even display prejudice toward those differences.

These two identified problematic components of the course represent the concern identified in Step 1 of the PTP model. The issues represent both problem and enhancement aspects. Risks could include opening a Pandora's box in terms of the complexity involved in trying to address more effectively the peer component of the course and the aspect of valuing difference. Potential benefits could be a greater connectedness among the students, instructor, and course material and more effective peer counselors.

In considering Step 2, desired educational goals and outcomes, the students who took the course were typically, but not exclusively, juniors and seniors who were majoring in a field related to counseling and who had an interest in helping. Typical classes included more women than men, more whites than nonwhites, and more traditional-aged than nontraditional-aged individuals. In terms of cognitive development, students typically displayed characteristics of multiplistic thinking, such as viewing the teacher as the source of the right process for finding the answer, valuing fairness, and giving attention to quantity issues (for example, time, effort, and number of pages to be read or written). Students seemed to have some regard for their peers as potential contributors to the learning process. Many also tended to be Holland (1985/1992) Social types; that is, "S" was the first letter in their Holland codes.

The course design followed Knefelkamp and Widick's Developmental Instruction model (Knefelkamp, 1984), discussed in Chapter Eight, with methods of learning and evaluation being varied. The basic model for the course was "knowledge of self plus knowledge of others plus knowledge of the environment plus skill development equals effective peer counseling." Two goals that emerged from a consideration of the issues described were to help students develop a conception of what peer counseling is and to help students expand the sphere of people and concerns toward which they could demonstrate empathy.

In relation to Step 3, investigating theories that might be helpful, several had the potential to be of use. Psychosocial theories could be useful in understanding and addressing identity issues and ramifications related to relationships and tolerance. Cognitive-structural theories could give insight into how the students were making meaning, as has already been indicated, as well as provide assistance in designing approaches that would appropriately challenge and support the students. Typology theory could aid in examining and understanding similarities and differences.

In analyzing student characteristics for Step 4, Chickering's theory (Chickering & Reisser, 1993) provides insight into the heightened challenge of relating to others when both the helpee's and helper's identities may be in flux. If I'm not quite sure who I am and you're not quite sure who you are, do we experience obstacles to connecting? Perry's theory (1968) can be helpful for anticipating who may be likely to use peer helpers as well as who may be likely to enroll in a peer counseling course. As mentioned earlier, students in the course tended to be multiplistic thinkers. It seems unlikely that students demonstrating dualistic thinking would either use peer counselors or enroll in a peer counseling course because peers would not be considered legitimate contributors to learning.

Gilligan's work (1977, 1982/1993) contains useful elements for trying to promote linkages among the students. For example, her message that different doesn't equal deficient can be helpful in raising consciousness and helping students understand issues of invisibility and misrepresentation.

In examining environmental characteristics, Step 5, it is also important to consider student characteristics. To aid students in exploring identity issues, an open environment for discussion is important. Similarly, the Developmental Instruction model provides guidance in designing environmental supports and challenges. Typology theory can aid in understanding person-environment fit issues and in addressing different learning styles.

In regard to developmental challenges and supports, Step 6, the DI model and attention to learning styles are both helpful, as is an understanding of the relationship between psychosocial issues, such as those represented in Chickering's seven vectors and the key influences in colleges, as described by Chickering and Reisser (1993), that can affect student development.

In Step 7, reanalyzing educational goals and outcomes, it can be determined that a developmental mismatch is desirable. Timing and approach are both important, and the nonthreatening nature of the classroom environment serves as a support. An overriding goal becomes that of challenging students' narrow definition of "peer," in the sense of who can help whom, to reduce exclusionary tendencies that may be based at least equally on feelings of inadequacy as on prejudice.

Several revisions were made in the design of the learning process, Step 8. One example is the creation of activities designed to get a preliminary indication of how students were conceptualizing peer counseling. These exercises were to be done during the first class. To add to the "knowledge of self" component of the course, an instrument was designed to solicit information on what types of people and issues students anticipated they would and would not relate to as peer counselors. The instrument could be used in a "pre and post" fashion at the beginning and conclusion of the course. The "pre" component was not to be administered until after students had received at least one written assignment with instructor comments in order to allow some time for the establishment of trust. In relation to the skill development component, the texts were supplemented with literature geared to peer counseling and the cases used were changed so that they described scenarios likely to be more typical of those encountered by peer counselors.

The "knowledge of others" component was modified to go beyond counseling theories and include readings and discussions geared to different student populations, and the cross-cultural counseling component was moved to an earlier position in the syllabus.

Using the PTP model as a support, substantial redesign work was done by the instructor. Use of the model provided an opportunity to be thorough, deliberate, and thoughtful in better understanding and addressing course concerns.

An Institutional Initiative

Midwest State University has recently hired a new vice president for student affairs to replace their former VP, who has recently retired. The former VP was well liked by the campus community, but the student affairs staff did recognize that he wasn't as on top of issues in the field as he might have been. He prided himself on being there for students but rarely initiated programs or advocated on behalf of student affairs for funding or recognition. As a result, most faculty and administrators saw the role of student affairs as handling crises and maintaining order, rather than contributing to the education of students. In recent years, several staff positions have been cut and morale in the division is low.

The new vice president is active in several student affairs professional associations, has frequently presented at conferences, and has had several articles published in student affairs journals. She served previously as the dean of students at a university in a neighboring state, has a doctorate from a nationally recognized student affairs graduate program, and comes highly recommended. The student affairs staff are excited; they feel that her hiring is a real coup. Members of the student affairs division attend the opening meeting of the fall division retreat, eagerly looking for direction from their new leader.

Dr. Sullivan, the new VP, greets the staff enthusiastically. She introduces a new initiative for the student affairs division. Her goal is to implement a "learning-oriented" student affairs division, based on the principles outlined in the Student Learning Imperative ("Student Learning Imperative," 1996, pp. 119–121). She wants to change the mission of the division from providing students with basic services, such as comfortable housing and placement assistance, to being actively involved in the educational mission of the university. Dr. Sullivan outlines the five basic characteristics of a learning-oriented student affairs division ("Student Learning Imperative,"):

1. "The student affairs division mission complements the institution's mission, with the enhancement of student learning and personal development being the primary goal of student affairs programs and services."
2. "Resources are allocated to encourage student learning and personal development."
3. "Student affairs professionals collaborate with other institutional agents and agencies to promote student learning and personal development."
4. "The division of student affairs includes staff who are experts on students, their environments, and teaching and learning processes."
5. "Student affairs policies and programs are based on promising practices from the research on student learning and institution-specific assessment data."

The staff are a bit overwhelmed. This is the first time they have heard of the Student Learning Imperative. They wondered what had happened to the idea of student development that many of them had studied in college and a few had even tried to use in their work with students. Student learning sounded like the purview of the faculty, not student affairs practitioners. Some of them were even having second thoughts about their new vice president as well as her ideas about what student affairs work was all about.

The concept of student learning is receiving a great deal of attention in the student affairs field (see Ender, Newton, & Caple, 1996; Schroeder, 1996). Like the student affairs staff at Midwest State University, many student affairs practitioners are wondering if this concept supersedes student development. Debates can be heard at professional conferences and on many campuses concerning the relative merits of the "two approaches." We argue that in reality, student learning and student development are one and the same. At the very least, student learning has been an integral part of the development movement since its inception (Brown, 1996).

A thorough grounding in student development theory can be extremely valuable when implementing a learning-based approach to student affairs work. The following suggestions for relating student development theory to the Student Learning Imperative (1996) are ones the staff at Midwest State and other universities may want to consider.

Enhancement of Student Learning and Personal Development Goals

Student development theories provide particularly helpful guidance toward achieving the objective of enhancing student learning and personal development. Both psychosocial and cognitive-structural theories point toward learning goals to be accomplished in college. For instance, Chickering and Reisser (1993) suggested seven areas of development students face during college, including developing competence, moving through autonomy toward interdependence, and developing purpose. Each area could serve as a measurable learning outcome around which student affairs could build its interventions (see Hurst, 1978). The racial and ethnic and gay, lesbian, and bisexual identity development models suggest that development of group and personal identity are additional growth areas for college students. Goals related to facilitating development in these areas should also be included in the strategic plans of student affairs divisions.

Cognitive-structural theories outline how individuals progress from simple ways of making meaning and understanding the world to more complex ways. Certainly, assisting students to move toward relativistic thinking (Perry, 1968), constructed knowledge (Belenky et al., 1986), reflective thinking (Kitchener & King, 1994), or contextual knowing (Baxter Magolda, 1992) is an important outcome to which student affairs staff should attend. Development of advanced levels of moral reasoning (Gilligan, 1982/1993; Kohlberg, 1976) is also a legitimate and too often neglected goal that student affairs educators should address.

Typology theories, while not pointing directly to outcomes, do guide the development of interventions to achieve outcomes. Educators must attend to learning style and personality differences with regard to how students take in and process information if they are to successfully implement programming to achieve the developmental goals suggested by cognitive-structural and psychosocial theories.

Both psychosocial and cognitive-structural theories also suggest ways to facilitate development. Sanford's concept of challenge and support (1967) is a basic guide for all programming. Chickering and Reisser (1993) emphasized strategies in areas such as faculty-student interaction, teaching practices, and student communities that can be implemented in conjunction with the rest of the academic community. The cognitive-structural theories include discussion of ways in which more complex reasoning processes can be encouraged. These principles include allowing students to experience cognitive dissonance and modeling reasoning processes slightly more complex than those used by students.

The Developmental Intervention model (Evans, 1987), introduced in Chapter Two, could be used as a framework for organizing interventions designed to achieve the goals suggested by developmental theory. Use of such a model ensures that a broad range of strategies are used to address student learning objectives comprehensively. For instance, a career center might include among its programming three types of interventions: (1) individual counseling (identified as an individual intervention, responsive to the needs students bring, and explicitly designed to foster career development); (2) a peer counseling program in which students trained by the professional staff hold informal discussions with students in the lounge of the student center about their future plans (identified as an intervention targeted to individual students, responsive to the needs students express, and designed to implicitly address career development issues); and (3) a formal presentation to the board of trustees on the career development needs of students designed to support a request for additional funding (an institutional intervention, planned to address specific identified needs, that implicitly addresses career development concerns of students by securing more resources). Additional programs could be designed by the staff to address developmental needs by targeting the institution or individual students, explicitly or implicitly, using either planned strategies or responding to needs as they arise.

Allocation of Resources

Student development theory provides guidance in sorting out which programs, interventions, and services are important and which are not. Based on such an assessment, resources can be allocated for activities that will have a positive impact on students.

Existing student affairs initiatives should be assessed to determine what, if any, developmental goals they are designed to achieve and how well they are achieving them. In this process, it is important to recognize that services such as providing a high-quality food service, social activities such as pizza parties or movie nights, and phone-in registration can be just as "developmental" as a leadership development program or a service learning opportunity. To learn, students' basic needs, such as nutrition, physical well-being, social support, and a sense of community, must be met (Chickering & Reisser, 1993). Efforts to eliminate "chronic hassle" (Schlossberg, 1984), such as long registration lines, are also important to student development.

Assessment is a complex process that requires careful analysis of both process and outcomes associated with specific programs. Use of both quantitative and qualitative measures is needed to provide a comprehensive description of the effectiveness of programs. For example, to determine omissions and overlap, staff might be asked to provide a list of the various programs offered in their areas and the goals of each. Questionnaires distributed to visitors to various offices as they leave might be used to determine what students thought of the service they received. Observations of particular programs could provide a sense of the material being covered, the manner in which it is covered, and student reactions to the presentation. Resident assistants could be interviewed to gather their impressions of what programs and services were popular with students and the effects these programs had on the residents of their floors. Academic advisers might conduct similar interviews with selected student advisees. More formal developmental assessments using validated instruments might be conducted to determine the impact of a few specific programs of particular interest.

Once assessments have been completed, the data should be examined to determine which goals are not being adequately addressed. Resources should be reassigned to new or expanded efforts in these areas. Likewise, programs with similar goals should be reevaluated to determine if they are all really needed. For instance, an analysis might determine that no efforts are being made to address the development of gay, lesbian, or bisexual identity but several programs and interventions for developing interpersonal competence are in place. Resources might be reallocated from some of the latter efforts to the former.

Collaboration with Other Institutional Agents

Student development goals can also guide the establishment of collaborative activities between student affairs and academic affairs. For instance, Kolb (1984) identified concrete experience as an important strategy to enhance student learning. Concrete experience refers to active involvement in the learning process. Service learning experiences sponsored by student affairs and tied to specific classes are one way to provide hands-on educational opportunities (see Jacoby & Associates, 1996).

Cosponsorship by academic departments and student affairs of lectures, cultural events, theatrical performances, and other educationally meaningful activities is another way to encourage developmental outcomes. Internships and programs connecting students with professionals in various fields could also be jointly sponsored by career services, alumni affairs, and academic units. Such programs would facilitate development of purpose (Chickering & Reisser, 1993).

Student and faculty involvement in the student judicial process is another educationally meaningful intervention that could assist in moral development as well as psychosocial and cognitive development. Such innovations as living-learning centers in residence halls, including interest houses; classes conducted in the living unit; resident faculty; and academic advisers located in the halls also provide the "seamless learning opportunities" advocated by Kuh (1996).

Identity development theories, as well as information related to gender differences in learning, can be used to support the efforts of advocacy offices to develop cultural opportunities, lecture series, and awareness-building activities for students. Centers for lesbian, gay, and bisexual students, students of color, and women, along with respective academic programs in gay studies, racial and ethnic studies, and women's studies, can effectively collaborate on such programming.

Fried and Associates (1995) provided excellent examples of intentionally designed, developmentally based collaborative programs that have a powerful impact on student development. For instance, the University of Hartford's All University Curriculum (AUC) involves active modes of learning emphasizing skill building in areas such as critical thinking, problem solving, and social interaction. Student affairs staff work with AUC instructors to develop educational programs related to material covered in the classroom.

Providing Expertise on Students

Most faculty, trained only in their academic disciplines, are unfamiliar with developmental theory. Nor are they aware that student affairs practitioners possess this knowledge. Yet when introduced to developmental concepts, faculty find them helpful in their efforts to understand students and design beneficial educational experiences. Student affairs professionals must be more willing to share their knowledge base with faculty and actively seek out opportunities to do so.

Talking with the staff of the faculty development office is a good place to begin, since their goal is to improve teaching and they are usually interested in theories and strategies to assist them in their work. For instance, a faculty development session that presented an introduction to personality type and the relevance of Myers's work (1980) to teaching and learning was well received by faculty at Western Illinois University. As a result of this response, information on learning styles and cognitive-structural theories was included in new faculty orientation the following year, and a number of follow-up sessions were requested by specific departments.

Classes designed to introduce teaching assistants to teaching principles would also be an ideal place to introduce potential faculty members to developmental theories. Faculty development offices are often involved in such efforts. For instance, at the Pennsylvania State University, identity development theory was used as a basis for developing scenarios about the classroom experiences of students of color and disabled students. These case studies were prepared for use in a class for teaching assistants.

Media such as videos, Web sites, newsletters, and informational brochures reach many faculty who do not attend programs. Creators of such media are often pleased to receive contributions. At Penn State, the Educational Equity Office developed a series of videos focusing on issues faced by gay, lesbian, and bisexual students and staff on campus. These were designed for use in the classroom as well as in educational workshops for faculty and staff.

Even informal, private conversations can serve as a vehicle for providing faculty with information on developmental issues students face, environmental factors that influence development, and strategies for enhancing teaching and learning. Such conversations can occur at the recreation center, in an on-campus eating establishment, or at a campus reception if student affairs practitioners take the initiative to get to know and interact with faculty.

Research and Assessment

Research based on student development theory, such as that reported in earlier chapters, can be used to guide development of programs and practices on college campuses. In particular, reported evaluations of the effectiveness of developmentally based programs and interventions on other campuses can be useful as various options are considered during the early stages of program development. For instance, knowing that a roommate-matching program that used Myers-Briggs Type Indicator data was successful in improving residence hall retention rates (Kalsbeek, Rodgers, Marshall, Denny, & Nicholls, 1982) might encourage residence life staff at a similar campus to explore such an option.

Sharing research findings with faculty, administrators, and other institutional agents also provides support when arguing for the need for developmentally based interventions. Such constituencies are generally more impressed by empirically driven evidence than by persuasive argument. For example, being able to document that a first-year orientation class based on the Developmental Instruction model (Knefelkamp, 1984) improves students' academic competence and increases students' confidence in their academic abilities would certainly do more to encourage widespread adoption of such an approach than merely suggesting to faculty that they need to personalize their teaching.

Student development theory also provides a base for design and implementation of comprehensive research initiatives on campus. Previously we noted the importance of assessment to determine whether developmental goals were being achieved. Such assessment is important not only to determine where to allocate resources but also to determine the overall effectiveness of the educational program. Though this is not an easy task, it can be worth the effort. Too often, outcomes assessment information provided by institutions is limited to graduation rates, placement of graduates, and other easily quantifiable data. Evidence that significant student learning and development are taking place at a particular institution can be a major selling point to prospective students, their parents, potential donors, and state legislators.

Student development theories suggest outcomes to measure, as noted earlier. Many also point to instrumentation or assessment techniques that can be used in assessment and evaluation efforts—for example, the Reflective Judgment Interview (King & Kitchener, 1994) and the Defining Issues Test (Rest, 1986a). Qualitative approaches can also be used to examine the effectiveness of various environments in promoting learning. For instance, classrooms that students report as exemplary could be observed, and students in those classes could be interviewed to determine just what learning is occurring and the factors that are specifically contributing to that learning. The information obtained could then be disseminated to faculty, students, and administrators to enhance other environments.

The Student Learning Imperative ("Student Learning Imperative," 1996) is a helpful statement of student affairs philosophy that can assist student affairs educators in focusing their efforts and creating a coherent program to enhance student development and learning on campus. It is also an excellent public relations tool to use with faculty and administrators in that it uses language that they can relate to and understand. In implementing a learning-based approach, however, we must not lose track of the important foundation that student development theory provides. In her efforts to update the student affairs program at Midwest State University, Dr. Sullivan will want to go back to the ideas and concepts with which her staff are familiar and work with them to apply these approaches in the comprehensive manner that is called for in the Student Learning Imperative.

With each of the preceding examples, the use of theory is intended to be representative rather than exhaustive in regard to approaches that could be taken. Other helpful discussions of how various student development theories can be used in a comprehensive manner are provided in Fried and Associates (1995), Rodgers (1990a), and Ricci, Porterfield, and Piper (1987).

Promoting Responsible Use of Theory

A question is sometimes raised as to whether the use of developmental theory requires too much of student affairs practitioners' already limited time. This question can be countered with a consideration of whether trial-and-error approaches are likely to be any less time-consuming or any more effective. When a graduate class taking a student development theory course was asked early on, "Why do we study theory?" one student responded, "So we can fly by navigation rather than by the seats of our pants." In a similar vein, a former student passed on a quote he attributed to Lofti Vadeh: "When your only tool is a hammer, every problem looks like a nail." Both statements serve to underscore the value of knowing and appropriately using student development theory. Having more tools in the tool box affords more options to guide our practice. Appropriate use of theories requires that they be used tentatively rather than prescriptively and that the potential for individual variations is kept in mind.

Brown and Barr (1990) have noted that the task of translating theory to practice can be made to seem more complicated than it has to be. Eleven steps in a process model may seem overwhelming to some people. Terminology that is unfamiliar can prompt a reluctant practitioner to think that learning a new language is a prerequisite to being able to incorporate theory. Those of us who may find ourselves in the role of formal or informal teacher need to be mindful of the legitimacy of such reservations. We need to present theory to others in an accessible fashion.

Forney, Eddy, Gunter, and Slater (1992) identified issues and challenges that individuals who seek to promote and use student development theory may encounter. These include less than supportive attitudes from others (such as supervisors and colleagues); the dynamics of change (its slowness and potentially threatening nature); less than effective approaches by the would-be translator, such as the "bull in a china shop" (well intentioned but clumsy) and the "know-it-all"; language issues in trying to translate; competing priorities; politics; and budgetary constraints (including the perception that being developmental is more expensive).

Forney et al. (1992) also presented several strategies that can be used in dealing with such issues and challenges. Some of these are providing solid rationales, avoiding jargon, using language and strategies appropriate to the audience (for example, using theory and research to promote ideas with faculty), building alliances, dividing and conquering (recruiting one staff member at a time), being unobtrusive versus blatant (doing first and drawing attention later), being on the lookout for and using windows of opportunity, using pilot programs, demonstrating perseverance, and recognizing and celebrating successes.

Helping others, such as professional staff, faculty, graduate students, and peer helpers, become familiar with the content of theory and its potential uses in a straightforward, down-to-earth manner can render theory more user-friendly. Minimizing jargon, helping potential users see connections between theory and their own experiences, and showing (versus telling) how we have successfully used theory in our own work can all facilitate an openness to theory among those who are unfamiliar with the material and its value.

Knefelkamp (1984) asserted that as educators, we have an intellectual and ethical responsibility to study theory to improve our understanding of students, colleagues, and environments. Moreover, we have an obligation to make appropriate use of what we know. Professionalism would seem to demand such expertise. In light of the increasing diversity of our student populations, with their many and varied needs, this responsibility has certainly not diminished.

CHAPTER SIXTEEN

FUTURE DIRECTIONS FOR THEORY IN STUDENT DEVELOPMENT PRACTICE

The preceding chapters in this book represent the "state of the art" regarding student development theory, research, and practice. As is readily evident, significant progress has been made in the past several decades toward understanding the growth and development that students experience during college. In this concluding chapter, challenges to student development theory as presented in the literature are followed by an overall evaluation of the current status of student development theory, research, and practice. Recommendations are made regarding future efforts to understand students and the impact of their experiences in college. Finally, we provide a response to critics who question the utility of student development as a foundation for student affairs practice.

Challenges to Student Development Theory

Although student development theory plays a central role in educational practice, particularly in student affairs, it is not without its critics. Criticism in any field is positive in that it suggests new directions and can lead to research and refinement of theoretical statements to incorporate new ideas and respond to questions that have been raised.

An important concern about student development theory has been the narrowness of the populations on which most theory has been based (Garland &

Grace, 1993; King, 1994). Earlier research, especially, centered on white, male, upper- and upper-middle-class, traditional-aged students (McEwen, 1996a; Strange, 1994). Later researchers and theorists have attempted to address this bias by extending their studies to include women, people of color, nonheterosexual students, and older adults, but more work in these areas is still needed (Strange). King stressed the importance of identifying factors that individuals from various backgrounds have in common as well as their differences. She also urged researchers to look beyond obvious differences and consider the influence of factors such as motivation, mastered skills, and disabling conditions.

Garland and Grace (1993) faulted student development theories for not adequately detailing how growth actually takes place. As a result, they noted, the utility of theory to guide practice is limited. King (1994) pointed out, however, that "theory construction is an evolving process" (p. 418) and that initial work is typically descriptive. She called for the more advanced research that would more clearly outline the mechanisms by which development occurs.

Terenzini (1994) noted that we know very little about the timing of development or whether it occurs in a linear progression or a more discontinuous fashion. He stressed that to answer this question, research studies extending over a number of years are needed.

Many writers have suggested that student development theorists have not paid enough attention to the role of the environment in developmental change (Kuh, Whitt, & Shedd, 1987; Terenzini, 1994). Kuh et al., for example, stressed the mutual shaping that results from the interaction of person and environment.

Terenzini (1994) noted that few theories have been adequately tested with regard to their conceptual validity. He argued, "If meaningful advances in understanding student change and college's effects on those changes are to be made, studies will be needed that purposefully evaluate the validity of both current and emerging models explaining student change among different student groups" (p. 426). Upcraft (1994) also criticized theorists for failing to incorporate findings from practice into their theories.

Strange (1994) pointed out that student development theory is rooted in "Western rationalism and American pragmatism" (p. 410). This philosophical base leads to a limited set of assumptions and values related to education and development. King (1994) gave as an example the focus in student development theories on individual development to the almost total exclusion of attention to development of community-oriented values such as altruism and interdependence. (Jones, 1990, stated that only the Western cultural tradition emphasizes the needs of the individual over the needs of the group.) Strange (1994) proposed that a broader range of cultural perspectives be considered to reveal the impact of the multicultural and global context in which student development will increasingly occur.

Bloland, Stamatakos, and Rogers (1994) presented a critique of the entire student development movement and suggested that the student affairs field move away from student development as the philosophical underpinning of the profession, focusing instead on aligning itself with the educational mission of higher education and facilitation of student learning. Upcraft (1994) also stressed the importance of connecting student affairs work to the academic mission of the university and wondered if student development principles made this connection in a clear enough fashion.

In the following two sections of this chapter, these points will be considered and an overall evaluation of the status of the student development movement will be presented.

What Has Been Achieved

Fifteen years ago, student affairs educators who were familiar with the "big three theorists"—Chickering, Perry, and Kohlberg—considered themselves well versed in developmental theory. Today, the theory base of the field has grown to include numerous other important perspectives that challenge educators to expand their thinking, particularly related to the development of women, adult students, students from various racial and ethnic groups, and gay, lesbian, and bisexual students.

Indeed, educators who teach student development theory face the challenging task of determining which theories to cover and which to omit from their syllabi. Many master's-level student affairs preparation programs (including those at Western Illinois University, Iowa State University, and the Ohio State University) have expanded their offerings to include at least two classes examining student development theory, and some (like the University of Georgia) also offer a course on designing student development interventions.

Likewise, significant research has been conducted to critically examine the propositions associated with existing theories, to explore the applicability of theories to different populations of students, and to develop new theories. As a result, some theories are receiving less attention in the field (for example, the work of Douglas Heath, 1968; Roy Heath, 1964; and Jane Loevinger, 1976), others have been modified to take new information into account (the theories of Chickering and Holland are good examples), and new theories are being introduced as a basis for student affairs practice (for example, D'Augelli's 1994 life span model of gay, lesbian, and bisexual identity development).

The application of student development theory to student affairs practice has also become more sophisticated and intentional over the past two decades. Theory-to-practice models, such as those of Rodgers and Widick (1980) and Knefelkamp,

Golec, and Wells (1985), which were discussed in Chapter Two, have provided guidance for practitioners in using theories as a foundation for their work. Examples reported in the literature and at professional conferences suggest that student affairs practitioners are creatively using theory as a tool for understanding the issues faced by today's students and for intervening to structure a more positive campus environment to enhance student development. Theories are being effectively and insightfully used to work with individual students, to advise and train student groups and organizations, to design classroom experiences, and to evaluate and develop policy and procedures on college campuses.

Limitations of the Existing Knowledge Base

Although the knowledge base that can be subsumed under the label of "college student development theory" is rich and informative, limitations exist. Most of the theories reviewed in this book fit contextually within the positivist tradition that assumes that there is an objective reality that holds regardless of time or situation. As a result, developmental processes are assumed to be similar for every individual in any environment or culture. Research evidence and observation suggest that this is a narrow view.

In addition, existing developmental theories are for the most part based on the values of Euro-American, middle-class, educated people. Such values may contribute to a limited sense of what is important in the lives of students, especially those from other traditions.

Another important point to recall is that developmental theory has its base in the field of psychology. As such, internal developmental processes tend to be emphasized and insufficient attention is paid to the role of environmental forces that influence development.

Finally, existing theories tend to fragment development rather than view it holistically. For example, King and Kitchener (1994) discussed reflective judgment; Kohlberg (1976) studied moral development; Cross (1991) examined African American identity development. Little is known about how these various aspects of development interrelate.

Stage theories, in particular, suffer from all of the problems just noted. The underlying assumptions on which these theories are based lead the reader to conclude that the developmental path is similar for all individuals, leading to an end point, at which the individual has achieved maximum growth. The descriptions of various stages reflect values and perspectives that are relevant in the dominant Euro-American culture. Environmental influences are given little attention by most stage theorists. Although conditions in the environment may facilitate or hold back development through the stages, these influences never change the developmental process itself. For example, a white student attending Harvard in 1960 is assumed to have faced the same developmental challenges as a Native American student attending a tribal college in 1998. And each theory, as noted, outlines only one particular aspect of development (for example, moral reasoning or racial identity development).

Several problem areas must also be noted with regard to student development research. First, although it is growing, our research base is limited. Since most existing research grows out of the positivist tradition, it is quantitative in nature. Such an approach limits phenomena that can be examined and ways in which data are interpreted. Much energy goes into testing predetermined hypotheses and controlling experimental conditions. It is difficult to predict and control all the variables that contribute to or interfere with human growth and development. As a result, bits and pieces of development are examined, and it is often difficult to see how the obtained information contributes to the bigger picture. All too often, what is studied is what is easiest to study, rather than what is important to study.

Research findings are often based on small, homogeneous samples that preclude generalization to other populations. Unfortunately, sufficient caution in interpreting the results of such studies is often missing. Too little research has focused on developmental processes for students of color; older students; students from different cultural backgrounds; students with disabilities; gay, lesbian, and bisexual students; and students from various religious traditions and socioeconomic classes.

Instrumentation remains a significant problem in developmental research. Very few reliable and valid instruments are available to measure any aspect of development. Those that do exist frequently require specialized training to administer or to score and interpret. Often they must be individually administered and hand-scored. These are costly and time-intensive procedures that limit the number of participants in studies. For many theories, no standardized instruments exist to test related propositions and hypotheses. For other theories, such as that of Chickering, existing instruments relate to only certain components of the theory. To compound the problem further, some existing instruments are becoming dated. For example, the Defining Issues Test (Rest, 1986a) includes a dilemma that references the Students for a Democratic Society, an organization active in the 1960s that many individuals today would not recognize. Obviously, the lack of appropriate instrumentation limits how research is conducted and what can be studied.

The preponderance of studies reported in the literature are cross-sectional. (For example, such a study might compare the developmental level of first-year and fourth-year students.) It is difficult to determine much about the process of development over time and the factors that contribute to development without longitudinal studies (for example, studies that follow the same group of students from the first year through the fourth year).

Although the literature presents some elegant applications of theoretical principles to student affairs practice (for example, Rodgers, 1990a), too few comprehensive examples are available. Those that do exist are most likely to be hypothetical rather than reports of actual interventions. In addition, most reported applications of theory have been in the area of programming. Though important, programming is only one aspect of student affairs practice that is informed by theory. Finally, few discussions of actual theory-to-practice efforts have included systematic evaluation data. Discussions of ways that theory can be used in practice are helpful in providing ideas, but solid evidence from well-designed evaluation studies demonstrating the effectiveness of an intervention is much more persuasive in convincing student affairs administrators of the utility of an approach. It also does much to further the theoretical knowledge base by demonstrating that hypotheses drawn from theory can be validated in practice.

Recommendations for the Future

Taking account of the critique of the student development knowledge base presented in the preceding section, we make the following recommendations.

1. *Development must be considered in a more comprehensive and less linear manner.* Kathy Allen (1989) suggested that assumptions about development need to be modified in a number of ways. Her ideas reflect a constructivist perspective and include the following modifications of traditional thought: (a) There are multiple pathways to development rather than a single developmental path. Not everyone will get from point A to point B in the same way. (b) Development consists of themes and patterns, rather than stages. Certain themes may be more or less reflective of individuals from different backgrounds. (c) Development is both internally and externally triggered. While maturation certainly plays a role in determining what issues will become salient at particular times and how the individual will respond to them, environmental conditions also contribute to this process in significant ways. (d) Cohort patterns exist with regard to development. Culture, gender, and generation all play a role in how development occurs and what it looks like. Developmental patterns and themes would be more similar for individuals from the same cohort than for persons from different cohorts. For example, developing a life's purpose would be a different process for women born in 1930 than for women born in 1980 because opportunities and values related to the roles of women in society have changed over time. Because of differences in cultural worldviews, the experiences of African

American women and Caucasian women might also be different. Differing societal expectations of men and women could also affect the developmental paths of each gender group. (e) Aspects of development are interconnected. It is impossible to separate cognitive development from psychosocial development and personality style. As such, development must be studied in a holistic manner. Allen's propositions are intriguing and certainly worthy of further exploration. They influence many of the recommendations noted here.

2. *Researchers must examine what development looks like for various student populations independent of Eurocentric models.* A student in a student development class offered the following comment in a critique of Chickering's theory: "I wonder how we would think about development if the students on which Chickering based his theory had all been African American." A good question indeed! Although the knowledge base is expanding to consider the generalizability of developmental theories to students from different backgrounds, most often researchers and practitioners still start from the existing theoretical base and examine how students of color, women, and other groups differ from that base. Implicitly, as Gilligan (1977) suggested, "different" is viewed as "deficient," and the white Euro-American male experience is still considered the norm. Researchers need to start afresh in exploring the development of students from various racial and ethnic groups, sexual orientations, and other students whose life experiences have shaped them in different ways. Qualitative research approaches, including ethnographic interviews, participant observation, and other techniques used in anthropology and sociology, are particularly appropriate for determining what development is really like for students from diverse backgrounds.

3. *Representatives of groups that have been unacknowledged in our theory base must be given a voice.* Related to recommendation 2, student affairs professionals need to become more aware of the missing voices in the student development literature (see Madrid, 1988). How often do educators read about or consider the developmental experiences of students with disabilities, Jewish students, Islamic students, fundamentalist Christians, or students raised in poverty? What about the children of migrant workers, veterans, or displaced faculty workers returning to college? Greater understanding of the role played by background and culture in the lives of students from diverse populations is crucial if student affairs professionals are to be inclusive in creating meaningful experiences to facilitate development for all students. In reality, addressing issues of invisibility and voicelessness in the theory base may be the most pressing need. Educators cannot assume that development is the same process for all students or that the concepts that apply to a narrowly defined group of students work equally well for others. Identifying what factors influence development by learning from students who have been previously overlooked will help in determining what makes students unique and special, as well as what they have in common with others.

4. *Development must be studied throughout the life span.* No longer are students all between eighteen and twenty-two years old. Nor does development end at twenty-two. If educators are to truly understand student development, they must learn more about the changes that take place in later life and the impact of those changes on the ways in which older students negotiate the college environment. Understanding development throughout the life span is also crucial if student affairs professionals are to understand their own life experiences and effectively work with staff to enhance personal as well as professional development.

5. *Longitudinal research that examines development over time is needed.* Development is not a static variable. It cannot be studied in the same way researchers study things like who gets admitted to college and who graduates. Researchers must follow people as they move through their lives and see what unfolds in the process. Although such research is time-consuming and difficult, the benefits are great. Work such as that being conducted by Marcia Baxter Magolda (1995), who is now following her previously interviewed college students into their careers and lives after college, will tell us much about not only the process of development during college but also the impact of college experiences on later development.

6. *The impact of the environment on development must be considered.* As Lewin (1936) stated long before the advent of the student development movement, behavior is a function of the interaction of the person and the environment. For too long, researchers and theorists have focused on the person by concentrating on internal maturational processes and downplayed the role of the environment in the determination of developmental outcomes. Investigators must balance their efforts more evenly so that environmental forces are given their just due.

"Environment" has many meanings. As noted, it can be the familial, cultural, and social circumstances of a person's life before college. Pascarella and Terenzini (1991) concluded from their review of the literature that the most significant determinants of students' success in college are their experiences prior to college. Environment can be the type of institution in which a student is enrolled. For example, Fleming (1984) discovered that the development of African American students attending predominantly white universities was quite different from the development of their counterparts in historically black universities. Particular settings on college campuses must also be considered when examining the environment. In a study of the development of gay, lesbian, and bisexual students in residence halls (Evans, Broido, Dragon, Eberz, & Richards, 1997), students reported very different experiences in various hall settings that either facilitated or retarded the development of their identities.

7. *What factors influence development must be examined.* As King (1994) has noted, developmental theory as it currently exists is mainly descriptive. More information is needed about "movement" in developmental processes. Researchers must identify factors that contribute to growth and learn more about how development

can be facilitated. Educators also need to understand more about forces that inhibit development and how those forces might be countered. Case study and in-depth interviewing over time are preferred methods for conducting such research.

8. *The ways in which various aspects of development are interconnected must be investigated.* Exploratory research has indicated that various components of development are interconnected. For example, level of cognitive development and personality type as measured by the MBTI both appear to influence how developmental tasks are approached and mastered (Anchors & Robinson, 1992; Polkosnik & Winston, 1989). Cognitive style as defined by Belenky, Clinchy, Goldberger, and Tarule (1986) and MBTI personality type were found to correlate in another study (Carter, 1990). And gay and lesbian identity development appears to interact in complex ways with accomplishment of other developmental tasks (Levine & Bahr, 1989). Researchers must continue to explore ways in which different aspects of development influence each other. They must also search for new approaches to the study of development that look at processes holistically. Again, in-depth interviews conducted over extended time periods may be one answer to exploring the complexity of development in a more comprehensive manner.

9. *Better methods to assess development must be developed.* More accessible and inexpensive assessment techniques are needed, particularly for large-scale evaluation studies. If educators are to determine if programs, services, and other interventions are having an impact on students, they must have ways of measuring development. Programmatic efforts to develop and refine instrumentation, such as those at the University of Iowa and the University of Georgia, are crucial if progress is to be made in this area. Too many studies use "home-grown" assessment tools that may have face validity but that have not been thoroughly examined for reliability or validity in any systematic way.

Educators must also respect the validity of qualitative approaches to assess development. Such approaches are particularly appropriate when building new theory and extending theory to previously unconsidered populations. Researchers must, of course, hold themselves to high standards in the use of qualitative techniques, recognizing that qualitative research methodology involves much more than just "talking to people."

10. *Educators must challenge themselves to be creative in the use of theory.* Developmental interventions, as noted by Evans (1987), can be targeted at the individual or the institution. Too often, practitioners think only of programming when they think of ways to use theory in practice. While programming is important, theory is also extremely helpful when advising or counseling students, advising student organizations, designing classroom instruction and training initiatives, and formulating policy. The Cube model (Morrill, Oetting, & Hurst, 1974) and the Developmental Intervention model (Evans, 1987), both discussed in Chapter Two,

are particularly helpful tools for stretching one's thinking about ways in which theory can guide practice.

11. *Educators must intelligently design interventions that are sensitive to the unique needs of specific environments.* The following scenario is played out far too often in student affairs: A practitioner attends a student affairs conference presentation in which the presenters outline a program they have implemented successfully on their campus. The practitioner is impressed. She believes that this program is just what is needed to address a similar issue on her campus. She comes home and sells the new program to the staff of her unit. They implement it the next year. It bombs.

What the practitioner and her fellow staff members failed to recognize is that each campus is unique. The issue may seem the same, but the environment is different. Programs cannot be transplanted without a careful assessment of the environment and modifications to adapt the program to the particular situation.

12. *Assessment and evaluation must be a part of every intentionally designed developmental intervention.* Interventions must be intentionally planned and based on sound assessment data reflecting the needs of the student community. They must also be carefully evaluated to determine their effectiveness. Focus groups, targeted interviewing based on purposive sampling, examination of archival data, and other qualitative means of assessment can be used effectively in program evaluation along with more traditional quantitative approaches (Upcraft & Schuh, 1996).

13. *More effort must be made to publish reports of studies evaluating developmental interventions.* Few evaluative studies of theory-based interventions are available in the literature. Such work is extremely important for advancing the field. Evaluation studies, of course, provide information to practitioners about what efforts are worthy of continuation and where resources should be allocated. In addition, well-designed evaluation studies can also lead to refinements of theory and provide direction for future investigation. Holland's program of research evaluating career counseling interventions, discussed in Chapter Thirteen, is an excellent example of the impact that such endeavors can have.

14. *The use of theory in educational practice must be encouraged.* In an applied field such as student affairs, a knowledge base would seem to be valuable only to the extent that it informs practice. In the same way, theoretical information that can enhance the teaching and learning process is of limited value if it does not find a home in the classroom. More must be done to disseminate information about how student development theory informs educational practice. Collaborative efforts between student affairs educators and faculty are particularly powerful in enhancing the climate for learning and development on college campuses. In this book, case studies and practical scenarios have been systematically included to demonstrate ways in which theory informs practice in a variety of student affairs and classroom settings. Further efforts in this vein are needed.

15.   *Educators must remember that all theory reflects the values of its authors and the times in which they live.* In both research and practice, educators have to remain sensitive to the implications of theory's being socially constructed, as McEwen (1996a) has emphasized. She advocated peeling away layers to discover "hidden and unstated bases and intentions" (p. 159). The role of power and oppression in theory development and use must be identified and understood if theory is to be used with wisdom and caring.

A Response to the Critics

Student development theory, particularly its use as a foundation for student affairs practice, has recently been under attack. Bloland et al. (1994, 1996) presented what some have viewed as a scathing indictment of the student development philosophy (see R. D. Brown, 1995, 1996). Specifically, Bloland et al. (1994, 1996) claimed that many student affairs educators have inappropriately elevated student development theory to something resembling icon status. *If* this has happened or is happening in our profession, the act deserves to be challenged. No single resource stands alone as *the* foundation for professional practice. Student development theory, for example, is one of several knowledge bases that can inform our practice. Considering additional theoretical bases, areas such as environmental theory and organizational theory, are important resources also. And knowledge beyond theory is obviously important as well (for example, awareness of and ability to use ethical principles and codes). Moreover, as noted earlier in this chapter and throughout this book, student development theory has its limitations. The need for information that is inclusive of the diversity and cohort differences that have come to characterize today's students and will continue to change with tomorrow's students will be ongoing. However, the fact that student development theory is missing some information and will continue to require updating and intelligent usage is not a reason to throw out the baby with the bath water. Student development theory doesn't tell us everything, but it tells us much.

Bloland et al. (1994, 1996) also discussed learning and development as though these are mutually exclusive phenomena. As was highlighted throughout this book, particularly in Chapter Fifteen, several student development theories directly address learning. An individual student's level of cognitive complexity and preferred learning style have important implications for the student's ability to learn. In addition, struggles that individual students experience with psychosocial development come to bear on their learning processes. For example, drawing on Chickering's theory (Chickering & Reisser, 1993), we note that developing intellectual competence is intertwined with the learning process, and issues of identity development (particularly those related to gender, sexual orientation, and ethnicity) can become so pronounced as to overshadow and limit participation in the learning process. Clearly, for the individual student, learning and development are not neat and discrete personal dynamics that operate in isolation in easily compartmentalized processes. Given the manner in which these processes interact, higher education professionals need to be skeptical of false dichotomies.

Knefelkamp (1982) once promoted the value of student development theory as a source of common language. Such language can facilitate empathic listening, a crucial process for anyone in higher education who works with students. From Knefelkamp's work, the following question can be derived: If people cannot hear each other's voices, how can they possibly understand each other's natures? Educators must honor this language as well as recognize its limitations. They need to help this common language evolve, particularly in regard to expanding its scope to be inclusive of all students. Educators must help others learn to speak the language and understand it when it is spoken to them. A spirit of collaboration is essential if individuals are to be effective in contributing to the education of both today's and tomorrow's students.

Finally, all educators need to be encouraged to consider the truth that having more information would always seem to be more advantageous than having less information. Use of this information in a generative fashion is a mutually shared responsibility.

RECOMMENDATIONS
FOR FURTHER READING

Individuals new to a body of knowledge are often uncertain where to begin in their efforts to develop a sound grounding in the literature. This appendix provides our recommendations concerning the most comprehensive and helpful literature for students who wish to explore particular theories and concepts in greater depth, organized to correspond to the chapters in this book.

Chapter One

Brown, R. D. (1972). *Student development in tomorrow's higher education—a return to the academy.* Alexandria, VA: American College Personnel Association.

Carpenter, D. S. (1996). The philosophical heritage of student affairs. In A. Rentz (Ed.), *Student affairs functions in higher education* (2nd ed., pp. 3–27). Springfield, IL: Thomas.

Guba, E. G. (1990). The alternative paradigm dialog. In E. G. Guba (Ed.), *The paradigm dialog* (pp. 17–30). Newbury Park, CA: Sage.

Miller, T. K., & Prince, J. S. (1976). *The future of student affairs: A guide to student development for tomorrow's higher education.* San Francisco: Jossey-Bass.

Strange, C. C. (1994). Student development: The evolution and status of an essential idea. *Journal of College Student Development, 35,* 399–412.

Chapter Two

McEwen, M. K. (1996). The nature and uses of theory. In S. R. Komives, D. B. Woodard Jr., & Associates, *Student services: A handbook for the profession* (3rd ed., pp. 147–163). San Francisco: Jossey-Bass.

Parker, C. A. (1977). On modeling reality. *Journal of College Student Personnel, 18,* 419–425.

Rodgers, R. F., & Widick, C. (1980). Theory to practice: Using concepts, logic and creativity. In F. B. Newton & K. L. Ender (Eds.), *Student development practice: Strategies for making a difference* (pp. 5–25). Springfield, IL: Thomas.

Strange, C. C., & King, P. M. (1990). The professional practice of student development. In D. G. Creamer & Associates, *College student development: Theory and practice for the 1990s* (pp. 9–24). Alexandria, VA: American College Personnel Association.

Chapter Three

Chickering, A. W., & Reisser, L. (1993). *Education and identity* (2nd ed.). San Francisco: Jossey-Bass.

Hurst, J. C. (1978). Chickering's vectors of development and student affairs programming. In C. A. Parker (Ed.), *Encouraging the development of college students* (pp. 113–126). Minneapolis: University of Minnesota Press.

McEwen, M. K., Roper, L., Bryant, D., & Langa, M. (1990). Incorporating the development of African-American students into psychosocial theories of student development. *Journal of College Student Development, 31,* 429–436.

Miller, T. K., & Winston, R. B., Jr. (1990). Assessing development from a psychosocial perspective. In D. G. Creamer & Associates, *College student development: Theory and practice for the 1990s* (pp. 99–126). Alexandria, VA: American College Personnel Association.

Thomas, R., & Chickering, A. W. (1984). *Education and identity* revisited. *Journal of College Student Personnel, 25,* 392–399.

Chapter Four

Erikson, E. H. (1980). *Identity and the life cycle.* New York: Norton. (Original work published 1959)

Josselson, R. (1987). *Finding herself: Pathways to identity development in women.* San Francisco: Jossey-Bass.

Josselson, R. (1992). *The space between us: Exploring the dimensions of human relationships.* San Francisco: Jossey-Bass.

Marcia, J. E. (1966). Development and validation of ego-identity status. *Journal of Personality and Social Psychology, 3,* 551–558.

Marcia, J. E. (1980). Identity in adolescence. In J. Adelson (Ed.), *Handbook of adolescent psychology* (pp. 159–187). New York: Wiley.

Chapter Five

Cross, W. E., Jr. (1991). *Shades of black: Diversity in African American identity*. Philadelphia: Temple University Press.

Helms, J. E. (1992). *A race is a nice thing to have: A guide to being a white person or understanding the white persons in your life*. Topeka, KS: Content Communications.

Helms, J. E. (Ed.). (1993). *Black and white racial identity: Theory, research, and practice*. Westport, CT: Praeger.

Phinney, J. S. (1990). Ethnic identity in adolescents and adults: Review of research. *Psychological Bulletin, 108*, 499–514.

Ponterotto, J. G., Casas, J. M., Suzuki, L. A., & Alexander, C. M. (Eds.). (1995). *Handbook of multicultural counseling*. Thousand Oaks, CA: Sage.

Ponterotto, J. G., & Pedersen, P. B. (1993). *Preventing prejudice: A guide for counselors and educators*. Multicultural Aspects of Counseling, Series 2. Newbury Park, CA: Sage.

Chapter Six

D'Augelli, A. R. (1994). Identity development and sexual orientation: Toward a model of lesbian, gay, and bisexual development. In E. J. Trickett, R. J. Watts, & D. Birman (Eds.), *Human diversity: Perspectives on people in context* (pp. 312–333). San Francisco: Jossey-Bass.

D'Augelli, A. R. (1996). Enhancing the development of lesbian, gay, and bisexual youths. In E. D. Rothblum & L. A. Bond (Eds.), *Preventing heterosexism and homophobia* (pp. 124–150). Thousand Oaks, CA: Sage.

D'Augelli, A. R., & Patterson, C. J. (Eds.). (1995). *Lesbian, gay, and bisexual identities over the lifespan: Psychological perspectives*. New York: Oxford University Press.

Evans, N. J., & Wall, V. A. (Eds.). (1991). *Beyond tolerance: Gays, lesbians and bisexuals on campus*. Alexandria, VA: American College Personnel Association.

Chapter Seven

Chickering, A. W., & Schlossberg, N. K. (1995). *How to get the most out of college*. Boston: Allyn & Bacon.

Schlossberg, N. K. (1989). *Overwhelmed: Coping with life's ups and downs*. Lexington, MA: Lexington Books.

Schlossberg, N. K., Lynch, A. Q., & Chickering, A. W. (1989). *Improving higher education environments for adults: Responsive programs and services from entry to departure*. San Francisco: Jossey-Bass.

Schlossberg, N. K., Waters, E. B., & Goodman, J. (1995). *Counseling adults in transition* (2nd ed.). New York: Springer.

Chapter Eight

Cosgrove, T. J. (1987). Understanding how college students think. *Campus Activities Programming, 20* (3), 56–60.

Perry, W. G., Jr. (1978). Sharing in the costs of growth. In C. A. Parker (Ed.), *Encouraging development in college students* (pp. 267–273). Minneapolis: University of Minnesota Press.

Perry, W. G., Jr. (1981). Cognitive and ethical growth: The making of meaning. In A. W. Chickering & Associates, *The modern American college: Responding to the new realities of diverse students and a changing society* (pp. 76–116). San Francisco: Jossey-Bass.

Piper, T. D., & Rodgers, R. F. (1992). Theory-practice congruence: Factors influencing the internalization of theory. *Journal of College Student Development, 33,* 117–123.

Ricci, J. P., Porterfield, W. D., & Piper, T. D. (1987). Using developmental theory in supervising residential staff members. *NASPA Journal, 24* (4), 32–41.

Stonewater, B. B. (1988). Informal developmental assessment in residence halls: A theory to practice model. *NASPA Journal, 25,* 267–273.

Chapter Nine

Baxter Magolda, M. B. (1992). *Knowing and reasoning in college: Gender-related patterns in students' intellectual development.* San Francisco: Jossey-Bass.

Belenky, M. F., Clinchy, B. M., Goldberger, N. R., & Tarule, J. M. (1986). *Women's ways of knowing: The development of self, voice, and mind.* New York: Basic Books.

King, P. M., & Kitchener, K. S. (1994). *Developing reflective judgment: Understanding and promoting intellectual growth and critical thinking in adolescents and adults.* San Francisco: Jossey-Bass.

Chapter Ten

Colby, A., & Kohlberg, L. (Eds.). (1987). *The measurement of moral judgment: Vol. 1. Theoretical foundations and research validation.* New York: Cambridge University Press.

Kohlberg, L. (1984). *Essays on moral development: Vol. II. The psychology of moral development.* San Francisco: Harper & Row.

Rest, J. R. (1979). *Development in judging moral issues.* Minneapolis: University of Minnesota Press.

Rest, J. R. (1986). *Moral development: Advances in research and theory.* New York: Praeger.

Walker, L. J. (1988). The development of moral reasoning. *Annals of Child Development, 5,* 33–78.

Chapter Eleven

Delworth, U., & Seeman, D. (1984). The ethics of care: Implications of Gilligan for the student services profession. *Journal of College Student Development, 25,* 489–492.

Gilligan, C. (1977). In a different voice: Women's conceptions of self and morality. *Harvard Educational Review, 47,* 481–517.

Gilligan, C. (1993). *In a different voice: Psychological theory and women's development.* Cambridge, MA: Harvard University Press. (Original work published 1982)

Hotelling, K., & Forrest, L. (1985). Gilligan's theory of sex-role development: A perspective for counseling. *Journal of Counseling and Development, 64,* 183–186.

Picard, I. A., & Guido-DiBrito, F. (1993). Listening to the voice of care: Women's moral development and implications for student affairs practitioners. *Iowa Student Personnel Journal, 8,* 21–34.

Porterfield, W. D., & Pressprich, S. T. (1988). Carol Gilligan's perspectives and staff supervision: Implications for the practitioner. *NASPA Journal, 25,* 244–248.

Chapter Twelve

Anderson, J. A., & Adams, M. (1992). Acknowledging the learning styles of diverse student populations: Implications for instructional design. In L. L. B. Border & N. V. N. Chism (Eds.), *Teaching for diversity* (New Directions for Teaching and Learning, No. 49, pp. 19–33). San Francisco: Jossey-Bass.

Claxton, C. S., & Murrell, P. H. (1987). *Learning styles: Implications for improving educational practices* (ASHE-ERIC Higher Education Report 4). Washington, DC: Association for the Study of Higher Education.

Kolb, D. A. (1981). Learning styles and disciplinary differences. In A. W. Chickering & Associates, *The modern American college: Responding to the new realities of diverse students and a changing society* (pp. 232–255). San Francisco: Jossey-Bass.

Svinicki, M. D., & Dixon, N. M. (1987). The Kolb model modified for classroom activities. *College Teaching, 35,* 141–146.

Chapter Thirteen

Holland, J. L. (1992). *Making vocational choices: A theory of vocational personalities and work environments* (2nd ed.). Odessa, FL: Psychological Assessment Resources. (Original published 1985.)

Jacoby, B., Rue, P., & Allen, K. T. (1984). UMaps: A person-environment approach to helping students make critical choices. *Personnel and Guidance Journal, 62,* 426–428.

Walsh, W. B., & Holland, J. L. (1992). A theory of personality types and work environments. In W. B. Walsh, K. H. Craik, & R. H. Price (Eds.), *Person-environment psychology: Models and perspectives* (pp. 35–69). Hillsdale, NJ: Erlbaum.

Weinrach, S. G., & Srebalus, D. J. (1990). Holland's theory of careers. In D. Brown, L. Brooks, & Associates, *Career choice and development: Applying contemporary theories to practice* (2nd ed., pp. 37–67). San Francisco: Jossey-Bass.

Chapter Fourteen

Bayne, R. (1995). *The Myers-Briggs Type Indicator: A critical review and practical guide.* London: Chapman & Hall.

Lawrence, G. (1993). *People types & tiger stripes* (3rd ed.). Gainesville, FL: Center for Applications of Psychological Type.

Myers, I. B. (1980). *Gifts differing.* Palo Alto, CA: Consulting Psychologists Press.

Provost, J. A., & Anchors, S. (Eds.). (1987). *Applications of the Myers-Briggs Type Indicator in higher education.* Palo Alto, CA: Consulting Psychologists Press.

REFERENCES

Abbey, D. S., Hunt, D. E., & Weiser, J. C. (1985). Variations on a theme by Kolb: A new perspective for understanding counseling and supervision. *Counseling Psychologist, 13,* 477–501.

Adams, G. R., Bennion, L., & Huh, K. (1987). *Objective measures of ego identity status: A reference manual.* Logan: Utah State University.

Adams, G. R., & Fitch, S. A. (1982). Ego stage and identity status development: A cross-sequential analysis. *Journal of Personality and Social Psychology, 43,* 574–583.

Akbar, N. (1989). Nigrescence and identity: Some limitations. *Counseling Psychologist, 17,* 258–263.

Alexander, C. M. (1993). Construct validity and reliability of the White Racial Identity Attitude Scale (WRIAS). *Dissertation Abstracts International, 53,* 3799A.

Allen, K. E. (1989, June). *A non-linear model of student development: Implications for assessment.* Paper presented at the American Association of Higher Education Assessment Forum.

American Council on Education. (1994a). The student personnel point of view. In A. L. Rentz (Ed.), *Student affairs: A profession's heritage* (American College Personnel Association Media Publication No. 40, 2nd ed., pp. 66–77). Lanham, MD: University Press of America. (Original work published 1937)

American Council on Education. (1994b). The student personnel point of view. In A. L. Rentz (Ed.), *Student affairs: A profession's heritage* (American College Personnel Association Media Publication No. 40, 2nd ed., pp. 108–123). Lanham, MD: University Press of America. (Original work published 1949)

Anchors, S. (1987). Academic advising. In J. A. Provost & S. Anchors (Eds.), *Applications of the Myers-Briggs Type Indicator in higher education* (pp. 109–123). Palo Alto, CA: Consulting Psychologists Press.

Anchors, S., & Dana, R. (1992). Substance abuse patterns and personality type among first-year residence hall students. *Journal of College and University Student Housing, 22* (1), 7–11.

Anchors, W. S., & Robinson, D. C. (1992). Psychological type and the accomplishment of student development tasks. *NASPA Journal, 29,* 131–135.

Anderson, J. A., & Adams, M. (1992). Acknowledging the learning styles of diverse student populations: Implications for instructional design. In L. L. B. Border & N. V. N. Chism (Eds.), *Teaching for diversity* (New Directions for Teaching and Learning, No. 49, pp. 19–33). San Francisco: Jossey-Bass.

Apostal, R. A. (1991). College students' career interests and sensing-intuition personality. *Journal of College Student Development, 32,* 4–7.

Arbuckle, D. S. (1953). *Student personnel services in higher education.* New York: McGraw-Hill.

Arce, C. A. (1981). A reconsideration of Chicano culture and identity. *Daedalus, 110,* 177–192.

Arvizu, D. R. (1995). The care voice and American Indian college students: An alternative perspective for student development professionals. *Journal of American Indian Education, 34,* 1–17.

Assouline, M., & Meir, E. (1987). Meta-analysis of the relationship between congruence and well-being measures. *Journal of Vocational Behavior, 31,* 319–332.

Astin, A. W. (1964). Distribution of students among higher educational institutions. *Journal of Educational Psychology, 55,* 276–287.

Astin, A. W. (1965a). Effects of different college environments on the vocational choices of high aptitude students. *Journal of Counseling Psychology, 12,* 28–34.

Astin, A. W. (1965b). *Who goes where to college?* Chicago: Science Research Associates.

Astin, A. W. (1984). Student involvement: A developmental theory for higher education. *Journal of College Student Personnel, 25,* 297–308.

Astin, A. W., & Holland, J. L. (1961). The Environmental Assessment Technique: A way to measure college environments. *Journal of Educational Psychology, 52,* 308–316.

Atkinson, D. R., Morten, G., & Sue, D. W. (1993). *Counseling American minorities: A cross-cultural perspective* (4th ed.). Madison, WI: Brown and Benchmark Publishers.

Atkinson, G., Jr., & Murrell, P. H. (1988). Kolb's experiential learning theory: A meta-model for career exploration. *Journal of Counseling and Development, 66,* 374–377.

Avens, C., & Zelley, R. (1992). *QUANTA: An interdisciplinary learning community (four studies).* Daytona Beach, FL: Daytona Beach Community College. (ERIC Document Reproduction Service No. ED 349 073)

Bakken, L., & Ellsworth, R. (1990). Moral development in adulthood: Its relationship to age, sex, and education. *Educational Research Quarterly, 14* (2), 2–9.

Baldwin, J. A., & Bell, Y. R. (1985). The African Self-Consciousness Scale: An Africentric personality questionnaire. *Western Journal of Black Studies, 9,* 61–68.

Baltes, P. B. (1987). Theoretical perspectives on life-span developmental psychology: On the dynamics between growth and decline. *Developmental Psychology, 23,* 611–626.

Banning, J. H. (1989). Creating a climate for successful student development: The campus ecology manager role. In U. Delworth, G. Hanson, & Associates, *Student services: A handbook for the profession* (2nd ed., pp. 304–322). San Francisco: Jossey-Bass.

Barr, L., & Barr, N. (1989). *The leadership equation: Leadership, management, and the Myers-Briggs.* Austin, TX: Eakin.

Barrett, W. R. (1978). *Construction and validation of the Developing Purposes Inventory.* Technical report. Iowa City: University of Iowa, Iowa Student Development Project.

Bateman, D., & Donald, J. G. (1987). Measuring the intellectual development of college students: Testing a theoretical framework. *Canadian Journal of Higher Education, 17,* 27–45.

Baxter Magolda, M. B. (1987). Comparing open-ended interviews and standardized measures of intellectual development. *Journal of College Student Personnel, 28,* 443–448.

Baxter Magolda, M. B. (1989). Gender differences in cognitive development: An analysis of cognitive complexity and learning styles. *Journal of College Student Development, 30,* 213–220.

Baxter Magolda, M. B. (1992). *Knowing and reasoning in college: Gender-related patterns in students' intellectual development.* San Francisco: Jossey-Bass.

Baxter Magolda, M. B. (1995). The integration of relational and impersonal knowing in young adults' epistemological development. *Journal of College Student Development, 36,* 205–216.

Baxter Magolda, M. B., & Porterfield, W. D. (1985). A new approach to assess intellectual development on the Perry scheme. *Journal of College Student Personnel, 26,* 343–350.

Bayne, R. (1995). *The Myers-Briggs Type Indicator: A critical review and practical guide.* London: Chapman & Hall.

Belenky, M. F., Clinchy, B. M., Goldberger, N. R., & Tarule, J. M. (1986). *Women's ways of knowing: The development of self, voice, and mind.* New York: Basic Books.

Bell, A. P., Weinberg, M. S., & Hammersmith, S. K. (1981). *Sexual preference: Its development in men and women.* Bloomington: Indiana University Press.

Bem, S. L. (1974). The measurement of psychological androgyny. *Journal of Consulting and Clinical Psychology, 4,* 155–162.

Bernal, M. E., & Knight, G. P. (Eds.). (1993). *Ethnic identity: Formation and transmission among Hispanics and other minorities.* Albany: State University of New York Press.

Bertaux, D. (1982). The life course approach as a challenge to the social sciences. In T. K. Hareven & K. J. Adams (Eds.), *Aging and life course transitions: An interdisciplinary perspective* (pp. 127–150). New York: Guilford Press.

Bilsker, D., Schiedel, D., & Marcia, J. E. (1988). Sex differences in identity status. *Sex Roles, 18,* 231–236.

Black, J. D. (1980). Publisher's forward. In I. B. Myers, *Gifts differing* (pp. ix-xii). Palo Alto, CA: Consulting Psychologists Press.

Blackhurst, A. B. (1995). The relationship between gender and student outcomes in a freshman orientation course. *Journal of the Freshmen Year Experience, 7,* 63–80.

Blasi, A. (1980). Bridging moral cognition and moral action: A critical review of the literature. *Psychological Bulletin, 88,* 1–45.

Bloland, P. A., Stamatakos, L. C., & Rogers, R. R. (1994). *Reform in student affairs: A critique of student development.* Greensboro, NC: ERIC Counseling and Student Services Clearinghouse.

Bloland, P. A., Stamatakos, L. C., & Rogers, R. R. (1996). Redirecting the role of student affairs to focus on student learning. *Journal of College Student Development, 37,* 217–226.

Borgen, F. H. (1991). Megatrends and milestones in vocational behavior: A 20–year counseling psychology retrospective. *Journal of Vocational Behavior, 39,* 263–290.

Bourassa, D., & Shipton, B. (1991). Addressing lesbian and gay issues in residence hall environments. In N. J. Evans & V. A. Wall (Eds.), *Beyond tolerance: Gays, lesbians and bisexuals on campus* (pp. 79–96). Alexandria, VA: American College Personnel Association.

Bourne, E. (1978a). The state of research on ego identity: A review and appraisal. Part I. *Journal of Youth and Adolescence, 7,* 223–251.

Bourne, E. (1978b). The state of research on ego identity: A review and appraisal. Part II. *Journal of Youth and Adolescence, 7,* 371–392.

Boyatzis, R. E., & Kolb, D. A. (1991). Assessing individuality in learning: The Learning Skills Profile. *Educational Psychology, 11,* 279–295.

Boyatzis, R. E., & Kolb, D. A. (1993a). *The Adaptive Style Inventory.* Boston: McBer.

Boyatzis, R. E., & Kolb, D. A. (1993b). *Learning Skills Profile workbook*. Boston: McBer.

Brabeck, M. (1983). Moral judgment: Theory and research on differences between males and females. *Developmental Review, 3,* 274–291.

Bradby, D., & Helms, J. E. (1993). Black racial identity attitudes and white therapist cultural sensitivity in cross-racial therapy dyads: An exploratory study. In J. E. Helms (Ed.), *Black and white racial identity: Theory, research, and practice* (pp. 165–175). Westport, CT: Praeger.

Brady, S. (1983). The relationship between differences in stages of homosexuality identity formation and background characteristics, psychological well-being and homosexual adjustment. *Dissertation Abstracts International, 45,* 3328 (10B).

Brady, S., & Busse, W. J. (1994). The Gay Identity Questionnaire: A brief measure of homosexual identity formation. *Journal of Homosexuality, 26* (4), 1–21.

Branch-Simpson, G. (1984). *A study of the patterns in the development of black students at the Ohio State University.* Unpublished doctoral dissertation, Ohio State University, Columbus.

Brand, M. (1988, Fall). Toward a better understanding of undergraduate music education majors: Perry's perspective. *Bulletin of the Council for Research in Music Education,* 22–31.

Broughton, J. M. (1975). *The development of natural epistemology in years 11 to 16.* Unpublished doctoral dissertation, Harvard University.

Brown, D. (1987). The status of Holland's theory of vocational choice. *Career Development Quarterly, 36* (1), 13–30.

Brown, L. M., & Gilligan, C. (1991). Listening for voice in narratives of relationship. In M. B. Tappan & M. J. Packer (Eds.), *Narrative and storytelling: Implications for understanding moral development* (New Directions for Child Development, No. 54, pp. 43–62). San Francisco: Jossey-Bass.

Brown, L. M., & Gilligan, C. (1992). *Meeting at the crossroads: Women's psychology and girls' development.* Cambridge, MA: Harvard University Press.

Brown, L. S. (1995). Lesbian identities: Concepts and issues. In A. R. D'Augelli & C. J. Patterson (Eds.), *Lesbian, gay, and bisexual identities over the lifespan: Psychological perspectives* (pp. 3–23). New York: Oxford University Press.

Brown, R. D. (1972). *Student development in tomorrow's higher education—a return to the academy.* Alexandria, VA: American College Personnel Association.

Brown, R. D. (1995). Reform in student affairs: A counterpoint comment. *ACPA Developments, 4,* 12.

Brown, R. D. (1996). We've been there. We've done that. Let's keep it up. *Journal of College Student Development, 37,* 239–241.

Brown, R. D., & Barr, M. J. (1990). Student development: Yesterday, today and tomorrow. In L. V. Moore (Ed.), *Evolving theoretical perspectives on students* (New Directions for Student Services, No. 51, pp. 83–92). San Francisco: Jossey-Bass.

Brown, V. L., & DeCoster, D. A. (1991). The Myers-Briggs Type Indicator as a developmental measure: Implications for student learners. *Journal of College Student Development, 32,* 378–379.

Browning, C. (1987). Therapeutic issues and intervention strategies with young adult lesbian clients: A developmental approach. *Journal of Homosexuality, 14* (2), 45–52.

Brownsword, A. W. (1987). *It takes all types!* San Anselmo, CA: Baytree.

Bruch, M. A. (1978). Holland's typology applied to client-counselor interaction: Implications for counseling men. *Counseling Psychologist, 7* (4), 26–32.

Bruner, J. S., Goodnow, I. J., & Austin, G. A. (1956). *A study of thinking.* New York: Wiley.

Buczynski, P. L. (1991). The relationship between identity and cognitive development in college freshmen: A structural equation modeling analysis. *Journal of College Student Development, 32,* 212–222.

Buczynski, P. L. (1993). The development of a paper-and-pencil measure of Belenky, Clinchy, Goldberger, and Tarule's (1986) conceptual model of women's ways-of-knowing instrument. *Journal of College Student Development, 34,* 197–200.

Buhrke, R. A., & Stabb, S. D. (1995). Gay, lesbian, and bisexual student needs. In S. D. Stabb & J. E. Talley (Eds.), *Multicultural needs assessment for college and university student populations* (pp. 173–201). Springfield, IL: Thomas.

Burnham, C. C. (1986). The Perry scheme and the teaching of writing. *Rhetoric Review, 4,* 152–158.

Cain, R. (1991). Stigma management and gay identity development. *Social Work, 36,* 67–73.

Cairo, T. A. (1992). Applications of the Myers-Briggs Type Indicator with returning adult students. *Journal of Continuing Higher Education, 40* (1), 25–28.

Callan, E. (1992). Finding a common voice. *Educational Theory, 42,* 429–441.

Calliotte, J. A., Helms, S. T., & Wells, E. A. (1975). *The education and vocational orientations of UMBC freshmen.* Baltimore: University of Maryland, Counseling Center.

Canon, H. J., & Brown, R. D. (1985). How to think about professional ethics. In H. J. Canon & R. D. Brown (Eds.), *Applied ethics in student services* (New Directions for Student Services, No. 30, pp. 81–87). San Francisco: Jossey-Bass.

Carey, J. C., Hamilton, D. L., & Shanklin, G. (1986). Does personality similarity affect male roommates' satisfaction? *Journal of College Student Personnel, 27,* 65–69.

Carlson, J. G. (1989). Affirmative: In support of researching the Myers-Briggs Type Indicator. *Journal of Counseling and Development, 67,* 484–486.

Carpenter, D. S. (1996). The philosophical heritage of student affairs. In A. Rentz (Ed.), *Student affairs functions in higher education* (2nd. ed., pp. 3–27). Springfield, IL: Thomas.

Carskadon, T. G. (1979). Clinical and counseling aspects of the Myers-Briggs Type Indicator: A research review. *Research in Psychological Type, 2,* 2–31.

Carskadon, T. G. (1982). Myers-Briggs Type Indicator characteristics: A Jungian horoscope? *Research in Psychological Type, 5,* 87–88.

Carskadon, T. G. (1994). Student personality factors: Psychological type and the Myers-Briggs Indicator. In K. W. Prichard & R. M. Sawyer (Eds.), *Handbook of college teaching: Theory and applications* (pp. 69–81). Westport, CT: Greenwood.

Carson, A. D. (1994). Applications of Holland's vocational theory to counselling practice related to vocational education. *McGill Journal of Education, 29,* 281–294.

Carter, J. A. (1990). A comparison of personality types as determined by the Myers-Briggs Type Indicator with the process of separate-knowing and connected-knowing procedural processing among female, undergraduate, and nontraditional students. *Dissertation Abstracts International, 51* (05), 1475A.

Carter, K. (1997). *Transgenderism and college students: Issues of gender orientation and its role on our campuses.* Unpublished master's paper, Pennsylvania State University, University Park, PA.

Carter, R. T. (1993). Does race or racial identity attitudes influence the counseling process in black and white dyads? In J. E. Helms (Ed.), *Black and white racial identity: Theory, research, and practice* (pp. 145–163). Westport, CT: Praeger.

Casas, J. M. (1984). Policy, training, and research in counseling psychology: The racial/ethnic minority perspective. In S. D. Brown & R. Lent (Eds.), *Handbook of counseling psychology* (pp. 785–831). New York: Wiley.

Casas, J. M., & Pytluk, S. D. (1995). Hispanic identity development: Implications for research and practice. In J. G. Ponterotto, J. M. Casas, L. A. Suzuki, & C. M. Alexander (Eds.), *Handbook of multicultural counseling* (pp. 155–180). Thousand Oaks, CA: Sage.

Cass, V. C. (1979). Homosexual identity formation: A theoretical model. *Journal of Homosexuality, 4,* 219–235.

Cass, V. C. (1983–1984). Homosexual identity: A concept in need of definition. *Journal of Homosexuality, 9* (2–3), 105–126.

Cass, V. C. (1984). Homosexual identity formation: Testing a theoretical model. *Journal of Sex Research, 20,* 143–167.

Cella, D. F., DeWolfe, A. S., & Fitzgibbon, M. (1987). Ego identity status, identification, and decision-making style in late adolescents. *Adolescence, 22,* 849–861.

Certo, S., & Lamb, S. (1979). Identification and measurement of instrument bias within the Learning Style Instrument through a Monte Carlo technique. *Southern Management Proceedings, 1979,* 22–24.

Champagne, D. E., & Petitpas, A. (1989). Planning developmental interventions for adult students. *NASPA Journal, 26,* 265–271.

Chan, C. S. (1989). Issues of identity development among Asian-American lesbians and gay men. *Journal of Counseling and Development, 68,* 16–20.

Chan, C. S. (1995). Issues of sexual identity in an ethnic minority: The case of Chinese American lesbians, gay men, and bisexual people. In A. R. D'Augelli & C. J. Patterson (Eds.), *Lesbian, gay, and bisexual identities over the lifespan: Psychological perspectives* (pp. 87–101). New York: Oxford University Press.

Chap, J. B. (1985–1986). Moral judgment in middle and late adulthood: The effects of age-appropriate moral dilemmas and spontaneous role-taking. *International Journal of Aging and Human Development, 22,* 161–172.

Charner, I., & Schlossberg, N. K. (1986). Variations by theme: The life transitions of clerical workers. *Vocational Guidance Quarterly, 34,* 212–224.

Chartrand, J. M., Strong, S. R., & Weitzman, L. M. (1995). The interactional perspective in vocational psychology: Paradigms, theories, and research practices. In W. B. Walsh & S. H. Osipow (Eds.), *Handbook of vocational psychology: Theory, research, and practice* (2nd ed., pp. 35–65). Mahwah, NJ: Erlbaum.

Cheatham, H. E., Slaney, R. B., & Coleman, N. C. (1990). Institutional effects on the psychosocial development of African-American college students. *Journal of Counseling Psychology, 37,* 453–458.

Chickering, A. W. (1969). *Education and identity.* San Francisco: Jossey-Bass.

Chickering, A. W. (1977). Potential contributions of college unions to student development. *Association of College Unions–International Conference Proceedings,* pp. 23–27.

Chickering, A. W., & O'Connor, J. (1996). The University Learning Center: A driving force for collaboration. *About Campus, 1,* 16–21.

Chickering, A. W., & Reisser, L. (1993). *Education and identity* (2nd ed.). San Francisco: Jossey-Bass.

Chickering, A. W., & Schlossberg, N. K. (1995). *How to get the most out of college.* Boston: Allyn & Bacon.

Chodorow, N. (1978). *The reproduction of mothering: Psychoanalysis and the sociology of gender.* Berkeley: University of California Press.

Choney, S. K., Berryhill-Paapke, E., & Robbins, R. R. (1995). The acculturation of American Indians: Developing frameworks for research and practice. In J. G. Ponterotto, J. M. Casas, L. A. Suzuki, & C. M. Alexander (Eds.), *Handbook of multicultural counseling* (pp. 73–92). Thousand Oaks, CA: Sage.

Claney, D., & Parker, W. M. (1989). Assessing white racial consciousness and perceived comfort with black individuals: A preliminary study. *Journal of Counseling and Development, 67,* 449–451.

Clark, A. J., & Dobson, J. E. (1980). Moral development: A factor in the group counseling process. *Journal for Specialists in Group Work, 5,* 81–86.

Claxton, C. S., & Murrell, P. H. (1987). *Learning styles: Implications for improving educational practices* (ASHE-ERIC Higher Education Report No. 4). Washington, DC: Association for the Study of Higher Education.

Clayton, S. A., & Jones, A. (1993). Multiculturalism: An imperative for change. *Iowa Student Personnel Association Journal, 8,* 35–49.

Clopton, N. A., & Sorell, G. T. (1993). Gender differences in moral reasoning: Stable or situational? *Psychology of Women Quarterly, 17,* 85–101.

Cohen, K. M., & Savin-Williams, R. C. (1996). Developmental perspectives on coming out to self and others. In R. C. Savin-Williams & K. M. Cohen (Eds.), *The lives of lesbians, gays, and bisexuals: Children to adults* (pp. 113–151). Fort Worth, TX: Harcourt Brace.

Colby, A., & Kohlberg, L. (1987). Reliability and validity of Standard Issues scoring. In A. Colby & L. Kohlberg (Eds.), *The measurement of moral judgment: Vol. 1. Theoretical foundations and research validation* (pp. 63–75). New York: Cambridge University Press.

Colby, A., Kohlberg, L., Gibbs, J., & Lieberman, M. (1983). A longitudinal study of moral judgment. *Monographs of the Society for Research in Child Development, 48* (1–2, Serial No. 200).

Colby, A., Kohlberg, L., & Kauffman, K. (1987a). Instructions for moral judgment interviewing and scoring. In A. Colby & L. Kohlberg (Eds.), *The measurement of moral judgment: Vol. 1. Theoretical foundations and research validation* (pp. 151–239). New York: Cambridge University Press.

Colby, A., Kohlberg, L., & Kauffman, K. (1987b). Theoretical introduction to the measurement of moral judgment. In A. Colby & L. Kohlberg (Eds.), *The measurement of moral judgment: Vol. 1. Theoretical foundations and research validation* (pp. 1–61). New York: Cambridge University Press.

Colby, A., Kohlberg, L., Speicher, B., Hewer, A., Candee, D., Gibbs, J., & Power, C. (1987). *The measurement of moral judgment: Vol. 2. Standard Issue scoring manual.* New York: Cambridge University Press.

Coleman, E. (1981–1982). Developmental stages of the coming out process. *Journal of Homosexuality, 7* (2–3), 31–43.

Committee on the Student in Higher Education. (1968). *The student in higher education.* New Haven, CT: Hazen Foundation.

Constantinople, A. (1969). An Eriksonian measure of personality development in college students. *Developmental Psychology, 1,* 357–372.

Constantinou, S., & Harvey, M. (1985). Dimensional structure and intergenerational differences in ethnicity: The Greek Americans. *Sociology and Social Research, 69,* 234–254.

Coomes, M. D. (1992). Understanding students: A developmental approach to financial aid services. *Journal of Student Financial Aid, 22* (2), 23–31.

Coomes, M. D. (1994). Using student development to guide institutional policy. *Journal of College Student Development, 35,* 428–437.

Cormier, L. S., & Hackney, H. (1993). *The professional counselor: A process guide to helping* (2nd ed.). Needham Heights, MA: Allyn & Bacon.

Cosgrove, T. J. (1987). Understanding how college students think. *Campus Activities Programming, 20* (3), 56–60.

Council of Student Personnel Associations in Higher Education. (1994). Student development services in postsecondary education. In A. Rentz (Ed.), *Student affairs: A profession's heritage* (American College Personnel Association Media Publication No. 40, 2nd ed., pp. 428–437). Lanham, MD: University Press of America. (Original work published 1975)

Crawford, J. S. (1989, May). *Perry levels and Belenky's findings: Their possibilities in the teaching of art and art history.* Paper presented at the Getty Conference on Discipline-Based Art Education, Austin, TX. (ERIC Document Reproduction Service No. ED 310 698)

Creamer, D. G. (1990). *College student development: Theory and practice for the 1990s.* Alexandria, VA: American College Personnel Association.

Crockett, J. B., & Crawford, R. L. (1989). The relationship between Myers-Briggs Type Indicator (MBTI) scale scores and advising style preferences of college freshmen. *Journal of College Student Development, 30,* 154–161.

Cross, K. P. (1981). *Adults as learners.* San Francisco: Jossey-Bass.

Cross, W. E., Jr. (1971). Toward a psychology of black liberation: The Negro-to-black conversion experience. *Black World, 20* (9), 13–27.

Cross, W. E., Jr. (1978). The Thomas and Cross models of psychological Nigrescence: A review. *Journal of Black Psychology, 5,* 13–31.

Cross, W. E., Jr. (1991). *Shades of black: Diversity in African American identity.* Philadelphia: Temple University Press.

Cross, W. E., Jr. (1995). The psychology of Nigrescence: Revising the Cross model. In J. G. Ponterotto, J. M. Casas, L. A. Suzuki, & C. M. Alexander (Eds.), *Handbook of multicultural counseling* (pp. 93–122). Thousand Oaks, CA: Sage.

Crowley, P. M. (1989). Ask the expert: A group teaching tool. *Journal for Specialists in Group Work, 14,* 173–175.

Cutietta, R. A. (1990). Adapt your teaching style to your students. *Music Educators Journal, 76* (6), 31–36.

Damarin, S. K. (1994). Equity, caring and beyond: Can feminist ethics inform educational technology? *Educational Technology, 34* (2), 34–39.

Daniel, G. R. (1996). Black and white identity in the new millennium: Unsevering the ties that bind. In M. P. P. Root (Ed.), *The multiracial experience: Racial borders as the new frontier* (pp. 121–151). Thousand Oaks, CA: Sage.

Dank, B. M. (1971). Coming out in the gay world. *Psychiatry, 34,* 180–197.

Darley, J. G. (1938). A preliminary study of relations between attitude, adjustment, and vocational interest tests. *Journal of Educational Psychology, 29,* 467–473.

D'Augelli, A. R. (1991). Gay men in college: Identity processes and adaptations. *Journal of College Student Development, 32,* 140–146.

D'Augelli, A. R. (1994a). Identity development and sexual orientation: Toward a model of lesbian, gay, and bisexual development. In E. J. Trickett, R. J. Watts, & D. Birman (Eds.), *Human diversity: Perspectives on people in context* (pp. 312–333). San Francisco: Jossey-Bass.

D'Augelli, A. R. (1994b). Lesbian and gay male development: Steps toward an analysis of lesbians' and gay men's lives. In B. Greene & G. M. Herek (Eds.), *Lesbian and gay psychology: Theory, research, and clinical implications* (Psychological Perspectives on Lesbian and Gay Issues, Vol. 1, pp. 118–132). Thousand Oaks, CA: Sage.

D'Augelli, A. R. (1996). Enhancing the development of lesbian, gay, and bisexual youths. In E. D. Rothblum & L. A. Bond (Eds.), *Preventing heterosexism and homophobia* (pp. 124–150). Thousand Oaks, CA: Sage.

Davidson, J. R. (1992). Evaluation of an education model for race-ethnic social work and critique of the White Racial Identity Attitude Scale. *Dissertation Abstracts International, 53,* 304A.

Dawis, R. V. (1992). The structure(s) of occupations: Beyond RIASEC. *Journal of Vocational Behavior, 40,* 171–178.

de Charms, R., & Rosenbaum, M. E. (1960). Status variables and matching behavior. *Journal of Personality, 28,* 492–502.

Delworth, U., & Seeman, D. (1984). The ethics of care: Implications of Gilligan for the student services profession. *Journal of College Student Personnel, 25,* 489–492.

Denzin, N. K., & Lincoln, Y. S. (1994). *Handbook of qualitative research.* Thousand Oaks, CA: Sage.

Deveaux, M. (1995). Shifting paradigms: Theorizing care and justice in political theory. *Hypatia, 10,* 115–119.

Devito, A. J. (1985). Review of Myers-Briggs Type Indicator. In J. V. Mitchell (Ed.), *The ninth mental measurements yearbook* (pp. 1030–1032). Lincoln: University of Nebraska, Buros Institute of Mental Measurements.

Dewey, J. (1933). *How we think: A restatement of the relation of reflective thinking to the educative process.* Lexington, MA: Heath.

Dewey, J. (1958). *Experience and nature* (2nd ed.). La Salle, IL: Open Court.

Dewey, J. (1960). *Logic: The theory of inquiry.* New York: Holt, Rinehart & Winston. (Original work published 1938)

DiCaprio, N. S. (1974). *Personality theories: Guides to living.* Philadelphia: Saunders.

Dillon, M., & Weissman, S. (1987). Relationship between personality types on the Strong-Campbell and Myers-Briggs instruments. *Measurement and Evaluation in Counseling and Development, 20,* 68–79.

Dinitz, S., & Kiedaisch, J. (1990). Persuasion from an eighteen-year-old's perspective: Perry and Piaget. *Journal of Teaching Writing, 9,* 85–97.

Dirks, D. H. (1988). Moral development in Christian higher education. *Journal of Psychology and Theology, 16,* 324–331.

DuBay, W. H. (1987). *Gay identity: The self under ban.* Jefferson, NC: McFarland.

du Bois, W. E. B. (1995). *The souls of black folk.* New York: Signet. (Original work published 1903)

Egan, G. (1982). *The skilled helper* (2nd ed.). Monterey, CA: Brooks/Cole.

Egan, G. (1994). *The skilled helper* (5th ed.). Pacific Grove, CA: Brooks/Cole.

Eldridge, N. S., & Barnett, D. C. (1991). Counseling gay and lesbian students. In N. J. Evans & V. A. Wall (Eds.), *Beyond tolerance: Gays, lesbians and bisexuals on campus* (pp. 147–178). Alexandria, VA: American College Personnel Association.

Elliott, D. (1991). Moral development theories and the teaching of ethics. *Journalism Educator, 46* (3), 18–24.

Ellis, L. (1996). Theories of homosexuality. In R. C. Savin-Williams & K. M. Cohen (Eds.), *The lives of lesbians, gays, and bisexuals: Children to adults* (pp. 11–34). Fort Worth, TX: Harcourt Brace.

Ender, S. C., Newton, F. B., & Caple, R. B. (Eds.). (1996). *Contributing to learning: The role of student affairs* (New Directions for Student Services, No. 75). San Francisco: Jossey-Bass.

Enns, C. Z. (1991). The new relationship models of women's identity: A review and critique for counselors. *Journal of Counseling and Development, 69,* 209–217.

Erickson, D. B. (1993). The relationship between personality type and preferred counseling model. *Journal of Psychological Type, 27*, 39–41.

Erikson, E. H. (1950). *Childhood and society.* New York: Norton.

Erikson, E. H. (1963). *Childhood and society* (2nd ed.). New York: Norton.

Erikson, E. H. (1964). *Insight and responsibility.* New York: Norton.

Erikson, E. H. (1968). *Identity: Youth and crisis.* New York: Norton.

Erikson, E. H. (1980). *Identity and the life cycle.* New York: Norton. (Original work published 1959)

Erwin, T. D. (1979). The validation of the Erwin Identity Scale. *Dissertation Abstracts International, 34*, 4818A–4819A. (University Microfilms No. 7902899)

Erwin, T. D. (1982). Academic status as related to the development of identity. *Journal of Psychology, 110*, 163–169.

Erwin, T. D. (1983). The Scale of Intellectual Development: Measuring Perry's scheme. *Journal of College Student Personnel, 24*, 6–12.

Erwin, T. D., & Delworth, U. (1982). Formulating environmental constructs that affect students' identity. *NASPA Journal, 20* (1), 47–55.

Erwin, T. D., & Kelly, K. (1985). Changes in students' self-confidence in college. *Journal of College Student Personnel, 26*, 395–400.

Erwin, T. D., & Schmidt, M. R. (1982). The convergent validity of the Erwin Identity Scale. *Educational and Psychological Measurement, 41*, 1307–1310.

Espin, O. M. (1987). Issues of identity in the psychology of Latina lesbians. In Boston Lesbian Psychologies Collective (Eds.), *Lesbian psychologies* (pp. 35–51). Urbana: University of Illinois Press.

Evans, N. J. (1982). Using developmental theory in needs assessment. *Journal of the National Association for Women Deans, Administrators, and Counselors, 45* (3), 34–39.

Evans, N. J. (1987). A framework for assisting student affairs staff in fostering moral development. *Journal of Counseling and Development, 66*, 191–194.

Evans, N. J. (1996). Theories of student development. In S. R. Komives, D. B. Woodard Jr., & Associates, *Student services: A handbook for the profession* (3rd ed., pp. 164–187). San Francisco: Jossey-Bass.

Evans, N. J., Bradley, R., & Bradley, J. (1985, March). *An overview and comparison of student development theory to practice models.* Paper presented at the meeting of the American College Personnel Association, Boston.

Evans, N. J., Broido, E., Dragon, M., Eberz, A., & Richards, K. (1997, March). *Gay, lesbian, and bisexual students' development in residence halls.* Paper presented at the joint conference of the American College Personnel Association and the National Association of Student Personnel Administrators, Chicago.

Evans, N. J., & D'Augelli, A. R. (1996). Lesbians, gay men, and bisexual people in college. In R. C. Savin-Williams & K. M. Cohen (Eds.), *The lives of lesbians, gays, and bisexuals: Children to adults* (pp. 201–226). Fort Worth, TX: Harcourt Brace.

Evans, N. J., & Wall, V. A. (Eds.). (1991). *Beyond tolerance: Gays, lesbians and bisexuals on campus.* Alexandria, VA: American College Personnel Association.

Fassinger, R. E., & Schlossberg, N. K. (1992). Understanding the adult years: Perspectives and implications. In S. D. Brown & R. W. Lent (Eds.), *Handbook of counseling psychology* (2nd ed., pp. 217–249). New York: Wiley.

Feldman, K. A., & Newcomb, T. M. (1969). *The impact of college on students.* 2 vols. San Francisco: Jossey-Bass.

Ferrell, B. G. (1983). A factor analytic comparison of four learning-style instruments. *Journal of Educational Psychology, 75*, 33–39.

Fiske, M., & Chiriboga, D. A. (1990). *Change and continuity in adult life.* San Francisco: Jossey-Bass.

Fleming, J. (1984). *Blacks in college: A comparative study of students' success in black and white institutions.* San Francisco: Jossey-Bass.

Ford, M. R., & Lowery, C. R. (1986). Gender differences in moral reasoning: A comparison of the use of justice and care orientations. *Journal of Personality and Social Psychology, 50*, 777–783.

Forney, D. S. (1991a). Learning style information: A support for service delivery, Part I. *Career Waves: Leading Ideas for Career Development Professionals, 4* (1), 2–3.

Forney, D. S. (1991b). Learning style information: A support for service delivery, Part II. *Career Waves: Leading Ideas for Career Development Professionals, 4* (2), 1, 7.

Forney, D. S. (1994). A profile of student affairs master's students: Characteristics, attitudes, and learning styles. *Journal of College Student Development, 35*, 337–345.

Forney, D. S., Eddy, W. L., Gunter, G. S., & Slater, R. E. (1992, March). *Student development as a subversive activity.* Paper presented at the annual meeting of the American College Personnel Association, San Francisco.

Forney, D. S., & Gingrich, D. D. (1983, March). *Transitions: Making the break to life after college.* Paper presented at the American College Personnel Association National Conference, Houston.

Forrest, L. (1988). [Review of the book *Women's ways of knowing: The development of self, voice, and mind*]. *Journal of College Student Development, 29*, 82–84.

Fouad, N. A. (1994). Annual review, 1991–1993: Vocational choice, decision-making, assessment, and intervention. *Journal of Vocational Behavior, 45*, 125–176.

Fowler, J. (1981). *Stages of faith: The psychology of human development and the quest for meaning.* San Francisco: Harper & Row.

Fox, N. S., Spooner, S. E., Utterback, J. W., & Barbieri, J. A. (1996). Relationships between autonomy, gender, and weekend commuting among college students. *NASPA Journal, 34*, 19–28.

Fox, R. C. (1995). Bisexual identities. In A. R. D'Augelli & C. J. Patterson (Eds.), *Lesbian, gay, and bisexual identities over the lifespan: Psychological perspectives* (pp. 48–86). New York: Oxford University Press.

Frankenberg, R. (1993). *The social construction of whiteness: White women, race matters.* Minneapolis: University of Minnesota Press.

Freedburg, S. (1993). The feminine ethic of care and the professionalization of social work. *Social Work, 38*, 535–540.

Freire, P. (1973). *Education for critical consciousness.* New York: Continuum.

Freire, P. (1974). *Pedagogy of the oppressed.* New York: Continuum.

Freud, S. (1965). *Three essays on the theory of sexuality.* (J. Strachey, Trans.). New York: Basic Books. (Original work published 1905)

Fried, J. (1988). Women's ways of knowing: Some additional observations [Review of the book *Women's ways of knowing: The development of self, voice, and mind*]. *Journal of College Student Development, 29*, 84–85.

Fried, J. (Ed.). (1994). *Different voices: Gender and perspective in student affairs administration.* Washington, DC: National Association of Student Personnel Administrators.

Fried, J., & Associates (1995). *Shifting paradigms in student affairs: Culture, context, teaching, and learning.* Lanham, MD: American College Personnel Association.

Friedman, M. (1993). *What are friends for? Feminist perspectives on personal relationships and moral theory.* Ithaca, NY: Cornell University Press.

Frye, M. (1990). The possibility of feminist theory. In D. L. Rhode (Ed.), *Theoretical perspectives on sexual difference* (pp. 174–184). New Haven, CT: Yale University Press.

Galbraith, R. E., & Jones, T. M. (1976). *Moral reasoning: A teaching handbook for adapting Kohlberg to the classroom.* Minneapolis, MN: Greenhaven Press.

Garcia, J. (1982). Ethnicity and Chicanos: Measurement of ethnic identification, identity, and consciousness. *Hispanic Journal of Behavioral Sciences, 4,* 295–314.

Garfield, N. J., & David, L. B. (1986). Arthur Chickering: Bridging theory and practice in student development. *Journal of Counseling and Development, 64,* 483–491.

Garland, P. H., & Grace, T. W. (1993). *New perspectives for student affairs professionals: Evolving realities, responsibilities, and roles* (ASHE-ERIC Higher Education Report No. 7). Washington, DC: George Washington University, School of Education and Human Development.

Gay, G. (1985). Implications of selected models of ethnic identity development for educators. *Journal of Negro Education, 54,* 43–55.

Geiger, M. A., Boyle, E. J., & Pinto, J. (1992). A factor analysis of Kolb's revised Learning Style Inventory. *Educational and Psychological Measurement, 52,* 753–759.

Geiger, M. A., & Pinto, J. K. (1991). Changes in learning style preference during a three-year longitudinal study. *Psychological Reports, 69,* 755–762.

Gelwick, B. P. (1985). Cognitive development of women. In N. J. Evans (Ed.), *Facilitating the development of women* (New Directions for Student Services, No. 29, pp. 29–44). San Francisco: Jossey-Bass.

Gibbs, J. T. (1974). Patterns of adaptation among black students at a predominantly white university: Selected case studies. *American Journal of Orthopsychiatry, 44,* 728–740.

Gilchrest, G. G. (1994). Racial identity and cultural worldviews among ethnically diverse white college students: A quantitative and qualitative analysis. *Dissertation Abstracts International, 54,* 2804A.

Gilligan, C. (1977). In a different voice: Women's conceptions of self and morality. *Harvard Educational Review, 47,* 481–517.

Gilligan, C. (1981). Moral development in the college years. In A. W. Chickering & Associates, *The modern American college: Responding to the new realities of diverse students and a changing society* (pp. 139–157). San Francisco: Jossey-Bass.

Gilligan, C. (1986). Reply (to critics). *Signs: Journal of Women in Culture and Society, 11,* 324–333.

Gilligan, C. (1987a). Moral orientation and moral development. In E. F. Kittay & D. T. Myers (Eds.), *Women and moral theory* (pp. 19–33). Totowa, NJ: Rowman & Littlefield.

Gilligan, C. (1987b). Remapping development: The power of divergent data. In C. Farnham (Ed.), *The impact of feminist research in the academy* (pp. 77–107). Bloomington: Indiana University Press.

Gilligan, C. (1991). Women's psychological development: Implications for psychotherapy. *Women and Therapy, 11* (3–4), 5–31.

Gilligan, C. (1993). *In a different voice: Psychological theory and women's development.* Cambridge, MA: Harvard University Press. (Orignal work published 1982)

Gilligan, C. (1995). Hearing the differences: Theorizing connection. *Hypatia, 10,* 120–127.

Gilligan, C. (1996). The centrality of relationship in human development: A puzzle, some evidence and a theory. In G. G. Noam & K. W. Fischer (Eds.), *Development and vulnerability in close relationships* (pp. 237–261). Mahwah, NJ: Erlbaum.

Gilligan, C., & Belenky, M. F. (1980). A naturalistic study of abortion decisions. In R. Selman & R. Yando (Eds.), *Clinical-developmental psychology* (New Directions for Child Development, No. 7, pp. 69–90). San Francisco: Jossey-Bass.

Gilligan, C., Lyons, N. J., & Hanmer, T. J. (Eds.). (1990). *Making connections: The relational world of adolescent girls at Emma Willard School.* Cambridge, MA: Harvard University Press.

Gilligan, C., & Murphy, J. M. (1979). Development from adolescence to adulthood: The philosopher and the "dilemma of the fact." In D. Kuhn (Ed.), *Intellectual development beyond childhood* (New Directions for Child Development, No. 5, pp. 85–99). San Francisco: Jossey-Bass.

Gilligan, C., Ward, J. V., & Taylor, J. M. (Eds.). (1988). *Mapping the moral domain: A contribution of women's thinking to psychological theory and education.* Cambridge, MA: Harvard University Press.

Gilligan, C., & Wiggins, G. (1987). The origins of morality in early childhood relationships. In J. Kagan & S. Lamb (Eds.), *The emergence of morality in young children* (pp. 277–305). Chicago: University of Chicago Press.

Ginsburg, S. D., & Orlofsky, J. L. (1981). Ego identity status, ego development, and locus of control in college women. *Journal of Youth and Adolescence, 10,* 297–307.

Golden, C. (1996). What's in a name? Sexual self-identification among women. In R. C. Savin-Williams & K. M. Cohen (Eds.), *The lives of lesbians, gays, and bisexuals: Children to adults* (pp. 229–249). Fort Worth, TX: Harcourt Brace.

Golden, V. J., & Provost, J. A. (1987). The MBTI and career development. In J. A. Provost & S. Anchors (Eds.), *Applications of the Myers-Briggs Type Indicator in higher education* (pp. 151–179). Palo Alto, CA: Consulting Psychologists Press.

Gooden, W. E. (1989). Development of black men in early adulthood. In R. L. Jones (Ed.), *Black adult development and aging* (pp. 63–90). Berkeley, CA: Cobb & Henry.

Gose, B. (1995, February 10). "Women's ways of knowing" form the basis of Ursuline curriculum. *Chronicle of Higher Education,* p. A25.

Gose, B. (1996, February 9). The politics and images of gay students. *Chronicle of Higher Education,* pp. A33–A34.

Gottfredson, G. D., & Holland, J. L. (1989). *Dictionary of Holland occupational codes* (2nd ed.). Odessa, FL: Psychological Assessment Resources.

Gramick, J. (1984). Developing a lesbian identity. In T. Darty & S. Potter (Eds.), *Women-identified women* (pp. 31–44). Palo Alto, CA: Mayfield.

Grandner, D. F. (1992). The relationship between white racial identity attitudes and moral development of college students. *Dissertation Abstracts International, 53,* 1055A.

Greeley, A., & Tinsley, H. (1988). Autonomy and intimacy development in college students: Sex differences and predictors. *Journal of College Student Development, 29,* 512–520.

Griffin, T. D., & Salter, D. W. (1993). Psychological type and involvement in a university residence hall judicial system. *Journal of Psychological Type, 27,* 32–38.

Grotevant, H. D., Scarr, S., & Weinberg, R. A. (1977). Patterns of interest similarity in adoptive and biological families. *Journal of Personality and Social Psychology, 35,* 667–676.

Groves, P. A., & Ventura, L. A. (1983). The lesbian coming out process: Therapeutic considerations. *Personnel and Guidance Journal, 62,* 146–149.

Guba, E. G. (1990). The alternative paradigm dialog. In E. G. Guba (Ed.), *The paradigm dialog* (pp. 17–30). Newbury Park, CA: Sage.

Guba, E. G., & Lincoln, Y. S. (1994). Competing paradigms in qualitative research. In N. K. Denzin & Y. S. Lincoln (Eds.), *Handbook of qualitative research* (pp. 105–117). Thousand Oaks, CA: Sage.

Guido-DiBrito, F., Noteboom, P. A., Nathan, L. E., & Fenty, J. (1996). Traditional and new paradigm leadership: The gender link. *Initiatives, 58* (1), 27–38.

Guilford, J. P., Christensen, P. R., Bond, N. A., Jr., & Sutton, M. A. (1954). A factor analysis study of human interests. *Psychological Monographs, 64* (4, Whole No. 375).

Gypen, J. (1980). *Learning style adaptation in professional careers: The case of engineers and social workers.* Unpublished doctoral dissertation, Case Western Reserve University, Cleveland, Ohio.

Haan, N. (1985). Processes of moral development: Cognitive or social disequilibrium? *Developmental Psychology, 21,* 996–1006.

Hackett, G., Lent, R. W., & Greenhaus, J. H. (1991). Advances in vocational theory and research: A 20–year retrospective. *Journal of Vocational Behavior, 38,* 3–38.

Hagberg, J., & Leider, R. (1982). *The inventurers: Excursions in life and career renewal.* Reading, MA: Addison-Wesley.

Hagestad, G. O., & Neugarten, B. L. (1985). Age and the life course. In R. Binstock & E. Shanar (Eds.), *Handbook of aging and the social sciences* (2nd ed., pp. 35–61). New York: Van Nostrand Reinhold.

Hammer, A. L., & Mitchell, W. D. (1996). The distribution of MBTI types in the US by gender and ethnic group. *Journal of Psychological Type, 37,* 2–15.

Hansen, J. C. (1987). Cross-cultural research on vocational interests. *Measurement and Evaluation in Counseling and Development, 19,* 163–176.

Hansen, J. C. (1992). Does enough evidence exist to modify Holland's theory to accommodate the individual differences of diverse populations? *Journal of Vocational Behavior, 40,* 188–193.

Hansen, J. C., Collins, R. C., Swanson, J. L., & Fouad, N. A. (1993). Gender differences in the structure of interests. *Journal of Vocational Behavior, 42,* 200–211.

Hardiman, R., & Jackson, B. W. (1992). Racial identity development: Understanding racial dynamics in college classrooms and on college campuses. In M. Adams (Ed.), *Promoting diversity in college classrooms: Innovative responses for the curriculum, faculty, and institutions* (New Directions for Teaching and Learning, No. 52, pp. 21–37). San Francisco: Jossey-Bass.

Hare-Mustin, R. T., & Marcek, J. (1988). The meaning of difference: Gender theory, postmodernism, and psychology. *American Psychologist, 43,* 455–464.

Hareven, T. K. (1992). Family and generational relations in the later years: A historical perspective. *Generations, 16* (3), 7–12.

Harmon, L. W., Hansen, J. C., Borgen, F. H., & Hammer, A. L. (1994). *Strong Interest Inventory: Applications and technical guide.* Stanford, CA: Stanford University Press.

Harvey, L. J., Hunt, D. E., & Schroder, H. M. (1961). *Conceptual systems and personality organization.* New York: Wiley.

Haskins, C. H. (1957). *The rise of the universities.* Ithaca, NY: Cornell University Press.

Hays, J. N. (1988). Socio-cognitive development and argumentative writing: Issues and implications from one research project. *Journal of Basic Writing, 7* (2), 42–67.

Hayward, P. A. (1993, November). *The intersection of critical pedagogy and developmental theory for public speaking.* Paper presented at the annual meeting of the Speech Communication Association, Miami Beach, FL. (ERIC Document Reproduction Service No. ED 372 423)

Healy, C. G. (1989). Negative: The MBTI: Not ready for routine use in counseling. *Journal of Counseling and Development, 67,* 487–488.

Hearn, J. C., & Moos, R. H. (1976). Social climate and major choice: A test of Holland's theory in university student living groups. *Journal of Vocational Behavior, 8,* 293–305.

Heath, D. (1968). *Growing up in college.* San Francisco: Jossey-Bass.

Heath, D. (1977). *Maturity and competence: A transcultural view.* New York: Gardner.

Heath, R. (1964). *The reasonable adventurer.* Pittsburgh, PA: University of Pittsburgh Press.

Heath, R. (1973). Form, flow, and full-being. *Counseling Psychologist, 4,* 56–63.

Heckman, S. J. (1995). *Moral voices, moral selves: Carol Gilligan and feminist moral theory.* University Park: Pennsylvania State University Press.

Helgesen, S. (1995). *The web of inclusion.* New York: Doubleday Currency.

Helms, J. E. (1992). *A race is a nice thing to have: A guide to being a white person or understanding the white persons in your life.* Topeka, KS: Content Communications.

Helms, J. E. (Ed.). (1993a). *Black and white racial identity: Theory, research and practice.* Westport, CT: Praeger.

Helms, J. E. (1993b). Introduction: Review of racial identity terminology. In J. E. Helms (Ed.), *Black and white racial identity: Theory, research and practice* (pp. 3–8). Westport, CT: Praeger.

Helms, J. E. (1993c). The measurement of black racial identity attitudes. In J. E. Helms (Ed.), *Black and white racial identity: Theory, research and practice* (pp. 33–47). Westport, CT: Praeger.

Helms, J. E. (1993d). Toward a model of white racial identity development. In J. E. Helms (Ed.), *Black and white racial identity: Theory, research and practice* (pp. 49–66). Westport, CT: Praeger.

Helms, J. E. (1995). An update of Helms's white and people of color racial identity models. In J. G. Ponterotto, J. M. Casas, L. A. Suzuki, & C. M. Alexander (Eds.), *Handbook of multicultural counseling* (pp. 181–198). Thousand Oaks, CA: Sage.

Helms, J. E., & Carter, R. T. (1991). Relationships of white racial attitudes and demographic similarity to counselor preferences. *Journal of Counseling Psychology, 38* (4), 446–457.

Helms, J. E., & Carter, R. T. (1993). Development of the White Racial Identity Inventory. In J. E. Helms (Ed.), *Black and white racial identity: Theory, research and practice* (pp. 67–80). Westport, CT: Praeger.

Helms, J. E., & Parham, T. A. (1996). The development of the Racial Identity Attitude Scale. In R. L. Jones (Ed.), *Handbook of tests and measurements for black populations, 2* (pp. 167–174). Berkeley, CA: Cobb & Henry.

Helms, S. T. (1973). Practical applications of the Holland occupational classification in counseling. *Communique, 2,* 69–71.

Hencken, J. D., & O'Dowd, W. T. (1977). Coming out as an aspect of identity formation. *Gai Saber, 1* (1), 18–22.

Hepburn, E. R. (1994). Women and ethics: A "seeing" justice. *Journal of Moral Education, 23* (1), 27–38.

Hesketh, B., & Rounds, J. B. (1995). International cross-cultural approaches to career development. In W. B. Walsh & S. H. Osipow (Eds.), *Handbook of vocational psychology: Theory, research, and practice* (2nd ed., pp. 367–390). Mahwah, NJ: Erlbaum.

Hess, W. D., & Winston, R. B., Jr. (1995). Developmental task achievement and students' intentions to participate in developmental activities. *Journal of College Student Development, 36,* 314–321.

Hetherington, C. (1991). Life planning and career counseling with gay and lesbian students. In N. J. Evans & V. A. Wall (Eds.), *Beyond tolerance: Gays, lesbians and bisexuals on campus* (pp. 131–145). Alexandria, VA: American College Personnel Association.

Heubner, A. M., & Garrod, A. C. (1993). Moral reasoning among Tibetan monks: A study of Buddhist adolescents and young adults in Nepal. *Journal of Cross-Cultural Psychology, 24,* 167–185.

Heyer, D. L., & Nelson, E. S. (1993). The relationship between parental marital status and the development of identity and emotional autonomy in college students. *Journal of College Student Development, 34,* 432–436.

Hill, O. W., & Clark, J. L. (1993). The personality typology of black college students: Evidence for a characteristic cognitive style? *Psychological Reports, 72,* 1091–1097.

Hillman, L., & Lewis, A. (1980). *The AER model of effective advising.* Unpublished manuscript, University of Maryland, College Park.

Hirsh, S. K., & Kummerow, J. M. (1990). *Introduction to type in organizations* (2nd ed.). Palo Alto, CA: Consulting Psychologists Press.

Hodgson, J. W., & Fischer, J. L. (1979). Sex differences in identity and intimacy development in college youth. *Journal of Youth and Adolescence, 8,* 37–50.

Holland, J. L. (1958). A personality inventory employing occupational titles. *Journal of Applied Psychology, 42,* 336–342.

Holland, J. L. (1959). A theory of vocational choice. *Journal of Counseling Psychology, 6,* 35–45.

Holland, J. L. (1966). *The psychology of vocational choice.* Waltham, MA: Blaisdell.

Holland, J. L. (1971). A theory-ridden, computerless, impersonal vocational guidance system. *Journal of Vocational Behavior, 1,* 167–176.

Holland, J. L. (1985). *Vocational Preference Inventory (VPI): Professional manual.* Odessa, FL: Psychological Assessment Resources.

Holland, J. L. (1992). *Making vocational choices: A theory of vocational personalities and work environments* (2nd ed.). Odessa, FL: Psychological Assessment Resources. (Original work published 1985)

Holland, J. L. (1994). *The Self-Directed Search (SDS).* Odessa, FL: Psychological Assessment Resources.

Holland, J. L., Fritzsche, B. A., & Powell, A. B. (1994). *The Self-Directed Search (SDS) technical manual.* Odessa, FL: Psychological Assessment Resources.

Holland, J. L., & Gottfredson, G. D. (1992). Studies of the hexagonal model: An evaluation (or, The perils of stalking the perfect hexagon). *Journal of Vocational Behavior, 40,* 158–170.

Holland, J. L., Powell, A. B., & Fritzsche, B. A. (1994). *The Self-Directed Search (SDS) professional user's guide.* Odessa, FL: Psychological Assessment Resources.

Holley, J. H., & Jenkins, E. K. (1993). The relationship between student learning style and performance on various test question formats. *Journal of Education for Business, 68,* 301–308.

Hood, A. B. (Ed.). (1986). *The Iowa Student Development Inventories.* Iowa City, Iowa: Hitech Press.

Hood, A. B., & Jackson, L. M. (1983a). *Assessing the development of competence.* Technical report. Iowa City: University of Iowa, College of Education.

Hood, A. B., & Jackson, L. M. (1983b). *The Iowa Developing Autonomy Inventory.* Technical report. Iowa City: College of Education, University of Iowa.

Hood, A. B., & Jackson, L. M. (1983c). *The Iowa Managing Emotions Inventory.* Technical report. Iowa City: College of Education, University of Iowa.

Hood, A. B., Riahinejad, A. R., & White, D. B. (1986). Changes in ego identity during the college years. *Journal of College Student Personnel, 27,* 107–113.

Hopcke, R. H. (1989). *A guided tour of the collected works of C. G. Jung.* Boston: Shambhala.

Hopkins, L. (1982). Assessment of identity status in college women using outer space and inner space interviews. *Sex Roles, 8,* 557–565.

Hotelling, K., & Forrest, L. (1985). Gilligan's theory of sex-role development: A perspective for counseling. *Journal of Counseling and Development, 64,* 183–186.

Hughes, M. S. (1987). Black students' participation in higher education. *Journal of College Student Personnel, 28,* 532–545.

Huitt, W. G. (1988). Personality differences between Navajo and non-Indian college students. *Equity and Excellence, 24* (1), 71–74.

Hunt, D. E. (1978). Theorists are persons, too: On preaching what you practice. In C. A. Parker (Ed.), *Encouraging the development of college students* (pp. 250–266). Minneapolis: University of Minnesota Press.

Hunt, S., & Rentz, A. L. (1994). Greek-letter social group members' involvement and psychosocial development. *Journal of College Student Development, 35,* 289–295.

Hurst, J. C. (1978). Chickering's vectors of development and student affairs programming. In C. A. Parker (Ed.), *Encouraging the development of college students* (pp. 113–126). Minneapolis: University of Minnesota Press.

Huss, J. K. (1983). Developing competence and autonomy for disabled students. *AHSSPPE Bulletin, 1,* 81–92.

Icard, L. (1985–1986). Black gay men and conflicting social identities: Sexual orientation vs. racial identity. *Journal of Social Work and Human Sexuality, 4* (1–2), 83–93.

Illich, I. (1972). *Deschooling society.* New York: Harrow Books.

Iwasa, N. (1992). Postconventional reasoning and moral education in Japan. *Journal of Moral Education, 21,* 2–16.

Jacobus, E. F., Jr. (1989). *The relationship between cognitive development and foreign language proficiency.* Unpublished manuscript. (ERIC Document Reproduction Service No. ED 313 894)

Jacoby, B., & Associates. (1996). *Service-learning in higher education: Concepts and practices.* San Francisco: Jossey-Bass.

Jacoby, B., Rue, P., & Allen, K. T. (1984). UMaps: A person-environment approach to helping students make critical choices. *Personnel and Guidance Journal, 62,* 426–428.

Jensen, G. H., & DiTiberio, J. K. (1984). Personality and individual writing processes. *College Composition and Communication, 35,* 285–300.

Jones, H. J., & Newman, I. (1993, April). *A mosaic of diversity: Vocationally undecided students and the Perry scheme of intellectual and ethical development.* Paper presented at the annual meeting of the American Educational Research Association, Atlanta. (ERIC Document Reproduction Service No. ED 360 488)

Jones, J. M. (1972). *Prejudice and racism.* Reading, MA: Addison-Wesley.

Jones, J. M. (1981). The concept of racism and its changing reality. In B. P. Bowser & R. G. Hunt (Eds.), *Impacts of racism on white Americans* (pp. 27–49). Beverly Hills, CA: Sage.

Jones, S. R. (1995). *Voices of identity and difference: A qualitative exploration of the multiple dimensions of identity development in women college students.* Unpublished doctoral dissertation, University of Maryland, College Park.

Jones, W. T. (1990). Perspectives on ethnicity. In L. V. Moore (Ed.), *Evolving theoretical perspectives on students* (New Directions for Student Services, No. 51, pp. 59–72). San Francisco: Jossey-Bass.

Jordan-Cox, C. A. (1987). Psychosocial development of students in traditionally black institutions. *Journal of College Student Personnel, 28,* 504–511.

Josselson, R. (1973). Psychodynamic aspects of identity formation in college women. *Journal of Youth and Adolescence, 2,* 3–52.

Josselson, R. (1982). Personality structure and identity status in women as viewed through early memories. *Journal of Youth and Adolescence, 11,* 293–299.

Josselson, R. (1987a). *Finding herself: Pathways to identity development in women.* San Francisco: Jossey-Bass.

Josselson, R. (1987b). Identity diffusion: A long-term follow-up. *Adolescent Psychology, 14,* 230–258.

Josselson, R. (1992). *The space between us: Exploring the dimensions of human relationships.* San Francisco: Jossey-Bass.

Josselson, R. (1996). *Revising herself: The story of women's identity from college to midlife.* New York: Oxford University Press.

Josselson, R., Greenberger, E., & McConochie, D. (1977). Phenomenological aspects of psychosocial maturity in adolescence. Part II: Girls. *Journal of Youth and Adolescence, 6,* 145–167.

Jung, C. G. (1960). *The structure and dynamics of the psyche.* New York: Bollingen Foundation.

Jung, C. G. (1971). *Psychological types.* (R. F. C. Hull, Ed.; H. G. Baynes, Trans.). Volume 6 of *The collected works of C. G. Jung.* Princeton, NJ: Princeton University Press. (Original work published 1923)

Kacerguis, M. A., & Adams, G. R. (1980). Erikson stage resolution: The relationship between identity and intimacy. *Journal of Youth and Adolescence, 9,* 117–126.

Kahn, M. J. (1991). Factors affecting the coming out process for lesbians. *Journal of Homosexuality, 21* (3), 47–70.

Kahn, R. L., & Antonucci, T. C. (1980). Convoys over the life course: Attachment, roles, and social support. In P. B. Baltes & C. O. Brim (Eds.), *Life-span development and behavior* (pp. 383–405). New York: Academic Press.

Kalsbeek, D., Rodgers, R., Marshall, D., Denny, D., & Nicholls, G. (1982). Balancing challenge and support: A study of degrees of similarity in suitemate personality type and perceived difference in challenge and support in a residence hall environment. *Journal of College Student Personnel, 23,* 434–442.

Kanter, R. M. (1977). *Men and women of the corporation.* New York: Basic Books.

Kastenbaum, R. (1985). When aging begins: A lifespan developmental approach. *Research on Aging, 6* (1), 105–117.

Kaufman, A. S. (1993). Profiles of Hispanic adolescents and adults on the Myers-Briggs Type Indicator. *Perceptual and Motor Skills, 76,* 628–630.

Kegan, R. (1982). *The evolving self.* Cambridge, MA: Harvard University Press.

Keirsey, D. (1987). *Portraits of temperament.* Del Mar, CA: Prometheus Nemesis.

Keirsey, D., & Bates, M. (1984). *Please understand me: Character and temperament types.* Del Mar, CA: Prometheus Nemesis.

Kerber, L., Greeno, C. G., Maccoby, E. E., Luria, Z., Stack, C. B., & Gilligan, C. (1986). Viewpoint: On *In a different voice:* An interdisciplinary forum. *Signs: Journal of Women in Culture and Society, 11,* 304–333.

Kerwin, C., & Ponterotto, J. G. (1995). Biracial identity development. In J. G. Ponterotto, J. M. Casas, L. A. Suzuki, & C. M. Alexander (Eds.), *Handbook of multicultural counseling* (pp. 199–217). Thousand Oaks, CA: Sage.

Kilgannon, S. M., & Erwin, T. D. (1992). A longitudinal study about the identity and moral development of Greek students. *Journal of College Student Development, 33,* 253–259.

Kim, J. (1981). *The process of Asian American identity development: A study of Japanese American women's perceptions of their struggle to achieve positive identities.* Unpublished doctoral dissertation, University of Massachusetts at Amherst.

King, P. M. (1978). William Perry's theory of intellectual and ethical development. In L. L. Knefelkamp, C. Widick, & C. A. Parker (Eds.), *Applying new developmental findings* (New Directions for Student Services, No. 4, pp. 35–51). San Francisco: Jossey-Bass.

King, P. M. (1987). [Review of *Women's ways of knowing: The development of self, voice, and mind*]. *Journal of Moral Education, 16*, 249–251.

King, P. M. (1990). Assessing development from a cognitive developmental perspective. In D. G. Creamer (Ed.), *College student development: Theory and practice for the 1990s* (pp. 81–98). Alexandria, VA: American College Personnel Association.

King, P. M. (1994). Theories of college student development: Sequences and consequences. *Journal of College Student Development, 35*, 413–421.

King, P. M., & Kitchener, K. S. (1994). *Developing reflective judgment: Understanding and promoting intellectual growth and critical thinking in adolescents and adults.* San Francisco: Jossey-Bass.

Kitchener, K. S., & King, P. M. (1981). Reflective judgment: Concepts of justification and their relationship to age and education. *Journal of Applied Developmental Psychology, 2,* 89–116.

Kitchener, K. S., & King, P. M. (1990). The reflective judgment model: Ten years of research. In M. L. Commons et al. (Eds.), *Adult development: Vol. II. Models and methods in the study of adolescent and adult thought* (pp. 63–78). New York: Praeger.

Kitzinger, C. (1995). Social constructionism: Implications for lesbian and gay psychology. In A. R. D'Augelli & C. J. Patterson (Eds.), *Lesbian, gay, and bisexual identities over the lifespan: Psychological perspectives* (pp. 136–161). New York: Oxford University Press.

Klein, F. (1990). The need to view sexual orientation as a multivariate dynamic process: A theoretical perspective. In D. P. McWhirter, S. A. Sanders, & J. M. Reinisch (Eds.), *Homosexuality/heterosexuality: Concepts of sexual orientation* (pp. 277–282). New York: Oxford University Press.

Klepper, W. M., & Kovacs, E. (1978, December). What is the impact of the college union program on today's student? *Association of College Unions–International Bulletin,* pp. 17–20.

Knefelkamp, L. L. (1974). *Developmental instruction: Fostering intellectual and personal growth in college students.* Unpublished doctoral dissertation, University of Minnesota, Minneapolis.

Knefelkamp, L. L. (1978). *A reader's guide to student development theory: A framework for understanding, a framework for design.* Unpublished manuscript.

Knefelkamp, L. L. (1982). Faculty and student development in the '80s: Renewing the community of scholars. In H. F. Owens, C. H. Witten, & W. R. Bailey (Eds.), *College student personnel administration: An anthology* (pp. 373–391). Springfield, IL: Thomas.

Knefelkamp, L. L. (1984). *A workbook for the practice-to-theory-to-practice model.* Unpublished manuscript, University of Maryland, College Park.

Knefelkamp, L. L., & Cornfeld, J. L. (1979, March). *Combining student stage and style in the design of learning environments.* Paper presented at the annual meeting of the American College Personnel Association, Los Angeles.

Knefelkamp, L. L., Golec, R. R., & Wells, E. A. (1985). *The practice-to-theory-to-practice model.* Unpublished manuscript, University of Maryland, College Park.

Knefelkamp, L. L., Parker, C. A., & Widick, C. (1978). Roy Heath's model of personality typologies. In L. L. Knefelkamp, C. Widick, & C. A. Parker (Eds.), *Applying new developmental findings* (New Directions for Student Services, No. 4, pp. 93–105). San Francisco: Jossey-Bass.

Knefelkamp, L. L., & Slepitza, R. (1976). A cognitive-developmental model of career development: An adaptation of the Perry scheme. *Counseling Psychologist, 6* (3), 53–58.

Knefelkamp, L. L., Widick, C., & Parker, C. A. (1978). Editors' notes: Why bother with theory? In L. L. Knefelkamp, C. Widick, & C. A. Parker (Eds.), *Applying new developmental findings* (New Directions for Student Services, No. 4, pp. vii-xvi). San Francisco: Jossey-Bass.

Knefelkamp, L. L., Widick, C., & Stroad, B. (1976). Cognitive-developmental theory: A guide to counseling women. *Counseling Psychologist, 6* (2), 15–19.

Knock, G. (1988). The philosophical heritage of student affairs. In A. L. Rentz & G. L. Saddlemire (Eds.), *Student affairs functions in higher education* (pp. 3–20). Springfield, IL: Thomas.

Kohlberg, L. (1958). *The development of modes of moral thinking and choice in the years ten to sixteen.* Unpublished doctoral dissertation, University of Chicago.

Kohlberg, L. (1969). Stage and sequence: The cognitive developmental approach to socialization. In D. A. Goslin (Ed.), *Handbook of socialization theory and research* (pp. 347–480). Chicago: Rand McNally.

Kohlberg, L. (1971). Stages of moral development as a basis for moral education. In C. Beck, B. S. Crittenden, & E. V. Sullivan (Eds.), *Moral education: Interdisciplinary approaches* (pp. 23–92). Toronto: University of Toronto Press.

Kohlberg, L. (1972). A cognitive-developmental approach to moral education. *Humanist, 6,* 13–16.

Kohlberg, L. (1976). Moral stages and moralization: The cognitive-developmental approach. In T. Lickona (Ed.), *Moral development and behavior: Theory, research, and social issues* (pp. 31–53). New York: Holt, Rinehart & Winston.

Kohlberg, L. (1979). Foreword. In J. R. Rest, *Development in judging moral issues* (pp. vii-xvi). Minneapolis: University of Minnesota Press.

Kohlberg, L. (Ed.). (1981a). *Essays on moral development: Vol. I. The philosophy of moral development.* San Francisco: Harper & Row.

Kohlberg, L. (1981b). *The meaning and measurement of moral development.* Worcester, MA: Clark University Press.

Kohlberg, L. (Ed.). (1984). *Essays on moral development: Vol. II. The psychology of moral development.* San Francisco: Harper & Row.

Kohlberg, L., & Candee, D. (1984). The relationship of moral judgment to moral action. In L. Kohlberg (Ed.), *Essays on moral development: Vol. II. The psychology of moral development* (pp. 498–581). San Francisco: Harper & Row.

Kohlberg, L., & Hersh, R. H. (1977). Moral development: A review of the theory. *Theory into Practice, 16,* 53–59.

Kohlberg, L., & Higgins, A. (1984). Continuities and discontinuities in childhood and adult development revisited—again. In L. Kohlberg (Ed.), *Essays on moral development: Vol. II. The psychology of moral development* (pp. 426–497). San Francisco: Harper & Row.

Kohlberg, L., & Kramer, R. (1969). Continuities and discontinuities in childhood and adult moral development. *Human Development, 12,* 93–120.

Kohlberg, L., Levine, C., & Hewer, A. (1984a). The current formulation of the theory. In L. Kohlberg (Ed.), *Essays on moral development: Vol. II. Psychology of moral development* (pp. 212–319). San Francisco: Harper & Row.

Kohlberg, L., Levine, C., & Hewer, A. (1984b). Synopses and detailed replies to critics. In L. Kohlberg (Ed.), *Essays on moral development: Vol. II. Psychology of moral development* (pp. 320–386). San Francisco: Harper & Row.

Kolb, D. A. (1976). *The Learning Style Inventory: Technical manual.* Boston: McBer.

Kolb, D. A. (1981). Learning styles and disciplinary differences. In A. W. Chickering & Associates, *The modern American college: Responding to the new realities of diverse students and a changing society* (pp. 232–255). San Francisco: Jossey-Bass.

Kolb, D. A. (1984). *Experiential learning: Experience as the source of learning and development.* Englewood Cliffs, NJ: Prentice Hall.

Kolb, D. A. (1985). *The Learning Style Inventory.* Boston: McBer.

Kolb, D. A. (1993). *LSI-IIA Learning Style Inventory.* Boston: McBer.

Kolb, D. A. (1994). *Bibliography of research on experiential learning theory and the Learning Style Inventory.* Unpublished manuscript, Case Western Reserve University, Cleveland, Ohio.

Komives, S. R. (1994). New approaches to leadership. In J. Fried & Associates, *Different voices: Gender and perspective in student affairs administration* (pp. 46–61). Washington, DC: National Association of Student Personnel Administrators.

Krieshok, T. S. (1987). Review of the Self-Directed Search. *Journal of Counseling and Development, 65,* 512–514.

Krivoski, J. F., & Nicholson, R. M. (1989). An interview with Arthur Chickering. *Journal of College and University Student Housing, 19* (2), 6–11.

Kroger, J. (1985). Separation-individuation and ego identity status in New Zealand university students. *Journal of Youth and Adolescence, 14,* 133–147.

Krogman, W. M. (1945). The concept of race. In R. Linton (Ed.), *The science of man in world crisis* (pp. 38–61). New York: Columbia University Press.

Kuh, G. D. (1996). Guiding principles for creating seamless learning environments for undergraduates. *Journal of College Student Development, 37,* 135–148.

Kuh, G. D., Whitt, E. J., & Shedd, J. D. (1987). *Student affairs work, 2001: A paradigmatic odyssey.* Alexandria, VA: American College Personnel Association.

Kuhn, T. S. (1970). *The structure of scientific revolutions* (2nd ed.). Chicago: University of Chicago Press.

Kuk, L. (1992). Perspectives on gender differences. In L. V. Moore (Ed.), *Evolving theoretical perspectives on students* (New Directions for Student Services, No. 51, pp. 25–36). San Francisco: Jossey-Bass.

Larrabee, M. J. (Ed.). (1993). *An ethic of care: Feminist and interdisciplinary perspectives.* New York: Routledge.

Lavallée, M., Gourde, A., & Rodier, C. (1990). The impact of lived experience on cognitive-ethical development of today's women. *International Journal of Behavioral Development, 13,* 407–430.

Lawrence, G. (1993). *People types & tiger stripes* (3rd ed.). Gainesville, FL: Center for Applications of Psychological Type.

Lazarus, R. S., & Folkman, S. (1984). *Stress, appraisal, and coping.* New York: Springer.

Lea, H. D., & Leibowitz, Z. (1986). The program developer as learner. In Z. Leibowitz & D. Lea (Eds.), *Adult career development: Concepts, issues, and practices* (pp. 50–62). Alexandria, VA: American Association for Counseling and Development.

Lee, J. A. (1977). Going public: A study in the sociology of homosexual liberation. *Journal of Homosexuality, 3* (1), 49–78.

Lemons, L. J., & Richmond, D. R. (1987). A developmental perspective of sophomore slump. *NASPA Journal, 24* (3), 15–19.

Leong, F. T. L., & Brown, M. T. (1995). Theoretical issues in cross-cultural career development: Cultural validity and cultural specificity. In W. B. Walsh & S. H. Osipow (Eds.), *Handbook of vocational psychology: Theory, research, and practice* (2nd ed., pp. 143–180). Mahwah, NJ: Erlbaum.

Leung, S. A., Ivey, D., & Suzuki, L. A. (1994). Factors affecting the career aspirations of Asian Americans. *Journal of Counseling and Development, 72,* 404–410.

Levine, H. (1997). A further exploration of the lesbian identity development process and its measurement. *Journal of Homosexuality, 32,* 67–78.

Levine, H., & Bahr, J. (1989). *Relationship between sexual identity formation and student development.* Unpublished manuscript.

Levine, H., & Evans, N. J. (1991). The development of gay, lesbian, and bisexual identities. In N. J. Evans & V. A. Wall (Eds.), *Beyond tolerance: Gays, lesbians and bisexuals on campus* (pp. 1–24). Alexandria, VA: American College Personnel Association.

Levinson, D. J. (1986). A conception of adult development. *American Psychologist, 41,* 3–13.

Levy, N., Murphy, C., Jr., & Carlson, R. (1972). Personality types among Negro college students. *Educational and Psychological Measurement, 32,* 641–653.

Levy, N., & Ridley, S. E. (1987). Stability of Jungian personality types within a college population over a decade. *Psychological Reports, 60,* 419–422.

Lewin, K. (1935). *A dynamic theory of personality.* New York: McGraw-Hill.

Lewin, K. (1936). *Principles of topological psychology.* New York: McGraw-Hill.

Lewin, K. (1951). *Field theory in the social sciences.* New York: Harper & Row.

Liddell, D. L. (1990). *Measure of moral orientation: Construction of an objective instrument measuring care and justice, with an investigation of gender differences.* Unpublished doctoral dissertation, Auburn University, Auburn, Alabama.

Liddell, D. L. (1995). [Review of *Developing reflective judgment: Understanding and promoting intellectual growth and critical thinking in adolescents and adults*]. *Journal of College Student Development, 36,* 94–96.

Liddell, D. L., & Davis, T. (1996). The measure of moral orientation: Reliability and validity evidence. *Journal of College Student Development, 37,* 485–493.

Liddell, D. L., Halpin, G., & Halpin, W. G. (1992). The measure of moral orientation: Measuring the ethics of care and justice. *Journal of College Student Development, 33,* 325–330.

Lind, G. (1986). Growth and regression in cognitive-moral development of young university students. In C. Harding (Ed.), *Moral dilemmas: Philosophical and psychological issues in the development of moral reasoning* (pp. 99–114). Chicago: Precedent.

Linton, R. (1945). *The cultural background of personality.* New York: Century.

Loevinger, J. (1976). *Ego development: Conceptions and theories.* San Francisco: Jossey-Bass.

Loevinger, J. (1993). Ego development: Questions of method and theory. *Psychological Inquiry, 4* (1), 56–63.

Logan, R., Snarey, J., & Schrader, D. (1990). Autonomous versus heteronomous moral judgment types. *Journal of Cross-Cultural Psychology, 21,* 71–89.

Loiacano, D. K. (1989). Gay identity issues among black Americans: Racism, homophobia, and the need for validation. *Journal of Counseling and Development, 68,* 21–25.

Long, B. E., Sowa, C. J., & Niles, S. G. (1995). Differences in student development reflected by the career decisions of college seniors. *Journal of College Student Development, 36,* 47–52.

Looney, J. (1988). Ego development and black identity. *Journal of Black Psychology, 15,* 41–56.

Lorde, A. (1983). There is no hierarchy of oppressions. *Interracial Books for Children, 14* (3–4), 9.

Lott, J. K. (1986). Freshman home reentry: Attending to a gap in student development. *Journal of Counseling and Development, 64,* 456.

Lowman, R. L. (1987). Occupational choice as a moderator of psychotherapeutic approach. *Psychotherapy, 24,* 801–808.

Lyons, J. (1980). *The effect of a structural group experience in the transition from the role of college student to the role of working professional.* Unpublished master's thesis, University of Maryland, College Park.

Lyons, N. P. (1983). Two perspectives: On self, relationships, and morality. *Harvard Educational Review, 53,* 125–145.

Lyons, N. P. (1987). Ways of knowing, learning and making moral choices. *Journal of Moral Education, 16,* 226–239.

Ma, H. K. (1989). Moral orientation and moral judgment in adolescents in Hong Kong, mainland China, and England. *Journal of Cross-Cultural Psychology, 20,* 152–177.

Madrid, A. (1988, May-June). Missing people and others: Joining together to expand the circle. *Change, 20,* 55–59.

Malcolm X. (1965). *Autobiography of Malcolm X.* New York: Golden Press.

Manalansan, M. F., IV. (1996). Double minorities: Latino, black, and Asian men who have sex with men. In R. C. Savin-Williams & K. M. Cohen (Eds.), *The lives of lesbians, gays, and bisexuals: Children to adults* (pp. 393–415). Fort Worth, TX: Harcourt Brace.

Marcia, J. E. (1966). Development and validation of ego-identity status. *Journal of Personality and Social Psychology, 3,* 551–558.

Marcia, J. E. (1980). Identity in adolescence. In J. Adelson (Ed.), *Handbook of adolescent psychology* (pp. 159–187). New York: Wiley.

Marcia, J. E. (1989). Identity and intervention. *Journal of Adolescence, 12,* 401–410.

Marcia, J. E., & Friedman, M. L. (1970). Ego identity status in college women. *Journal of Personality, 38,* 249–263.

Mayer, K. U., & Schoepflin, U. (1989). The state and the life course. *Annual Review of Sociology, 15,* 187–209.

McBride, M. C. (1990). Autonomy and the struggle for female identity: Implications for counseling women. *Journal of Counseling and Development, 69,* 22–26.

McBride, M. C., & Martin, G. E. (1988). The relationship between psychological type and preferred counseling theory in graduate counseling students. *Journal of Psychological Type, 15,* 46–48.

McCarley, N. G., & Carskadon, T. G. (1983). Test-retest reliabilities of scales and subscales of the Myers-Briggs Type Indicator and of criteria for clinical interpretive hypotheses involving them. *Research in Psychological Type, 6,* 24–36.

McCartney, C. E., Steffens, K. M., Imbra, C. M., & Slack, P. J. F. (1992). Moral development: Interviews with young Ojibwa women. *Initiatives, 55* (1), 11–21.

McCaulley, M. H. (1990). The Myers-Briggs Type Indicator: A measure for individuals and groups. *Measurement and Evaluation in Counseling and Development, 22,* 181–195.

McCaulley, M. H. (1991). Additional comments regarding the Myers-Briggs Type Indicator: A response to comments. *Measurement and Evaluation in Counseling and Development, 23,* 182–185.

McDonald, G. J. (1982). Individual differences in the coming out process for gay men: Implications for theoretical models. *Journal of Homosexuality, 8* (1), 47–60.

McEwen, M. (1994). [Review of *Knowing and reasoning in college: Gender-related patterns in students' intellectual development*]. *NASPA Journal, 31,* 153–157.

McEwen, M. K. (1996a). The nature and uses of theory. In S. R. Komives, D. B. Woodard Jr., & Associates, *Student services: A handbook for the profession* (3rd ed., pp. 147–163). San Francisco: Jossey-Bass.

McEwen, M. K. (1996b). New perspectives on identity development. In S. R. Komives, D. B. Woodard Jr., & Associates, *Student services: A handbook for the profession* (3rd ed., pp. 188–217). San Francisco: Jossey-Bass.

McEwen, M. K., Roper, L., Bryant, D., & Langa, M. (1990). Incorporating the development of African-American students into psychosocial theories of student development. *Journal of College Student Development, 31,* 429–436.

McIntosh, P. (1989, July–August). White privilege: Unpacking the invisible knapsack. *Peace and Freedom*, 10–12.

McNeer, E. J. (1991). Learning theories and library instruction. *Journal of Academic Librarianship*, *17*, 294–297.

McNickle, P. J., & Veltman, G. C. (1988). Gathering the force fields of energy in student affairs: Staff development using the Myers-Briggs Type Indicator. *NASPA Journal*, *25*, 202–208.

Mednick, M. T. (1989). On the politics of psychological constructs: Stop the bandwagon, I want to get off. *American Psychologist*, *44*, 1118–1123.

Mennuti, R. B., & Creamer, D. G. (1991). Role of orientation, gender, and dilemma content in moral reasoning. *Journal of College Student Development*, *32*, 241–248.

Mentkowski, M., Moeser, M., & Strait, M. J. (1983). *Using the Perry scheme of intellectual and ethical development as a college outcomes measure: A process and criteria for judging student performance.* 2 vols. Milwaukee, WI: Alverno College Productions.

Merenda, P. F. (1991). Additional comments regarding the Myers-Briggs Type Indicator. *Measurement and Evaluation in Counseling and Development*, *23*, 179–181.

Merikangas, M. (1980). *The next step: A retirement planning seminar.* Unpublished master's thesis, University of Maryland, College Park.

Merritt, S. L., & Marshall, J. C. (1984). Reliability and construct validity of ipsative and normative forms of the Learning Style Inventory. *Educational and Psychological Measurement*, *44*, 463–472.

Meyer, P. (1977). Intellectual development: Analysis of religious content. *Counseling Psychologist*, *6* (4), 47–50.

Miller, J. B. (1976). *Toward a new psychology of women.* Boston: Beacon Press.

Miller, J. G., & Bersoff, D. M. (1992). Culture and moral judgment: How are conflicts between justice and interpersonal responsibilities resolved? *Journal of Personality and Social Psychology*, *62*, 541–554.

Miller, T. K., & Prince, J. S. (1976). *The future of student affairs: A guide to student development for tomorrow's higher education.* San Francisco: Jossey-Bass.

Miller, T. K., & Winston, R. B., Jr. (1990). Assessing development from a psychosocial perspective. In D. G. Creamer & Associates, *College student development: Theory and practice for the 1990s* (pp. 99–126). Alexandria, VA: American College Personnel Association.

Miller, T. K., & Winston, R. B., Jr. (1991). Human development and higher education. In T. K. Miller & R. B. Winston Jr. (Eds.), *Administration and leadership in student affairs: Actualizing student development in higher education* (pp. 3–35). Muncie, IN: Accelerated Development.

Milliones, J. (1973). *Construction of the developmental inventory of black consciousness.* Unpublished doctoral dissertation, University of Pittsburgh.

Mines, R. A. (1977). *Development and validation of the Mines-Jensen Interpersonal Relationships Inventory.* Technical report. Iowa City: University of Iowa, Student Development Project.

Mines, R. A. (1982). Student development assessment techniques. In G. R. Hanson (Ed.), *Measuring student development* (New Directions for Student Services, No. 20, pp. 65–91). San Francisco: Jossey-Bass.

Mines, R. A. (1985). Measurement issues in evaluating student development programs. *Journal of College Student Personnel*, *26*, 101–106.

Minton, H. L., & McDonald, G. J. (1983–1984). Homosexual identity formation as a developmental process. *Journal of Homosexuality*, *9* (2–3), 91–104.

Mitchell, S. L., & Dell, D. M. (1992). The relationship between black students' racial identity attitude and participation in campus organizations. *Journal of College Student Development, 33,* 39–43.

Mobley, M., & Slaney, R. B. (1996). Holland's theory: Its relevance for lesbian women and gay men. *Journal of Vocational Behavior, 48,* 125–135.

Moore, L. V., & Upcraft, M. L. (1990). Theory in student affairs: Evolving perspectives. In L. V. Moore (Ed.), *Evolving theoretical perspectives on students* (New Directions for Student Services, No. 51, pp. 3–23). San Francisco: Jossey-Bass.

Moore, W. S. (1989). The Learning Environment Preferences: Exploring the construct validity of an objective measure of the Perry scheme of intellectual development. *Journal of College Student Development, 30,* 504–514.

Morales, E. S. (1989). Ethnic minority families and minority gays and lesbians. *Marriage and Family Review, 14,* 217–239.

Morrill, W. H., Hurst, J. C., & Oetting, E. R. (1980). A conceptual model of intervention strategies. In W. H. Morrill, J. C. Hurst, E. R. Oetting, et al., *Dimensions of intervention for student development* (pp. 85–95). New York: Wiley.

Morrill, W. H., Oetting, E. R., & Hurst, J. C. (1974). Dimensions of counselor functioning. *Personnel and Guidance Journal, 52,* 354–359.

Mullis, R. L., Martin, R. E., Dosser, D. A., & Sanders, G. F. (1988). Using cognitive developmental theory to teach home economics courses. *Journal of Home Economics, 80* (1), 35–39.

Murphy, J. M., & Gilligan, C. (1980). Moral development in late adolescence and adulthood: A critique and reconstruction of Kohlberg's theory. *Human Development, 23,* 77–104.

Murrell, P. H., & Claxton, C. S. (1987). Experiential learning theory as a guide for effective teaching. *Counselor Education and Supervision, 27,* 4–14.

Mustapha, S. L., & Seybert, J. A. (1990). Moral reasoning in college students: Effects of two general education courses. *Education Research Quarterly, 14,* 32–40.

Myers, I. B. (1980). *Gifts differing.* Palo Alto, CA: Consulting Psychologists Press.

Myers, I. B. (1987). *Introduction to type: A description of the theory and applications of the Myers-Briggs Type Indicator* (4th ed.). Palo Alto, CA: Consulting Psychologists Press.

Myers, I. B., & McCaulley, M. H. (1985). *Manual: A guide to the development and use of the Myers-Briggs Type Indicator.* Palo Alto, CA: Consulting Psychologists Press.

Neugarten, B. L. (1979). Time, age, and the life cycle. *American Journal of Psychiatry, 136,* 887–894.

Neugarten, B. L. (1982, August). *Successful aging.* Paper presented at the annual meeting of the American Psychological Association, Washington, DC.

Neugarten, B. L., & Neugarten, D. A. (1987, May). The changing meanings of age. *Psychology Today,* pp. 29–33.

Newcomb, T. M., & Wilson, E. K. (Eds.). (1966). *College peer groups: Problems and prospects for research.* Chicago: Aldine.

Niles, S. G., Sowa, C. J., & Laden, J. (1994). Life role participation and commitment as predictors of college student development. *Journal of College Student Development, 35,* 159–163.

Noddings, N. (1984). *Caring: A feminine approach to ethics and moral education.* Berkeley: University of California Press.

Obear, K. (1991). Homophobia. In N. J. Evans & V. A. Wall (Eds.), *Beyond tolerance: Gays, lesbians and bisexuals on campus* (pp. 39–66). Alexandria, VA: American College Personnel Association.

Orlofsky, J. L. (1977). Sex role orientation, identity formation, and self-esteem in college men and women. *Sex Roles, 6,* 561–575.

Orlofsky, J. L. (1978). Identity formation, achievement, and fear of success in college men and women. *Journal of Youth and Adolescence, 7,* 49–62.

Orlofsky, J. L., & Frank, M. (1986). Personality structure as viewed through the early memories and identity status in men and women. *Journal of Personality and Social Psychology, 50,* 580–586.

Ortman, P. E. (1993). A feminist approach to teaching learning theory with educational applications. *Teaching of Psychology, 20,* 38–40.

Osipow, S. H. (1990). Convergence in theories of career choice and development: Review and prospect. *Journal of Vocational Behavior, 36,* 122–131.

Ottavi, T. M., Pope-Davis, D. B., & Dings, J. G. (1994). Relationship between racial identity attitudes and self-reported multicultural counseling competencies. *Journal of Counseling Psychology, 41,* 149–154.

Pace, C. R. (1984). *Measuring the quality of college student experiences: An account of the development and use of the College Student Experiences Questionnaire.* Los Angeles: University of California, Higher Education Research Institute.

Padilla, A. M. (1995). On the nature of Latino ethnicity. In A. S. Lopez (Ed.), *Historical themes and identity: Mestizaje and labels* (pp. 439–452). New York: Garland.

Parham, T. A. (1989). Cycles of psychological Nigrescence. *Counseling Psychologist, 17,* 187–226.

Parham, T. A., & Helms, J. E. (1981). The influence of black students' racial identity attitudes on preference for counselor's race. *Journal of Counseling Psychology, 28,* 250–257.

Parham, T. A., & Helms, J. E. (1985). Attitudes of racial identity and self-esteem of black students: An exploratory investigation. *Journal of College Student Personnel, 26,* 143–147.

Parker, C. A. (1974). Student development: What does it mean? *Journal of College Student Personnel, 15,* 248–256.

Parker, C. A. (1977). On modeling reality. *Journal of College Student Personnel, 18,* 419–425.

Parker, C. A. (Ed.). (1978). *Encouraging development in college students.* Minneapolis: University of Minnesota Press.

Parker, C. A., Widick, C., & Knefelkamp, L. L. (1978). Why bother with theory? In L. L. Knefelkamp, C. Widick, & C. A. Parker (Eds.), *Applying new developmental findings* (New Directions for Student Services, No. 4, pp. vii-xvi). San Francisco: Jossey-Bass.

Parsons, F. (1909). *Choosing a vocation.* Boston: Houghton-Mifflin.

Pascarella, E. T., & Terenzini, P. T. (1991). *How college affects students: Findings and insights from twenty years of research.* San Francisco: Jossey-Bass.

Paul, J. P. (1984). The bisexual identity: An idea without social recognition. In J. P. DeCecco & M. G. Shively (Eds.), *Bisexual and homosexual identities: Critical theoretical issues* (pp. 45–63). New York: Haworth Press.

Paul, J. P. (1996). Bisexuality: Exploring/exploding the boundaries. In R. C. Savin-Williams & K. M. Cohen (Eds.), *The lives of lesbians, gays, and bisexuals: Children to adults* (pp. 436–461). Fort Worth, TX: Harcourt Brace.

Pearlin, L. I. (1982). Discontinuities in the study of aging. In T. K. Hareven & K. J. Adams (Eds.), *Aging and life course transitions: An interdisciplinary perspective* (pp.55–79). New York: Guilford Press.

Pearlin, L. I., & Schooler, C. (1978). The structure of coping. *Journal of Health and Social Behavior, 19,* 2–21.

Pearson, R. E., & Petitpas, A. J. (1990). Transitions of athletes: Developmental and preventative perspectives. *Journal of Counseling and Development, 69,* 7–10.

Penn, W. Y., Jr. (1990). Teaching ethics: A direct approach. *Journal of Moral Education, 19,* 124–138.

Perreault, G. (1996). Sharing the vision: Leadership as friendship and feminist care ethics. *Leadership Journal, 1,* 33–49.

Perreira, D. C., & Dezago, J. L. (1989). College student development: Is it different for persons with disabilities? *Proceedings of the 1989 AHSSPPE Conference,* 51–54.

Perry, W. G., Jr. (1968). *Forms of intellectual and ethical development in the college years: A scheme.* New York: Holt, Rinehart & Winston.

Perry, W. G., Jr. (1978). Sharing in the costs of growth. In C. A. Parker (Ed.), *Encouraging development in college students* (pp. 267–273). Minneapolis: University of Minnesota Press.

Perry, W. G., Jr. (1981). Cognitive and ethical growth: The making of meaning. In A. W. Chickering & Associates, *The modern American college: Responding to the new realities of diverse students and a changing society* (pp. 76–116). San Francisco: Jossey-Bass.

Peter, E., & Gallop, R. (1994). The ethic of care: A comparison of nursing and medical students. *IMAGE: Journal of Nursing Scholarship, 26* (1), 47–50.

Pharr, S. (1988). *Homophobia: A weapon of sexism.* Little Rock, AR: Chardon.

Phinney, J. S. (1989). Stages of ethnic identity development in minority group adolescents. *Journal of Early Adolescence, 9,* 34–49.

Phinney, J. S. (1990). Ethnic identity in adolescents and adults: Review of research. *Psychological Bulletin, 108,* 499–514.

Phinney, J. S. (1992). The Multigroup Ethnic Identity Measure: A new scale for use with diverse groups. *Journal of Adolescent Research, 7,* 156–176.

Phinney, J. S., & Alipuria, L. L. (1990). Ethnic identity in college students from four ethnic groups. *Journal of Adolescence, 13,* 171–183.

Phinney, J. S., & Tarver, S. (1988). Ethnic identity and search and commitment in black and white eighth graders. *Journal of Early Adolescence, 8,* 265–277.

Piaget, J. (1950). *The psychology of intelligence* (M. Piercy & D. E. Berlyne, Trans.). London: Routledge & Kegan Paul. (Original work published 1947)

Piaget, J. (1952). *The origins of intelligence in children.* New York: International Universities Press.

Piaget, J. (1971). *Psychology and epistemology.* Harmondsworth, England: Penguin.

Piaget, J. (1973). *The child and reality* (A. Rosin, Trans.). New York: Viking. (Original work published 1956)

Piaget, J. (1977). *The moral judgment of the child* (M. Gabain, Trans.). Harmondsworth, England: Penguin. (Original work published 1932)

Picard, I. A., & Guido-DiBrito, F. (1993). Listening to the voice of care: Women's moral development and implications for student affairs practitioners. *Iowa Student Personnel Journal, 8,* 21–34.

Pinkney, J. W. (1983). The Myers-Briggs Type Indicator as an alternative in career counseling. *Personnel and Guidance Journal, 62,* 173–177.

Piper, T. D., & Rodgers, R. F. (1992). Theory-practice congruence: Factors influencing the internalization of theory. *Journal of College Student Development, 33,* 117–123.

Pitt, A. (1991). The expression of experience: Code's critique of Gilligan's abortion study. *Journal of Moral Education, 20,* 177–190.

Pittenger, D. J. (1993). The utility of the Myers-Briggs Type Indicator. *Review of Educational Research, 63,* 467–488.

Placier, P., Moss, G., & Blockus, L. (1992). College student personal growth in perspective: A comparison of African American and white alumni. *Journal of College Student Development, 33*, 462–471.

Plummer, K. (1975). *Sexual stigma: An interactionist account.* London: Routledge & Kegan Paul.

Plummer, T. G. (1988). Cognitive growth and literacy analysis: A dialectical model for teaching literature. *Unterrichtspraxis, 21* (1), 68–80.

Polkosnik, M. C., & Winston, R. B., Jr. (1989). Relationships between students' intellectual and psychosocial development: An exploratory investigation. *Journal of College Student Development, 30*, 10–19.

Pollard, K. D., Benton, S. E., & Hinz, K. (1983). The assessment of developmental tasks of students in remedial and regular programs. *Journal of College Student Personnel, 24*, 20–23.

Ponse, B. (1980). Lesbians and their worlds. In J. Marmor (Ed.), *Homosexual behavior: A modern reappraisal* (pp. 157–175). New York: Basic Books.

Ponterotto, J. G., & Casas, J. M. (1991). *Handbook of racial/ethnic minority counseling research.* Springfield, IL: Thomas.

Ponterotto, J. G., & Wise, S. (1987). Construct validity study of the Racial Identity Attitude Scale. *Journal of Counseling Psychology, 34*, 218–223.

Popper, K. R. (1969). *Conjectures and reflections.* New York: Harper & Row.

Porterfield, W. D., & Pressprich, S. T. (1988). Carol Gilligan's perspectives and staff supervision: Implications for the practitioner. *NASPA Journal, 25*, 244–248.

Poston, W. S. C. (1990). The biracial identity development model: A needed addition. *Journal of Counseling and Development, 69*, 152–155.

Prager, K. J. (1986). Identity development, age and college experience in women. *Journal of Genetic Psychology, 147* (1), 31–36.

Pratt, M. W., Golding, G., & Hunter, W. J. (1983). Aging as ripening: Character and consistency of moral judgment in young, mature, and older adults. *Human Development, 26*, 277–288.

Prince, J. S., Miller, T. K., & Winston, R. B., Jr. (1974). *Student Developmental Task Inventory.* Athens, GA: Student Development Associates.

Provost, J. A. (1985). "Type watching" and college attrition. *Journal of Psychological Type, 9*, 16–23.

Provost, J. A. (1987). Psychological counseling. In J. A. Provost & S. Anchors (Eds.), *Application of the Myers-Briggs Type Indicator in higher education* (pp. 125–148). Palo Alto, CA: Consulting Psychologists Press.

Quinn, M. T., Lewis, R. J., & Fischer, K. L. (1992). A cross-correlation of the Myers-Briggs and Keirsey instruments. *Journal of College Student Development, 33*, 279–280.

Ramirez, M., III. (1983). *Psychology of the Americas: Mestizo perspective on personality and mental health.* New York: Pergamon Press.

Rapaport, N. J. (1984). Critical thinking and cognitive development. *Proceedings and Addresses of the American Philosophical Association, 57*, 610–615.

Reardon, R. C., & Minor, C. W. (1975). Revitalizing the career information service. *Personnel and Guidance Journal, 54*, 169–171.

Reardon, R. C., Psychological Assessment Resources, & Holland, J. L. (1985). *Self-Directed Search: Computer version.* Odessa, FL: Psychological Assessment Resources.

Reimer, J. (1981). Moral education: The just community approach. *Phi Delta Kappan, 62*, 485–487.

Reisser, L. (1995). Revisiting the seven vectors. *Journal of College Student Development, 36*, 505–511.

Rendón, L. I. (1994). Validating culturally diverse students: Toward a new model of learning and student development. *Innovative Higher Education, 19,* 33–51.

Rest, J. R. (1969). *Hierarchies of comprehension and preference in a developmental stage model of moral thinking.* Unpublished doctoral dissertation, University of Chicago.

Rest, J. R. (1979a). *Development in judging moral issues.* Minneapolis: University of Minnesota Press.

Rest, J. R. (1979b). *Revised manual for the Defining Issues Test.* MMRP Technical Report. Minneapolis: University of Minnesota.

Rest, J. R. (1985). Moral reasoning methodology. In S. Modgil & C. Modgil (Eds.), *Lawrence Kohlberg: Consensus and controversy* (pp. 455–459). Philadelphia: Falmer Press.

Rest, J. R. (1986a). *The Defining Issues Test* (3rd ed.). Minneapolis: University of Minnesota, Center for the Study of Ethical Development.

Rest, J. R. (1986b). *Moral development: Advances in research and theory.* New York: Praeger.

Rest, J. R. (1988). Why does college promote development in moral judgment? *Journal of Moral Education, 17,* 183–194.

Rhoads, R. A. (1994). *Coming out in college: The struggle for a queer identity.* Westport, CT: Bergin & Garvey.

Rhodes, M. L. (1985). Gilligan's theory of moral development as applied to social work. *Social Work, 37,* 101–105.

Ricci, J. P., Porterfield, W. D., & Piper, T. D. (1987). Using developmental theory in supervising residential staff members. *NASPA Journal, 24* (4), 32–41.

Rice, M. B., & Brown, R. D. (1990). Developmental factors associated with self-perceptions of mentoring competence and mentoring needs. *Journal of College Student Development, 31,* 293–299.

Richards, J. M., Jr., Seligman, R., & Jones, P. K. (1970). Faculty and curriculum as measures of college environment. *Journal of Educational Psychology, 61,* 324–232.

Rideout, C. A., & Richardson, S. A. (1989). A team-building model: Appreciating differences using the Myers-Briggs Type Indicator with developmental theory. *Journal of Counseling and Development, 67,* 529–533.

Roberts, P., & Newton, P. M. (1987). Levinsonian studies of women's adult development. *Psychology and Aging, 2,* 154–163.

Rodgers, R. F. (1980). Theories underlying student development. In D. G. Creamer (Ed.), *Student development in higher education* (pp. 10–95). Cincinnati, OH: American College Personnel Association.

Rodgers, R. F. (1990a). An integration of campus ecology and student development: The Olentangy project. In D. G. Creamer & Associates, *College student development: Theory and practice for the 1990s* (pp. 155–180). Alexandria, VA: American College Personnel Association.

Rodgers, R. F. (1990b). Recent theories and research underlying student development. In D. Creamer & Associates, *College student development: Theory and practice for the 1990s* (pp. 27–79). Alexandria, VA: American College Personnel Association.

Rodgers, R. F. (1990c). Student development. In U. Delworth, G. R. Hanson, & Associates, *Student services: A handbook for the profession* (2nd ed., pp. 117–164). San Francisco: Jossey-Bass.

Rodgers, R. F., & Widick, C. (1980). Theory to practice: Using concepts, logic and creativity. In F. B. Newton & K. L. Ender (Eds.), *Student development practice: Strategies for making a difference* (pp. 5–25). Springfield, IL: Thomas.

Rodriguez, R. (1982). *Hunger of memory: The education of Richard Rodriguez.* New York: Bantam Books.

Rogers, J. L. (1989). New paradigm leadership: Integrating the female ethos. *Initiatives, 52* (4), 1–8.

Romer, N. (1991). A feminist view of moral development: Criticisms and applications. *Initiatives, 54* (3), 19–32.

Root, M. P. P. (1992). Within, between, and beyond race. In M. P. P. Root (Ed.), *Racially mixed people in America* (pp. 3–11). Newbury Park, CA: Sage.

Rosenbaum, J. E. (1979). Tournament mobility: Career patterns in a corporation. *Administrative Science Quarterly, 24,* 220–241.

Rosenberg, M., & McCullough, B. C. (1981). Mattering: Inferred significance to parents and mental health among adolescents. In R. Simmons (Ed.), *Research in community and mental health* (Vol. 2, pp. 163–182). Greenwich, CT: JAI Press.

Ross, D. B. (1984). A cross-cultural comparison of adult development. *Personnel and Guidance Journal, 62,* 418–421.

Ross, M. W. (1989). Gay youth in four cultures: A comparative study. In G. Herdt (Ed.), *Gay and lesbian youth* (pp. 299–314). New York: Haworth Press.

Rothbart, M. K., Hanley, D., & Albert, M. (1986). Gender differences in moral reasoning. *Sex Roles, 15,* 645–653.

Rounds, J. B. (1995). Vocational interests: Evaluating structural hypotheses. In D. Lubinski & R. V. Dawis (Eds.), *Assessing individual differences in human behavior: New concepts, methods, and findings* (pp. 177–232). Palo Alto, CA: Davies-Black.

Rounds, J. B., & Tracey, T. J. (1996). Cross-cultural structural equivalence of RIASEC models and measures. *Journal of Counseling Psychology, 43,* 310–329.

Rounds, J. B., Tracey, T. J., & Hubert, L. (1992). Methods for evaluating vocational interest structural hypotheses. *Journal of Vocational Behavior, 40,* 239–259.

Rowe, W., Behrens, J. T., & Leach, M. M. (1995). Racial/ethnic identity and racial consciousness: Looking back and looking forward. In J. G. Ponterotto, J. M. Casas, L. A. Suzuki, & C. M. Alexander (Eds.), *Handbook of multicultural counseling* (pp. 218–235). Thousand Oaks, CA: Sage.

Ruble, T. L., & Stout, D. E. (1990). Reliability, construct validity, and response-set bias of the revised Learning-Style Inventory (LSI–1985). *Educational and Psychological Measurement, 50,* 619–629.

Ruble, T. L., & Stout, D. E. (1991). Reliability, classification stability, and response-set bias of alternate forms of the Learning-Style Inventory (LSI–1985). *Educational and Psychological Measurement, 51,* 481–489.

Ruble, T. L., & Stout, D. E. (1992). Changes in learning-style preferences: Comments on Geiger and Pinto. *Psychological Reports, 70,* 697–698.

Ruddick, S. (1995). *Maternal thinking: Toward a politics of peace.* Boston, MA: Beacon Press. (Original work published 1989)

Ruiz, A. S. (1990). Ethnic identity: Crisis and resolution. *Journal of Multicultural Counseling and Development, 18,* 29–40.

Rust, P. C. (1993). "Coming out" in the age of social constructionism: Sexual identity formation among lesbian and bisexual women. *Gender and Society, 7* (1), 50–77.

Saidla, D. D. (1990). Cognitive development and group stages. *Journal for Specialists in Group Work, 15* (1), 15–20.

Salter, D. W. (1994, March). Implications of psychological and environmental type congruence in educational settings. *Proceedings of an International Symposium: Orchestrating Education Change in the '90s: The Role of Psychological Type* (pp. 157–168). Gainesville, FL: Center for Applications of Psychological Type.

Salter, D. W. (1995a, July). Gender bias in the classroom: How much is "type bias"? *Proceedings of the APT XI International Conference: Diversity and Expression of Type* (pp. 131–134). Kansas City, MO: Association for Psychological Type.

Salter, D. W. (1995b). A Jungian view of the dimensions of behavioral environments. *Journal of Psychological Type, 34,* 24–28.

Salter, D. W. (1997, March). *Carl Gustav Jung: Big theorist on campus.* Paper presented at the joint meeting of the American College Personnel Association and the National Association of Student Personnel Administrators, Chicago.

Sanford, N. (1962). Developmental status of the entering freshman. In N. Sanford (Ed.), *The American college* (pp. 253–282). New York: Wiley.

Sanford, N. (1966). *Self and society.* New York: Atherton Press.

Sanford, N. (1967). *Where colleges fail: A study of the student as a person.* San Francisco: Jossey-Bass.

Savin-Williams, R. C. (1995). Lesbian, gay male, and bisexual adolescents. In A. R. D'Augelli & C. J. Patterson (Eds.), *Lesbian, gay, and bisexual identities over the lifespan: Psychological perspectives* (pp. 165–189). New York: Oxford University Press.

Schenkel, S. (1975). Relationship among ego identity status, field independence and traditional femininity. *Journal of Youth and Adolescence, 4,* 73–82.

Schenkel, S., & Marcia, J. E. (1972). Attitudes toward premarital intercourse in determining ego identity status in college women. *Journal of Personality, 40,* 472–482.

Schlossberg, N. K. (1981). A model for analyzing human adaption to transition. *Counseling Psychologist, 9* (2), 2–18.

Schlossberg, N. K. (1984). *Counseling adults in transition.* New York: Springer.

Schlossberg, N. K. (1989a). Marginality and mattering: Key issues in building community. In D. C. Roberts (Ed.), *Designing campus activities to foster a sense of community* (New Directions for Student Services, No. 48, pp. 5–15). San Francisco: Jossey-Bass.

Schlossberg, N. K. (1989b). *Overwhelmed: Coping with life's ups and downs.* Lexington, MA: Lexington Books.

Schlossberg, N. K., & Leibowitz, Z. B. (1980). Organizational support systems as a buffer to job loss. *Journal of Vocational Behavior, 18,* 204–217.

Schlossberg, N. K., Lynch, A. Q., & Chickering, A. W. (1989). *Improving higher education environments for adults: Responsive programs and services from entry to departure.* San Francisco: Jossey-Bass.

Schlossberg, N. K., & Robinson, S. P. (1996). *Going to plan B.* New York: Simon & Schuster.

Schlossberg, N. K., Waters, E. B., & Goodman, J. (1995). *Counseling adults in transition* (2nd ed.). New York: Springer.

Schreier, B. A. (1995). Moving beyond tolerance: A new paradigm for programming about homophobia/biphobia and heterosexism. *Journal of College Student Development, 36,* 19–26.

Schroeder, C. C. (1976). New strategies for structuring residential environments. *Journal of College Student Personnel, 17,* 386–391.

Schroeder, C. C. (1993, September-October). New students—new learning styles. *Change,* pp. 21–26.

Schroeder, C. C. (Guest Ed.). (1996). The student learning imperative [Special issue]. *Journal of College Student Development, 37* (2).

Schroeder, C. C., & Jackson, S. (1987). Designing residential environments. In J. A. Provost & S. Anchors (Eds.), *Applications of the Myers-Briggs Type Indicator in higher education* (pp. 65–88). Palo Alto, CA: Consulting Psychologists Press.

Schroeder, C. C., Warner, R., & Malone, D. (1980). Effects of assignment to living units by personality types on environmental perceptions and student development. *Journal of College Student Personnel, 21,* 443–449.

Schuh, J. H. (1994). [Review of *Education and identity* (2nd ed.)]. *Journal of College Student Development, 35,* 310–312.

Schurr, K. T., & Ruble, V. (1988). Psychological type and the second year of college achievement: Survival and the gravitation toward appropriate and manageable major fields. *Journal of Psychological Type, 14,* 57–59.

Schwartz, R. H. (1991). Achievement-orientation of personality type: A variable to consider in tests of Holland's congruence-achievement and other hypotheses. *Journal of Vocational Behavior, 38,* 225–235.

Schwartz, R. H. (1992). Is Holland's theory worthy of so much attention, or should vocational psychology move on? *Journal of Vocational Behavior, 40,* 179–187.

Scott, D. (1991). Working with gay and lesbian student organizations. In N. J. Evans & V. A. Wall (Eds.), *Beyond tolerance: Gays, lesbians and bisexuals on campus* (pp. 117–130). Alexandria, VA: American College Personnel Association.

Sears, J. T. (1991). *Growing up gay in the South: Race, gender, and journeys of the spirit.* New York: Haworth Press.

Sedlacek, W. E. (1987). Black students on white campuses: 20 years of research. *Journal of College Student Personnel, 28,* 484–495.

Selman, R. (1980). *Growth of interpersonal understanding: Developmental and clinical analysis.* New York: Academic Press.

Sergent, M. T., & Sedlacek, W. E. (1990). Volunteer motivations across student organizations: A test of person-environment fit theory. *Journal of College Student Development, 31,* 255–261.

Sheehan, O. T. O., & Pearson, F. (1995). Asian international and American students' psychosocial development. *Journal of College Student Development, 36,* 523–530.

Sichel, B. A. (1985). Women's moral development in search of assumptions. *Journal of Moral Education, 14,* 149–161.

Simmons, G., & Barrineau, P. (1994). Learning style and the Native American. *Journal of Psychological Type, 28,* 3–10.

Sims, R. R., Veres, J. G., III, Watson, P., & Bruckner, K. E. (1986). The reliability and classification stability of the Learning Style Inventory. *Educational and Psychological Measurement, 46,* 753–760.

Skoe, E. E., & Diessner, R. (1994). Ethic of care, justice, identity and gender: An extension and replication. *Merrill-Palmer Quarterly, 40,* 272–289.

Skoe, E. E., & Marcia, J. E. (1991). A measure of care-based morality and its relation to ego identity. *Merrill-Palmer Quarterly, 37,* 289–304.

Smith, D. M., & Kolb, D. A. (1986). *User's guide for the Learning Style Inventory.* Boston: McBer.

Smith, E. J. (1991). Ethnic identity development: Developing a theory within the context of majority/minority status. *Journal of Counseling and Development, 70,* 181–188.

Snarey, J. R. (1985). Cross-cultural universality of social-moral development: A critical review of Kohlbergian research. *Psychological Bulletin, 97,* 202–232.

Snead, R. F., & Caple, R. B. (1971). Some effects of the environmental press in university housing. *Journal of College Student Personnel, 12,* 189–192.

Sodowsky, G. R., Kwan, K. K., & Pannu, R. (1995). Ethnic identity of Asians in the United States. In J. G. Ponterotto, J. M. Casas, L. A. Suzuki, & C. M. Alexander (Eds.), *Handbook for multicultural counseling* (pp. 123–154). Thousand Oaks, CA: Sage.

Sophie, J. (1982). Counseling lesbians. *Personnel and Guidance Journal, 60,* 341–345.

Sophie, J. (1985–1986). A critical examination of stage theories of lesbian identity development. *Journal of Homosexuality, 12* (2–3), 39–51.

Sowa, C. J., & Gressard, C. F. (1983). Athletic participation: Its relationship to student development. *Journal of College Student Development, 24,* 236–239.

Spann, S., Newman, D., & Matthews, C. (1991). The Myers-Briggs Type Indicator and student development: An analysis of relationships. *Journal of Psychological Type, 22,* 43–47.

Spokane, A. R. (1985). A review of research on person-environment congruence in Holland's theory of careers. *Journal of Vocational Behavior, 26,* 306–343.

Spoto, A. (1989). *Jung's typology in perspective.* Boston: SIGO Press.

Stalvey, L. M. (1989). *The education of a WASP.* Madison: University of Wisconsin Press. (Original work published 1970).

Stander, V., & Jensen, L. (1993). The relationship of value orientation to moral cognition: Gender and cultural differences in the U.S. and China explored. *Journal of Social Psychology, 69,* 407–414.

Stiller, N. J., & Forrest, L. (1990). An extension of Gilligan's and Lyons' investigation of morality: Gender differences in college students. *Journal of College Student Development, 31,* 54–63.

Stimpson, D., Jensen, L., & Neff, W. (1992). Cross-cultural gender differences in preference for a caring morality. *Journal of Social Psychology, 132,* 317–322.

Stonewater, B. B. (1988). Informal developmental assessment in residence halls: A theory to practice model. *NASPA Journal, 25,* 267–273.

Stonewater, B. B. (1989). Gender differences in career decision making: A theoretical integration. *Initiatives, 52* (1), 27–34.

Strahan, R. F. (1987). Measures of consistency for Holland-type codes. *Journal of Vocational Behavior, 31,* 37–44.

Strange, C. C. (1994). Student development: The evolution and status of an essential idea. *Journal of College Student Development, 35,* 399–412.

Strange, C. C. (1996). Dynamics of campus environments. In S. R. Komives, D. B. Woodard Jr., & Associates, *Student services: A handbook for the profession* (3rd ed., pp. 244–268). San Francisco: Jossey-Bass.

Strange, C. C., & King, P. M. (1990). The professional practice of student development. In D. G. Creamer & Associates, *College student development: Theory and practice for the 1990s* (pp. 9–24). Alexandria, VA: American College Personnel Association.

Straub, C. (1987). Women's development of autonomy and Chickering's theory. *Journal of College Student Personnel, 28,* 198–205.

Straub, C., & Rodgers, R. F. (1986). An exploration of Chickering's theory and women's development. *Journal of College Student Personnel, 27,* 216–224.

Strickler, L. J., & Ross, J. (1962). *A description and evaluation of the Myers-Briggs Type Indicator* (Research Bulletin No. RB–62–6). Princeton, NJ: Educational Testing Service.

Student Learning Imperative: Implications for student affairs. (1996). *Journal of College Student Development, 37,* 118–122.

Subich, L. M. (1992). Holland's theory: "Pushing the envelope." *Journal of Vocational Behavior, 40,* 201–206.

Sue, D., & Sue, D. W. (1990). *Counseling the culturally different: Theory and practice* (2nd ed.). New York: Wiley.

Sue, D. W. (1995). Multicultural organizational development: Implications for the counseling profession. In J. G. Ponterotto, J. M. Casas, L. A. Suzuki, & C. M. Alexander (Eds.), *Handbook of multicultural counseling* (pp. 474–492). Thousand Oaks, CA: Sage.

Sugarman, L. (1985). Kolb's model of experiential learning: Touchstone for trainers, students, counselors, and clients. *Journal of Counseling and Development, 64,* 264–268.

Super, D. E. (1985). Validating a model and a method. *Contemporary Psychology, 30,* 771.

Svinicki, M. D., & Dixon, N. M. (1987). The Kolb model modified for classroom activities. *College Teaching, 35,* 141–146.

Swain, D. A. (1991). Withdrawal from sport and Schlossberg's model of transitions. *Sociology of Sport Journal, 8,* 152–160.

Swick, H. M. (1991, April). *Fostering the professional development of medical students.* Paper presented at the annual meeting of the American Educational Research Association, Chicago. (ERIC Document Reproduction Service No. ED 330 283)

Szapocznik, J., & Kurtines, W. (1980). Acculturation, biculturalism, and adjustment among Cuban Americans. In A. M. Padilla (Ed.), *Acculturation theories, models, and some new findings* (pp. 139–159). Boulder, CO: Westview Press.

Tatum, B. D. (1992). Talking about race, learning about racism: The application of racial identity development theory in the classroom. *Harvard Educational Review, 62,* 1–24.

Taub, D. J. (1995). Relationship of selected factors to traditional-age undergraduate women's development of autonomy. *Journal of College Student Development, 36,* 141–151.

Taub, D. J., & McEwen, M. K. (1991). Patterns of development of autonomy and mature interpersonal relationships in black and white undergraduate women. *Journal of College Student Development, 32,* 502–508.

Taub, D. J., & McEwen, M. K. (1992). The relationship of racial identity attitudes to autonomy and mature interpersonal relationships in black and white undergraduate women. *Journal of College Student Development, 33,* 439–446.

Taylor, J. M., Gilligan, C., & Sullivan, A. M. (1995). *Between voice and silence: Women and girls, race and relationship.* Cambridge, MA: Harvard University Press.

Tedesco, J. (1991). Women's ways of knowing/women's ways of composing. *Rhetoric Review, 9,* 246–252.

Terenzini, P. T. (1994). Good news and bad news: The implications of Strange's proposals for research. *Journal of College Student Development, 35,* 422–427.

Teske, R., & Nelson, B. (1973). Two scales for the measurement of Mexican-American identity. *International Review of Modern Sociology, 3,* 192–203.

Thayer-Bacon, B. J. (1993). Caring and its relationship to critical thinking. *Educational Theory, 43,* 323–340.

Thoma, G. A. (1993). The Perry framework and tactics for teaching critical thinking in economics. *Journal of Economic Education, 24,* 128–137.

Thoma, S. J. (1986). Estimating gender differences in the comprehension and preference of moral issues. *Developmental Review, 6,* 165–180.

Thomas, C. W. (1971). *Boys no more.* Beverly Hills, CA: Glencoe.

Thomas, R., & Chickering, A. W. (1984). *Education and identity* revisited. *Journal of College Student Personnel, 25,* 392–399.

Thorne, A., & Gough, H. (1991). *Portraits of type: An MBTI research compendium.* Palo Alto, CA: Consulting Psychologists Press.

Ting-Tomey, S. (1981). Ethnic identity and close friendship in Chinese-American college students. *International Journal of Intercultural Relations, 5,* 383–406.

Tischler, L. (1994). The MBTI factor structure. *Journal of Psychological Type, 31,* 24–31.

Todaro, E. (1993). The impact of recreational sports on student development: A theoretical model. *NIRSA Journal, 17* (3), 23–26.

Tokar, D. M., & Swanson, J. L. (1991). An investigation of the validity of Helms's (1984) model of white racial identity development. *Journal of Counseling Psychology, 38,* 296–301.

Torres, V. (1996, March). *Empirical studies in Latino/Latina ethnic identity.* Paper presented at the National Association of Student Personnel Administrators National Conference, Baltimore.

Torres, V. (1997, March). *Understanding Latino students through a bicultural development model.* Paper presented at the joint national conference of the American College Personnel Association and the National Association of Student Personnel Administrators, Chicago.

Touchton, J. G., Wertheimer, L. C., & Cornfeld, J. L., & Harrison, K. H. (1977). Career planning and decision-making: A developmental approach to the classroom. *Counseling Psychologist, 6* (4), 42–47.

Tranberg, M., Slane, S., & Ekeberg, S. E. (1993). The relation between interest congruence and satisfaction: A meta-analysis. *Journal of Vocational Behavior, 42,* 253–264.

Transition coping guide. (1993). Minneapolis: Personnel Decisions.

Transition coping questionnaire. (1993). Minneapolis: Personnel Decisions.

Troiden, R. R. (1989). The formation of homosexual identities. *Journal of Homosexuality, 17* (1–2), 43–74.

Tronto, J. (1993). *Moral boundaries: A political argument for the ethic of care.* New York: Routledge.

Tuckman, B. W. (1965). Developmental sequence in small groups. *Psychology Bulletin, 63,* 384–399.

Twohey, D., & Ewing, M. (1995). The male voice of emotional intimacy. *Journal of Mental Health Counseling, 17,* 54–62.

TwoTrees, K. (1997). *Somebody always singing you.* Jackson: University Press of Mississippi.

U.S. Department of Labor. (1977). *Dictionary of occupational titles* (4th ed.). Washington, DC: U.S. Government Printing Office.

Upcraft, M. L. (1994). The dilemmas of translating theory to practice. *Journal of College Student Development, 35,* 438–443.

Upcraft, M. L., & Barr, M. J. (1990). Identifying challenges for the future in current practice. In M. J. Barr, M. L. Upcraft, & Associates, *New futures for student affairs: Building a vision for professional leadership and practice* (pp. 3–21). San Francisco: Jossey-Bass.

Upcraft, M. L., & Moore, L. V. (1990). Evolving theoretical perspectives of student development. In M. J. Barr, M. L. Upcraft, & Associates, *New futures for student affairs: Building a vision for professional leadership and practice* (pp. 41–68). San Francisco: Jossey-Bass.

Upcraft, M. L., & Schuh, J. H. (1996). *Assessment in student affairs: A guide for practitioners.* San Francisco: Jossey-Bass.

Utterback, J. W., Spooner, S. E., Barbieri, J. A., & Fox, S. N. (1995). Gender and ethnic issues in the development of intimacy among college students. *NASPA Journal, 32,* 82–89.

Van Hecke, M. L. (1987, May). *Cognitive development during the college years.* Paper presented at the annual meeting of the Midwest Psychological Association, Chicago. (ERIC Document Reproduction Service No. ED 288 477)

Veblen, T. B. (1946). *The higher learning in America: A memorandum on the conduct of universities by business men.* New York: Hill & Wang. (Original work published 1918)

Veres, J. G., III, Sims, R. R., & Shake, L. G. (1987). The reliability and classification stability of the Learning Style Inventory in corporate settings. *Educational and Psychological Measurement, 47,* 1127–1133.

Vreeke, G. J. (1991). Gilligan on justice and care: Two interpretations. *Journal of Moral Education, 20,* 33–46.

Wadeson, H. (1989). In a different image: Are "male" pressures shaping the "female" arts therapy professions? *Arts in Psychotherapy, 16,* 327–330.

Wadsworth, B. J. (1979). *Piaget's theory of cognitive development* (2nd ed.). New York: Longman.

Walker, L. J. (1980). Cognitive and perspective-taking prerequisites for moral development. *Child Development, 51,* 131–139.

Walker, L. J. (1983). Sources of cognitive conflict for stage transition in moral development. *Developmental Psychology, 19,* 103–110.

Walker, L. J. (1984). Sex differences in the development of moral reasoning: A critical review. *Child Development, 55,* 677–691.

Walker, L. J. (1988). The development of moral reasoning. *Annals of Child Development, 5,* 33–78.

Walker, L. J. (1989). A longitudinal study of moral reasoning. *Child Development, 60,* 157–166.

Walker, L. J., & Taylor, J. H. (1991). Stage transitions in moral reasoning: A longitudinal study of developmental processes. *Developmental Psychology, 27,* 330–337.

Wall, V. A., & Evans, N. J. (1991). Using psychosocial development theories to understand and work with gay and lesbian persons. In N. J. Evans & V. A. Wall (Eds.), *Beyond tolerance: Gays, lesbians and bisexuals on campus* (pp. 25–38). Alexandria, VA: American College Personnel Association.

Wall, V. A., & Washington, J. (1991). Understanding gay and lesbian students of color. In N. J. Evans & V. A. Wall (Eds.), *Beyond tolerance: Gays, lesbians and bisexuals on campus* (pp. 67–78). Alexandria, VA: American College Personnel Association.

Walsh, W. B. (1973). *Theories of person-environment interaction: Implications for the college student.* Iowa City, IA: American College Testing Program.

Walsh, W. B., & Holland, J. L. (1992). A theory of personality types and work environments. In W. B. Walsh, K. H. Craik, & R. H. Price (Eds.), *Person-environment psychology: Models and perspectives* (pp. 35–69). Hillsdale, NJ: Erlbaum.

Warren, C. A. B. (1974). *Identity and community in the gay world.* New York: Wiley.

Waterman, A. S., Geary, P. S., & Waterman, C. K. (1974). A longitudinal study of changes in ego identity status from the freshman to the senior year at college. *Developmental Psychology, 10,* 387–392.

Waterman, A. S., & Waterman, C. K. (1971). A longitudinal study of changes in ego identity status during the freshmen year at college. *Developmental Psychology, 5,* 167–173.

Waterman, C. K., & Nevid, J. (1977). Sex differences in the resolution of the identity crisis. *Journal of Youth and Adolescence, 6,* 337–342.

Weick, K. E. (1964). Reduction of cognitive dissonance through task enhancement and effort expenditure. *Journal of Abnormal and Social Psychology, 68,* 533–539.

Weinberg, M. S., Williams, C. J., & Pryor, D. W. (1994). *Dual attraction: Understanding bisexuality.* New York: Oxford University Press.

Weinberger, S. L., Yacker, N. L., Orenstein, S. H., & DeSarbo, W. (1993). Care and justice reasoning: A multidimensional scaling approach. *Multivariate Behavioral Research, 28,* 435–465.

Weinrach, S. G., & Srebalus, D. J. (1990). Holland's theory of careers. In D. Brown, L. Brooks, & Associates, *Career choice and development: Applying contemporary theories to practice* (2nd ed., pp. 37–67). San Francisco: Jossey-Bass.

Weise, R. B. (1992). *Closer to home: Bisexuality and feminism.* Seattle, WA: Seal Press.

Weith, R. (1985). *A student development scenario.* Unpublished manuscript.

Weston, L. C., & Stein, S. L. (1977). The relationship of identity achievement of college women and campus participation. *Journal of College Student Personnel, 18,* 21–24.

Whitbourne, S. (1985). The psychological construction of the life span. In J. E. Birren & K. W. Schaie (Eds.), *Handbook of the psychology of aging* (2nd ed., pp. 594–618). New York: Van Nostrand Reinhold.

Whitbourne, S. K., Jelsma, B. M., & Waterman, A. S. (1982). An Eriksonian measure of personality development in college students: A reexamination of Constantinople's data and a partial replication. *Developmental Psychologist, 18,* 369–371.

White, D. B., & Hood, A. B. (1989). An assessment of the validity of Chickering's theory of student development. *Journal of College Student Development, 30,* 354–361.

White, K., & Strange, C. C. (1993). Effects of unwanted childhood sexual experiences on psychosocial development of college women. *Journal of College Student Development, 34,* 289–294.

Whiteley, J. (1982). *Character development in college students* (Vol. 1). Schenectady, NY: Character Research Press.

Widick, C. (1975). *An evaluation of developmental instruction in a university setting.* Unpublished doctoral dissertation, University of Minnesota, Minneapolis.

Widick, C., Knefelkamp, L. L., & Parker, C. A. (1975). The counselor as a developmental instructor. *Counselor Education and Supervision, 14,* 286–296.

Widick, C., Knefelkamp, L. L., & Parker, C. A. (1980). Student development. In U. Delworth, G. R. Hanson, & Associates, *Student services: A handbook for the profession* (pp. 75–116). San Francisco: Jossey-Bass.

Widick, C., Parker, C. A., & Knefelkamp, L. L. (1978a). Douglas Heath's model of maturing. In L. L. Knefelkamp, C. Widick, & C. A. Parker (Eds.), *Applying new developmental findings* (New Directions for Student Services, No. 4, pp. 79–91). San Francisco: Jossey-Bass.

Widick, C., Parker, C. A., & Knefelkamp, L. L. (1978b). Erik Erikson and psychosocial development. In L. L. Knefelkamp, C. Widick, & C. A. Parker (Eds.), *Applying new developmental findings* (New Directions for Student Services, No. 4, pp. 1–17). San Francisco: Jossey-Bass.

Widick, C., & Simpson, D. (1978). Developmental concepts in college instruction. In C. A. Parker (Ed.), *Encouraging development in college students* (pp. 27–59). Minneapolis: University of Minnesota Press.

Wiggins, J. S. (1989). Review of the Myers-Briggs Type Indicator. In J. C. Close & J. J. Kramer (Eds.), *The tenth mental measurements yearbook* (pp. 536–538). Lincoln: University of Nebraska Press.

Will, K. (1994). The courage of their convictions: Empowering voices of girls. *Journal of Emotional and Behavioral Problems, 3* (2), 46–47.

Williams, J. E. (1967). *Conflict between freshman male roommates.* (Research Report No. 10–67.) College Park: University of Maryland, Counseling Center.

Williams, M. E., & Winston, R. B., Jr. (1985). Participation in organized student activities and work: Differences in developmental task achievement of traditional-aged college students. *NASPA Journal, 22*(3), 52–59.

Williams, M. Q., Williams, T. F., Xu, Q., & Li, X. (1992). A glimpse of the psychological types of mainland Chinese undergraduates. *Journal of Psychological Type, 23,* 3–9.

Williams, W. C., & Nelson, S. I. (1986). Residence hall discipline as a function of personality type. *NASPA Journal, 24* (2), 38–48.

Williams, W. L. (1996). Two-spirit persons: Gender nonconformity among Native American and Native Hawaiian youths. In R. C. Savin-Williams & K. M. Cohen (Eds.), *The lives of lesbians, gays, and bisexuals: Children to adults* (pp. 416–435). Fort Worth, TX: Harcourt Brace.

Wingfield, L., & Haste, H. (1987). Connectedness and separation: Cognitive style or moral orientation? *Journal of Moral Education, 16,* 214–225.

Winston, R. B., Jr. (1990). The Student Developmental Task and Lifestyle Inventory: An approach to measuring students' psychosocial development. *Journal of College Student Development, 31,* 108–120.

Winston, R. B., Jr., & McCaffrey, S. S. (1983). Ethical practice in student affairs administration. In T. K. Miller, R. B. Winston Jr., & W. R. Mendenhall (Eds.), *Administration and leadership in student affairs* (pp. 167–191). Muncie, IN: Accelerated Development.

Winston, R. B., Jr., & Miller, T. K. (1987). *Student Developmental Task and Lifestyle Inventory manual.* Athens, GA: Student Development Associates.

Winston, R. B., Jr., Miller, T. K., & Prince, J. S. (1979). *Student Developmental Task Inventory* (Rev. 2nd ed.). Athens, GA: Student Development Associates.

Winston, R. B., Jr., Miller, T. K., & Prince, J. S. (1987). *Student Developmental Task and Lifestyle Inventory.* Athens, GA: Student Development Associates.

Wooden, W. S., Kawasaki, H., & Mayeda, R. (1983). Lifestyles and identity maintenance among gay Japanese-American males. *Alternative Lifestyles, 5,* 236–243.

Woods, D. R. (1990). Nurturing intellectual development. *Journal of College Science Teaching, 19,* 250–252.

Yeh, S., & Creamer, D. G. (1995). Orientations to moral reasoning among men and women leaders of higher education in Taiwan. *Journal of College Student Development, 36,* 112–122.

Yinger, J. M. (1976). Ethnicity in complex societies. In L. A. Coser & O. N. Larsen (Eds.), *The uses of controversy in sociology* (pp. 197–216). New York: Free Press.

Zak, I. (1973). Dimensions of Jewish-American identity. *Psychological Reports, 33,* 891–900.

Zemke, R. (1992). Second thoughts about the MBTI. *Training, 29* (4), 43–47.

Zuschlag, M. K., & Whitbourne, S. K. (1994). Psychosocial development in three generations of college students. *Journal of Youth and Adolescence, 23,* 567–577.

NAME INDEX

A

Abbey, D. S., 222
Adams, G. R., 61, 66, 83
Adams, M., 220
Albert, M., 183
Alexander, C. M., 82
Alipuria, L. L., 83
Allen, K. T., 240
American Council on Education, 5, 6
Anchors, W. S., 253, 254, 258, 288
Anderson, J. A., 220
Antonucci, T. C., 114
Apostal, R. A., 255
Arbuckle, D. S., 6
Arce, C. A., 73
Arvizu, D. R., 197, 198
Assouline, M., 237
Astin, A. W., 21, 26, 235, 236
Atkinson, D. R., 73
Atkinson, G., Jr., 218

B

Bahr, J., 47, 101, 288
Bakken, L., 180

Baltes, P. B., 96
Banning, J. H., 25
Barbieri, J. A., 46, 48
Barnett, P. C., 104
Barr, L., 257
Barr, M. J., 5, 279
Barr, N., 259
Barrett, W. R., 45
Barrineau, P., 253
Bateman, D., 136
Bates, M., 245, 248, 249, 252
Baxter Magolda, M. B., 11, 13, 126, 134, 144, 153, 154, 155, 156, 157, 158, 159, 199, 217, 273, 287
Bayne, R., 251, 252, 258
Behrens, J. T., 82
Belenky, M. F., 11, 126, 144, 147, 148, 149, 150, 151, 152, 158, 160, 189, 190, 199, 254, 268, 273, 288
Bell, A. P., 103
Bell, Y. R., 81
Bem, S. L., 197
Bennion, L., 83
Benton, S. E., 48
Bernal, M. E., 73

Berryhill-Paapke, E., 73
Bersoff, D. M., 182
Bertaux, D., 108
Bilsker, D., 56
Black, J. D., 245
Blackhurst, A. B., 46
Blasi, A., 172
Blockus, L., 84
Bloland, P. A., 280, 282
Bond, N. A., Jr., 227
Borgen, F. H., 232, 241
Bourassa, D., 105
Bourne, E., 61
Boyatzis, R. E., 216
Boyle, E. J., 215
Brabeck, M., 190
Bradby, D., 84
Bradley, J., 19
Bradley, R., 19
Brady, S., 98, 100
Branch-Simpson, G., 47
Brand, M., 140
Broido, E., 287
Broughton, J. M., 161
Brown, D., 228, 241
Brown, L. M., 195
Brown, L. S., 90, 103

SUBJECT INDEX